Who's Who
in World War II

Who's Who
in World War II

David Mason

Weidenfeld and Nicolson
London

Designed by Sheila Sherwen
for George Weidenfeld and Nicolson Limited
11 St John's Hill, London SW11
ISBN 0 297 77376 3

Colour Separations by Newsele Litho Ltd
Printed in Great Britain by
Butler & Tanner Ltd, Frome and London

Contents

A

ALEXANDER, Harold (1891–1969). British general who commanded with great success in the North African and Italian campaigns. Alexander joined the Irish Guards after education at Harrow and Sandhurst, and served in France in the first world war, commanding his battalion at the age of twenty-five. He was wounded three times and extensively decorated. He also commanded the Baltic *Landwehr* in northern Russia during 1919. During the inter-war years he held a variety of commands, including service on the northern frontier in India.

His second world war service began as commander of 1 Division of the British Expeditionary Force, and after Gort (q.v.) had returned to Britain Alexander took over the supervision of the final evacuation at Dunkirk. He made a tour of the beaches and harbour with the senior naval commander to ensure that no British troops remained. He was subsequently placed in charge of Southern Command, the most important force concerned with the ground defence against the expected German invasion. He made great contributions in updating training methods and devising the army's new battle drill.

When the threat of invasion receded, but events in the Far East promised disaster, he was sent out early in 1942 to take over command in Burma. It was too late to save the situation there, and he organized a second major withdrawal.

His opportunity to play a more positive part in the war came in August 1942, when Churchill (q.v.) called on him to take over command of the Middle East theatre from Auchinleck (q.v.). It was at a time when Rommel's (q.v.) advance had been stopped at El Alamein, and the British were receiving substantial reinforcements. He had as his subordinate commander, head of Eighth Army, General Montgomery (q.v.). It was to Alexander's credit that he found the ideal way of dealing with the autocratic Montgomery, which was broadly to give Montgomery support when he needed it but otherwise to leave him alone. A less flexible theatre commander would almost certainly have had clashes with the army commander. In February 1943, with the Anglo–American force advancing from the west and Eighth Army approaching Tunisia from the east, he was appointed deputy commander-in-chief to General Eisenhower (q.v.), and was responsible for overseeing the land campaigns in the theatre which led to the destruction of the Axis armies in North Africa and the capture of 200,000 Axis troops.

Alexander remained deputy to Eisenhower for the Sicily operations, and after the Italian mainland landings he became commander-in-chief of the Allied armies in his own right. For several months he therefore commanded the only operation by the western Allies on the Axis-dominated mainland of Europe. His conduct of the Italian campaign was criticized when it became bogged down, especially in the unsuccessful early assaults on the Cassino stronghold. But in May 1944 he produced a highly successful answer by moving Eighth Army across the Apennines and throwing the combined strength of the British Eighth and American Fifth Armies against the German front, which led to the capture of Rome.

The Allied invasion of France in 1944 led to the drastic reduction of the role of the Mediterranean

theatre and the allocation of resources to it. Alexander was forced to take second place to the commanders in north-west Europe, but he continued to conduct his campaign successfully and was the first Allied commander to take the surrender of a German army group at the end of the war.

Alexander went on to serve as governor-general of Canada after the war and was for a two-year period from 1952–4 Britain's minister of defence. His reputation depended on two strands of his character – the aggressive determination to attack whenever possible, even when his force was on the defensive, and his considerable personal charm and likeability which enabled him to command forces of mixed nationalities with success, and to exact willing loyalty from his subordinate commanders.

AMERY, Leo (1873–1955). British statesman. Amery was severely critical of Chamberlain's (q.v.) appeasement policy, and attacked Chamberlain in the House of Commons in 1940 with Cromwell's words, 'Depart I say, and let us have done with you. In the name of God, go.' Amery hoped for an important wartime post in the Churchill Cabinet, but was appointed to the India Office. His elder son John was executed in 1945 for treason, after trying to recruit British internees in Germany to fight against Communist Russia.

ANDERSON, (Sir) John (1882–1958). British politician credited with inspiring the Anderson shelter, widely used in private gardens throughout Britain to protect civilians during air raids. It was a simple, cheap, and easily erected structure of concrete and corrugated iron, and was credited with saving thousands of lives by protecting its occupants from the blast of bomb explosions. The detailed design was largely the work of the Scottish engineer Sir William Paterson. Anderson was re-

Opposite General Alexander (right), Allied commander in Italy, talks to the American general, Lucian Truscott, in the war-damaged town of Nettuno in 1944.

Above Leo Amery (left), prominent British politician, secretary of state for India and Burma in Churchill's government, 1940–45.

An Anderson shelter being assembled. It was a simple corrugated steel structure designed to protect civilians from blast injuries in bombing raids, and named after the man who introduced it, Sir John Anderson.

The British War Cabinet photographed in the garden of 10 Downing Street in October 1941. Left to right are (seated) Sir John Anderson, Winston Churchill, Clement Attlee, Anthony Eden, and (standing) Arthur Greenwood, Ernest Bevin, Lord Beaverbrook, Sir Kingsley Wood.

sponsible for a great part of Britain's civilian and economic affairs during the war, and for overseeing the programme of atomic development including Britain's bomb. He became chancellor of the exchequer in 1943, and was Churchill's (q.v.) choice to replace him as prime minister in the event of Churchill and Eden (q.v.) being killed during the 1943 journey to Yalta.

ANDERSON, (Sir) Kenneth (1891–1959). British general who commanded an infantry brigade and then 3 Division in the withdrawal to Dunkirk, before serving in his most important post in the Anglo–American invasion of northwest Africa. After holding posts in England from 1940 to 1942 Anderson was appointed to command the Allied force subsequent to the landings at Algiers in Operation Torch. Three days after the landings, on 11 November 1942, he took over the British First Army, which included 2 United States Corps and shortly afterwards 19 French Corps. His task was to take Tunis, 500 miles to the east, and after severe difficulties his force stood, by 28 November, only twelve miles short of the target. He made the assault on 28 December but the force was held up in torrential rain. After a build-up of Axis forces during the winter, there were further clashes, including Rommel's (q.v.) victory at the Kasserine Pass, before Tunis fell to Alexander's and Montgomery's forces (qq.v.) (under the overall control of Alexander's Twelfth Army Group) in May 1943. Anderson was the first choice to command the British Second Army for the Normandy invasion, but after a few months preparing for that operation he was replaced by Dempsey (q.v.), and given Eastern Command. After the war he served in East Africa and also as governor of Gibraltar.

ANTONESCU, Ion (1882–1946). Wartime dictator of Romania. A soldier in the first world war who rose to become chief of staff in 1937, Antonescu was suspended in 1938 for opposing King Carol and later that year arrested as a leader of the revolt against the king. He was soon released, appointed war minister, and imprisoned again in 1940 for opposing the cession of Bessarabia and northern Bucovina to the USSR. Released once more, he became premier on 5 September 1940, with the support of the pro-Fascist Iron Guard and the Peasant party. He became military dictator on 27 January 1941, forced King Carol to abdicate in favour of his son Michael, and declared war against the Allies on 22 June that year. In 1944, with the Russians approaching the Romanian border, he was forced to seek peace terms, and on 23 August King Michael staged a coup and had Antonescu arrested. Romania declared war on Germany two days later. In 1946 Antonescu was tried as a war criminal, and on 1 June was shot.

ANTONOV, Alexei (1896–1962). Soviet general, concerned mainly with staff work in Moscow during the second world war. The son of an artillery officer and member of the tsar's army, Antonov rose to occupy several staff posts in the early years of the war, as chief of staff successively of the Southern Army Group, North Caucasian, then Transcaucasian Army Groups. In December 1942 he was appointed chief of operations, holding at the same time the post of deputy chief of the general staff under Vasilevsky (q.v.). As Vasilevsky, at Stalin's (q.v.) insistence, was frequently away visiting fighting units at the various fronts, Antonov carried full responsibility for almost the entire range of staff problems, involving daily and sometimes twice-daily reports to the supreme commander, Stalin. He was closely involved in the planning of all Soviet operations from December 1942. Antonov took over Vasilevsky's post as chief of the general staff in February 1945.

General Shtemenko (q.v.), his deputy as chief of operations, has written an illuminating memoir of Antonov, describing his great erudition, painstaking preparation for staff conferences, patience and even temper, clarity of thought and methodical approach to his job. He was obviously the quintessential staff officer, and Stalin valued his accurate, precise and uncompromising reports.

AOSTA, Duke of (1898–1942). Commander-in-chief of Italian forces in East Africa at the beginning of the war. He was also governor-general of Italian East Africa, viceroy of Abyssinia, and a

'Hap' Arnold (right), five-star general and commander of United States Army Air Force. He was a staunch advocate of an independent and overwhelmingly powerful air force.

cousin of the king of Italy. He commanded the invasion of Somaliland on 4 August 1940, but failed to hold the territory against British-led campaigns in 1941, and was captured by the Allies when his forces surrendered on 16 May 1941. Respected by the Allies as a chivalrous commander, but not noted by either the Allies or Mussolini for his skill as a soldier, since he was conspicuously lacking in ruthlessness, the Duke of Aosta died in a prisoner-of-war camp in Nairobi, Kenya, in 1942.

ARNOLD, Henry Harley (1886–1950). United States army air force general, and the senior American air figure of the second world war. Arnold was a pioneer army aviator, and learnt his flying from the Wright brothers. From that time on his career covered, and in many ways brought about, the development of military air power into the era of jet flight and the massed bomber raids. In his early years Arnold won a number of flying trophies. He was appointed chief of the Air Corps in 1938, and paved the way for the rapid increase in the role of aircraft by instituting extensive programmes of aircraft manufacture, as well as a scheme for training civilian pilot cadets. The basis of his military philosophy was that air power would render mass armies and navies obsolete, and enemy countries could be reduced to surrender without the intervention of occupying ground forces. For this purpose he strove to create the best and most powerful air force possible, remarking that the second best air force was no more use than the second best hand at poker. He also fought to bring about the independence of the air force from the army, but this remained unattainable until 1947. However, although nominally integrated with the army, the technical independence of the force was recognized in a separate and equal seat for Arnold on the combined chiefs of staff. It was also recognized in Arnold's promotion to full general in 1944. When the force became independent, Arnold was appointed the first five-star general of the United States Air Force. He was widely known as 'Hap' Arnold, reportedly a contraction of the nickname 'Happy' which he was given by virtue of his cheerful and humorous disposition.

ATTLEE, Clement (1883–1967). British prime minister who replaced Winston Churchill (q.v.) shortly before the end of the second world war. As early as May 1945 Britain had been suffering from election fever. There had been no election for ten years, and as the war in Europe drew to a close the people were conscious that their opportunity to elect their first new government in a decade was imminent. Winston Churchill as prime minister deliberated on the right time to hold the election, and invited his deputy, the Labour party leader Clement Attlee, to agree to preserving the wartime coalition government until Japan had been defeated. At the time, the best estimates indicated that the end of the war in the Far East would take as much as eighteen months. Attlee therefore declined the offer. Churchill was forced to resign the coalition, and formed a caretaker government without the Labour leaders until the election.

Clement Attlee, leader of the British Labour party. He led his party in the coalition government until the end of the European fighting, when an election made him prime minister.

The election was held in June but, since many of the electors were spread around the world in various theatres of war, the counting of votes was delayed and the result was not due to be announced until 26 July. In the interim Churchill, conscious that Attlee might soon occupy the post of premier, invited him to attend the conference at Potsdam in the capacity of observer. The election gave the Labour Party a majority in the House of Commons, and as its leader Attlee was asked by the king to form the new government. Attlee returned to Potsdam as the British representative, and was responsible for the last major wartime duty – the announcement of the Japanese surrender.

AUCHINLECK, (Sir) Claude (born 1884). British general, distinguished both by his service in India and as the man who stopped Rommel (q.v.) in North Africa. He received little acknowledgment at the time for this achievement, and was replaced, just as he was on the point of bringing his plans to their culmination, by the Alexander–Montgomery (qq.v.) combination.

Claude Auchinleck was born at Aldershot into a soldier's family, and was of Scottish and Irish descent. He was educated at Wellington School and Sandhurst. He joined the Indian Army, served in the Middle East in the first world war, and after returning to India for a period was recalled to take charge of 4 Corps, due for service in France. Instead they were ordered to Norway to take part in the Narvik operation (May–June 1940), in which Auchinleck commanded the land and air forces. After the withdrawal from Norway, Auchinleck took command first of 5 Corps and later of Southern Command, in which his task was to build up as rapidly as possible Britain's anti-invasion capability. As the summer of 1940 passed under the threat of invasion, Auchinleck worked hard to engender an appropriate warlike spirit among his troops, and especially among the home guard who formed an integral part of the defence system. One of his most significant problems during this period was to control the activities of General Montgomery, who had taken over Auchinleck's post with 5 Corps, and who frequently ignored Auchinleck and approached the War Office direct over his head. In this, and in his practice of 'poaching' the officers he wanted from other units, Montgomery caused Auchinleck considerable trouble.

In November 1940, as the threat of invasion that year receded, Auchinleck was given a new appointment as commander-in-chief India. While he was serving in India, British attention was focused mainly on the Mediterranean theatre: in North Africa in January and February 1941 the Western Desert Force won a startling victory over the Italian Tenth Army. Then Wavell (q.v.) was ordered to mount an operation in Greece against the threat of a German invasion; this ended in April in withdrawal. This was followed by the German capture of Crete in May. And finally in June the British offensive, Battleaxe, failed against Rommel's Afrika Korps. In the wake of these losses Wavell, who had lost the confidence of the

prime minister, was sacked. He was sent out to India as commander-in-chief, and in a direct exchange of posts on 5 July 1941 Auchinleck took over from him as commander-in-chief Middle East. He immediately came under pressure, as Wavell had done, from the prime minister in London to renew the offensive at the earliest possible moment. He told Churchill (q.v.) brusquely that launching an offensive with inadequate means was not a justifiable operation of war. He was called to London, where he explained the delay at length and convinced the service chiefs (but not Churchill) that he was right. Eventually the date for the new offensive, Crusader, was fixed for 1 November 1941. Auchinleck selected General Alan Cunningham (q.v.) to command the Eighth Army, which came into being on 26 September. Because he considered his resources of armour inadequate, and he was short of time for training, Auchinleck postponed D-Day until 15 November, and then for a further three days, even though he still considered his army's equipment and training barely adequate. The delays, though necessary, did not help to satisfy the prime minister's demand for drive and aggression. The battle, under Cunningham, went badly, and by 23 November the Eighth Army had lost two-thirds of its armour to the German guns around Sidi Rezegh outside Tobruk. Auchinleck flew to Cunningham's headquarters and found the army commander exhausted, suffering from battle fatigue, and barely able to make a coherent decision. Cunningham was in favour of withdrawal but Auchinleck, sensing that Rommel and his troops were as exhausted as his own troops, pressed for further action. He urged the Eighth Army to 'hang on and bite deeper and deeper and hang on till he is finished'. Auchinleck decided to relieve Cunningham, who went into hospital suffering from overstrain, and replace him with Ritchie (q.v.). Between then and 6

General Claude Auchinleck (right). He was successful in the desert once he had taken personal command, but was removed by Churchill before seeing the fruits of his efforts.

January 1942, these two defeated Rommel in the extended Crusader operation, and Rommel retreated to El Agheila. It was then that the Japanese entry into the war changed the picture, as both reinforcements and armour (some of it already with the Eighth Army) were diverted to the Far East.

At the same time, although the British staffs refused to believe it, Rommel received substantial tank reinforcements, and on 21 January launched one of his typical incisive attacks which destroyed the British 1 Armoured Division. Auchinleck again flew in to steady the Eighth Army, but there was no alternative to retreat. The routed army fell back to Gazala, leaving Cyrenaica in Rommel's hands. Inevitably a period of recuperation followed on both sides, which Auchinleck used to restructure his forces into balanced formations of armour, artillery and motorized infantry. Before these changes, together with a new programme of intense training, could produce concrete results, Churchill was again pressing from London for a new offensive. Auchinleck remained adamant that he would not attack again until he had built up adequate resources. On 10 May Churchill ordered him to attack or resign. In fact Auchinleck's planned attack was pre-empted by a new advance by Rommel on 26 May. Largely because General Ritchie, in contravention of Auchinleck's advice, had laid down static defence lines instead of a mobile defence plan appropriate to the desert, Rommel's advance continued almost unimpeded. The outcome was the loss of the fortress of Bir Hacheim on 10 June and, after further battles around Gazala, the fall of Tobruk on 21 June 1942. On 25 June, faced with the disintegration of Britain's hold on the Middle East, Auchinleck flew in from Cairo to relieve Ritchie of his post and take command of the Eighth Army himself. He had already written to Churchill taking full responsibility for the failure, and offering to resign. Churchill assured him of his full confidence.

Auchinleck's first decision after taking operational control of the Eighth Army was to abandon the plan to stand at Mersah Matruh, which Ritchie

had ordered, and prepare to fall back to El Alamein. He also showed the quality and style of his generalship, though it was too late for it to have any great effect, by issuing orders impressing on his troops the need for mobility, fast and bold counter-attack, and co-operation between divisional commanders to ensure that one formation should aid another which came under threat, especially by attacking the enemy in the flank. It was, of course, impossible to bring about a radical change in the outlook and methods of an army in the hours before the start of the impending battle. On 26 June Rommel launched his attack, and in the confused battle of Mersah Matruh, by a combination of audacity and speed, his Afrika Korps routed the British force. The two exhausted armies raced eastwards, in some places actually intermingled, the Eighth Army in confusion and the Afrika Korps running ahead of both its intelligence and supplies. In Cairo, the British were flung into a panic as they anticipated having to cede Egypt to Rommel. The scene is remembered clearly for the black pall of smoke that hung over the city as officials burned their papers. At Alexandria, the Royal Navy put to sea in a hurry. Then Rommel made the uncharacteristic mistake of pausing in his pursuit, and Auchinleck was able to organize his defence in the forty-mile 'bottleneck' between the Qattara depression and the sea at El Alamein. Despite the demoralization in the capital, Auchinleck was full of renewed optimism. He had read the battle accurately and realized that Rommel's force was stretched beyond its limits, and on 1 July he confidently told his chief of staff, Eric Dorman-Smith (q.v.): 'I am going to win.' As Auchinleck well recognized, this was his last chance to save the Middle East. Defeat here would have dire consequences. By 30 June 1942 the British were back at El Alamein, waiting for the next thrust from the Afrika Korps. It came on 1 July, but the Afrika Korps were held up by a severe artillery hammering, and Rommel himself was pinned down by a British bomber attack as he went forward to sort out the problems of his harassed troops. That night, and throughout 2

July, the artillery pounding continued. By then Rommel recognized that he had lost the battle. On 3 July he tried to mount another offensive, but failed to break through. And on that day Rommel conceded temporary defeat.

Auchinleck also had his failures. He planned a counter-stroke which his forces could not carry out. In fact both sides were suffering from exhaustion and, however much they were urged on by their respective commanders, they could not comply. During the first two weeks of July the fighting around El Alamein developed into a fierce battle of attrition, in which Auchinleck gradually secured the advantage. His 9 Australian Division was especially successful in over-running the Italian Sabratha Division, which forced Rommel to overstretch his meagre resources of German formations. Rommel wrote home to his wife complaining that the enemy was using his infantry superiority to destroy the Italian formations one by one, and saying that the German formations were much too weak to stand alone. 'It's enough to make one weep,' he added. On 21 July, partly as the result of a new prompting from Churchill and partly to prevent Rommel establishing unassailable defensive positions, Auchinleck attempted to resume the offensive. The attack failed with heavy losses. A follow-up attack on 26 July similarly came to nothing. But as the German commander Bayerlein later averred, that day was decisive. The Afrika Korps was out of artillery ammunition and Rommel was preparing to withdraw to the frontier if Auchinleck continued the attack. Two days' further pressure would have made the difference. But on 27 July Auchinleck decided to call off the attack. He began to plan for a new offensive, to begin about the middle of September. By the time this first battle of El Alamein drew to a close, however, Churchill in London had become infuriated and exasperated at the position in the Middle East. He had wanted to fly out to Cairo a month earlier, and eventually he arrived there on 3 August with a contingent of important military figures which included Brooke, Wavell, Smuts and Tedder (qq.v.). During his tour of the army positions, he seriously misread the extent of the Eighth Army's domination over their enemy at this time, and once more pressed for offensive action. Making imaginary thrusts with his thumb and fingers on the wall map at Auchinleck's desert headquarters he urged: 'Attack, attack.' That was on 5 August. On 6 August Churchill sent a message back to London for consideration by the War Cabinet, proposing a complete revision of the command structure. Auchinleck would be moved out of the present Middle East Command to a new command covering Persia and Iraq. For Auchinleck it meant dismissal.

Churchill's first idea for his successor was Brooke, but already that morning Brooke had turned down the appointment. Instead Churchill proposed that Alexander should take over from Auchinleck. His choice as commander of the Eighth Army was General Gott (q.v.), then one of its corps commanders. Gott had already pleaded for three months' leave in England because he was tired out, and had suggested that what was needed in the area was some new blood, as he himself had already 'tried out most of his ideas on the Boche'. Churchill turned down his objections and insisted on appointing him. Then on 7 August Gott's aircraft was shot down and he was killed. Churchill wanted Maitland Wilson (q.v.) to replace him, but both Brooke and General Smuts pressed for Montgomery. Churchill gave way and agreed to appoint the man whose name from then on became synonymous with that of the Eighth Army. As it happened, Montgomery was even more resolute than Auchinleck in his refusal to be hustled by Churchill into a premature offensive. He delayed until October, then fought the battle largely according to the plan originated by Auchinleck and his chief of staff Eric Dorman-Smith. For a variety of reasons – his talent for publicity, the British need for a propaganda success, the fact that when he did take the offensive it was a winning one – Montgomery came to enjoy massive public esteem for defeating Rommel and throwing the Axis out of North Africa.

On 8 August Auchinleck was given the letter informing him of his removal. He read it two or three times in silence, and remained calm and in control of himself. He also declined the offer of the post in Persia. On the following day, 9 August, he came out of the desert and visited Churchill in the ambassador's office in Cairo, where they had an hour's conversation graphically described by Churchill as 'bleak and impeccable'. Auchinleck flew to India, where he remained without an appointment for ten months. Then on 20 June 1943 he was appointed to replace Wavell as commander-in-chief India, while Wavell became viceroy. It was a return to Auchinleck's old post, but again it was a reduced command, as it was proposed to hive off the responsibility for the war against Japan and give it to a new South-east Asia Command with Mountbatten (q.v.) as supreme commander. India then became something of a base and training area for SEAC, but Auchinleck still threw himself enthusiastically into this work, which he rightly regarded as of vital importance. He remained c-in-c India under both Wavell and then Mountbatten during India's troubled transition to peace and independence, and saw through the dissolution of the Indian Army in which he had spent the bulk of his career.

Auchinleck's reputation suffered severely after the war, largely through neglect of his achievements. He was overshadowed by his successor in the desert. Certainly he made mistakes, perhaps most significantly in the area of man-management and selection, notably in leaving the unfortunate Ritchie in command of the Eighth Army through a period when the difficulties were beyond Ritchie's experience and ability to cope with them. But once he decided to take personal command his generalship was almost faultless. He stopped Rommel's forces at the gateway to Egypt, and

would certainly have defeated his adversary had he been left to see his plan through to fulfilment. Many commentators have observed that the year 1942 saw the two great events which may be regarded as turning points in the European war. One was Stalingrad; the other the first battle of El Alamein. For winning that battle Auchinleck deserves the greatest possible credit. Unjustly the credit went largely to his successor. In personal terms, Auchinleck was extremely popular with his men. While remaining a simple personality with none of Montgomery's flair for publicity or public relations, he nevertheless won a deep affection from the Eighth Army. He lived with the men out in the desert, sleeping like them in a sleeping bag laid out on the sand. With water supplies short he washed, like his men, once a week. He ate the same meals that they ate, even when entertaining visiting dignitaries, and suffered from the same sandstorms and the same desert flies. The men therefore liked and respected him and were happy to be led by the tall imposing figure with the aggressive jutting jaw and the penetrating blue eyes.

AUNG SAN (1914–1947). Burmese nationalist leader who headed the Burmese Independence Army fighting with the Japanese against the British. After a career spent promoting the independence of his country through revolutionary activity, Aung San fled to Japan to avoid arrest but returned in 1941 to aid the Japanese by creating a force of guerrillas which he called the Burmese Independence Army. Towards the end of the war he lost faith in the Japanese through their treatment of his own troops and through their apparent intentions regarding post-war independence for his country, and in March 1945, when a victory for the Japanese was no longer a possibility, he brought his army over to the Allied side. After the war he refused to incorporate his forces into the British army, and in 1947 secured an agreement for Burma's independence and withdrawal from the Commonwealth. Still only 33 years old, Aung San was assassinated in the council chamber in Rangoon during a parliamentary session, along with six of his colleagues.

Aung San (at head of procession in white costume), youthful commander of the Burmese Independence Army, leads his supporters through Rangoon to the Constituent Assembly.

B

BADER, Douglas (born 1910). British squadron leader and Battle of Britain pilot. Bader achieved a spurious fame as the 'legless air ace'. In fact his part in the battle was far greater than that faintly theatrical notoriety, and he made significant contributions by his teaching of aerial tactics and by his aggressive leadership. His disability came about in 1931, when after serving for a year as an RAF officer he crashed and lost both legs. He was invalided out in 1933. In 1939, wearing artificial legs, he rejoined the service, but refused to accept a desk job. He proved his fitness and returned to flying duties with 12 Group of fighter command, and commanded 242 Squadron. His men were exhausted and dispirited after service in France, but under Bader's leadership they rapidly

Squadron leader Douglas Bader, the legless air ace who commanded a squadron in the Battle of Britain. He was a leading figure in the 'big wing controversy' which helped lead to Dowding's removal.

Badoglio

recovered, and when Bader approached the Air Ministry with testy messages his squadron quickly received the equipment it needed. They then served with distinction throughout the battle from their base at Coltishall. He was personally credited with twenty enemy aircraft destroyed. He came down in France after a mid-air collision with an Me109 on 9 August 1941, was captured, escaped from hospital, but was recaptured. During his internment the Royal Air Force dropped a replacement artificial leg on to the airfield at St Omer. (*See also* Dowding, Leigh-Mallory, Park)

BADOGLIO, Pietro (1871–1956). Italian general, chief of staff during the early part of the war. He resigned from that post in December 1940 after Italy's failure in the attempted invasion of Greece. An ardent anti-Fascist, Badoglio became premier in July 1943 when Mussolini (q.v.) was removed. He signed the Italian surrender document at Malta on 28 September 1943 and declared war on Germany in the following month. He resigned from office in June 1944.

BAGRAMIAN, Ivan Cristoforovich (born 1897). Soviet cavalry general: commander of the First Baltic Army Group 1943–5. As chief of operations and deputy chief of staff of the Southwestern Army Group in September 1941 Bagramian was involved in the fighting in the Ukraine. He was almost captured in the encirclement of Kiev, but succeeded in breaking out with a column of 2000 men. He commanded the Eleventh Guards Army at the battle of Kursk. During the summer offensive of 1944 Bagramian commanded the First Baltic Front in Belorussia. On 31 July his front broke through the German lines to the Gulf of Riga, isolating the German Army Group Nord in Estonia and Latvia. However he was unable to maintain the pressure, and when three weeks later the German army group counter-attacked, they re-established contact with German forces in Lithuania.

BARUCH, Bernard Mannes (1870–1965). American economist and financial expert. Baruch was chairman of the War Industries Board during the first world war, when he greatly influenced the

Marshal Pietro Badoglio (right), Italian chief of staff, and premier after the downfall of Mussolini in 1943.

Bernard M. Baruch (right), American financier and a leading figure in wartime political circles. Here he receives the 1944 Churchman's Award for distinguished service to humanity from General George C. Marshall.

performance of the American war industries. Despite his strong opposition to Nazi Germany, he refused to accept any public office during the second world war (although he continued as an 'elder statesman' and adviser), as he had been accused by Henry Ford of being part of a Jewish conspiracy to control the world's economy. However he still had a great influence on the American government as he was closely associated with the Office of War Mobilization. He served as President Roosevelt's (q.v.) personal emissary in England and was a friend of Winston Churchill (q.v.).

BATOV, Pavel Ivanovich (born 1897). Soviet general. Batov commanded a rifle corps in the Soviet invasion of Poland, and in the war against Finland. He subsequently rose to command of the Third Army in the Briansk sector during 1941–2, and commanded the Sixty-fifth Army at Stalingrad and Kursk. His army took part in the great offensive of 1943 as part of Rokossovsky's (q.v.) Central Front. When Rokossovsky's command was renamed the First Belorussian Front, Batov's Sixty-fifth Army remained part of it, and served in the drive into Belorussia in the summer of 1944. He further followed Rokossovsky to the Second Belorussian Front in the attack against East Prussia in January and February 1945.

BAYERLEIN, Fritz (born 1883). German general who served with distinction in the North African theatre. Bayerlein fought as a private in the first world war, left the army, and rejoined in 1921. In the second world war he fought first in the Russian campaign, then in October 1941 was transferred to North Africa to be chief staff officer with the Afrika Korps. In May 1942 he became chief of staff to General Rommel (q.v.), then occupying the post of commander-in-chief of Panzer Group Afrika, with the Afrika Korps and two Italian corps under his command. Bayerlein took over temporary command of the Afrika Korps at the end of August 1942 when its commander, General Nehring, was wounded, and achieved his ambition of taking over formal command in November, when the Afrika Korps was reduced to a skeleton force of only eighty tanks and

was on the verge of surrender to Montgomery's (q.v.) Eighth Army. Bayerlein escaped from captivity and commanded the excellent Panzer Lehr Division in France at the time of the Allied invasion. This division was holding the ground chosen by General Bradley (q.v.) for the breakout from the Normandy beach-head, and suffered severe casualties in the Anglo–American air bombardment which prepared the way for that attack. The division under Bayerlein also took part in the Ardennes offensive. Bayerlein was an astute and aggressive commander who clearly understood the role of air power in neutralizing the effect of armoured formations and trained his tank commanders to use of camouflage and concealment.

BEAVERBROOK (First Lord Beaverbrook, born Maxwell Aitken) (1879–1964). Minister of aircraft production in the British war administration during 1940 and 1941, and a close confidant of Winston Churchill (q.v.). During the critical early war period, Beaverbrook greatly increased the rate of production of aircraft for the RAF. His programme, concentrating on finished aircraft, met opposition from some officers who thought he was neglecting spare-parts production and prejudicing future operational capability. Beaverbrook's view was that the urgency of 1940 demanded a short-term policy dedicated to increasing the flow of front-line aircraft for the immediate battle. Under Beaverbrook the aircraft industry produced a remarkable increase in output from 719 in February 1940 (282 short of the target) to 1601 in August (291 more than the target). Beaverbrook helped to achieve this success by ignoring red tape, temporarily abandoning closely controlled programmes, and relying on his personal inspiration of the workforce. He was also well known for his campaign to persuade housewives to give pots and pans to build Spitfires. The effort was more use in building morale than in producing aircraft, as the metal was unsuitable. He held other Cabinet posts between 1941 and 1945, and was responsible for negotiating military supplies to the Soviet Union and arranging Lend-Lease from the United States. Born in Canada, he was a British

Lord Beaverbrook (right), Canadian newspaper tycoon who as minister of aircraft production kept up the flow of fighters during the Battle of Britain. Here he signs an agreement on oil supplies for the post-war period with US acting secretary of state Edward Stettinius, 8 October 1944.

newspaper magnate and proprietor of the *Daily Express*.

BECK, Ludwig (1880–1944). German general who served as chief of staff in 1938. He was against the war, for which he thought Germany was not ready, and against the Nazis. He resigned office in 1938 because he resented the increasing power of Hitler's (q.v.) ss compared with the army, and became an opponent of Hitler. He was involved in the plot on Hitler's life of 20 July 1944, and was the general designated to be head of state on Hitler's disposal. When captured at the conspirators' headquarters after the failure of the attempt, Beck realized that he would be executed. Instead he chose suicide, attempted to shoot himself in the temple, but missed and caused only a graze; he pleaded with his captors to be allowed another try, asking for help if that failed. It did, and he was finally helped to his death by a third shot from a German army sergeant.

BEDELL-SMITH, Walter (born 1895). American general, one of the most influential staff officers of the war. In 1939 he became secretary to the War Department general staff in Washington, and in February 1942 secretary to the United States joint chiefs of staff and the Allied combined chiefs of staff. In September of that year he became chief of staff to General Eisenhower (q.v.), and was thus closely involved in all strategic decisions from North Africa, through Sicily, to the invasion of Normandy and operations in north-west Europe. He was highly regarded by all Allied commanders for his clear-sighted grasp of strategy and his command of detail, and was greatly responsible for the smooth running of the Allied enterprise. He signed the German surrender document with General Jodl (q.v.) at Eisenhower's HQ at Rheims on 7 May 1945.

BELOV, Pavel Alekseevich (1897–1962). Soviet cavalry general: served as commander of

1 Guards Cavalry Corps during the defence of Moscow. In the early counter-offensive of 5 and 6 December 1941 he organized many of the new mobile combined formations of cavalry, tanks and infantry aimed at cutting behind German lines. The operations were not a success and the cavalry suffered severe losses. Belov was promoted to command of the Sixty-first Army at the battle of Kursk, and served as their leader right up to the assault on Berlin.

BENES, Eduard (1884–1948). Czechoslovakian political leader acknowledged to be one of the founders of his country. When the Germans invaded in 1938 Benes fled to France, where he set up his national committee; in 1940 he moved to

President Eduard Benes, head of the Czechoslovakian government-in-exile in London during the second world war, and co-founder of his country with Tomas Masaryk in 1918.

London where he became president of the provisional government which the British recognized in July 1941. He worked to secure the participation of his countrymen in the war, and many of them fought as either airmen or soldiers with the British forces. After visiting the United States and Canada, where he made speeches to Congress and Parliament, Benes went to Moscow in December 1941 and secured an alliance with the Soviet Union. His work during the war had brought him enormous popular support, and he returned to his own country in 1945, re-entering Prague on 16 May to an enthusiastic reception. He was the only east European leader of a government-in-exile whom the Russians permitted to return home after the war. However he could not resist the Communist pressures from Russia or from within Czechoslovakia itself, and on 7 June 1948 he resigned. He died three months later, on 3 September. (*See also* Masaryk)

BENNETT, Henry Gordon (1887–1962). Commander of the 8 Australian Division in Malaya during the Japanese invasion. Bennett's division, augmented by three Indian brigades, was given the title West Force with the task of defending against the Japanese thrust on the Malayan west coast. Although a resourceful commander, his forces could not match the two Japanese divisions sent against him, and his division was forced southwards in a general retreat. On Singapore Island he was in command of Western Area. There he unwittingly contributed to the loss of the island when he passed on to his brigade commanders an order that the defence would fall back on Singapore town if the forward lines could not be held. One brigade commander took this order to be operational as opposed to provisional, and ordered his units to fall back. Other units found their flanks exposed by this withdrawal, and also fell back, leaving the Japanese in position to cross the Johore Straits on to the island unopposed. On the night of 10 February 1942 the GOC Malaya, General Percival (q.v.), ordered Bennett to counter-attack, but his exhausted troops suffered heavy losses. Bennett was among the first divisional commanders to advocate surrender to Percival as the only way of saving the troops and civilians in Singapore town.

BERNADOTTE OF WISBORG, Count Folke (1895–1948). Swedish soldier and humanitarian, who headed the Swedish Red Cross during the second world war and saved the lives of countless thousands of inmates of concentration camps by his intervention, as well as organizing the exchange of large numbers of prisoners of war. These humanitarian activities made him *persona grata* with both the Allies and the Axis and in February 1945 he travelled to Berlin to confer with Himmler (q.v.) and other Nazi leaders, who wanted him to mediate in securing the surrender of German forces to the British and Americans instead of to the Russians. The idea was rejected. Count Bernadotte was acting in a similar capacity as mediator for the United Nations Security Council between the Arabs and Israelis during the conflict of 1948 when he was assassinated in Palestine by Jewish extremists.

BEVIN, Ernest (1881–1951). British Labour party politician who served in the wartime coalition led by Churchill (q.v.). As minister of labour and national service, with far-reaching emergency powers, he was responsible for directing labour where it was needed, and by 1943 had transferred nearly 7 million men and women into the armed forces, munitions and other essential industries.

The Swedish aristocrat and humanitarian Count Bernadotte, whose activities crossed the boundaries of war and ultimately cost him his life.

Ernest Bevin, Britain's wartime minister of labour. A socialist member of Churchill's government, he was responsible for the direction of manpower.

Two of Australia's greatest war leaders: General Sir Thomas Blamey and Major-General Gordon Bennett.

After Churchill's defeat in the 1945 election he accompanied the new prime minister Attlee (q.v.) to the Potsdam conference.

BLAMEY, (Sir) Thomas (1884–1951). Australian general. After serving in Gallipoli and France in the first world war, and in the Australian police service, Blamey was appointed to command the Australian Corps in the Middle East at the outbreak of war. He served in the corps in Libya and Greece. He became c-in-c Australian Army in March 1942, responsible for measures against a possible Japanese invasion, including bringing a raw and inefficient army up to a state of war readiness. He was also Allied land forces commander under General MacArthur (q.v.), taking personal command from September 1942 to January 1943, and leading operations in New Guinea, Buna, Papua and the Solomons. After 1943, when the Australian part in the Pacific operations was gradually being reduced, Blamey's role as Allied land forces commander became purely nominal.

BLASKOWITZ, Johannes (1883–1948). German general who commanded the Eighth Army in the invasion of Poland, when his forces were subjected to a severe flank attack from Poland's Poznan and Pomorze armies at the battle of Bzura (10–13 September 1939). His position was recovered by Rundstedt's (q.v.) decision to send the Tenth Army (Reichenau) to give support, and the Poles were forced back across the Bzura. Blaskowitz received the surrender of Warsaw on 27 September. He then remained out of the limelight until he was appointed to command Army Group G, preparing to defend against the invasion in France. His area covered the bay of Biscay and the Mediterranean. He was relieved in September 1944 after the defeat in Lorraine, not because of any military deficiency but because he was independently minded. He committed suicide while waiting to be tried for war crimes at Nuremberg.

BLOMBERG, Werner von (1878–1946). German field-marshal and war minister 1935–8. Blomberg was a key figure in Hitler's (q.v.) rise to power. As minister for war, along with the heads of the three services, he was called in by Hitler on the death of President Hindenburg to swear the oath of allegiance to the Führer. Blomberg in turn imposed the oath on his fellow officers, and thereby helped confirm Hitler's control of the armed forces.

Blomberg became commander-in-chief of the armed forces as well as war minister in 1935, when Hitler created a unified overall command. Blomberg was widely accused by his fellow generals of being too pliant to Hitler's aims, evinced by his wearing of Nazi insignia. His chief antagonist at this stage was Himmler (q.v.), who was zealously promoting the interests of his armed *ss* formations. Himmler's opportunity to outflank Blomberg came in January 1938, when he presented Hitler with 'evidence' that the woman Blomberg had married a few weeks earlier (with Hitler as an approving witness) had been a prostitute. The scandal shocked the officer corps, who demanded their chief's resignation. Shortly afterwards Blomberg's natural successor, Fritsch, was ruined by a charge of homosexuality fabricated by Himmler,

Werner von Blomberg, minister of war between 1935 and 1938, and a key figure in the pre-war rise of the German army. He was discredited by a false scandal concocted by Himmler.

and Hitler neatly solved the problem of a successor to Blomberg by taking over command of the armed forces and the office of minister of defence himself. The Blomberg–Fritsch episode therefore spelled the end of any power the armed forces might have retained of acting independently of Hitler and the Nazi regime.

BLUM, Léon (1872–1950). French socialist leader. Blum was a fervent opponent of the surrender of France in 1940, and travelled to Vichy to rally socialists to continue the fight. He was arrested by the Vichy government and tried in 1942 for leading France unprepared towards war during his two periods as premier. He defended himself so eloquently that he discredited his accusers and the Germans stopped the trial. He was moved to Buchenwald concentration camp and continued to write while constantly expecting execution. He was freed by the Allies in 1945 and returned to politics, heading a caretaker government from December 1946 to January 1947.

BOCK, Fedor von (1880–1945). German general, one of the old Prussian school who served in the army from the age of seventeen. He commanded the German armies in the invasion of Poland, and was chief of Army Group B for the invasion of 1940, which operated on the northern flank in the Netherlands and Belgium. Promoted field-marshal, he commanded Army Group Centre for the invasion of the Soviet Union, but was retired after the failure to capture Stalingrad.

BOR-KOMOROWSKI, Tadeusz (1895–1966). Commander of the Polish home army from 1943, and the general who gave the order for the tragic Warsaw rising on 1 August 1944. When the Germans invaded Poland in 1939 Komorowski, an experienced cavalry officer and brilliant horseman, persuaded his friend General Sikorski (q.v.) in exile in France to allow the formation of an underground army. Komorowski took the name Bor as a cover and subsequently retained it. He commanded the home army in the Cracow area, then became deputy commander of the Polish home

Bor-Komorowski (left), the Polish general who commanded the underground resistance army. He was captured after the Warsaw rising, and is seen surrendering to an *ss* general, Bach-Zelewski.

army, and finally its commander in July 1943. He was considered a major target for the German occupation forces, who put a price of £400,000 on his head. He was captured on one occasion, but escaped before he could be identified.

The tragedy of the Warsaw rising began when the Russians approached the city and Moscow radio called for an uprising. Bor-Komorowski gave the order, but the Russians remained outside Warsaw and the home army was crushed in two months of bitter fighting. Bor-Komorowski was captured, but was released by the American forces at Innsbruck, and later settled in England.

He was severely attacked for the loss of life incurred in the rising at a time when the Russian armies were not ready to take the city. There is now considerable evidence that he naïvely allowed himself to be outmanœuvred by the Russian command, who were only too happy to stand by and watch the German army of occupation and the independent Polish forces destroy each other as completely as possible before they took over. Stalin (q.v.) in fact impeded all British and American efforts to drop supplies to the Polish home army.

BORMANN, Martin (born 1900). Leading Nazi who became Hitler's (q.v.) deputy after the defection of Rudolf Hess (q.v.) in 1941. Bormann was one of the most sinister members in the Nazi inner circle during the war, and one of the most mysterious figures after it. On 1 May 1945, as the Russians closed in on the Reich chancellery, he set out with a small number of associates to break through the Russian lines behind a screen of German tanks. One witness stated that he was seen dead, but his body was never recovered. Since that time major efforts have been made to trace him in South America, where it has been alleged he escaped with the help of loyal Nazis through Austria, using vast Nazi party funds. He has never been identified in South America, although several innocent people have been arrested and questioned on suspicion of being Bormann.

BOSE, Subhas Chandra (1897-1945). Indian nationalist leader who organized a force to fight against the Allies during the second world war.

Martin Bormann (right), Hitler's deputy, in company with Hitler and Ribbentrop in 1944. His fate has remained one of the outstanding wartime mysteries.

Subhas Chandra Bose, the Indian National Army leader
who fought with the Axis in Burma, intending to take
over India in the wake of Japanese victory.

Brendan Bracken (right, with Churchill), one of
Churchill's closest confidants. A mysterious and elusive
figure, he occupied the post of minister of information
for most of the war.

After a lifetime spent in gaols and in exile Bose,
at one time a supporter of Gandhi, became head
of the Indian National Congress in 1938. He was
imprisoned again by the British in 1940, but,
released a short time later, he fled to Afghanistan
and from there to Germany. He raised a force to
fight with the Axis as the Indian National Army.
In 1943 he turned to Japan for support, and took
his army into Burma, with the intention of advancing on India and setting up an independent
government with Japanese support. His force was
defeated along with the Japanese armies in Burma.
Bose was killed in an aircraft accident in Formosa
in 1945.

BRACKEN, Brendan (1901–58). British politician and newspaper publisher. Bracken, Irish by
birth, served as parliamentary private secretary to
Churchill (q.v.) in 1940–1, and was then appointed
minister of information, a post which he occupied
until 1945. In Churchill's brief caretaker government of 1945 Bracken was made first lord of the
Admiralty. Throughout the war he was one of
Churchill's inner circle of advisers.

A cartoon published in *Pravda* depicts Allied
confidence in early victory after the Anglo–Soviet
alliance of 1942. The Allied thunderbolt strikes at the
cowering and weakly defended Axis leaders, while the
original caption proclaimed 1942 as 'the year of the
enemy's final rout'.

BRADLEY, Omar (born 1893). United States general, commander of the US First Army in the invasion of Normandy and of the Twelfth US Army Group for the subsequent operations in Europe. Born in Missouri, Omar Bradley entered West Point military academy in 1911 and graduated four years later in the same class as Dwight D. Eisenhower (q.v.). He missed active service in the first world war, and in the inter-war years held a variety of appointments, notably as head of the weapons section at the infantry school, serving under George Marshall (q.v.), then a lieutenant-colonel. In 1940, when Marshall had become chief of staff, Bradley was appointed commandant of the infantry school at Fort Benning. It was only after Pearl Harbor in 1941 that Bradley began to obtain field commands, first as commander of the 82 Infantry Division, later of the 28 Infantry Division. For the next two years he held a variety of commands, all arranged by General Marshall to extend the variety of his experience. He was attached to General Eisenhower's staff for the landings in Algeria in Operation Torch. The American 2 Corps, under General Fredendall, suffered badly at the battle of the Kasserine Pass, and General Patton (q.v.) was appointed its new commander. He asked that Bradley should be his assistant. Eisenhower agreed, and when Patton was subsequently promoted, Bradley took over the corps. The corps under Bradley served in the Sicily campaign, and in October 1943 Bradley was withdrawn, ordered to England, and given the job of commanding the First Army in preparation for the cross-Channel invasion of France. In the course of preparations for the invasion, the commanders were appointed for the exploitation phase, and

Opposite above Ernest Bevin, British minister of labour and national service. He became foreign minister in Attlee's Labour government in 1945, and was a delegate at the Potsdam conference.

Below General Charles de Gaulle, who rallied the Free French from his base in exile in London, and entered Paris with the Allies on 25 August 1944 to become head of the provisional government.

Bradley learned that he was to command the Twelfth US Army Group. The prospect gave him some anxiety, since one of the army commanders serving under him would be his former boss General Patton, reinstated after the disgrace caused by the celebrated 'slapping' incidents in Sicily. It was Marshall himself who inspired this command structure, remarking that Bradley had the administrative talent needed for the army group command, while Patton was the aggressive commander needed to exploit the breakout from the beach-head.

At the time the invasion took place in June 1944, Bradley was far from well known, and his commands in North Africa and Sicily had given little public indication of his abilities. But in the course of the campaign the newspaper correspondents, led by Ernie Pyle, promoted him on a world-wide basis as 'the GI's general'. As commander of the US First Army, Bradley served under Montgomery during and immediately after the invasion. In the early weeks, Montgomery's declared strategy was to hold the German armour on the eastern end of the Allied lodgment area – the 'hinge' – and use the highly mobile American army on the right to break out into Normandy and swing round towards Germany for the exploitation – the 'door'. Bradley's task was to effect the breakout. He chose the coastal corridor, aiming for Coutances. The first critical battle was not a success. Faced with the difficulties of the *bocage* country – Normandy's patchwork of small fields divided by hedges growing on top of strong high earth ridges – the armour was unable to exploit its strength and mobility. The hedges provided ideal defensive cover, and the tank undersides were badly exposed to fire from German defences every time they tried to cross a hedgerow. Bradley had also made the mistake of dispersing his strength across a wide front for the attempt to break out, using Middleton's 8 Corps and Collins's (q.v.) 7 Corps. The result was that the offensive gained only a few miles. Bradley's next attempt, on 24 July, was mounted on a narrow front in the wake of a concentrated bombing attack against the defences, and within two days the German line virtually broke. Patton's newly activated Third Army was able to advance at speed and spread out into northern France. General Bradley was promoted commander of the Twelfth US Army Group on 1 August 1944. And from then until the end of the war his career was notable as much for his relations with his fellow generals as for his contribution to the military success. To the extremely large press corps serving with the armies in Europe Bradley presented a bland and uninteresting picture, concerned as he was with the command of an army group, compared with the more exciting General Patton with his penchant for the audacious armoured thrust. It was a comparison from which Bradley suffered: as Eisenhower remarked, Bradley's only weakness was that he lacked the capacity, possibly the willingness, to dramatize himself. His other inter-Allied conflict was with Montgomery (q.v.), now promoted to the rank of field-marshal but serving in a parallel role to Bradley's as Twenty-first Army Group commander. Both were responsible to Eisenhower, who had assumed ground command for the European theatre as head of SHAEF on 1 September.

During September the stresses of personality and protocol, and the problems of keeping under control the armed forces of two nations fighting as allies, became acute. Bradley was generally the sufferer. The basis of the friction was the division of opinion on whether the Allied advance beyond the Seine should be mounted on a broad front, or by a concentrated thrust on a narrow front. From the early days of planning for the battle in Europe, Eisenhower had envisaged the entire Allied armed forces – two army groups advancing from Normandy and the third from the south of France – arriving on the Rhine before the final concerted push into the German heartland. Montgomery, once the Allies had advanced beyond the Seine, put to Eisenhower his recommendation for a single thrust by one army group. It was impossible, he said, to continue to supply both army groups, and one should be halted while the other drove hard into the German rear areas. It was a philosophy

which fell more into the pattern expected of generals like Patton than into the conventional picture of Montgomery as a cautious, plodding, setpiece battle commander. Of course, Montgomery's plan included the suggestion that his Twenty-first Army Group should receive the supplies and mount the advance on the left of the Allied front, where it would take the Channel ports, particularly Antwerp, over-run the v-weapon sites, and go on to the Ruhr, where the vast majority of German war production was located. On the other hand, credit should be given to Montgomery for putting the plan before his own part in it, and he twice offered to place himself subordinate to Bradley if Eisenhower would agree to a single commander for the single thrust which he so urgently recommended.

Bradley at this stage still did not feel secure enough to exert himself in the struggles between the Allies. He was disadvantaged by two geographical circumstances. Firstly, the form of the landing and breakout had left him commanding the army group on the right, with his advance due east towards the Saar basin and southern Germany covering the less important objectives. Secondly, the geographical obstacle of the Ardennes forest made it necessary to filter off two corps from his First Army, 19 and 7 Corps, and put them under Montgomery's operational control. Bradley was therefore left in operational control of only one corps of the First Army and the Third Army. His position was made even more difficult by the determination of the Third Army commander, General Patton, to move on to the Moselle at the greatest possible speed, irrespective of the supply position. On 1 September Bradley had ordered that the First Army should have 5000 tons a day of the available supplies, because of the priority of the advance to the north-east, and Patton's Third Army should receive 2000 tons per day. Patton's forceful argument, however, persuaded Eisenhower, at a conference on 2 September at Chartres, to agree that the Third Army could advance to the Moselle and secure the crossings as soon as they had the fuel to move. It was obvious

General Omar Bradley (centre), senior United States land commander during the battles in north-west Europe, with fellow (and rival) commanders Patton and Montgomery after a presentation of medals by Montgomery, 7 July 1944. Bradley was shortly to take command of Twelfth Army Group.

that such a policy would prejudice the chance of a decisive breakthrough by Montgomery's forces on the left flank, by depriving them of the limited supplies available. By 4 September, Montgomery's forces had captured Antwerp intact and, after an advance of 250 miles in ten days, were well placed to drive on for the Ruhr. At the same time it was known that Hitler (q.v.) had ordered reinforcements to be sent to the Moselle area to defend against Patton's advance, which left German defences in the north extremely weak. Montgomery, anxious to capitalize on these advantages, suggested that Patton's advance should be halted altogether, and the whole of the available fuel given to sustain the drive in the north. With reduced forces and a reduced role, and with Montgomery and Patton fighting for priority for their own missions, Bradley was being squeezed out of the picture. Worse, Patton's eastward advance, and the north-east advance of the two separated corps, were pulling his army group badly out of shape.

Meanwhile, in the course of October, Hitler recognized the fundamental weakness of the Allied position in the Ardennes, the fork of the Allied advance where a sixty-mile front was being held by only four American divisions. This offered the chance of the counter-attack which could restore

Germany's position in the west. Bradley was with Eisenhower at his headquarters in Versailles when news of the German attack arrived. At first Bradley made the mistake of judging it to be a local German spoiling effort, and he retained this misconception for fully three days, until on 18 December he ordered Patton to stop planning for an offensive in the Saar and prepare to attack the southern flank of 'the bulge'. Two days later, when it was decided that the main attack against the bulge would be made from the north, Eisenhower's chief of staff telephoned Bradley to say that Bradley's two armies north of the Ardennes, the us First and Ninth Armies, were to be brought under Montgomery's control. Although the move was logical, bringing all the troops operating north of the salient under a single unified command, Bradley understandably found it objectionable. It was open to unfavourable interpretation, as a loss of confidence in him personally and in the American command in general, and as implying that when the Americans got into trouble they had to be baled out by a British commander. But the changeover went ahead, on a temporary basis, and Bradley was left with command of only one army, Patton's Third Army, while Montgomery had command of four – the Canadian First and British Second, and the us First and Ninth Armies. Bradley was even more enraged by what he considered to be Montgomery's reluctance to commit his troops from the north of the bulge, while Patton's troops attacked from the south. Bradley was annoyed at this lack of activity, and urged Bedell-Smith to spur Montgomery to action. Ultimately the German offensive failed to break the Allied line, and lost momentum. And then public statements by Montgomery exacerbated the differences in the Allied command. The one thing that Bradley insisted on was that Montgomery should not be given command of all the ground forces. To this Eisenhower acceded. But Bradley was still not able to escape from his position at the centre of the Allied personality clashes. On 29 December, when Patton's army had relieved Bastogne and the

German counter-offensive had been contained, Montgomery wrote to Eisenhower suggesting that the Twelfth Army Group (Bradley's) should come under the control and co-ordination of c-in-c Twenty-first Army Group (Montgomery) 'subject to such instruction as may be issued by the Supreme Commander from time to time'. He made this suggestion, he said, 'only because I am so anxious not to have another failure'. Eisenhower wrote back that he found this implication 'disturbing', with its predictions of failure unless Montgomery's opinions on giving him command of Bradley were met in detail. When Bradley learned of this new threat to his rump of a command, he was naturally angered. He told Eisenhower that he would be unable to retain the confidence of his troops if Montgomery's request was granted, and Eisenhower would have to send him home. Eisenhower was surprised by Bradley's reaction, saying that Bradley had been the one officer he thought he could rely on to do as he was asked. But Bradley declared bluntly that this was the one thing he could not take. General Patton also sided with Bradley, and declared that he would quit with him in support if necessary. Then Montgomery further insulted the Americans by issuing a statement outlining how he had stopped the German offensive, and omitting any mention of the American commander's part in the operation. Two days later Bradley tried to redress the balance by issuing a statement of his own, stating clearly that the changeover of the us First and Ninth Armies to Montgomery's command had been only temporary. But the problem was never satisfactorily resolved. Although the us First Army was returned to Bradley's control, the Ninth Army remained under Montgomery for a further three months. And the problems of whose forces should play the major part in the advance against Germany continued into the new year.

When the autumn stalemate was broken and the plan was being formed for the advance beyond the Rhine, Eisenhower still favoured a double attack. The main drive into the Reich was to be made by Montgomery, north of the Ruhr and into the north

German plain, which offered the best opportunity for mobile operations and was the quickest means of denying the Germans the vital Ruhr industries. At the same time a complementary attack was to be made by Bradley's forces from the Mainz–Frankfurt area, producing a massive double envelopment to be followed by a great thrust to join up with the Russians. The British chiefs of staff examined this plan and objected, on the grounds that Eisenhower would not have enough strength to mount more than one full-blooded attack. As the combined chiefs of staff had already agreed that the main attack should be made north of the Ruhr, they proposed that the forces to the south of the Ruhr should be put on the defensive. In this discussion, a variation on the broad-front or narrow-front debate of the previous autumn, the disagreement proved to be one of the most serious of the war. Marshall went so far as to say that if the British did not accept Eisenhower's plan, he would recommend Eisenhower to ask to be relieved of his command. The British had no choice but to accept. And a corollary of the plan was that Montgomery was not to take over the position of sole ground force commander. Bradley's position was still intact, though he had come close to being swamped again in the strategic discussions that went on over his head. It was at this stage that he began to assert himself and fight for a stronger role than that envisaged even in Eisenhower's plan. This plan called for an approach to the Rhine by Montgomery's forces, while Bradley's were to maintain an 'aggressive defence'. Only when Montgomery had secured the west bank of the Rhine north of Düsseldorf was Bradley to advance to the Rhine south of Düsseldorf. This plan clearly consigned Bradley's army group, which had already been deprived of the Ninth Army, to a supporting role, while Montgomery played the major part. Bradley therefore put an alternative plan to Eisenhower. He told his supreme commander bluntly that if SHAEF wanted to destroy the whole operation they could do so and be damned. It was, he said, the prestige of the American army that was at stake. Instead of the

thrust to the north of the Ruhr, Bradley asked that the Ninth Army should be returned to his command, and that the main force of the advance should be in the centre of the Allied line, not in the north, with his own First and Third Armies advancing to the Rhine between Cologne and Coblenz, and on towards the centre of Germany as opposed to the north. Montgomery's role would be to cover the flanks of this fundamentally American advance. Eisenhower turned down this idea, and the two army groups proceeded according to Eisenhower's original conception. As it turned out, this was no great handicap to Bradley. He had the advantage of General Patton as one of his army commanders: Patton interpreted the extraordinarily ambiguous term 'aggressive defence' with his usual liberality, and proceeded to exploit as far east as he could in the Eifel region. On 7 March, out of conformity with orders, a combat command of the 9 Armoured Division (part of General Hodges's, q.v., First Army) reached the Ludendorff bridge at Remagen, and found it intact. Dozens of other bridges had been demolished by the retreating *Wehrmacht* as the Allies approached, but this one remained intact, although two demolition charges set the bridge vibrating. The Americans dashed across and secured a small bridgehead. Bradley was jubilant at being able to tell SHAEF that his men had crossed the Rhine. But the staff at supreme headquarters were not pleased, and told Bradley that Remagen had no part in the plan. Bradley angrily asked if they wanted him to pull the troops back and blow the bridge themselves. Fortunately the man who mattered, Eisenhower, was as delighted as Bradley, and told him to throw across whatever he needed to hold the bridgehead. Even so, Bradley still feared, justifiably, that he could lose more divisions to Montgomery for the advance in the north, and he ordered his two army commanders, Patton and Hodges, to get involved in crossings of the Rhine. Patton needed little urging. He drove his divisional commanders hard, and by 22 March was ready. General Irwin's 5 Division slipped across the river at Oppenheim, thereby

pre-empting Montgomery's much-vaunted set-piece crossing. Bradley himself wrote that he thought this battle to approach the Rhine a model textbook manœuvre, and the one campaign that brought him the greatest professional pride. His aggressive campaigning in the south meant that Bradley was allowed to keep the divisions ear-marked for Montgomery, and continue to exploit to the east and subsequently to the north, ulti-mately meeting Montgomery's Twenty-first Army Group and trapping the bulk of Field-Marshal Model's (q.v.) Army Group B in the Ruhr. Bradley had survived a difficult patch and his stock was again high.

Bradley improved his position even further dur-ing the last phase of the war, when the con-troversial question arose of what strategy to pursue to eliminate the last German resistance. For this phase Eisenhower elected to concentrate the main effort on Bradley's army group in the south, giving Montgomery not much more than a flanking role. The American thrust, towards Leipzig and Dresden, was aimed at over-running the remain-ing German industrial areas, and meeting up with the Russians on the Elbe. The axis of this advance was also aimed eastwards to attack the German command, who were reported to be moving south-wards towards a supposed 'last redoubt' in the Alps. But the principal consequence of the plan was that it left the Russians to take over Berlin. In coming to his decision, and backing it despite furious objections from the British, Eisenhower was undoubtedly influenced by Bradley. The approach to the Rhine had enhanced Bradley's reputation as a forceful and aggressive com-mander, while Montgomery's comparative caution in the north had consolidated his reputa-tion (unwelcome at this stage in the war) as a set-piece battle commander. Eisenhower therefore listened to Bradley's reasoning, and when Eisen-hower asked how they could avert an accidental clash between Russian and Allied troops, Bradley

The invasion has succeeded, and Bradley reviews the war with General Collins after the capture of Cherbourg, 27 June 1944.

looked for a clearly defined barrier. He too was anxious to avoid a collision which might flare into a fight, and was unwilling to trust to radio signals. Together Bradley and his chief studied the map and settled on the line of the Elbe as the best choice of a meeting line, extending along the Mulde south of Magdeburg. Bradley's reasoning was prompted by several considerations. He wrote in his post-war memoirs that he 'could see no political advan-tage accruing from the capture of Berlin that would offset the need for quick destruction of the German army on our front'. He was also prompted at the time by the calculated likelihood of 100,000 further casualties in a dash for Berlin, by the fact that the Russians were already far closer to the Elbe than the Allies, and by the fact that the Elbe itself lay ninety miles to the east of the agreed line of demarcation for the occupation. Against the urgings of Winston Churchill (q.v.), Eisenhower endorsed Bradley's view. The First and Ninth Armies were ordered to spread defensively with their front facing the Czech border and the Elbe, while Patton's Third Army was to mount an offen-sive south along the valley of the Danube, to join up with the Russians and break up the southern redoubt. Eisenhower specifically excluded Berlin from his plan. In the last days of the war, some of Patton's troops actually entered Prague and, although Bradley tried to persuade Eisenhower to let them mount a full occupation, Eisenhower in-sisted on avoiding international complications and they were ordered to withdraw. The one advan-tage of Patton's drive to the south was to dispel at last all fears of the last redoubt, and Bradley was able to transfer 18 Airborne Corps to aid Montgo-mery's forces in their dash to the Baltic, which pre-vented a Russian occupation of Denmark.

A summary of Bradley's contribution to the war falls neatly into two pockets: his diffidence and in-feriority to the more experienced Montgomery in the months up to the approach to the Rhine, and a sudden surge of assertiveness in the final weeks of the war. In that period he achieved his proper influence as the senior American army officer in direct command of ground troops. Whether he used that influence to effective ends is open to doubt. He was one of the men on whom Eisenhower placed great reliance for advice, and therefore a key member of the quartet of personalities (Bradley, Eisenhower, Marshall and Roosevelt, with Roosevelt eventually replaced by Truman, qq.v.) who determined the pattern of subsequent history. And the characteristic of the American approach to the end of the war was that fighting was a military matter, and political questions could be worked out separately when the fighting had been brought to an end. The basic mistake was in trusting that the Russians would adopt the same moral standpoint, and the result was a Soviet-dominated eastern Europe. Bradley himself

wrote: 'As soldiers we looked naïvely on this British inclination to contemplate the war with political foresight and non-military objectives.' No hostile critic could have been more outspoken than Bradley himself in summarizing thus the limitations of the American military command in failing to recognize the blurred line where strategy (the means) merges into politics (the end). After the war Bradley served for two years as administrator of veterans' affairs in Washington, and in 1948 he became chief of staff. In August 1949 he was appointed the first chairman of the joint chiefs of staff, and in succeeding years served with distinction in a variety of posts, mainly connected with military aspects of NATO.

BRAUCHITSCH, Walter von (1881–1948). Commander-in-chief of the German army from 1938 until December 1941. Brauchitsch was very much a subordinate of Hitler (q.v.) and enjoyed considerable prestige during the early stages of the war with the defeats of Poland, France and the Low Countries, and the Russian invasion. After setbacks in Russia, during which he warned Hitler of the dangers of neglecting to take Moscow before the onset of winter, he lost his influence. That and increasing ill-health forced him to resign his post and Hitler took over this command himself. Brauchitsch died while being held as a prisoner of war by the British.

BRAUN, Eva (1912–45). Hitler's (q.v.) companion and, for the last few hours of their lives, his wife. She met Hitler in 1930 and set up home with him in Munich. She stayed with him throughout the pre-war and war years, acting occasionally as hostess but otherwise playing no significant part in the war except by keeping herself and Hitler amused. Their domestic life remained almost completely private, and they seldom appeared in public together. Hitler married her on 29 April 1945 in the Führer's bunker in Berlin. They committed suicide the next day, she by taking poison and he by shooting himself, and their bodies were allegedly taken out into the garden of the Reich chancellery, soaked in petrol, and burned.

A determined Bradley strides into London as head of the United States First Army, in January 1944, to plan for the Normandy invasion.

BRAUN, Wernher von (1912–1977). Born into a distinguished family – his father was Baron Magnus von Braun, minister of agriculture and founder of the German savings bank, and his mother a talented musician – Wernher von Braun failed mathematics and physics at the French Gymnasium, but later at another school developed an interest in astronomy which inspired him with the desire to master space flight. He tackled maths and physics with new enthusiasm and became highly proficient in both subjects. He made contact with other rocket enthusiasts while studying at the Charlottenburg Institute of Technology in Berlin, and set up rudimentary experimental units both outside Berlin and in Switzerland. On 1 October 1932 he was appointed to the German Army Ordnance Office to work on their rocket programme. (There were no restrictions on rockets as weapons in the treaty of Versailles.) By 1937, when the rocket centre had moved to Peenemünde on the Baltic coast, Braun had become its director. By the outbreak of war Braun and his staff were working on the development of the v-2 rocket, forty-six feet long and having 55,000 lb of thrust. The new rocket demanded significant advances in the areas of guidance, aerodynamics and propulsion. All those problems the genius of Braun was able to solve, but the political difficulties remained intractable. Firstly he was thwarted by Hitler (q.v.) who drew off men and resources from rocket research for the Luftwaffe. Then he was arrested by the *ss* on suspicion of concentrating on space travel and not giving his entire energy to making war weapons. Braun's v-2 (v stands for *Vergeltungswaffe*, or reprisal weapon) was first launched in action on 8 September 1944, and some 3600 were used in the seven months of the campaign against England before the launching sites were captured. At the end of the war Braun ordered the evacuation of his staff and their families from the Peenemünde area to the south-west, to avoid falling into the hands of the Russians and ensure capture by the Americans. He was taken to America as a 'ward of the army' with 112 of his scientists, 100 rockets,

The German rocket scientist Wernher von Braun, architect of the belated v-weapons campaign, and subsequently of the United States space programme.

and all their technical data, and became a leading figure in the American space programme. He and forty of his associates became naturalized us citizens in 1965.

BRERETON, Lewis Hyde (1890–1967). American air commander. A veteran of naval, army and air service, Brereton was a pioneer aviator in 1913. He held commands in the Pacific and European theatres in the second world war, including the Far East Air Force in the Philippines, the Tenth Air Force in India, and the Middle East Air Force. He organized the raid from Libya on the Ploesti oil refineries in Romania. He commanded the Ninth Air Force covering the Normandy campaign, and the First Allied Airborne Army from August 1944 for operations in north-west Europe. Men from his force fought the battles of Nijmegen and Arnhem in September 1944.

BROOKE, Alan (First Viscount Alanbrooke of Brookeborough) (1883–1963). British general

Brooke-Popham

who served as chief of the imperial general staff
for most of the war. Brooke commanded 2 Corps
of the British Expeditionary Force until the withdrawal from Dunkirk, which he conducted with
acknowledged brilliance, and was appointed
c-in-c home forces responsible for the army's anti-
invasion preparations. He became CIGS in 1941,
and chairman of the British chiefs of staff committee in June 1942. With the other service chiefs
he was responsible for the running of the war and
the planning of strategy, and was Churchill's (q.v.)
closest adviser.

It was widely anticipated that he would command the invasion of France, but when it became
clear that the United States would provide the
greater part of the manpower and equipment for
the invasion Churchill suggested to Eisenhower
(q.v.) that an American commander would be
more appropriate, and Eisenhower was selected.
Brooke bore the disappointment stoically.

His grasp of strategy, clarity of thought, and
firmness of expression were qualities greatly
appreciated not only by his British colleagues but
also by Roosevelt (q.v.). Stalin (q.v.) provoked a
major disagreement with Brooke during the
summit conference at Teheran in 1943, but
Brooke's aggressive response won Stalin's support. Brooke's contribution to the war remained
largely unsung until his diaries were made public.
It then became obvious that he was the architect
of much of the strategic outline of the war in the
west, and also that he played an important role in
curbing and controlling the worst excesses of a
highly imaginative prime minister, whom he
regarded as the most difficult but rewarding man
he could possibly have worked with.

BROOKE-POPHAM, (Sir) Robert (1878–
1953). British air marshal, in charge of Allied air
defences in the Far East at the time of Japan's victorious entry into the war. After a long and distinguished career first as a soldier and then as an

A working lunch on the Rhine. Field-Marshal Alan
Brooke (centre) confers with Montgomery (right) and
Churchill on 26 March 1945, two days after the main
Rhine crossings had begun.

Sir Robert Brooke-Popham (left), British air marshal. He was unjustly attacked by critics for alleged neglect of the air defences in the Far East.

officer in the Royal Air Force from its formation, he retired in 1937 to a new career as governor of Kenya. He rejoined the RAF when war broke out in 1939, and went first to Canada to organize aircrew training there. Then in October 1940 he was made c-in-c Far East. He recognized the dangers of the inadequate air defences he was provided with, and fought doggedly for resources with which to improve them. Because of greater priorities, especially in the Middle East, he was denied. He also suffered from a dispersed and ambiguous command structure, and from political interference from London. One main point of his policy was to push the exiguous air defences forward into neutral Thailand, but he was not allowed to do so until it was too late. On 27 December 1941, in the middle of the battle for Malaya, he was relieved of his command. Inevitably, and totally unfairly, Brooke-Popham was attacked as responsible for British defeats in the Far East. He served in a figurehead post as inspector of the air training corps and retired for the second time in 1945.

BROWNING, Frederick (1896–1965). British airborne commander. A Grenadier Guards officer with long regimental experience, Browning was selected to command the new glider-borne parachute formation which was created after the Dun-

Lieutenant-General Sir Frederick 'Boy' Browning (left), commander of 1 British Airborne Corps. He is seen during preparations for the invasion of Normandy with the deputy supreme commander, Tedder. The glider wings bear the three white stripes used to identify Allied invasion aircraft.

kirk evacuation. It became 1 Airborne Division in 1941, and was employed, without great success, in the Mediterranean. Its first major operation was Sicily, where inexperience led to the landings being widely scattered and many men being unnecessarily lost. The formation was expanded to a corps under Browning's command and took part in the Normandy landings, when its 6 Airborne Division under Richard Gale dropped soon after midnight, several hours before the seaborne landings, to secure the left flank of the beach-head, carry out demolitions, and prevent the panzer formations from counter-attacking the troops in the beach-head.

In August 1944 the Allied Airborne Army was formed under the American general Brereton (q.v.), with Browning as his deputy, combining British and American airborne forces. A month later 10,000 men of 1 Airborne Division were dropped to form a corridor ahead of the British Second Army to secure the crossings of the canals and rivers as far as the Rhine. They were severely counter-attacked by German forces, and after a week of fighting, impeded by bad weather and lack of reinforcements and ammunition, the 2400 survivors were forced to withdraw.

Browning was later made chief of staff to Mountbatten (q.v.) in South-east Asia Command, and was not in command for the final great airborne operation of the war in the crossing of the Rhine. 'Boy' Browning, as he was familiarly known, was the major contributor to the formation of airborne forces in the west.

BUCKNER, Simon Bolivar (1886–1945). United States general. Buckner spent the immediate pre-war period building up the defences in Alaska against the threat of a Japanese advance across the Pacific. After the Japanese had invaded Attu and Kiska in the Aleutians Buckner was instrumental in recapturing them in May 1943. In June 1944 he was sent to take command of Tenth Army in preparation for the attack on Okinawa. He launched the attack on 1 April 1945, and six weeks of hard fighting followed in which the Japanese were forced to retreat to the south-west

corner of the island. On 18 June Buckner was at a forward observation post when he was hit in the chest by a fragment of shrapnel thrown up by a Japanese shell explosion. He died shortly afterwards. He was buried on Okinawa but four years after the war his body was transported to the family grave in Kentucky. Buckner was a stern disciplinarian, but had a humorous disposition, and was noted especially for his ability to work in harmony with officers and men from the other services.

BUDENNY, Semyon Mikhailovich (1883–1973). Soviet general, commander of the South-western Front defence against the southern sector of the German invasion of 1941 in the Ukraine. Born into a peasant family, Budenny began his army career when he was drafted into the cavalry in 1903, and he remained a cavalryman throughout. He served in the Russo–Japanese war, and rose to the rank of sergeant-major in the first world war. He joined the party in 1919, and was one of the creators of the First Cavalry Army. In the inter-war years he was associated mainly with the cavalry; in 1939 he became a deputy commissar for defence, and first deputy commissar for defence in 1940. When the German advance by Kleist's and Guderian's (qq.v.) panzers proved unstoppable in Operation Barbarossa in September 1941, and the city of Kiev was threatened, Budenny was relieved of his command of the South-western Front and replaced by Timoshenko (q.v.). The move did nothing to prevent total defeat in the battle of Kiev. Budenny was subsequently assigned to posts concerned with the recruiting and training of troops.

Heavily attacked for his ineptitude as a commander in the battle of Kiev, Budenny was cruelly described by one of his own officers as 'a man with an immense moustache, but a very small brain'. Even so, as one of a small group of Stalin's (q.v.) oldest associates and one of the best known of Soviet generals, he was well placed to remain

Lieutenant-General Simon Bolivar Buckner (right), commander of US Tenth Army on Okinawa. He was killed on 18 June 1945.

Marshal Budenny, one of the old guard of Stalin's generals. He remained close to the Soviet leader despite widespread doubts about his professional competence.

James Byrnes, American statesman and secretary of state in Truman's government.

nominally important, although being denied any further chance of holding a military command at the front.

BULL, Harold (born 1893). United States general who held the important post of chief of operations at SHAEF during the campaigns in north-west Europe. Bull was serving as secretary of the general staff in 1939, and became chief of operations with the United States War Department when the United States entered the war. In 1943 he was assigned to the North African theatre as a special observer for General Marshall (q.v.), after which he briefly took command of 3 Corps. In September 1943 he became deputy chief of the operations section with COSSAC, and in February 1944 was appointed operations chief at SHAEF.

BYRNES, James Francis (1879–1972). United States lawyer who became secretary of state for war on the death of President Roosevelt (q.v.) in 1945. Elected to the Senate in 1930 Byrnes was a promoter of the Cash and Carry Arms Act, and helped to push through legislation on selective service and Lend-Lease. Roosevelt appointed him associate

justice of the Supreme Court in June 1941, but on the outbreak of war he was made director of the Office of Economic Stabilization, and a year later chairman of the Mobilization Board. His main work was in looking after domestic affairs while the president concentrated on the war, and his success led Roosevelt to describe him as the 'assistant president on the home front'. Among his measures was the imposition of a ceiling on salaries of $25,000 to combat inflation, and a massive increase in war production. Byrnes was a candidate for selection as Roosevelt's vice-president in the elections of 1944, but he was passed over in favour of Truman (q.v.). Roosevelt took Byrnes to Yalta as adviser on shipping and other matters at the 'Big Three' conference, and as secretary of state under President Truman in 1945 he was responsible for dealing with the Russians during the immediate post-war period of the cold war.

Admiral Karl Dönitz, architect of Nazi Germany's U-boat operations, and naval commander-in-chief from 30 January 1943. Hitler designated Dönitz his successor as head of state.

C

CANARIS, Wilhelm (1888–1945). Head of the German *Abwehr* (military intelligence) 1935–44. Canaris played a key part in the Hitler (q.v.) bomb plot. A cultivated and intelligent man, Canaris had been a naval officer, was captured after the battle of the Falkland Islands, but escaped and served in espionage in Spain and Italy. He had commanded a submarine in the Mediterranean, and then became a staff officer in the navy. Although a politician of right-wing views, he became convinced that Hitler must be removed. Although he had no power to destroy Hitler himself he encouraged his staff, especially his deputy, Oster, in their efforts to build up a groundswell of opinion against Hitler, and he also did his best to warn the Allies of German intentions. The plot to remove Hitler attracted the support of several of the army generals, including Field-Marshal Kluge (q.v.), later to be commander of Army Group Centre in Russia, and Beck (q.v.), chief of the general staff 1933–8. But none of them was willing to take the lead, and Hitler's power remained unchallenged through the early part of the war. Canaris continued his involvement in the resistance to Hitler, until in January 1944 he was dismissed as head of the *Abwehr*. In the investigations that followed the failure of the bomb plot the Gestapo uncovered

Admiral Wilhelm Canaris, the anti-Nazi chief of the *Abwehr*, the OKW counter-intelligence service. He was hanged in the purges following the bomb attempt on Hitler's life in 1944.

Opposite above Major-General Ira C. Eaker, commander-in-chief US Eighth Army Air Force, who was responsible for the policy of daylight bombing raids over Germany. In August 1944 he became Air c-in-c for the invasion of southern France.

Below Anthony Eden, foreign secretary in the British government. He had resigned from the post in 1938 in protest against Chamberlain's policies, but was recalled by Churchill and remained Churchill's heir as wartime prime minister until the government fell in 1945.

a collection of incriminating documents in a secret safe belonging to an *Abwehr* member, which uncovered this group of conspirators. Canaris survived his interrogation, and was taken to Flossenburg concentration camp. There a summary court-martial was held by Huppenkothen in the camp laundry on 10 April, and with the sound of Allied gunfire in the background signalling the approach of the end of the war Canaris and his *Abwehr* deputy Oster, together with the pastor Dietrich Bonhoeffer, were taken out and hanged naked before daylight.

Neville Chamberlain celebrates his seventy-first birthday with an official portrait photograph on Horse Guards Parade, London, 18 March 1940. He was shortly to hand over to the new prime minister, Winston Churchill.

CHAMBERLAIN, Arthur Neville (1869–1940). British prime minister from 1937 to 1940 who was at the centre of the events leading up to war in 1939. Chamberlain entered Parliament in 1918 at the age of nearly fifty, after a career in industry and local government. His work during his years at 10 Downing Street was devoted to preserving the peace. He tried to establish contact with both Hitler and Mussolini (qq.v.), but dis-

agreements arising out the Spanish civil war made that impossible.

In March 1938 Hitler invaded Austria. In response to British protests Hitler undertook that there would be no further German aggression and stated specifically that there were no German designs on Czechoslovakia. Chamberlain made a speech in the House of Commons implying that Britain and France would not stand by if Czechoslovakia were attacked, and as the situation deteriorated throughout that summer he repeated that Britain would support France in any action against Germany to protect Czechoslovakia. However, when Hitler demanded self-government for the Sudetenland (the border district with Germany which contained three million Germans) France made it clear that they were not ready to act. Chamberlain's only recourse was to confer with Hitler, and on 15 September 1938 he flew to Berchtesgaden, where he wrung from Hitler a promise that Germany would not open hostilities, and in return conceded Sudeten self-government, subject to his own Cabinet's approval.

Having secured Cabinet approval for this step he returned to meet Hitler again, on 22 September, at Godesberg. At this stage Hitler denounced Britain's arrangements as dilatory and launched an attack on Czechoslovakia, stating at the same time that this was his last territorial ambition in Europe.

As a result of this attack, it was widely thought that war was inevitable, but while Chamberlain was speaking in the House of Commons he was handed a note from Hitler inviting him to a third conference, at Munich. Chamberlain flew to Germany and at 12.30 am on 30 September 1938 signed the agreement with Hitler which mollified the Czech government and persuaded it to accept Hitler's terms. The agreement between Britain and Germany was said to 'symbolize the desire of our two peoples never to go to war again'. Later that day, Chamberlain was welcomed home by crowds in London, when he waved at them a paper and declared that he had secured 'peace in our time'. Press and public alike proclaimed him the

Chamberlain returns from discussions with Hitler, carrying the agreement that promised 'peace in our time'.

saviour of European peace, and he was applauded by statesmen throughout the world.

However, German activity in Europe allowed no reduction in international tension and on 14 March 1939 Hitler invaded Czechoslovakia.

Poland, threatened with a similar fate at German hands, appealed to Britain and on 31 March Chamberlain announced support for Poland if her independence was threatened. Chamberlain still fought strenuously to avoid war, but when Germany invaded Poland on 1 September 1939, and ignored French and British calls for withdrawal, Chamberlain had no alternative but to announce, at 11.15 am on Sunday 3 September, that Britain was at war with Germany.

Chamberlain remained prime minister until May 1940. In April the British had made an inglorious attempt to intervene in Norway and were forced to withdraw after three weeks. On 10 May, after a debate in the House of Commons which ended in an unsatisfactory vote for his policies, Chamberlain decided to resign.

He continued to serve in Churchill's (q.v.) cabinet until 10 October when ill-health finally forced him from public office, and he died on 9 November.

Chamberlain has been characterized in the post-war years as the arch-appeaser whose weak and conciliatory policies allowed Hitler's early successes to go unchecked and led directly to war. It is a view which ignores the courageous and passionate work of a politician dedicated to saving Europe from repeating the destruction which had ended only two decades earlier. (*See also* Halifax)

CHENNAULT, Claire Lee (1890–1958). United States Air Force general. Chennault served in the army in the first world war, qualified as a flier in 1919 and rapidly became a leading if controversial air tactician. In 1935, when he was chief of fighter training at Maxwell Field, Alabama, he published a work arguing the role of fighters

Major-General Claire Chennault, leader of the 'Flying Tigers' and organizer of the famous air ferry service 'over the hump' from India to China.

in defence of bombers. His views were counter to current war-department thinking. He retired from the army in 1937 with a hearing defect, and became air adviser to Chiang Kai-shek (q.v.) in China, where he built up and trained the small Chinese air force, using United States-supplied planes. His theories were vindicated in successful combat with the Japanese. In 1941 he recruited a number of American volunteer pilots to his force. They became known as the 'Flying Tigers', and fought with great success against the Japanese from December 1941 to July 1942, shooting down more than 300 Japanese planes, although their own force never numbered more than 200. They eventually achieved and maintained complete air domination over Chinese territory. Chennault also organized the air ferry which flew supplies 'over the hump' from India to China. In April 1942 he was recalled to the army and commanded the US Air Force in China until almost the end of the war. He resigned on principle in July 1945 in protest against proposals to disband the joint Chinese–American wing of Chiang's air force.

CHERNIAKHOVSKY, Ivan Danilovich (1906–45). One of the youngest and most talented of Soviet wartime generals. He served as deputy commander and then commander of a tank division during the German invasion in 1941. His division lost practically all its armour in the retreat and was reformed as a rifle division. Cherniakhovsky served on the Leningrad Front until the summer of 1942, when he took over 18 Tank Corps and in July 1942 the Sixtieth Army. He was involved in the battle for Kursk in 1943. At the age of only thirty-eight, largely through the high recommendation of Marshal Vasilevsky (q.v.), he was given command of the Third Belorussian Front for the advances of 1944. He was the youngest officer ever to hold a post at such a high level. In January 1945 his forces advanced into East Prussia and took Tilsit. In February 1945 he was visiting his troops near Königsberg when he was hit and fatally wounded by shellfire.

CHIANG KAI-SHEK (born 1887). Chinese generalissimo and nationalist leader. After a life-

The difficult Chinese leaders Chiang Kai-shek and Madame Chiang in cordial conference with President Roosevelt in Cairo, 25 November 1943.

time of military involvement in revolutionary affairs, Chiang Kai-shek was leader of his country's armies on the outbreak of war against Japan in 1937. He organized the stubborn defensive actions at Shanghai and Nantung before the Chinese government withdrew to Chunking. He became party leader in March 1938. Chiang's fierce resistance against the Japanese won the support of the Americans. When they entered the war at the end of 1941 American aid served to strengthen his weakening position. It was Roosevelt's (q.v.) conviction that Chiang would become the leader of the fourth great power in the world after the end of the war, and was therefore the right man to support, although Churchill and Stalin (qq.v.) had little sympathy with this view. Chiang also proved extremely difficult for the Americans who were sent to China to work alongside him, notably Stilwell (q.v.). They enjoyed a prickly working relationship as Chiang continued to accept American aid while showing no inclination to accept American conditions. Chiang's wily personality and political manœuvres are well recorded in Stilwell's diaries, in which the American general constantly and contemptuously refers to the Chinese leader as 'the peanut'. The difficulty of dealing with Chiang was to a great extent exacerbated by the intervention of his equally politically-minded wife Madame Chiang. He took the title of president of China in 1943, but by the end of the second world war Chiang's government had weakened sufficiently to allow the Communist Mao Tse-tung to control large areas of China; in the civil war which followed Chiang was defeated and forced to retire to the island of Formosa where he set up his nationalist government.

CHOLTITZ, Dietrich von (1894–1966). German officer in command of Nazi-occupied Paris. He ordered the capitulation on 25 August 1944. Hitler (q.v.) is alleged to have ordered Choltitz to destroy the city rather than allow it to fall intact into Allied hands, and it is said that when the Allies approached the city the Führer asked his aides 'Is Paris burning?' Choltitz is credited with refusing to carry out the order, although post-war historical research has been unable to authenticate the entire episode.

CHUIKOV, Vasili Ivanovich (born 1900). Russian commander best known for his command of the Sixty-second Army at the siege of Stalingrad. At the age of only forty-two, Chuikov commanded the Sixty-fourth Army on the Stalingrad Front, but because of a problem in the command structure was transferred to the Sixty-second Army on 12 September 1942. His forces were cut off from the rest of the Soviet troops, but with the brave declaration 'We shall either hold the city or die there', he organized the defence against a powerful German offensive which began on 13 September. The Germans broke into the centre of the city, came within 800 yards of Chuikov's headquarters, and were confident they had the city sewn up. Then the arrival of reinforcements, beginning with the Rodimtsev Division, ended the German advance. In the savage street fighting that followed, the Rodimtsev Division lost so many men that they ceased to be a fighting force by the end of September. The climax of this early part of the battle came on 14 October when after a lull

of four days the Germans launched a massive offensive. It cost them 3000 dead and forty tanks, and Russian casualties included 3500 seriously wounded alone. This phase of the fighting continued for ten days, until exhaustion and losses brought a temporary standstill. The battle went on with unimaginable savagery and staggering losses through October, and by the end of that month the Russians felt they were winning. Nevertheless despite growing Russian pressure, made possible by a steady trickle of reinforcements and highly effective Katyusha rocket attacks from across the Volga, German resistance continued, and the struggle for the city went on house by house and factory by factory. The final German capitulation came only at the end of January 1943.

In the final campaign of the war Chuikov commanded the Eighth Guards Army in the advance on Poland, which formed the spearhead of Zhukov's (q.v.) army group in the advance on Berlin. His army covered 220 miles in fourteen days, reached the Oder, and on 3 February 1945 had established a bridgehead across the river. Chuikov was ready for the advance on Berlin, but he was then called to a conference with Zhukov. Chuikov claims that while he was there a telephone conversation took place between Zhukov and Stalin (q.v.), during which Stalin ordered Zhukov not to advance on Berlin, but to turn north and destroy German forces there. Zhukov denied after the war that this conversation ever took place, but the fact remains that the advance on Berlin was not completed until May. On 1 May Chuikov received the German officer who approached to negotiate the surrender of the city and its garrison, which took place on 2 May. It was troops of Chuikov's Eighth Guards Army who broke through to the Reich chancellery and allegedly found the bodies of Hitler and Eva Braun (qq.v.), burned in petrol-soaked rugs which were still smouldering. But Chuikov and his superior Zhukov were instrumental in obscuring the details of what happened to Hitler.

From 1946 to 1953 Chuikov was deputy commander and then commander of the Soviet

General Vasili Chuikov, veteran of battles from Stalingrad to Berlin, consults his officers outside Warsaw.

occupation forces of Germany, and later rose to be c-in-c Soviet ground forces from 1960–5. He was a thickset man with a red face, typical of the blunt, unsophisticated men of peasant origin who rose to command Soviet armed forces in the second world war. It is widely acknowledged that Chuikov's unshakeable courage and steadfastness saved Stalingrad, especially in the key battles which started on 14 October.

CHURCHILL, Winston (1874–1965). British prime minister and wartime minister of defence. Churchill's involvement in the second world war originated two decades before hostilities opened. Even before the Nazis came to power in Germany, he recognized the dangers of the largely secret German rearmament, and began a campaign of warning about it through innumerable articles in the press. In his book *The Aftermath*, published in 1928, he painted an awesome picture of the possibilities of war offered by the new weapons which had shown their potential during the first world war. It was then that he astutely summarized the inter-war years as 'that period of exhaustion which has been described as Peace'.

In 1932 he extended his campaign into Parliament, with the first in a long series of forecasts of a new European war if Germany were allowed to raise the level of her armaments to equal those of her European neighbours. He particularly stressed that Britain should concentrate on air power, and not be relegated to fifth place in terms of air strength. For a trained soldier with experience as a naval politician, even that acceptance of the air weapons was a modest indication of Churchill's extremely perceptive foresight.

During this period Churchill was without Cabinet office in the government, and his home in Kent, Chartwell, became the centre of his campaign. He poured out a stream of writings on the German military threat, and at the same time received at his home a growing list of politically informed visitors including German anti-Nazis, senior civil servants, and officers who felt as anxious as he did about the government's refusal to deal with the German threat. From them he gathered a vast body of information on defence affairs, and in due course his position became so powerful that some observers described Chartwell as a miniature Foreign Office.

In the 1935 General Election the Conservative element in the National government was even stronger than in 1931, and Churchill confidently anticipated being offered a post in the new government, but the prime minister Baldwin pointedly excluded him. In 1936, when Baldwin set up a ministry for the co-ordination of defence, it was widely thought that Churchill would get the job, but again Baldwin kept him out. Both men thought that this was a politically fatal stroke for Churchill. But in fact on both occasions it turned out to Churchill's advantage. He was able to carry on his independent campaign, while at the same time remaining unconnected with the appalling record of the government over its dealings with Germany.

On 26 May 1937 Neville Chamberlain (q.v.) succeeded Baldwin as prime minister, but Churchill was still excluded from the government. Privately he had large numbers of supporters, and there was widespread indignation that the best-informed and most able politician in the country was being kept out of office. But Chamberlain was determined to keep control of foreign policy in his own hands, and in addition subscribed to the popular view that Churchill, though brilliant, was unreliable and lacked judgment.

This was the period of appeasement, and of increasing despair for Churchill as Germany marched first into Austria and then into Czechoslovakia. Chamberlain secured his famous agreement with Hitler (q.v.) at Munich in September 1938, and British Parliament and people were relieved that he had averted a new European war.

Public opinion was so pro-Chamberlain and anti-Churchill that in November 1938 he only narrowly won a motion of censure in his own local constituency which might – if he had lost – have removed him from Parliament for good. In the course of March 1939 Britain moved slowly towards war, as Germany's annexation of the whole of Czechoslovakia shattered Chamberlain's faith in Hitler's trustworthiness, and Britain and France drew up a treaty guaranteeing help for Poland in the event of a threat to its independence.

It did not deter Hitler, and after settling a pact with the Soviet Union he proceeded to invade Poland on 1 September 1939.

Churchill's first action was comparatively mundane. He realized he might be the target for some of the 20,000 German Nazis known to be in England, so he called out his old bodyguard from his earlier days in government, retired Scotland Yard detective-inspector Thompson. Together they checked and loaded their old service revolvers, and prepared to sleep and keep watch by turns.

That afternoon, 1 September 1939, Chamberlain called Churchill to see him, told him that he saw no alternative to war with Germany, and invited him to join a small War Cabinet he was forming. Strangely enough Chamberlain still tried to keep total control in his own hands, and did not tell Churchill that he was about to issue the first of two ultimatums to Germany. Nor, despite Churchill's plea to put him in the picture, did he tell his colleagues that he was on the point of declaring war when those ultimatums were rejected. The first that Churchill knew about it was when he heard it in company with millions of other Britons over the radio.

Almost immediately the air-raid warning sounded, and Churchill and his wife went up on to the roof of their flat to see what was happening. There they saw the barrage of anti-aircraft balloons rising round the city, and after a few minutes' watching they went down to the air-raid shelter to sit out the raid among their neighbours. In fact it was a false alarm and the all-clear sounded ten minutes later.

Britain stands on the verge of war. A grim Winston Churchill leaves 10 Downing Street on 1 September 1939, the day he was appointed first lord of the Admiralty by Neville Chamberlain. Churchill became Britain's wartime supremo, as both prime minister and minister of defence.

That afternoon Churchill went to the House of Commons to listen to the speeches, and there, he wrote in his memoirs, a strong sense of calm came over him. He felt a serenity of mind and was conscious of a kind of uplifted detachment from human and personal affairs. While he was relishing the sense of relief from the strain of months of pre-war tension, he received a note asking him to see Chamberlain in his room at the House. There Churchill was offered the post of first lord of the Admiralty, which was to be a War Cabinet post.

Churchill was delighted, not only to have an active job as opposed to an unspecified advisory post, but to be back in his old first world war job at the Admiralty, where he had spent some of his happiest and most productive years. At six o'clock he went back to the room he had left 'in pain and sorrow' almost a quarter of a century earlier, when he was ousted from the Admiralty in the aftermath of the Dardanelles fiasco. There he found the same chair he had used before with the same map case he had fixed to the wall behind it, and his old octagonal table was resurrected from a store room. Furthermore the Admiralty were as glad to have Churchill at their head as he was to be there, and the signal went out to the entire fleet: 'Winston is back.'

Churchill remained at the Admiralty for eight months, during which his department was the most active of all the services. His dramatic introduction to this second period in office came that night when the liner *Athenia* was sunk by a U-boat in the Atlantic, and German propaganda accused Churchill of engineering the incident to discredit Germany. There followed the sinking of the aircraft carrier *Courageous* in the Bristol Channel, the sinking of the *Royal Oak* in Scapa Flow by the U-boat commanded by Gunther Prien, the trapping of the pocket-battleship *Graf Spee* off Montevideo, and the *Altmark* incident in February in which 299 British prisoners were released from the ship's hold by a Royal Navy boarding party acting on Churchill's personal order. Then in April and May 1940 the British mounted their unsuccessful expedition to Norway, and were forced to withdraw. The failure of the operation provoked a debate in Parliament and, although the government won the vote, Chamberlain felt obliged to resign. His first choice for successor, Lord Halifax (q.v.), declined to take over, and on 10 May, the day Germany attacked Holland, Belgium and Luxembourg, the king asked Churchill to form a government.

Churchill was profoundly relieved. He knew that his years in the political wilderness had freed him from the normal party antagonisms, and his warnings over the years had proved so accurate that he was above reproach, and could not be accused of making the war or of being unprepared for it. Now he had the authority to give directions over the whole scene, and he felt, he later wrote, as if he were walking with destiny.

The effect on the nation of Churchill taking over was electrifying. A flow of messages dictated by him began to pour out to every department of the government and the armed forces. Men who for years had quietly toiled away at their desks sud-

denly found themselves exposed to the glare of Churchill's scrutiny. If he sent out a message which needed urgent attention he pinned to it a small red label bearing the words: Action This Day.

He also circulated a note stating clearly that he would not be held responsible for any matters relating to defence unless he had made them in writing or confirmed them in writing immediately afterwards. It was a sensible precaution, designed not only to put all his instructions clearly on record, but also to clarify his own thoughts on the matter.

Churchill's method of working brought a minor revolution among those who worked around him. For Churchill, office hours did not exist, and there was no distinction between work and leisure. He began working in bed at eight in the morning, going rapidly through the papers which had been assembled in his Cabinet box, and dictating replies or memoranda to one of his secretaries. He seldom saw visitors until midday, when he began the day's meetings, which invariably carried on during lunch. In the afternoon he normally went to bed and slept soundly, so that he woke completely refreshed by that hour of 'blessed oblivion' and able, he said, to fit a day-and-a-half's work into each twenty-four hours. More meetings and dictation followed until dinner, which was used to discuss the running of the war, then he generally relaxed with a film in his private cinema, or by keeping his guests up talking into the small hours, before he returned to more work, and finally went to bed at two or three in the morning, to wake completely refreshed again the following morning at eight o'clock. It was a punishing routine, for which his energy never flagged, although some of those around him who did not share his taste for odd hours and could not enjoy an hour of afternoon sleep found it exhausting.

He could work, as he could sleep, almost anywhere – at home in bed, in the war rooms under

An army officer by training, Churchill's career ranged from the days of the cavalry charge to the era of jet aircraft. The RAF was a particular favourite of his. In April 1939 he became honorary air commodore to 615 Auxiliary Air Force Squadron.

In the dark days of 1939 and 1940 Churchill frequently visited the continent. Here, on 5 November 1939, he meets generals Gort (centre) and Pownall at the BEF headquarters in a French *château*.

Whitehall, at Ditchley or Chequers, the two country houses which he used when outside London, in a car, and on many of his journeys away from the capital in a special train which had been assembled for him. This useful device cut out the need for extensive security for personnel or documents in hotels in the provinces. It could be pulled up into a quiet siding overnight, and by a simple wiring operation connected into the telephone system so that the prime minister was in touch with his staff in London or elsewhere.

Generally, Churchill's great contribution during those early months of his premiership was in changing the gear: under him the war machine began to run at a new pace, as everybody recognized that a firm and confident hand had taken over the controls.

The public, of course, knew little of Churchill's working conduct of the war. But on them also he had a remarkable effect, achieved through his extraordinary impact as an orator. In a series of speeches made first to Parliament and then broadcast by radio, he rallied a confused and demoralized nation, and inspired the British people with an inflexible resolution not to accept defeat. The first of his speeches as prime minister he made on 13 May 1940, when he offered the nation nothing but 'blood, sweat, toil and tears'. That grim prediction was rapidly fulfilled with the breakthrough of the French defences at Sedan on 14 May, the surrender of the Netherlands on 15 May, and Churchill's own flying visits to Paris which left him in no doubt that the French were beaten. By 28 May the British had been forced to prepare for the withdrawal at Dunkirk, and on that day Churchill warned his Cabinet to prepare for bad news from the continent, but told them that whatever happened at Dunkirk, they would fight on. To Churchill's entire surprise, the Cabinet broke out in a spontaneous burst of cheering, applauding and congratulating him, and patting him on the back. For the first time he could confidently rely on the support of Parliament.

On 4 June the evacuation from Dunkirk was completed, and Churchill addressed Parliament again, then repeated his speech by radio to the British people. The words of this speech, as of so many others from that brief period, have become enshrined in the English language. He told them that they would fight on the beaches, on the landing grounds, in the fields and in the streets – 'We shall never surrender.' The effect was a transformation, as the British people recognized that they had a leader of a fundamentally new kind, who not only was himself resolved to fight, but who expressed their own determination to remain free from the 'grip of the Gestapo and all the odious apparatus of Nazi rule', under which most of Europe had fallen.

Whatever his merits as a war leader in succeeding years, Churchill's part in holding his country together through the perils of the German expansion of 1940 would entitle him to a high place among British leaders.

In fact the measure of his spirit may be judged by one of his typical actions during the darkest days of his country's misfortune. As early as 6 June 1940, before the German conquest of France was complete, and long before the problem of defending against a German invasion of England was solved, Churchill called for an end to the passive resistance war and for the creation of a variety of offensive devices. His suggestions included setting up 'striking companies' (which later emerged as the commandos), building landing craft to take tanks to enemy-held beaches, starting programmes of coastal espionage, training parachute troops, and locating heavy guns mounted to fire across the Channel. His commando proposal was the origin of a series of developments which led directly, through combined operations and amphibious attacks like the Dieppe raid, to the seaborne invasion of Normandy which marked the beginning of Hitler's downfall.

During the summer of 1940 the main preoccupation of the forces and government was with the Battle of Britain. Initially Churchill played little direct part, but when the Luftwaffe unwisely changed the target of its attacks from the Royal Air Force sector stations to the civilian populations of London and other major industrial cities Churchill's role as head of the government became increasingly important. Unlike the other European war leaders, Hitler and Stalin (q.v.), who both ran the war almost exclusively from the confines of their own headquarters, Churchill constantly roved about the country visiting the bombed areas. Occasionally he was not welcome, as when one group of citizens rummaging in the wreckage of their homes were irritated by his cheerful but inept war-cry 'London can take it.' But generally the people welcomed him warmly, called him 'Winnie' and urged him to 'give it back' to Hitler's Germany.

By the end of that year, described by Churchill as 'the most deadly year in our long English and British story', he had led his country through the threat of invasion, and had quite conceivably saved western Europe from permanent German domination. It is quite possible that not even the United States could have, or would have wanted to, free Europe from Hitler without the use of the British Isles as a base for an invasion. Churchill had also by the end of that year built up a great stock of goodwill and affection both in Parliament and in the country. It was a valuable asset, as serious reverses made it necessary for him to draw heavily on that stock of goodwill in the course of 1941. In

Churchill visits Bristol during the 'blitz'. The British people, even during the worst of the bombing raids, responded cheerfully to Churchill's aggressive optimism.

An indefatigable traveller both at home and on the world scene, Churchill visits an arms factory on the home front, talking to women engaged in war work.

March and April British and empire troops attempted to intervene in Greece and were forced to evacuate. On 10 May the bombing of London reached a new climax and three thousand people were killed. At the end of May the evacuation of Crete took place. Rommel, recently arrived in North Africa, pushed the Allies as far east as Tobruk.

Churchill at this time was widely criticized in the press and privately for running the war on his own, and he responded by asking for a vote of confidence in a parliamentary debate. He won convincingly, but the criticism was not silent for long.

In June the picture changed abruptly with Hitler's invasion of the Soviet Union, which relieved some of the pressure in the west and in North Africa, until German successes threatened even worse perils. On 9 August Churchill met Roosevelt (q.v.) in Placentia Bay, Newfoundland

and, although they struck up a warm personal friendship and signed a joint declaration known as the Atlantic Charter, the United States remained neutral, much to Churchill's disappointment. That problem was solved on 7 December when the Japanese attacked the United States fleet at Pearl Harbor. Churchill was so delighted that he galvanized the British government into declaring war on Japan even before the United States had a chance to do so. His conclusion at that early stage was: 'So we have won after all'. In Churchill's view it would now take no more than time before the Allies, representing four-fifths of the world's population, would end the Axis menace, and the long history of the island race would not come to an end. As Churchill saw it: 'All the rest was merely the proper application of overwhelming force.'

Churchill travelled again across the Atlantic to see Roosevelt in Washington, and during the voyage in the new battleship *Duke of York* he composed a set of three papers on the conduct of the war. The first dealt with the need to occupy the coast of North Africa to forestall a German–Japanese link-up and secure the Mediterranean for Allied shipping. The second called for the building of an aircraft carrier fleet big enough to secure the Pacific by May 1942. And the third argued the need for landing an Anglo–American invasion force to liberate occupied Europe, setting 1943 as the target date for this 'supreme stroke'. Churchill's capacity as a grand strategist has frequently been called into question by academic analysts, but his foresight in outlining the development of strategy almost precisely as it later developed shows considerable skill, and impressed Roosevelt so deeply that he asked to keep copies of Churchill's three papers. The western staffs were also happy to work to Churchill's outline. The only dissenting voice was that of Stalin, who continually pressed for a second front to be opened up in Europe at the earliest possible moment, totally ignoring American and British commitments elsewhere and the unproven technique of the major amphibious attack on which the invasion would depend.

During this visit to the United States and Canada, Churchill reproduced the effect of his British speeches of 1940, cementing the trans-Atlantic alliance, and allaying much of the British fear that American isolationism would lead them to prefer defeating Japan first. As it happened Roosevelt himself firmly dismissed all such suggestions, and showed himself determined to concentrate first on defeating Germany. To this end Churchill and Roosevelt agreed to set up the Combined Chiefs of Staff Committee consisting of their respective planners organizing the united Allied effort.

After this visit, Churchill showed clear changes in his mood, his outlook and his health. Already sixty-five years old when he became prime minister, he had lived through the frustrating pre-war years on the edge of affairs, watching the government squander the stability of Europe, then he had seen Europe fall, and finally he had lived through a year and a half with no strong ally, only the near-defeated Soviet Union. Now that he had seen the United States enter the war the tension broke. Churchill could barely bring himself to work, and although he was due to return to England he allowed himself to be persuaded to take a short holiday in Florida instead.

It was well that he took steps to improve his health, because the new year brought a further series of disasters and a great deal more criticism. In January the Japanese invaded Malaya, and Rommel (q.v.) went on to the offensive in Cyrenaica. February saw the escape of the *Scharnhorst* and *Gneisenau* through the Straits of Dover, the surrender of Singapore, and an alarming rise in the U-boat sinkings of merchant shipping in the Atlantic. The bad news continued, culminating on 21 June with the fall of Tobruk, and Churchill suffered the embarrassment of hearing the news from President Roosevelt during a second visit to Washington. Roosevelt asked Churchill what he could do to help, and Churchill immediately asked for as many Sherman tanks as could be spared. Three hundred new Shermans were immediately withdrawn from their American divisions and

Churchill

handed over, together with a hundred self-propelled guns and other material.

Back in England, on 1 July Churchill had to face a direct motion of censure in the House of Commons, expressing no confidence in the central direction of the war. He survived by an overwhelming margin, but not before serious attacks from both right and left. In fact his parliamentary survival marked the beginning of a new upward trend in his fortunes. He flew out to Egypt, enjoyed the sunshine of Cairo, and put his favourite general Alexander (q.v.) in command, with Montgomery (q.v.) shortly to join him as commander of the Eighth Army.

He then went on to Moscow and after a bristling early encounter established tolerably good relations with Stalin. He returned to Egypt, was impressed by a new mood of confidence to such a degree that he could hardly be persuaded to miss the coming battle, but eventually left for home. That autumn and winter the news was almost uniformly good. Montgomery steadily if slowly pushed the Afrika Korps back towards Tunisia, and the landings in north-west Africa went ahead in November with no serious difficulties. Churchill was able to tell an audience in the city of London that although this was not the end, nor even the beginning of the end, it was perhaps the end of the beginning.

On 13 January 1943 he flew to Casablanca for another conference with the American president, where they settled the next stage of strategy. They would attack Sicily to press home the advantage already gained, while at the same time building up forces for the cross-Channel invasion. Churchill went on to Marrakesh, taking Roosevelt with him, then continued alone with a tour of the Mediterranean theatre before flying home. On 16 February he fell ill with pneumonia, but recovered rapidly and crossed the Atlantic once more, arriving on 11 May, for a conference with Roosevelt.

The Allies in optimistic mood, at the Casablanca conference in January 1943. Churchill and Roosevelt pose for photographs with 'top brass' from British and American services. The civilian on the left is Harry Hopkins.

It was here that the first indications began to emerge of a serious divergence of opinion between Churchill and Roosevelt. It concerned the operation in Italy. Churchill saw Italy as the great prize which, if defeated, would cast a 'chill of loneliness' over the German people, besides bringing several other valuable strategic consequences. Roosevelt was sceptical, and suspected Churchill of pursuing imperialist ambitions in the Mediterranean to the detriment of the main attack on Germany through northern France. The American planners followed Roosevelt's lead, and made it clear that they were prepared to concentrate on the war against Japan so long as the British were unwilling to go ahead with the cross-Channel invasion. By 25 May patient negotiation had narrowed this difference of opinion, but no definite conclusion had yet been reached. Eventually it was settled away from the discussion tables of the chiefs of staff, when Churchill flew to North Africa after the conference, taking with him General Marshall (q.v.). They visited Eisenhower (q.v.), the North African commander-in-chief, who himself suggested going right ahead with the invasion of Italy as a natural consequence of the conquest of Sicily.

However the differences continued at the next conference, Quadrant, held in Quebec in August. There the Americans demanded that Overlord should have priority over operations in the Mediterranean, and asked for a firm commitment from the British. At one point in this conference the combined chiefs of staff were in such profound disagreement that they dismissed their advisers from the meeting and in the words of one participant 'really let their hair down'.

In the course of this conference Churchill suggested to Roosevelt that the British general Brooke (q.v.) should step down as commander-in-chief designate for the Overlord invasion, in place of an American commander. His justification was that there would be a preponderance of American troops participating in the operation, but it is likely that this was a concession Churchill was prepared to make as the price of preserving the creaking Anglo–American alliance.

It was at the next conference, at Teheran with Marshal Stalin in late November, that Churchill was finally obliged to accept a severely reduced role for his nation's forces and for his personal concept of strategic developments. Stalin pressed for a second front in mainland Europe, and Roosevelt agreed and promised May 1944 as the target date. Operations in the Mediterranean were to be limited to a supporting invasion of southern France, and Churchill's cherished notions of further major operations in Italy and the Balkans were passed over.

Churchill realized that he was rapidly becoming isolated, as Roosevelt struck up a relationship with Stalin in the belief that he could, as he put it, 'handle' the Russian leader.

Churchill was also ill again, and when they flew back to Tunisia he went down with a severe bout of pneumonia. He knew it was serious and told his daughter that it did not matter if he died, as the plans for the final victory had been laid. It was only a matter of time. He went on to Marrakesh to recover, and after two weeks was fit again. He flew back to Gibraltar, sailed home in a British battleship, and two hours after his arrival in London took his place to answer MPs' questions at the despatch box in the House of Commons.

Throughout 1944 and 1945 Churchill continued his tireless travelling, covering thousands of miles by train, ship and aircraft for further meetings with Roosevelt and Stalin. Once the foothold in France was successfully established (and Churchill was only narrowly prevented from sailing in the assault shipping to see what was going on) his concern moved away from military strategy to the area of politics, as he struggled from his ever-weakening position among the great powers to secure a stable situation once the fighting was finished. He was unsuccessful in his attempts to secure a compromise with Russian intentions over Poland. But he was more successful in his personal intervention in Greece, which he visited on Christmas Day 1944 at great personal danger.

In February 1945 he flew to Yalta for the most

His political tribulations at home largely behind him, Churchill inspects troops in training for D-Day.

important 'Big Three' conference of the war, called to discuss the post-war settlement, including the terms to be imposed on the defeated Germany, the establishment of the United Nations Organization, and the entry of Russia into the war with Japan.

Churchill was again isolated, as Roosevelt continued in his trusting attitude to Soviet intentions, and Churchill was forced to accept Russian and American terms in order to keep the Anglo–American alliance in being.

In the late stages of the war he urged the Americans to advance to meet the Russians as far east as possible, but the Americans, with the military hierarchy in effective charge following the death of Roosevelt and the accession to the presidency

of the inexperienced Truman, admitted to seeking the least costly military solution possible, and did not look earnestly at the political issues.

Churchill's final humiliation came after the end of the fighting in Europe. The Labour members of the coalition government declined to serve any longer, and he set up a caretaker government of Conservatives while waiting for the results of the general election. Churchill conducted his campaign badly from the start, making unconvincing attacks on the socialist system, and personal attacks on the men who had until recently been his colleagues in war. He completely misjudged the mood of the people, who were anxious for a change of politics as well as a relief from the war.

Churchill was attending the Potsdam con-

ference, with Attlee (q.v.) invited as an observer, when the results were due. He flew home to follow the counting, and on 26 June 1945, at six o'clock in the afternoon, the votes showed a Labour majority in the House of Commons. An hour later Churchill went to Buckingham Palace to tender his resignation to the king, and his part in the war was over.

During the second world war Churchill made, almost certainly, the second most significant personal contribution of any single individual. Only Adolf Hitler exerted a greater influence by his own decisions and outlook. Once the war, about which he had for so long warned, had begun he held the morale of the British people steady while they alone resisted the expansion of Hitler's imperialism. He also resisted very serious pressures in his own country to seek peace terms with Hitler. Until the entry of the United States into the war he directed its course, not always with good results. By the force of his personality and his unflagging energy, despite bouts of ill health, he kept the Grand Alliance in being, and made his own country's voice heard in the face of its near exhaustion of manpower and supplies. And up to the last days of the war he read as clearly as anyone the unwelcome historical consequences which could flow from the method by which it was being fought.

He did not do all this alone, of course, but was aided by a group of officers, led by the chief of the imperial general staff Brooke, who gave him advice, fed him the information he needed, and argued with him to the point of exhaustion, especially to dissuade him from the many outlandish proposals he made which they knew to be militarily unfeasible. It would be wrong to fall into the customary trap of eulogizing Churchill, and to ignore the one great fault – his impulsive desire to throw everything into the fight regardless of considerations of balance and preparedness. But perhaps his greatest quality was that he himself accepted his faults, and allowed himself to be guided by his

Churchill visits flying bomb defences in south-east England, when London again came under threat in the late stages of the war.

chiefs of staff. Hitler was the real megalomaniac, who surrounded himself with sycophants and admitted no denial of his own will. And it cost him the war. By comparison Churchill was a modest and reasonable human being.

CIANO, Galeazzo (1903–44). Italian foreign minister, son-in-law of Mussolini (q.v.), and one of Italy's chief opponents of the Axis connection. Count Ciano became foreign minister in 1936, no doubt helped by his marriage to Mussolini's daughter Edda. He met Hitler and Ribbentrop (qq.v.) in August 1939, and, only then realizing how close Europe was to war, tried to keep his country out of it and particularly to curb Hitler's influence on Mussolini. When that failed, and Italy declared war on the Allies, Ciano took command of a bomber squadron. His views as foreign minister were frequently in conflict with Mussolini's, and in February 1943 the dictator sent him out of the way as ambassador to the Holy See. Ciano was at the meeting of the Fascist grand council which deposed Mussolini on 25 July 1943, and recommended signing a separate peace with the Allies. After Mussolini's removal Ciano was

Galeazzo Ciano (left), Mussolini's son-in-law, seen here at a conference in Italy with Lord Halifax, Neville Chamberlain and Mussolini.

captured by the Germans, subjected to a mock trial after Mussolini's rescue, and shot in the back tied to a chair as a traitor. He left an invaluable diary recounting the meetings of the Fascist party.

CLARK, Mark Wayne (born 1896). United States general. The son of an army colonel, Mark Clark served in France in 1918, and held a variety of posts between the wars, but was only a major when the second world war began. By April 1942 he had risen to the rank of major-general and in May became chief of staff to army ground forces. Further spectacular promotion followed, as he was shortly afterwards appointed commander of United States ground forces in Europe. In November 1942, after Eisenhower (q.v.) had chosen him to plan the invasion of North Africa, Clark landed secretly in the British submarine *Seraph* to meet Free French officers near Algiers. He became deputy to Eisenhower for the North African invasion. His first army command came in January 1943, when he took over the US Fifth Army and commanded it in the landings at Salerno in September. After almost being repulsed, Clark established his beach-head and his troops drove north against fierce German resistance and took Rome in June 1944. He took over the Fifteenth Army Group from Alexander (q.v.) in November 1944, commanding all Allied forces in the Mediterranean. Clark was criticized for some aspects of his Italian campaign, not least the bombing of the monastery at Cassino, but was generally praised by his senior colleagues for his professionalism and for his skill as a diplomat. He continued in several high offices after the war, including commanding American occupation forces in Austria, and heading United Nations forces in Korea during the last fifteen months of operations and the complicated truce negotiations. He retired from the army in 1953.

COLLINS, Joseph Lawton (born 1896). United States general who commanded 7 Corps in the Normandy operations, capturing Cherbourg and leading the breakout at St Lô. Nicknamed 'Lightning Joe', Collins was also one of a number of holders of the familiar title 'the GI's

General Mark Clark, commander of the United States Fifth Army for the Salerno landings.

general'. He was in the typical American mould of aggressive exuberant commanders, was quick to remove anybody not up to his job and worked his battalions hard in short spells. In the tough battles of the closely packed Cotentin *bocage* he drove forward on narrow fronts, changing the leading formations several times in a day. He was basically a tough but flexible professional soldier. He

General 'Lightning Joe' Collins, one of the several American generals whose popularity earned them the title 'GI's general'.

continued to command 7 Corps in the same fast-moving style right up to the final battles in Germany.

CONINGHAM, (Sir) Arthur (1895–1948). Australian air marshal, noted mainly for his service in the desert campaigns in North Africa. Like many other senior Allied airmen of the second world war, he began service as a soldier and transferred to the Royal Flying Corps in the early days of air warfare. He flew as a fighter pilot over France during 1917, stayed in the Royal Air Force between the wars, and rose to the rank of air com-

modore by 1939. In 1941 he was given command of the Desert Air Force (part of the Middle East Air Force) responsible for supporting the Eighth Army. In January 1943, as head of the First Allied Tactical Air Force, he was in control of British and American air forces during the battles for Tunisia, Sicily and Italy. In January 1944 he transferred to England to command the Second Tactical Air Force, the British component of the Allied Expeditionary Air Force, covering the invasion in Normandy and the subsequent land operations in north-west Europe.

A sensitive man, Coningham resented the lack of credit given to the air forces in the public eye. This particularly led to clashes with Montgomery (q.v.), who openly viewed the air forces as mere support for his land operations. Ironically, this was the central theme of Coningham's vision of the air forces' role, that of destroying enemy air strength, then attacking tactical targets to aid the army advance on the ground. He attempted to foster the necessary co-operation by locating his own headquarters close to the army commander's, particularly in the desert. But it was the dismissive and arrogant attitude of Montgomery, who left his chief of staff to deal with the air force commander, that Coningham found objectionable. By the end of the war in Europe Coningham commanded an international air force of 1800 planes and 100,000 men of European and commonwealth nationalities. He was killed in a plane crash in 1948.

COOPER, Alfred Duff (1890–1954). British politician. Duff Cooper was first lord of the admiralty in Chamberlain's (q.v.) government, but resigned after denouncing the Munich agreement in the House of Commons as meaningless and dishonourable. Churchill (q.v.) made him minister of information briefly, and then in 1941 he went to Singapore to report on the state of the defences. He was unjustly forced to take some of the blame for Singapore's collapse. From January 1944 he occupied the post most congenial to him as British representative with de Gaulle's committee of national liberation, and later as ambassador to France. He was to a large extent respon-

Henry Crerar of Canadian First Army (left) and Miles Dempsey of British Second Army flank the Twenty-first British Army Group commander in Normandy, General Montgomery.

sible for healing Anglo–French differences and helping to rebuild post-war France.

CRERAR, Henry (1888–1965). Canadian general, commander of the Canadian First Army in the war in north-west Europe. Between the wars Crerar was concerned with building up Canada's army. He moved to London in 1939 to set up a Canadian military headquarters, returned to Canada in 1940 as chief of the general staff, but resigned a year later to take on a field post as commander of 1 Canadian Corps, which fought in Italy in 1943. He was appointed to command the Canadian First Army in the invasion of Normandy

and subsequent operations. These were on the left flank of the Allied bridgehead and the drive towards Germany, and included the capture of the v-rocket sites, the Pas de Calais and Antwerp. His army carried out the encirclement of all German forces in the Netherlands.

CRIPPS, (Sir) Stafford (1889–1952). British politician. Although a brilliant chemist as a young man, Cripps chose the law and then politics as a career. He visited India and Moscow in 1939, and Churchill (q.v.) made him ambassador to Russia in 1940, where in 1941 he organized the mutual assistance pact. He returned to Britain and was

Cunningham

leader of the House of Commons from February to November 1942, when he quarrelled with Churchill and left the War Cabinet. He then became a successful minister of aircraft production.

CUNNINGHAM, Andrew (1883–1963). British admiral who served in the Mediterranean, in Washington, and finally as first sea lord and the naval representative on the British chiefs of staff committee.

After his naval training in the *Britannia*, Cunningham commanded one of the first oil-fuelled ships in the Royal Navy, a torpedo boat. He commanded a destroyer during the Dardanelles operation in the first world war, and made a name as a highly competent and aggressive commander. He held a variety of posts between the wars and by 1937 faced an honourable retirement with the rank of vice-admiral. But a sudden succession of promotions left him holding the post of commander-in-chief Mediterranean in 1939, which became vitally important with the entry of Italy into the war in 1940. Cunningham immediately went on to the offensive against markedly superior forces, but by aggressive action rapidly tied up the Italian fleet, put half of its ships out of action in the fleet air arm attack at Taranto in November, and in March 1941 destroyed three Italian cruisers at the battle of Cape Matapan. The activity of the Royal Navy was then severely curtailed in the Mediterranean by Axis land gains which gave them the advantage of substantial land-based air cover.

In May 1942 Cunningham was sent to Washington as British representative to the joint chiefs of staff, but in that same year returned to the Mediterranean as naval commander-in-chief for the Torch landings under General Eisenhower (q.v.). In September 1943 he received the surrender of the whole Italian fleet. In October that

Admiral Sir Andrew Cunningham (standing, white uniform) at high-level conference in North Africa during 1943. His Anglo–American colleagues are (left to right) Eden, Brooke, Tedder, Churchill, Alexander, Marshall, Eisenhower and Montgomery.

year the first sea lord, Sir Dudley Pound, died in office and Cunningham was the universally popular choice to succeed him. From that time on until the end of the war he was the naval member of the trio of advisers who worked closely with the prime minister directing strategy.

CURTIN, John (1885–1945). Wartime prime minister of Australia. A member of Australia's Labour party, Curtin refused, in line with the rules of his party, to join in a coalition. He remained in opposition until the government resigned on 3 October 1941, and was then called on to take office. When Japan entered the war he shocked some Australians by openly declaring that his country looked to the United States for aid free of any pangs regarding Australia's traditional links or kinship with the United Kingdom. Far from abandoning the commonwealth connections as his detractors feared, Curtin was merely recognizing that, since his country's forces were heavily committed in the Middle East, only the United States could help protect Australia in the light of the rapid Japanese advance through the Pacific. Despite the appeal for American aid and the presence of large American forces in Australia, Curtin in fact fought to preserve his country's influence, maintaining firmly that Australia was a partner of the United States, not a satellite. The people's approval of his policies was confirmed by a clear victory in the elections of August 1943. Curtin was notable for introducing a measure of conscription into Australia's armed forces in view of the exigencies of war, even though he had served a term of imprisonment for opposing conscription during the first world war. He died in July 1945, only a month before the end of the war with Japan.

D

DALADIER, Edouard (1884–1970). French prime minister at the time of the outbreak of war. When the Germans invaded Poland and the British government declared war against Germany, Daladier followed a few hours later with the French declaration of war. In March 1940 he proposed sending a force of volunteers to aid Finland in their fight against the Russians, but Finland agreed terms before the plan could be put into effect. On 20 March 1940 Daladier's government collapsed, and he became war minister in the government of Paul Reynaud (q.v.). He resigned that post on 5 June when the battle of France had begun. Daladier was arrested on 17 November 1940 and in February 1942 was put on trial for his negligence in not bringing France to a state of readiness for war. The trial was suspended in April 1942, and Daladier was interned, first in France and after 1943 in Germany. He was released in 1945.

DARLAN, Jean (1881–1942). French admiral and political figure. Darlan was commander-in-chief of the French navy on the outbreak of war. When France fell he pursued a policy of limited co-operation with the Germans. Although he assured Churchill (q.v.) at a meeting that the French fleet would not be allowed to fall into German hands, he refused British requests to sail it to British, American or West Indian ports. The result was the engagement in July 1940 in which the British sank the bulk of the French fleet. Throughout 1941 Darlan was markedly pro-Nazi. He hoped for economic co-operation with Hitler (q.v.), and as vice-premier in the Vichy French government offered to fight with Germany against the British. Hitler declined both the offer and the requests which went with it. When Laval became head of the Vichy government in 1942 he put Darlan in command of French forces, at the same time depriving him of all political posts. When the Allies invaded Algeria in November 1942 Darlan was in Algiers. He decided then to co-operate with the Allies, and put all French forces in North Africa at their disposal. He was assassinated on 24 December 1942 by a young man believed to have been a supporter of de Gaulle (q.v.). The assassin was rapidly tried and executed. Although he was remembered with sympathy, Darlan's death was widely acknowledged to have simplified relations between the Vichy regime and the Allies.

DARNAND, Joseph (1897–1945). Pro-German French leader who fought openly for the German side. Working under Pétain (q.v.), Joseph Darnand set up the *Service d'Ordre Légionnaire*, or *Milice*, which functioned openly with German connivance as an internal security organization. Darnand was responsible for uncovering and sending to their deaths thousands of resistance workers in France. He took the oath of allegiance to Hitler (q.v.), and wore German uniform. When de Gaulle (q.v.) formed his government in 1944 Darnand and 6000 followers fled to Germany. Hitler thought of using them as a cohesive fighting force, but the idea was not taken up. At the end of the war Darnand was tried for treason and shot.

DEMPSEY, Miles (1896–1969). British general, commander of the British Second Army in the Normandy campaign and after. He came to prominence as a result of his close association with Montgomery (q.v.). He served as commander of

13 Corps in the Sicily and Italy campaigns. In north-west Europe Dempsey's army undertook some of the most punishing fighting in the battles of attrition around Caen, and carried out the drive to Antwerp which no other force could match for speed. A quiet and thoughtful man, Dempsey attracted little publicity but deserves great credit for his efficient command of the Second Army.

DEVERS, Jacob Loucks (born 1887). United States general. Devers served for the first eighteen months of the war as chief of armoured forces at Fort Knox. In May 1943 he was appointed to command United States forces in the European theatre, where he played an important part in planning the invasion of north-west Europe. He succeeded Eisenhower (q.v.) as commander in the North African theatre in December 1943 and rose to be deputy supreme commander in the Mediterranean. On 15 September 1944 he was appointed commander in chief of Sixth Army Group. He took over US Seventh and French First Armies, which had mounted the invasion of southern France (Operation Anvil) and formed the right

United States general Jacob Devers (left), commander of Sixth Army Group in operations in north-west Europe.

flank of the Allied force for the assault on Germany. His troops overran Hitler's (q.v.) headquarters at Berchtesgaden, and Devers received the surrender of the armies in southern Germany near Munich on 5 May 1945. (*See also* Patch)

DIETRICH, Sepp (1892–1966). Nazi officer, head of the *ss* Liebstandarte Adolf Hitler regiment during the early days of the Nazi party. Dietrich was among the first supporters of Hitler (q.v.) and as chief of the *Stabwache*, or staff guard, led the assassination squad which murdered Röhm (q.v.) and other *sa* leaders during the 'Night of the Long Knives' in 1934. Always one of Hitler's favourites, he rose to command I *ss* Panzer Corps in the battles to contain the Anglo–American beachhead in Normandy and Sixth *ss* Panzer Army in the Ardennes counter-offensive. In 1946 he was given a life sentence for his part in the massacre of captured American soldiers at Malmédy. He was released in 1955, and in 1957 given a further sentence of eighteen months by a German court for aiding Hitler to come to power.

DILL, (Sir) John (1881–1944). British fieldmarshal who gave valuable service as the British chiefs of staff's representative in Washington. An Ulsterman by birth, Dill saw service in the Boer war, and extensively in the first world war when he was wounded, decorated several times by France and Belgium as well as his own country, and won a high reputation as a staff officer. In the inter-war years he held a series of increasingly important appointments, including that of commandant of the staff college. He was clearly destined for the highest office of chief of the imperial general staff, but at the critical moment was passed over, as part of a new policy of appointing younger men, in favour first of Gort and then of Ironside (qq.v.). Dill was given the consolation of I Corps to command in France. In April 1940 the command structure was revised, and Dill was recalled as vice-CIGS, and then a mere month later was at last appointed CIGS in place of Ironside. Like many of the senior commanders at the beginning of the war he was in an unfortunate position, carrying the blame for the disasters while not being re-

Field-Marshal Sir John Dill (left), British representative in Washington, and a much-respected figure among American political and military leaders.

sponsible for the conditions which caused them. His position was further aggravated by a running quarrel with Winston Churchill (q.v.), who was desperate to return to the offensive, while Dill warned against premature operations which would waste resources better conserved for later action. He also first opposed, and then agreed to, the Greek operation, which did little to enhance his reputation. In December 1941 he was replaced as CIGS by Alan Brooke (q.v.).

Dill was due to take on the sinecure post of governor of Bombay, but when the Japanese attack brought the United States into the war, Dill went to Washington with Churchill, and remained there as representative of the British chiefs of staff. For him it was the ideal appointment, offering great (and steadily increasing) involvement in the strategic direction of the war, without the burden of daily executive activity which until then had seriously affected his uncertain health. He was rewarded with an unexpectedly high reputation among the American joint chiefs of staff, and especially with President Roosevelt (q.v.), all of whom liked him and gave him their complete

trust. As American participation grew, and with it the need for active co-ordination of the British and American efforts, Dill's role increased in importance until Roosevelt could call him the 'most important figure in the remarkable accord which has been developed in the combined operations of our two countries'. Dill became ill again late in 1944, died on 4 November, and was accorded the honour of burial in Arlington National Cemetery.

DÖNITZ, Karl (born 1891). German admiral. Head of the U-boat service, and commander-in-chief of the navy from 1943. Dönitz was named by Hitler (q.v.) as his successor during the last days of the war. After serving in cruisers and later U-boats in the first world war, Dönitz remained in the small German navy between the wars and when Hitler abandoned the restraints of the Versailles treaty in 1935 was appointed to raise and command the new U-boat arm. Dönitz was thus one of the most important figures in the war, as the U-boat came closer than any other single weapon to winning the war for Germany. Churchill (q.v.) confessed that the U-boat was the only thing that ever really frightened him during the war, and said that the Germans would have been wise to stake all upon it. Dönitz was an able tactician, notably in directing the battle of the Atlantic against the Allied supply shipping. His most effective innovation was the 'wolf pack' tactic in which U-boats waited for the convoys in groups. He became commander-in-chief when Raeder (q.v.) resigned in 1943. In the last days of the war, when Goering and Himmler (qq.v.) had been denounced as traitors by the Führer, Hitler made his last will in which he named Dönitz as president of the Reich. Dönitz took this suggestion seriously and attempted to negotiate an orderly end of the war with the Allies in the west, making strenuous efforts to protect the citizens of eastern Germany from Soviet barbarities, and accusing Eisenhower (q.v.) especially of 'inhuman' acts in preventing German troops and civilians escaping into Ameri-

Admiral Karl Dönitz (centre), architect of Germany's U-boat offensive, and one of the most important figures in the war.

can and British, as opposed to Russian, custody. The Allies took little notice of Dönitz as a national leader, arrested him, and tried him as a war criminal at Nuremberg. Like the other professional servicemen, he claimed in defence that he was merely a naval officer carrying out orders. He was convicted of crimes against peace and war crimes, and sentenced to ten years' imprisonment.

DOOLITTLE, James Harold (born 1896). American aviator and leader of the first air raid against the Japanese homeland. From the time of the entry of the United States into the war through the early months of 1942, little offensive action was possible by the Allies against Japan except carrier-based hit-and-run raids on the outlying islands of Japan's newly occupied Pacific territory, such as the Marshall Islands and New Guinea. But the American planners had high hopes of mounting a raid in retaliation for Pearl Harbor, and by early April the organization was ready. The operation would clearly have to be undertaken from a carrier, and would need to be flown from outside the patrol area of the Japanese picket boats, some 500 miles out of Tokyo. Because of the dangers of air attack, the carriers could not wait for recovery, and the aircraft would have to fly to a land airfield. In view of the range involved only army air force bombers would be able to tackle the job, and sixteen of them were assembled on the flight deck of the carrier *Hornet*, commanded by Captain Marc A. Mitscher (q.v.). It was not possible to carry a greater force on the flight-deck, and the aircraft were of course too large to be stowed below decks. The selected pilots practised short take-off procedures and long sea flights, and the *Hornet*, escorted by the carrier *Enterprise*, sailed from San Francisco on 2 April 1942. On 18 April they were sighted by a Japanese patrol boat, and because of the loss of surprise decided on an immediate take-off. Launching between 8.15 and 9.24 am, the bombers arrived over Tokyo at about noon, instead of in darkness, and thirteen of the crews bombed the capital with high explosive and incendiaries. Other crews raided Osaka, Nagoya and Kobe. After the raid they flew on to Chuchow on the Chinese main-

General James Doolittle (right), hero of the first bomber raid against Japan, a retaliation for Pearl Harbor and a great boost to American morale.

land, where because of the change in timing the airfield was not ready to receive them. The crews were forced to make crash landings in darkness or bale out, and several ditched in the sea close to the coast. Out of the eighty-two men who took part in the raid, twelve were lost. Two who were picked up by the Japanese were executed for bombing civilian targets. The carriers escaped and arrived back at Pearl Harbor on 25 April. The results of the Doolittle raid were in keeping with other early raids in both the Pacific and European theatres – small direct gains, but far-reaching strategic ramifications. This raid tied down large numbers of Japanese aircraft in Tokyo, and also induced the Japanese to attempt the Midway operation as a means of destroying the remnants of the American Pacific Fleet, which led them to diversify their efforts and dissipate their concentration of strength in the theatre. The raid also gave a healthy boost to American morale after the shock of Pearl Harbor four months earlier. It is worth noting that no further raids against Tokyo followed until 24 November 1944.

Doolittle went on to command the Twelfth Air Force in Operation Torch, and the Strategic Air Force which bombed Italian bases and shipping in 1943. He commanded the Eighth Air Force against Germany and led bombing attacks against many of the German v-weapon sites.

DORMAN-SMITH, Eric (1898–1969). Controversial British general and brilliant military thinker who was the brains behind many successful plans put into effect by General Sir Claude Auchinleck (q.v.) in the North African campaign. During the early part of his career Dorman-Smith was widely considered to be one of the best minds in the British army. But he was far too imaginative for the army authorities to feel comfortable with him holding an important field command; in the war he was twice demoted without explanation, and was finally removed from his last command at the successful climax of the Italian campaign. After service as a subaltern in the first world war, in which he was three times wounded and won the Military Cross before the age of twenty, Dorman-Smith rose through the ranks of the army with effortless speed. He was an instructor at Sandhurst, passed brilliantly out of the staff college at Camberley, and then held a series of key posts concerned with the development and modernization of the army in preparation for the new motorized and mechanized age of war: these posts were at the school of military engineering, in Wavell's (q.v.) 6 Experimental Brigade, and finally at the War Office. The essence of Dorman-Smith's military philosophy was that the linear infantry defences which were a feature of the first world war would be unable to stand the weight of a concentrated German armoured thrust, and that only by a high degree of mechanization and reorganization could the British deal with the problems of the coming war. After serving for a period as an instructor in the staff college, Dorman-Smith commanded an infantry battalion in Egypt, before

becoming director of military training in India, where he came to be associated with Auchinleck, then deputy chief of the general staff in India.

In 1940 he returned to the Middle East as commandant of the new Middle East staff college, where he came to Wavell's notice. From then until Montgomery's (q.v.) arrival in the theatre in August 1942 he was intimately concerned with the desert war. His contribution to it, even if only from the second rank in the hierarchy, was considerable. In February 1941 he was closely concerned with O'Connor (q.v.) in the pursuit that led to the defeat of the Italians at Beda Fomm. In April, May and June that year he held the post of director of military operations in Cairo, during which period Auchinleck, who had taken over from Wavell, sent him to report on the activities of the Eighth Army in the field. Dorman-Smith's recommendation was that the Eighth Army commander, General Ritchie (q.v.), should be removed as he was not quick-witted or imaginative enough for the job, and morale in the Eighth Army was low. Auchinleck had only recently sacked one commander and could not afford to act on his recommendation. However, Auchinleck continued to value Dorman-Smith's advice, and appointed him to the post of deputy chief of the general staff in May 1942. From then on Dorman-Smith produced a series of perceptive and analytically accurate reports on the desert fighting, many of which formed the basis of Auchinleck's recommendations to the army commander, Ritchie. In fact Auchinleck was already exercising close control of the battlefield over Ritchie's head, and by implication Dorman-Smith's advice was an influential factor in the British desert campaign. His position at the hub of the planning system was in due course formally acknowledged when Auchinleck flew in to take personal command of the Eighth Army after the loss of Tobruk. Dorman-Smith travelled with him in his plane, and became his personal chief of staff. Together they worked out the plan to fall back on El Alamein if the battle at Mersah Matruh went badly. Then on 27 July 1942, after the failure of the initial attempts to counter-attack following the first battle of El Ala-mein, Dorman-Smith wrote a study outlining the situation, and recommending a period of re-train-ing and reinforcement before the British would be able to go on to the offensive again during the latter part of September. A week later, on 3 August 1942, Churchill (q.v.) arrived in the desert, determined to make far-reaching changes in the command structure. They included the removal of Auchin-leck from office and his replacement by Alexander, and the removal of Dorman-Smith as deputy chief of the general staff. In the opinion of some histor-ians Dorman-Smith's report proved an accurate prediction of the course of the war in the next three months, and was adopted as the basis for Mont-gomery's operations both in the defensive battle of Alam Halfa and in the subsequent offensive which started with the second battle of El Alamein.

The controversy which surrounded Mont-gomery, Auchinleck and Dorman-Smith over this issue persisted after the war, when Dorman-Smith objected to some of the published accounts of the battles. He caused the publishers of Montgom-ery's memoirs to print a note acknowledging that Auchinleck had stabilized the front and enabled Montgomery to conduct the offensive of October 1942, and also that Auchinleck had no plans to retreat to the Nile delta. He also sued Winston Churchill for libel when Churchill stated that the command changes of early August 1942 would 're-store confidence in the Command, which I regret does not exist at the present time'. Churchill settled out of court and published a note in his memoirs acknowledging that Dorman-Smith bore no responsibility for the fall of Tobruk or the defeats at Gazala.

After his removal from the desert, Dorman-Smith was subjected to shabby treatment which has never been properly explained. He was reduced from the rank of major-general to colonel, then given command of an infantry brigade in England. Unfortunately in October 1943 General Ritchie arrived to become commander of 12 Corps, and therefore Dorman-Smith's boss. Dorman-Smith was sacked, and remained un-

employed until March 1944, when he again took over a brigade, this time fighting at the Anzio beach-head. After five months during which his tactics and leadership could not be faulted, he was again sacked, on the grounds that he was 'unfit for brigade command'. Then in November 1944 he was dismissed from the army altogether, and his name was removed from the active list. After the war he settled in his native Ireland, changed his name, and studied successfully for a new career as a lawyer. As with other individualists of intellect and imagination in the British army, the great weight of establishment orthodoxy had proved too formidable for Dorman-Smith to sustain the suc-cess of his early career.

DOUGLAS, (Sir) William Sholto (born 1893). British air marshal who took over fighter com-mand in November 1940 from Dowding (q.v.). His first task was to carry the air war back into the enemy camp, and he began flying offensive raids into France, designed not only to instil the British

William Sholto Douglas, British air marshal who took over fighter command at the end of 1940.

pilots with the confidence that they now held the initiative, but also to draw German fighters and defensive resources from south-east Europe. In June 1943 he became head of the Middle East air command, and a year later took over coastal command in England where he was responsible for defence against the rump of the U-boat effort. In the late days of the war he took the battle to the Germans by flying sorties into their U-boat working-up area in the Baltic.

DOWDING, Hugh (1882–1970). British air marshal who led fighter command during the Battle of Britain. Appointed c-in-c fighter command on 14 July 1936, Dowding, as much as any

Hugh Dowding moves on. The man who guided fighter command to victory in the Battle of Britain was under threat of removal throughout the battle, although he kept his post until it ended. Here Dowding (second from left) arrives in Ottawa to begin his new task on 31 December 1940.

other single man, can claim direct responsibility for ultimate Allied victory. It was through his foresight, and his recognition of the merits of the new invention of radar, that Britain was able to begin in 1935 building up the chain of early warning radar stations round the coast. Because of the radar, in conjunction with the efforts of the observer corps, the RAF was able to fly interception missions only when German fighters approached, thus eliminating the need for ceaseless and exhausting patrols. Dowding also backed the idea of a single-engined monoplane, which eventually gave Britain the Hurricane and Spitfire aircraft. Dowding further contributed to Britain's success in 1940 by refusing to send his Spitfire fighters to France. He insisted on retaining them in England as the spearhead of Britain's defence in the event of France's defeat, and appeared before Britain's Cabinet to plead his argument. He won his case, and his prediction proved accurate that the critical battle would be fought over Britain. An unemotional character familiarly known as 'Stuffy', Dowding was a masterly organizer, and had the resolution and confidence to resist powerful political pressures, for which his country owes a con-

siderable debt. After the Battle of Britain he was seconded to the United States Ministry of Aircraft Production. He retired in 1942. (*See also* Bader, Leigh-Mallory, Park)

DULLES, Allen (1893–1969). American lawyer who as the OSS representative in Switzerland was instrumental in maintaining contact with the German hierarchy during the war. After the Casablanca conference in 1943, where Churchill and Roosevelt (qq.v.) declared their intention to impose unconditional surrender on Germany, Dulles made contact with the German emissaries, Prince Maximillian Hohenlohe and Dr Schudekov, to discuss possible variations on this condition. The discussion also included Kaltenbrunner (q.v.) and other SS men, and covered questions of negotiated peace terms, the impossibility of Hitler (q.v.) leading a post-war government in Germany, and other aspects of a political solution to the late stages of the war. All this came to nothing, and Dulles's most concrete achievement appears to have been the orderly surrender of German forces in Italy in 1945. Allen Dulles was the brother of John Foster Dulles, Eisenhower's (q.v.) secretary of state.

E

EAKER, Ira (born 1898). American air commander. Eaker led a force of twelve B-17 bombers in the first bombing attack on Western Europe. He was instrumental in initiating daylight bombing raids by USAAF squadrons, which formed a twenty-four hour attack on Germany with the RAF's night raids. Eaker commanded the Allied air forces in the invasion of southern France in 1944.

EDEN, Anthony (First Earl of Avon) (1897–1977). British politician and wartime foreign minister. Eden was known in the early 1930s for his work to promote the League of Nations. In 1934 he met the two European dictators, Hitler and Mussolini (qq.v.), and when the Abyssinian crisis arose in 1935 Eden was one of the few to warn against Italian intentions. When the foreign

Anthony Eden (right) visits Montgomery's field headquarters in Normandy, June 1944. Eden was foreign minister and Churchill's heir apparent.

secretary resigned over the issue in December Eden succeeded him. There he found himself again isolated, as one of the few opponents of Chamberlain's (q.v.) appeasement policy, and on 19 February 1938 he resigned. He was recalled when the war began in September 1939, and in May 1940, when Churchill (q.v.) took over the premiership, Eden became secretary of state for war and Churchill's unofficial political heir. The work of the two men remained closely linked throughout the war. After seeing the armed services through the tense days of the Dunkirk evacuation, the Battle of Britain and the anti-invasion preparations, Eden again became foreign secretary. In February and March 1941 he was closely involved with the decision to send military aid to Greece, which resulted in a disaster for the British army. Eden also fought hard, but unsuccessfully, to preserve Polish independence, and early recognized that the future of France lay in de Gaulle. Although at times he bitterly disputed issues with Churchill, the partnership remained intact and Eden was a key figure with Churchill at all the major wartime conferences. In May 1945 he again reverted to the international policy which had occupied his earlier career, when he led the British delegation to San Francisco to work out the form of the new United Nations Organization. He served as British prime minister from 1955 to January 1957, when he resigned after the Suez crisis.

EICHELBERGER, Robert Lawrence (1886–1961). United States army general, commander of Eighth Army in the battles to clear the Japanese from the Philippines. Eichelberger served as commandant of the West Point military academy at the beginning of the war, and was appointed to command I Corps with the task of holding the Japanese advance towards Australia. He took over exhausted Australian and American troops at Buna, New Guinea, and revitalized them by reorganizing the command and training them in new tactics. Then in a lightning campaign, with instructions from MacArthur (q.v.) to 'take Buna or not come back alive', his troops recaptured Gona,

Lieutenant-General Robert Eichelberger (right), commander of United States forces on New Guinea and subsequently Eighth Army commander in the Philippines.

Buna and Sanananda between 9 December 1942 and 18 January 1943. After further clearance operations on New Guinea he took command in September 1944 of the newly activated Eighth Army and led them in the Philippines campaign. His forces carried out a series of amphibious operations which required thirty-eight landings in February and April 1945 in the central and southern Philippines. This form of warfare required immensely complex logistical arrangements, and its success was based on Eichelberger's own hard drive and courage, and a flexible approach which enabled him to take advantage of opportunities as they arose. (*See also* MacArthur and Wainwright)

EISENHOWER, Dwight David (1890–1969). United States general and supreme commander of all Allied forces in Europe from December 1943. Dwight Eisenhower was born in Texas, into a family which was too poor to send him to college. He earned the money as a cow-puncher and went to West Point where he graduated in 1915. He

Dwight D. Eisenhower, at work at his headquarters in January 1944 as Supreme Commander Allied Expeditionary Force, and commanding general of US forces in Europe.

missed the opportunity of serving in the first world war, and subsequently held a variety of staff and command posts. He served on the staff of General MacArthur (q.v.) in the early 1930s, and went with him to the Philippines as an assistant military adviser in 1935. In 1940 he returned to the United States to command an infantry regiment, and rose to the important post of chief of the war plans division.

Eisenhower was selected to command the American army in the European theatre in June 1942, and was in overall command of the North African landings. He had not until then held an army command in the field. In North Africa he had the vital experience of organizing an Allied effort with more experienced ground commanders serving under him, including General Alexander (q.v.). He also encountered de Gaulle (q.v.), whom he found difficult to deal with. The Americans were inclined to support General Giraud, de Gaulle's rival for Free French leadership.

In December 1943 Eisenhower was appointed to command the Allied Expeditionary Force for the invasion of Europe. He took over the post which had been earmarked for the British general, Brooke (q.v.), when the preponderance of American forces made an American appointment logical. Marshall (q.v.) was a more likely candidate for this supreme post, but Roosevelt (q.v.) could not spare him from Washington.

Eisenhower brought to the post an unusual but vital talent for welding a variety of powerful individuals, often with conflicting views and unharmonious personalities, into a co-ordinated Allied team. In this regard his own personality was a major contributing factor, acknowledged as being totally honest, sincere, warm and magnetic. As Montgomery (q.v.) (one of his principal antagonists at certain stages) stated, he had only to smile at you, and you could trust him at once.

Eisenhower organized the preparation for the invasion on 6 June 1944 with consummate administrative skill, and unexpectedly faced a critical test in the timing of D-Day itself. Weather forced a postponement of twenty-four hours, and prospects remained unfavourable for the next day. Eisenhower knew that tidal and moon conditions would force a postponement for several months if they did not go ahead, and he was forced to balance the risk of losses due to weather against that of loss of morale and possible damage to security. He consulted his advisers, then observed, 'This is a decision for me alone to make.' He decided to go ahead, and set the invasion in motion with the words, 'Okay, let 'er rip.' At the same time he wrote a letter stating that if the landings failed to gain a satisfactory foothold the fault was his alone.

In September 1944, according to a prearranged plan, Eisenhower took personal control of the land forces. Montgomery reverted to control of an army group, and Bradley (q.v.) was raised up to similar army group control parallel with Montgomery. Eisenhower thereby found himself at the crux of

General Eisenhower, anxious in the last hours before D-Day, talks with airborne troops about to take off for the initial landings in Normandy.

the arguments on strategy which bedevilled the late stages of the war. The principal battle was with Montgomery, who had little reticence about voicing his dissent, until in one showdown Eisenhower, ever patient and accommodating, patted Montgomery on the knee and told him, 'You can't talk to me like that, Monty, I'm your boss.' Although Eisenhower could be severe and ruthless with the incompetent, he was good-natured and humane almost to a fault. The main strand of the dispute between them was the question of the type of advance into Germany. Montgomery favoured a single narrow front thrust into northern Germany, carried out by his own Twenty-first Army Group. Eisenhower wanted a broad front advance by both the British Twenty-first and US Twelfth Army Groups. The broad-front strategy was the one he insisted on, and arguments about it have continued ever since. It is arguable that the single

thrust might have led to the defeat of Germany in the west in 1944, but equally might have brought a disaster. A similar controversy arose out of the question of whether the Allies should race on to take Berlin in advance of the Russians. Eisenhower later justified his not forcing on to Berlin on the grounds that the Russians were nearer, and large casualties would have been incurred. That is almost certainly not true, as it is now known that the Germans preferred to be defeated by the Anglo–American alliance and keep the Russians out of as much of their country as possible. However, the Allies had already drawn up agreed zones of occupation, and even if Eisenhower had gone on to take Berlin it is more than likely he would have been forced to withdraw his forces according to those treaties.

However, overall it is possible to criticize Eisenhower as being deficient in strategic grasp. On the other hand, that was not his main task: strategy was being settled by the respective political leaders and their respective chiefs of staff. Nor could he be called a great general, as he never had the opportunity to show his skill as a commander in the field. His job fell somewhere between these two, perhaps best summed up in Montgomery's definition as a 'military statesman'. And in that

he was superlatively successful. He was not prepared to tolerate a word of nationalistic prejudice from the men working with him. As he said, one general may call another a 'sonovabitch'. But no general could call an ally from another country a 'British sonovabitch', on pain of being sent home. As Churchill (q.v.) observed, he set the unity of the Allied armies above all nationalistic thoughts.

Eisenhower's own work combined two qualities: his personality, which made him one of the few men who could have kept the Allied machinery functioning without the grit in the works causing it to jam; and his administrative skill, which led to the faultless running of the greatest Allied war machine ever assembled.

Even General de Gaulle, with whom Eisenhower quarrelled both in North Africa and over the use of French troops in north-west Europe, paid tribute to Eisenhower's skill in dominating a military situation by method and perseverance, by choosing reasonable plans and sticking firmly to them, and for respecting logistics.

After the war Dwight D. Eisenhower went on to become United States chief of staff, supreme commander of NATO, and the thirty-fourth president of the United States.

Eisenhower visits the ruins of the citadel of Julich on the Ruhr in February 1945. Accompanying him are Major-General Raymond McLain, 19 Army Corps, and Lieutenant-General William Hood Simpson of US Ninth Army.

F

FALKENHAUSEN, Ernst von (1878–1966). German general who served as governor-general of occupied Belgium and northern France, and was a conspirator in the plot on Hitler's (q.v.) life on 20 July 1944. Falkenhausen had retired from the army in 1930, and went out to China to train the army for Chiang Kai-shek (q.v.) until Hitler recalled him and made him governor of France and Belgium. As an officer of the old Prussian school Falkenhausen found the methods of the *ss* and Gestapo unacceptable and did his utmost to protect the occupied people from the worst excesses of their rule. When he was suspected of complicity in the resistance movement he was dismissed. The attempt on Hitler's life took place a few days later. Falkenhausen was sent to Dachau concentration camp, liberated by the Americans, and handed back to the Belgians who sentenced him to twelve years in prison for allegedly ordering hostages to be executed. He was released after only three weeks as an act of clemency for his part in protecting Belgians from the *ss*. He wrote a bitter message in Latin in the book at the German customs station as he left Belgium: *Ingrata Belgia, non possedebis ossa mea*' – 'ungrateful Belgium, you will not possess my bones'.

FALKENHORST, Nikolaus von (1885–1968). German general who commanded 21 Corps in the invasion of Poland in 1939. He was commander-in-chief of German troops in Norway from 1940 to 1944 when he was dismissed for opposing the policies of the Norwegian Nazi commissioner. In 1946 a British military court sentenced him to be shot for handing over captured British commandos for execution following Hitler's (q.v.) order that commandos should not have the protection of international military convention. His sentence was reduced to twenty years' imprisonment and he was released in 1953 because of ill-health.

FORRESTAL, James Vincent (1892–1949). American administrator who served as first under-secretary of the navy during the second world war, and played a key role in building up United States naval strength. After a varied but extremely successful early career as a cub reporter, banker, and financial speculator, Forrestal entered political life in 1940 in a form of public service, as a low-paid assistant to President Roosevelt (q.v.). Six weeks later he was given the new post as first under-secretary of the navy and for the next four years was instrumental in the production and procurement of naval supplies. He did not avoid friction with senior naval officers, consistently maintaining that a civilian could carry out the task of building up the navy as well as a professional seaman. By the late stages of the war he had turned the United States navy into a larger organization than the combined fleets of the rest of the world. In 1944 secretary of the navy Knox (q.v.) died and Forrestal took his place. He expressed forceful political opinions from then on, having developed a passionate hatred of Communism and a determination to see his country contain it through strength. He was also against measures which would destroy the strength of Germany and Japan, and opposed proposals to share atomic knowledge. He fought to maintain budget spending on defence as a means of containing the Soviet threat and preserving world peace, but President Truman (q.v.),

The American naval chiefs: secretary of the navy James Forrestal, flanked by Fleet-Admiral Ernest King (left), and Fleet-Admiral Chester Nimitz, who took over from King as chief of naval operations.

whose views later came more into line with Forrestal's, initially reduced Forrestal's budget proposals. His career was crowned by the appointment as first secretary of defence, but he resigned after only a few months through ill health, and in 1949 entered Bethesda naval hospital for psychiatric treatment. It appears that his confidence had been undermined by what he saw as failure to impress President Truman with his views, and he was also suffering from overwork. He appeared to be responding to treatment, but on 21 May 1949 threw himself from a sixth-floor window and was killed.

FRANCO, Francisco (1892–1975). Spanish general and dictator. Having come to power with the aid of Axis help during the civil war, Franco was expected to side with the Axis during the second world war. Instead he astutely maintained a policy of neutrality. His reasons for this posture are complex. Without doubt he was anxious to avoid a repetition of the destruction his country had suffered in the civil war. No doubt he was keen to avoid joining the losing side. After the initial German successes of 1939 and 1940 he tended towards Axis co-operation, but at an interview with Hitler (q.v.) on 23 October 1939 he bargained so hard that Hitler was forced to abandon his request for a Spanish–German advance on Gibraltar and the Atlantic islands. Then when Britain held out and the United States entered the war the neu-

General Francisco Franco, Spanish dictator.

trality policy no doubt appeared the more judicious. His one contribution to the Axis was to send the 'Blue Division' to fight on the Russian front, but in October 1943 he broke off relations with the Axis.

FRANK, Hans (1900–46). Nazi party official and wartime governor of Poland. A lawyer by profession, Frank was the party's top legal expert throughout the 1930s and drafted most Nazi legislation. He was governor of Poland 1939–45, and at the Nuremberg trial was accused of crimes against the Polish people. He was penitent about his role in Poland's repression, and spent his time at the trial weeping or praying, having undergone a religious conversion. It did not save him. His own diaries detailing his sadistic crimes in Poland were heard in evidence, and he was hanged.

FRASER, Peter (1884–1950). New Zealand prime minister. Scottish-born Peter Fraser emigrated to New Zealand in 1911, and served a year's imprisonment in 1916 for sedition in opposing conscription. A lifelong Labour man, he carried out great reforms in the social field before becoming prime minister in 1940. He held his government together in the face of severe criticism from an opposition which refused to join a coalition, and he won an important general election at the height of the war in 1943. His great contribution to wartime leadership was as a willing member of the Allied team, leaving his troops in the Middle East even though it meant New Zealand being totally exposed at one stage to possible Japanese attack. At the same time he realized, as the Australians did, that New Zealand's war interests were closely tied up with those of the United States. In 1942 he travelled to Washington to discuss joint Pacific policy with President Roosevelt (q.v.).

FREYBERG, Bernard (1889–1963). New Zealand general, and commander-in-chief of his country's forces in the second world war. Freyberg was known as a soldier of phenomenal personal bravery who instilled his own fearlessness into the men under his command. He was himself wounded some thirty times in the first and second world wars, and won a large number of decorations including the Victoria Cross. He was appointed to command the New Zealand forces abroad in November 1939, and led them in the intervention in Greece, when he conducted a skilful withdrawal in the face of the German advance. In Crete he commanded all the Allied forces, and again conducted a creditable evacuation, saving about half of his force of 30,000 men.

He then commanded his forces in the desert battles in Libya and Egypt, and was severely wounded at Mersah Matruh in the attempt to stop Rommel's (q.v.) advance of the summer of 1942. The New Zealand Division was almost cut off but withdrew in a night march through German lines. Before he had fully recovered from his wounds Freyberg returned to action and took part in Montgomery's (q.v.) advance after the battle of El Alamein. In November 1944 he commanded the New Zealand Division in Italy at the battle of the Sangro river, and the New Zealand corps at Cas-

Major-General Bernard Freyberg, commander of the New Zealand Division in the North African desert.

sino. With his own division, an Indian division and other American and British troops serving under him he conducted the early operations against Cassino, which damaged the Germans' tenacious and well-secured defences sufficiently for Allied forces to overwhelm the position after Freyberg's corps had been withdrawn.

Perhaps the most notable tribute came from Rommel, who declared that he respected New Zealand troops above all others, and developed almost an affection for them. Freyberg was a believer in the bayonet charge, a fact which not only gave his men a reputation for unsurpassed bravery, but also illuminated Freyberg's limitations as a commander, bearing in the mind the bayonet's restricted potentialities in the mechanized warfare of the 1940s.

FRICK, Wilhelm (1877–1946). Reich minister of the interior, and a senior official in government under Hitler (q.v.). Already a senior civil servant in the Weimar Republic, Frick attached himself to Hitler's Nazi party, and was tried for treason with Hitler after the Munich putsch. When Hitler became chancellor, Frick was instrumental in drafting the legislation which kept Hitler in control. Once Hitler had consolidated his position of power and Germany had become a military state at war, Frick's importance declined. He was made protector of occupied Czechoslovakia. When indicted at Nuremberg, where he refused to testify, he claimed that he had been merely a civil servant working for a constitutionally elected government. He was found guilty and hanged.

FULLER, John (1878–1966). British general and military writer who served in the Tank Corps from July 1916, and after the first world war became deputy director of staff studies in the tanks section of the British War Office. He was from then on a prolific writer and, although he was not appointed to any command in the second world war because of his age, was one of the small group of military thinkers whose writings influenced the course of tank development in the inter-war years. (*See also* Hobart, Liddell-Hart)

FUNK, Walter (1890–1960). Economist and Nazi party official, and an important figure in the financial structuring of Hitler's (q.v.) Reich. A financial journalist by profession, Funk served in several party posts before the war, including press chief and state secretary for propaganda. In 1939 he was made president of the Reichsbank. He was tried at Nuremberg where he claimed he had been only an official implementing Nazi leaders' (particularly Goering's, q.v.) plans. He was found guilty and sentenced to life imprisonment.

G

German air ace Adolf Galland, veteran of the Battle of Britain, later commander-in-chief of the Luftwaffe fighter arm. At the end of the war he flew the jet-powered Me262 fighters which came off the production lines in August 1944.

GALLAND, Adolf (born 1912). Luftwaffe fighter pilot and air ace, credited with more than 100 aircraft destroyed. He led a fighter group in the Battle of Britain, and commanded the fighter force after the death of Mölders in November 1941. In 1942 he was promoted to become the youngest German general, at the age of thirty. He gradually fell out with Hitler (q.v.) and his own superiors and in January 1944 was relieved of his command. In 1943 he had test-flown the new German jet, the Me262, and had recommended its production as a fighter. Initially Hitler turned it down, but by January 1945 it was coming into production. Now, when Galland was no use to him as a senior commander, Hitler allowed his former ace to return to combat and made him head of the new *Jagdverband* 44, flying the new Me262 jets with other dismissed generals. The aircraft easily outflew the Allies' conventional machines, and their successes mounted remarkably, although they were too late and too few to influence the course of the war.

DE GAULLE, Charles André Joseph Marie (1890–1970). French general and leader of the Free French movement which resisted Germany after the occupation. A graduate of St Cyr, de Gaulle fought in the first world war, was wounded and left for dead at Verdun, but revived in a cart on the way to the graveyard, after which he escaped and was recaptured five times. After the war he gained a reputation for arrogance by criticizing his instructor during his staff college days, and became isolated in the army for his stance against the popular concept of static fortifications embodied in the building of the Maginot

General Charles de Gaulle, Free French leader and one of the most uncompromising Allied leaders. He was excluded from many of the major strategic and political decisions. He is seen visiting the Normandy beaches, against Churchill's advice, on 14 June 1944, eight days after the landings.

Line. Instead he fought for the creation of a mobile mechanized force of tanks and aircraft. He published his ideas in a series of essays and books, but they were ignored by the military hierarchy. De Gaulle was a colonel commanding 4 Armoured Brigade when the Germans invaded on 14 May 1940. Ten days later he was promoted to brigadier-general and put in command of the 4 Armoured Division, still not fully equipped. However, by energetic leadership he repulsed the enemy at Laon and Abbeville. In June prime minister Reynaud (q.v.) appointed him under-secretary of state for war and national defence. When Paris fell and the French sought an armistice de Gaulle escaped to London in a hazardous aircraft journey. Convinced that Hitler (q.v.) would be defeated by the Allies in due course, he broadcast to the French on 18 June a speech stating that France had lost merely the battle, not the war, and asking them to support him: 'The flame of French resistance must not die,' he told them. He was recognized as head of the Free French by the British government on 22 June, and on 7 July was sentenced to death in his absence by a French military court. The years that followed were marked by de Gaulle's unique patriotism, dedicated to freeing France from her enemies, whatever the cost in relations with the Allies themselves. He is said to have observed several times that he did not care who won the war so long as it was France. Early in June 1940 his position was tested by the British decision to sink the French fleet. De Gaulle was dismayed by the event, but understood the difficulty, and said he would rather have the *Dunkerque* aground than shelling English ports. He continued his campaign by rallying support in the French African colonies, and by December 1940 had amassed an army of 35,000 men. He was extremely angered by the British actions in Syria and the Lebanon, which he still thought of as French territory. His overall attitude was one of suspicion of the British and hatred of the Americans, and he persistently cultivated France's stance as one of the major Allied powers, while the British regarded defeated France as tem-

Accepted by the French people as their new leader, de Gaulle makes friends with a new generation.

porarily irrelevant to the main task of beating Nazi Germany. Further difficulties arose out of Roosevelt's (q.v.) refusal to allow French forces to take part in the North African landings, and Roosevelt's support for General Giraud, de Gaulle's rival for leadership of the Free French. For a time these two were made joint chairmen of the national liberation committee, but gradually de Gaulle emerged as the more likely leader, enjoying the support of the resistance in France, and Giraud was forced to withdraw. To de Gaulle's intense anger, he was not even told the date of the invasion of Normandy. Eight days after it, against opposition from Churchill (q.v.), he landed and was instantly acclaimed by the people. He entered Paris at the head of the liberating forces while fighting was still going on in the streets, and set up his government as the Fourth Republic, declaring Marshal Pétain's (q.v.) Vichy regime never to have existed legally. In the strategic decisions that arose towards the end of the war de Gaulle continued to quarrel with the Allies. He tried unsuccessfully to persuade Churchill to set up an Anglo–French front against the two major powers, the United States and the USSR, and was excluded from both the Yalta and Potsdam conferences. However, France was given a zone of Germany to administer and a permanent seat in the United Nations security council. After the war de Gaulle went on through succeeding vicissitudes to become president of a newly powerful France, but his relations with the Allies only became worse. He was essentially a man for whom little counted except the interests of France.

GIBSON, Guy (1918–44). Royal Air Force wing commander who led the squadron to attack the Möhne, Eder and other dams with Barnes Wallis's (q.v.) 'bouncing' bombs. The attack took place on 15 May 1943. The Möhne and Eder dams were breached and the Sorpe damaged, but two others survived intact. The Germans recognized the extent of the damage and worked hard to repair it. Eight aircraft were lost in the raid and fifty-four men killed. Gibson was awarded the Victoria Cross. He was killed in action on 29 September 1944.

GIFFARD, George (1886–1964). British general who commanded with quiet but unpublicized distinction during the Burma campaign in 1943 and 1944. At the beginning of the war Giffard was serving as military secretary to the war minister, Hore Belisha. He was sent to serve under Wavell (q.v.) in Palestine, but shortly afterwards

General Sir George Giffard (right), a popular if undemonstrative figure, affectionately known to the troops as 'Pop'. He was a master of jungle warfare, and served in West Africa and the Far East.

was posted to West Africa as commander-in-chief in that unglamorous but strategically important area. In 1943 he was transferred to India as GOC Eastern Army, as he was the only British senior officer with jungle fighting experience from the first world war. There his first task was to re-organize and train his forces to cope with unfamiliar jungle conditions in which the Japanese enemy until then had proved the master. He especially contributed by reorganizing the maintenance and administrative services and establishing a system of air supply. In August 1943 he was appointed commander-in-chief of Eleventh Army Group, with Slim's (q.v.) Fourteenth Army under his control. He was sacked at the height of the battle for Imphal, having had differences of opinion with the supreme commander Mountbatten (q.v.), but the battle was won, and his command vindicated, before a relief arrived.

GOEBBELS, Josef (1897–1945). Nazi leader, and propaganda minister responsible for stage-managing Hitler's (q.v.) impressive personal appearances. One of the most curiously contradictory personalities in the party, Goebbels came from poor origins. He was ill with poliomyelitis as a child, as a result of which he limped for the rest of his life, and almost entered into training for the Catholic priesthood. He was blessed with a hyperactive imagination, which led him to attempt the literary life, with novels and plays which failed to find a publisher. The Nazi party proved a much more suitable outlet for his creative energy, and in 1924 he became one of its star speakers. Two years later Hitler made him *Gauleiter* (local chief) of Berlin, and his career was launched. He had a genius for the arts of salesmanship and theatrical presentation. He designed posters, published his own aggressive propaganda sheet called *Der Angriff* (The Attack), staged parades with banners and Nazi songs, and exploited his own brilliant and carefully polished oratory. His skill and nerve were outstanding and undoubtedly helped mould the image of Hitler as a Messiah: he persuaded Hitler to fly in to meetings in a private plane to produce the then novel impact of an arrival from

Dr Goebbels, Hitler's master of propaganda. The Führer's astonishing popularity among the bulk of the German people owed much to Goebbels's instinctive expertise.

the sky. Once the Nazi party was established in power, Goebbels was free to extend his powers to almost total control of the area in which he was master – the media. As Hitler's minister of propaganda and public enlightenment he issued a series of decrees giving himself full power over radio, press and publishing, cinema and the other arts. Personnel in these fields were registered, and any suggestion of hostile criticism or unfavourable comment on the regime harshly dealt with. On 10 May 1933 he staged the great ritual 'burning of the books' in Berlin and other cities, in which books by Jewish authors were eradicated from public libraries. Much of Goebbels's career was devoted to his supporting role in promoting Hitler, but as the war progressed Hitler was more concerned with military matters and made fewer public appearances. Goebbels was then able to

Dr Goebbels shows some of the charm that brought him his personal and political success.

come more prominently into the picture, developing his own oratory and mastery of the microphone to manipulate public feeling. As he said, 'The great masses of a nation will always and only succumb to the force of the spoken word.' Goebbels's private life was as extraordinary as his public face. He was married with six children, but indulged in an endless series of love affairs, seemingly having a ready attraction for women, particularly beautiful young actresses. In 1938 his wife tried to divorce him and cited thirty women as his mistresses. But Hitler intervened and forbade the divorce.

Goebbels was instrumental in bringing the plot against Hitler's life of 20 July 1944 to a quick conclusion, when his house in Berlin became the centre of the counter-measures against the conspiracy, and he organized the arrest of several major participants.

He remained loyal to Hitler to the last, and stayed with him in the chancellery during the final days of Hitler's life. After Hitler's suicide, Goebbels ordered an ss doctor to kill his own six children with lethal injections, then had himself and his wife shot in the back of the head by an ss orderly.

Goebbels proved throughout his career a highly effective component in the Nazi machine, as the creator of its important and fatally appealing external trappings.

GOERDELER, Karl (1884–1945). A key figure in the conspiracy against Adolf Hitler (q.v.). Goerdeler was a civil servant, and served as mayor of Leipzig (a paid post) and Reich commissioner of prices. He was also a conservative nationalist and a fervent opponent of Nazism. By 1937 he had resigned both posts in protest against the Nazis, his resignation from the position of mayor being prompted by the Nazis removing the statue of the Jewish composer Mendelssohn from the public square in Leipzig. He then became a representative of the Bosch company and travelled widely in Europe and the United States, warning his associates of the dangers of Nazism. He was also extremely indiscreet, and wrote a pamphlet on the

Nazis, which he intended to distribute to the officers of the *Wehrmacht*. After the bomb plot of 20 July 1944 Goerdeler was designated to take over the post of chancellor. In the investigations following the failure of the assassination, Goerdeler was found to have in his possession several incriminating documents, including a list of members of his proposed future cabinet. He was put on trial, and hanged at Prinz Albrechtstrasse prison on 2 February 1945.

GOERING, Hermann (1883–1946). Chief of the Luftwaffe and Hitler's (q.v.) deputy; an important and commanding figure throughout the growth of Nazism and during the course of the war, and also the dominating personality at the trial of the leading Nazis. Goering died as dramatically as he had lived. Commissioned in the army in 1912, Goering transferred to the air arm in 1914 and rose to command the 'flying circus' after the death of Richthofen. He was an air ace himself, credited with twenty-two Allied aircraft shot down. After the war he became immersed in Nazi party affairs, and Hitler appointed him to command the *Sturmabteilung* (sa) brownshirts. Goering took part in the attempted Hitler putsch at Munich in 1923, was wounded in the shooting that followed, and was forced to flee Germany for four years. He returned on the amnesty in 1927 and re-established contact with Hitler. He became a successful businessman, was elected to the Reichstag, and worked successfully to reconcile the industrial leaders with Hitler. Hitler appointed him minister of the interior, and with Himmler (q.v.) he set up the Gestapo and early concentration camps. He and Himmler, along with the security chief Reinhardt Heydrich (q.v.), were responsible for the murders – the 'purge' – which eliminated Röhm (q.v.) and the other members of the sa in 1934. Running parallel with this political career was Goering's work with the Luftwaffe. He was put in command in 1935, and with Udet and Milch was responsible for the rapid expansion of the air force, the build-up of the aircraft industry, and the testing of new types of aircraft. In 1936 he added a third strand to his career, as trustee

Hermann Goering as he saw himself – the field-marshal resplendent in the uniform which he designed.

Goering enjoys a warm reception from a parade of the blackshirts, interrupted by an enthusiastic young supporter.

of the four-year plan, which gave him wide powers to direct the German economy. In 1938, when Hitler carried out a vast reorganization of the armed forces command, he promoted Goering to the rank of field-marshal. Goering had reached the top. And he was determined to live up to his rank. He devoted himself to the pursuit of pleasure, taking drugs, shooting on his estate where he had built himself a mansion named after his first wife Karin, designing himself flamboyant new uniforms, showing off his stolen art treasures, eating and hunting (he was even made master huntsman of the Reich). As a commander of the Luftwaffe he was almost a total failure. Promoted to the rank

of reich marshal after the Polish campaign, he was almost immediately thrown into the Battle of Britain. In that summer he dissipated the strength of his Luftwaffe in frenzied and uncontrolled attacks, accepted his pilots' exaggerated claims of British losses, and generally failed to keep control of the battle. In September he made his greatest mistake, in directing the Luftwaffe attacks at the British cities. The move proved a severe test of civilian morale, but saved the RAF sector control stations from destruction, and gave the British fighter defences time to recover. After that defeat for the Luftwaffe, Goering's position gradually declined.

As the war came to its close, on 22 April 1945

Hitler declared that he would remain in the bunker in Berlin and fight to the end, and if the capital fell he would shoot himself. When Goering heard this he took it to mean that Hitler had abdicated. Goering had already left for refuge in Bavaria, and as he was Hitler's designated deputy, he telegrammed the Führer suggesting that he should take over at once with full freedom of action at home and abroad. Hitler replied by having him arrested as a traitor, expelling him from the party, and stripping him of all his rights and titles. Goering was captured by the Allies shortly afterwards, and put on trial at Nuremberg. He dominated the proceedings, standing out above the other defendants as the commanding personality. His months in captivity had reduced his weight, taken him off drugs, and sharpened his wits, so that he recovered much of his earlier vigour. Even before he gave evidence, he tried to rally the other prisoners and expressed disgust at their confessions, which he considered treason. In his own testimony he was self-assured and lucid, and won many of the exchanges with the prosecuting counsel. Nevertheless he was found guilty on all four counts, of the conspiracy to wage war, crimes against peace, war crimes and crimes against humanity. He was sentenced to hang. Two hours before his execution was due to take place on the night of 14–15 October 1946, Goering committed suicide in his cell. He left a note saying he would do so because he had been refused a request to be executed by shooting. He had succeeded, despite the vigilance of the guards, in keeping two capsules of poison concealed throughout his captivity.

GOLIKOV, Filip Ivanovich (born 1900). Soviet general: commander of the Sixth Army in the invasion of Poland. Golikov was head of military intelligence in 1940–1, and leader of the Soviet military mission to London and Washington in 1941. His chief defect in intelligence work was a lack of objectivity: he graded intelligence according to its likely palatability to Stalin (q.v.). In this he undoubtedly contributed to the Soviet Union's misconception of Hitler's (q.v.) intentions, and its lack of preparedness for the war.

Lieutenant-General Filip Ivanovich Golikov, a sycophantic aide to Stalin in intelligence work, promoted to various group and defence ministry posts.

Nevertheless he was given command of the Tenth Army in the Moscow defence, and later served as commander of the Briansk and Voronezh Army Groups, and as deputy commander of Stalingrad Army Group during 1942 and 1943. He was subsequently recalled to Moscow as deputy defence minister and director of Red Army personnel from 1943 to 1950. In the post-war period he carried responsibility for the repatriation of German prisoners.

GORT, John Standish Surtees Prendergast Vereker (Sixth Viscount Gort) (1886–1946).

British general, commander-in-chief of the British Expeditionary Force at the time of the fall of France in 1940. Lord Gort was responsible for the decision to evacuate the BEF from Dunkirk, and must therefore be credited with saving the BEF from destruction and preserving it as the core round which the land defences against the threat of invasion could be organized, and the armies subsequently built up for operations against Germany.

Gort was a Sandhurst cadet, passing out in 1904, and he won a high reputation as a fighting man (as well as a VC, three DSOs and an MC) in the first world war. He was a student and later an instructor at the staff college at Camberley, and after a variety of other peacetime posts he returned there as commandant in 1936. His was in some respects a surprise appointment to the senior posts in the British army, first that of chief of the imperial general staff and then that of c-in-c BEF in 1939. Several critics felt that these appointments were far above his abilities as a commander. Montgomery (q.v.) complained that he carried out no exercises in France, and Brooke (q.v.) accused him of devoting excessive attention to detail while failing to see the whole picture. But few critics have been able to substantiate any criticism of his handling of the rescue of the BEF. In fact his conduct then showed great insight and resolution. For the defence against the German invasion in 1940, the BEF was subordinated to the French army's control under General Gamelin. In accordance with the French plan, the BEF advanced with three French armies also in the line into Belgium. Three days later, on 31 May, General Kleist's (q.v.) panzer group smashed through the Ardennes and crossed the Meuse, which immediately threatened the rear of the BEF. Lord Gort's only possible response was to withdraw from Belgium back towards the defences on the river Scheldt: he began to do so on 16 May. By 19 May it was obvious that the French had lost control of the situation. Gamelin was replaced by General Weygand (q.v.), but that produced no significant improvement.

Gort was faced with a choice of three courses of action. He could counter-attack to the south to close the gap, in concert with a counter-attack by the French armies to the north. He could withdraw to the line of the Somme. Or he could retreat north-west in concert with the French towards the Channel ports. He presented these three alternatives to London, and on 20 May was ordered to carry out the first – a march south to Amiens to take up a position on the left of the French army. By 23 May the BEF was back in its prepared positions on the frontier, but by that time the German advance had rendered the plan ineffective. The panzers had penetrated as far as the coast and had cut off British sea communications. Ammunition was short and the troops were put on half-rations. Senior commanders recognized that nothing short of a miracle could save the British army. Then, on the evening of 25 May, Gort took a remarkable decision. He had made up his mind that the possibility of a French attack to the north was a fiction. Despite still being under orders from London to attack to the south, he withdrew his 5 and 50 Divisions from that plan and sent them to the north to plug the gap caused by the failure of the Belgian defences. And he decided to order the BEF to fall back on Dunkirk. In doing so he acted on his own initiative and against orders, but on 26 May the government in London, with a clearer picture of the overall failure of the French forces, endorsed his decision. Having taken that courageous and historic decision, Gort's conduct of the withdrawal operation was masterly, and resulted in the rescue of 338,226 British and other Allied troops, though the bulk of their equipment was lost.

Despite his accomplishment being applauded in Britain, Lord Gort had apparently outlived his usefulness as a commander, and new men were given the important appointments from then on. Gort was first appointed inspector of training and the home guard, then in April 1941 governor of Gibraltar, and in May 1942 governor of Malta. He was promoted to the rank of field-marshal in 1943 and appointed high commissioner of Palestine in 1944. But this series of important quasi-political

Lord Gort, BEF commander in the débâcle in northern France, entertains Churchill in happier days as governor of Malta in 1943.

appointments counted as meagre compensation for the lack of a field command. Lord Gort died of cancer in 1946. (*See also* Ironside)

GOTT, William Henry Ewart ('Strafer') (1897–1942). British desert general: commander of the 7 Armoured Division and subsequently of 13 Corps in the North African desert campaign. In the early battles Gott, himself an infantry officer, failed to understand the full potential of the tank, and after the Crusader operation noted with apparent surprise that the Germans would not commit themselves to a tank-versus-tank battle, but preferred to co-ordinate anti-tank guns, artillery and infantry with tanks, and would not be diverted from this policy. Having observed the basis of the German successes, Gott suggested that good support from 25-pounder guns was an aid to the British tanks, and he was in some measure

'Strafer' Gott, a popular desert commander, designated to take over Eighth Army until his death made way for Montgomery.

responsible for the belated policy of integrating armour with artillery and infantry into all-arms brigade groups. When Ritchie (q.v.) took over the Eighth Army in August 1941 Gott became 13 Corps commander. He was more experienced than Ritchie himself, and by this time had built a considerable reputation as an energetic armoured commander. He was therefore inclined to move about the battlefield without much reference to the army command, a practice which made communication difficult. Gott's involvement in the series of defeats at the hands of Rommel (q.v.) that pushed the Eighth Army back from Gazala to El Alamein by July 1942 did not harm his esteem. He had become depressed by fatigue and defeat, but he remained 13 Corps commander during Auchin-

leck's (q.v.) early attempts to return to the offensive in July, then in August suddenly found himself on the verge of greatness. In the extensive changes in the command structure which Churchill (q.v.) insisted on making during his visit to the Middle East, Gott was selected for promotion to command of the Eighth Army. Gott protested that he was tired out, and suggested that he would like nothing more than three months' leave in England. He was, however, ready to take on any responsibilities asked of him. Churchill ignored his suggestion of leave and went ahead with the plan to give Gott the Eighth Army. Then on 7 August, in the midst of these upheavals, Gott was flying to Cairo from Eighth Army headquarters when a lone German fighter, flying at low level to escape the RAF, happened upon his Bombay transport aircraft. The Bombay pilot managed to land, but the Messerschmitt flier fired into the plane and Gott was killed. He was buried in the desert. On receiving the news of his death, Auchinleck, who at that time had no idea that he himself was to be removed, contacted Brooke (q.v.) in Cairo, and they arranged for Montgomery (q.v.) to fly out to take over the Eighth Army immediately. Gott's death, far more than his life, was the origin of historic events in European history.

GRAZIANI, Rodolfo (1882–1955). Italian general who was given command of the Italian armies in Libya in June 1940 after the death of Marshal Balbo. Commanding 200,000 men against a British force of 35,000, he attacked ponderously and on reaching Sidi Barrani dug in, relying on fixed defences in a desert where they were totally inappropriate. The result was that O'Connor's (q.v.) attack of 9 December 1940 cut in among the Italian defended positions, and within a week Graziani had lost 12,000 men, killed and wounded, and 38,000 prisoners. Two months later he had lost three-quarters of his original force, against British casualties amounting to no more than 500 dead and 1400 wounded. He resigned and went back to Italy. After the Italian capitulation he became defence minister in the pro-German republican government, was later tried by the post-

Marshal Rodolfo Graziani, Italian c-in-c North Africa. His armies were defeated in Cyrenaica in early 1941.

General Leslie Groves (right), overseer of atomic bomb development, follows up a test in company with Robert Oppenheimer.

war Italian government and sentenced to nineteen years in prison in 1950, of which he served only a few months.

GRECHKO, Andrei (born 1903). One of the younger Soviet generals, who rose to the command of four successive armies – the Twelfth, Eighteenth, Forty-seventh and Fifty-sixth – all in the Caucasian theatre. In 1944 and 1945 he led the First Guards Army in the advance on Czechoslovakia. After the war he commanded Warsaw Pact forces from 1950 to 1957, and was later appointed Soviet minister of defence.

GROVES, Leslie Richard (1896–1970). United States general who led the programme of development of the atomic bomb, the Manhattan project. An army engineer by profession, who was respon-

sible for a large part of the army's construction work, including building the Pentagon, Groves took over the atomic development project in September 1942. Although the basic scientific and design principles were established, the development of the project, including the assembly of a staff of 125,000 people, was largely the work of Groves, and its success, culminating in time to play a part in the ending of the war against Japan, was a tribute to his energy and administrative skill. (*See also* Oppenheimer)

GUDERIAN, Heinz (1888–1953). German panzer pioneer and successful tank commander on both Western and Russian Fronts. Although he made his reputation as a commander in the early operations of the war in 1939, 1940 and 1941,

Guderian's greatest contribution to German armed achievements was as the leading advocate of the development of armour and its use as a weapon in its own right, not in a supporting role. In the light of the part played by the tank in the *blitzkrieg* offensive, Guderian's influence was clearly a decisive factor in German success in the first two years of war. As a major in the restricted German army of the 1920s, Guderian and a handful of other officers observed and noted the pioneer work being done to develop armoured divisions in Britain. He quickly became convinced that the tank would have a role to play in future warfare far more significant than that conceived by conventional military thinkers. In 1929 he dismissed the concept of the tank working either on its own or in conjunction with infantry. He visualized the new weapon as the core of a powerful combined attack force: 'Tanks will never be able to produce their full effect until the other weapons on whose support they must inevitably rely are brought up to their standard of speed and cross-country performance. In such a formation of all arms the tanks must play the primary role, the other weapons being subordinated to the requirements of the armour.' Ideas like these were of course being tried out in other countries. The basic difference was that outside Germany orthodox military thinking prevailed and the developments envisaged by the tank proponents were held firmly in check. In Germany, also, orthodox soldiers attempted to curb Guderian's enthusiasm, but Hitler (q.v.), who was chancellor by 1933, fully supported the combined formation built around the tank, and backed Guderian in building up a tank force. Guderian was able to demonstrate the correctness of his ideas in the attack on Poland, when as commander of 19 Corps in Kluge's (q.v.) Fourth Army he acted as the spearhead in smashing the Polish armies defending the Danzig corridor. His technique was revolutionary. He was the first corps commander to direct a battle from a mobile radio communications vehicle at the front, and the first to use the tactic of a fast punching penetration on a narrow front, followed by driving on into the enemy's rear areas to sow panic and confusion and prevent a retreat, while leaving the strongholds to be mopped up by the following infantry. Strangely enough, Guderian's contribution was not universally acknowledged, as the infantry commanders perhaps understandably saw themselves left to clear up the more tenacious front-line resistance while the panzers went on their glamorous way to take over the key civilian centres. Then Guderian repeated the performance in France in 1940, when as part of Kleist's (q.v.) *Panzergruppe* his 19 Corps smashed through the Ardennes on 10 May and advanced to Sedan in three days. On 16 May Guderian was off again, aiming for the Channel. On this occasion, however, he fell out with Kleist who considered Guderian had gone further than ordered; Guderian resigned, only to be reinstated on Rundstedt's (q.v.) orders and given permission to carry out a reconnaissance in force. On 20 May his forces reached the Channel, and three days later were into both Boulogne and Calais. Then came Hitler's famous order to halt, and for two days the panzers were immobile while the British Expeditionary Force began their escape from Dunkirk. Following that episode the panzer formations were reorganized into three groups, with Guderian, Kleist and Hoth in command, and Guderian continued to astonish the *Wehrmacht* high command with the speed of his advance to the south-east as far as the Swiss border. Small wonder that he earned himself the nickname 'swift Heinz'. When Hitler turned to the east and attacked Russia, Guderian's *Panzergruppe* formed part of Bock's (q.v.) Army Group Centre, and performed even more devastating feats, driving forward to within 200 miles of Moscow. Then Hitler halted the attacks on Leningrad and Moscow, and ordered Guderian to move south and link up with Kleist's panzers in Army Group South. The result was the encirclement and capture of four Soviet armies in September – an astonishing bag. But the price was

General Heinz Guderian, the panzer pioneer and architect of the blitz operations in Poland, France and the Soviet Union.

paid in the following months as winter set in. The leading formations of panzers got to within twenty miles of Moscow, but then the autumn mud and winter cold reduced them to impotence, and the Russian winter counter-offensive ended their chance of success. By then Guderian had begun to fall out with his superiors, first with the Fourth Army commander, Kluge, who tried to slow the advance of his armour, and then with Hitler himself, who would not listen to Guderian's arguments that it was impossible to maintain the advanced positions through the winter. In December 1941 Guderian was dismissed.

He remained unemployed until February 1943, when he was recalled to become inspector-general of armoured forces. During this period his main concern was to stop Hitler committing precious resources of tanks to unproductive battle, notably the Kurst salient. He again encountered Kluge, now head of Army Group Centre, and their feud became so bitter that Kluge actually challenged Guderian to a duel and asked Hitler to be his second. Hitler ordered them to resolve their differences. As the German armies were forced into retreat in the autumn and winter of 1943, Guderian began to see the position as hopeless, and had the courage to canvass support for relieving Hitler of his command of the army. He even saw Goebbels (q.v.), which could have been dangerous, but he survived. And he was considered so 'clean' that after the attempt on Hitler's life of 20 July 1944 he was promoted to chief of staff of the Army High Command. As Hitler was now running the war personally through the OKW high command, with all three services under his control, Guderian's role was limited, and his main task was as a member of the court of honour which investigated officers implicated in the plot and handed them over to be dealt with by the people's court. In the course of 1945, when all sanity seemed to have gone out of the army command system, Guderian entered into a fierce series of arguments with Hitler, and by March was openly seeking support among the leading Nazis for the idea of seeking a peace. The result was inevitable. He was sacked again on 21 March. On 10 May he was captured by the Americans. Guderian had proved himself one of the finest German generals, an original mind with the courage not only to put his ideas on armoured warfare into practice, but also to argue them out in screaming matches with the Führer, perhaps in peril of his life.

DE GUINGAND, Francis (born 1900). British general whose main contribution was as chief of staff to Montgomery (q.v.) both with the Eighth Army in Africa and with Twenty-first Army Group in north-west Europe. In 1939 de Guingand was military assistant to the war minister. In 1942 he was made director of military intelligence in the Middle East, and from there went to serve as Montgomery's chief of staff, staying with him for the remainder of the war. He was highly regarded by Eisenhower (q.v.), and helped promote smooth relations between the Allies at a time when Montgomery's own behaviour was less than fully co-operative.

H

HALDER, Franz (1884–1971). German general who held the post of chief of the army general staff from 1938 to 1942. Halder was among the generals who wanted to see Hitler (q.v.) removed in 1938 in order to avoid war, and when he was made chief of staff went so far as to promise other opponents of Hitler that he was prepared to precipitate a putsch. It was even suggested by Halder and Brauchitsch (q.v.) of the army staff that if Hitler forced a policy that would lead to war with France and Britain, they should order the armies to turn about, march on Berlin and arrest Hitler. That particular plot came to nothing, and as Hitler's successes mounted up in Poland, France and initially in Russia, Halder and other generals were drawn into Hitler's orbit, and Halder became for a time a firm supporter of the Führer. As chief of staff he was closely concerned with planning those early battles. He was also concerned with the Russian invasion, but Hitler was increasingly running the war himself, as the OKW (high command of the entire armed forces) came to predominate over the

Colonel-General Franz Halder (second from right), chief of staff to the army high command (OKH) in 1940, seen with (left to right) Hitler, Keitel and Brauchitsch, the OKH commander-in-chief.

OKH (high command of the army). His planning produced the brilliant early successes of the summer campaign of 1942 on the Eastern Front. Halder's strategic aim was to take the oilfields of the Caucasus, but Hitler diverted forces to the prestige target of Stalingrad. After that Halder began to fall out with the Führer. When the campaign to take Stalingrad faltered, Halder argued that it should be called off. Such talk was unacceptable to Hitler, and as a result Halder was dismissed in September 1942. He was arrested after the bomb plot of 20 July 1944, but after being confined and interrogated over several months, narrowly avoiding execution, he was freed. A man of outstanding ability, who was a capable mathematician and botanist as well as a military writer and soldier, Halder failed – as all the other generals did – to influence Hitler. He consistently warned the Führer against over-extending the armies, allegedly telling him on one occasion: 'The trouble with us is that we win all the battles, except the last.'

HALIFAX (First Earl of, born Edward Frederick Lindley Wood) (1881–1959). British politician and statesman. Born into a landed family, Halifax became a peer in 1925. He was appointed foreign secretary in 1938, and on Chamberlain's (q.v.) resignation on 10 May 1940 was a natural successor as prime minister. Chamberlain and King George VI both supported him for the post, but Halifax himself turned it down, feeling that he did not have popular support and in any case could not run a wartime government successfully as a member of the House of Lords. He remained foreign secretary until December 1940 when he became ambassador in Washington. There he encountered considerable hostility on account of American isolationism (he even had eggs thrown at him in Detroit), but after the United States entered the war his role increased in importance and he became liked and respected in Washington government circles.

HALL, John Lesslie (born 1891). United States admiral and expert on amphibious operations, who commanded naval aspects of landing operations in the Mediterranean, Normandy and the Pacific. 'Jimmy' Hall was one of three commanders carrying forces for the invasions of Sicily. Landing the 1 Infantry Division at Gela, his ships were active in repelling tank counter-attacks by naval gunfire. General Eisenhower (q.v.) paid warm tribute to the gunfire, describing it as 'devastating in its effectiveness'. For the landings at Salerno, Hall commanded the ships transporting the southern attack force, landing on the beaches at Paestum. His amphibious experience fitted him well for operational command in the Normandy invasion. He was not only in command of the landings on Omaha beach, but because of his experience and expertise he was selected as the principal officer in charge of training all the US fire support ships, which he put through their shore bombardment exercises. He pressed for the provision of battleships, cruisers and destroyers for naval gunfire against the German coastal defences, which he knew would be largely impervious to bombing. Admiral Ernest J. King (q.v.), US navy chief of staff, was unwilling to provide them because of his strong preference for the Pacific theatre, but Hall's pressure resulted in the provision of three old battleships, three cruisers and thirty-one destroyers from American resources. These ships played a vital part in the D-Day landings, as the artillery landing behind the assault waves was largely sunk by choppy seas. The destroyers approached as close as 800 yards inshore, at severe risk of grounding, to aid the men on the beaches with their 5-inch guns. The chief of staff of the 1 Division later wrote to Hall that they could not have crossed the beaches without the naval gunfire. After his successful Normandy command Hall was assigned to the Pacific theatre where he commanded the southern attack force in the Okinawa landings. He was noted for his calm, even temperament and quiet confidence.

HALSEY, William Frederick (1882–1959). American admiral and commander in several victorious actions against the Japanese naval forces in the Pacific. During the Japanese attack on Pearl

with USAAF raids devastated many German cities. In 1943 he took advantage of technical developments such as airborne radar and pathfinder bombers to lay on night raids in which his pilots and aircraft were less vulnerable. His determination (backed by Churchill's, q.v.) maintained the policy of massive area bombing attacks when doubts were being widely expressed about its moral justification, and when some experts were even challenging its military influence on Germany's capacity or will to continue the war.

HART, Thomas Charles (1877–1971). United States admiral who commanded American forces in the Pacific from the beginning of the war until 1942. Hart was appointed commander-in-chief United States Asiatic Fleet in July 1939, and when the Japanese attacked at Pearl Harbor in December 1941 he took over all American naval forces in the Far East, which consisted of three cruisers, twelve old destroyers, and forty-two patrol aircraft. He was unable to make any serious obstacle to the Japanese expansion, but he did send his ships on a successful raid against the Japanese invasion forces at Balikpapan, Borneo, where in the battle of Makasser Strait they sank four transporters. After 1942 he was retired from service at sea, but returned to his pre-war post on the Navy General Board, finally retiring in 1945. He served for two years as United States senator for Connecticut.

HEINRICI, Gotthard (born 1889). German general who made his reputation as a brilliant defensive tactician in the great German defeats of 1943 and 1944 on the Eastern Front. After the war Heinrici graphically described his defensive techniques to Sir Basil Liddell-Hart (q.v.), who related them in his book *The Other Side of the Hill*. The initial key to successful defence was intelligence of Russian intentions, and for this he sent patrols out at night to capture Russian prisoners. When he knew where the attack would be concentrated he withdrew his force some two kilometres, so that the artillery preparation did no damage, and the attack hit nothing, with a resulting loss of momentum once the second phase of the attack met resist-

ance. Heinrici by this means demonstrated, he considered, the superiority of defence over attack. He never lost a defensive battle employing these methods, and never had to call on high command for reserves. The only reason the defensive campaign failed in the long run, he maintained, was because German strength had been wasted through earlier battles struggling to hold rigid defensive positions. Heinrici produced the opinion, startlingly significant in its implications if true, that an attacker needs a six- or seven-to-one numerical advantage to succeed against a well-knit defence, and his forces were able to hold out against odds of twelve- or eighteen-to-one at times. Heinrici, a small, mild-mannered man, rose from being 4 Corps commander in the west in 1940 to commanding Army Group West defending Berlin in March 1945.

HESS, Rudolf (born 1894). Adolf Hitler's (q.v.) deputy. Hess joined the Nazi party in 1920 after hearing Hitler address a meeting, and soon became his close friend. He was jailed in Landsberg fortress with Hitler for taking part in the Munich putsch and helped him with the writing of *Mein Kampf*. Hitler rewarded him with the post of deputy Führer in 1933 and in 1939 appointed him successor designate to Goering (q.v.). In 1941 Hess created a sensation when he took off from Germany in a Messerschmitt light plane and landed in Scotland, on a self-appointed and completely unofficial mission to try to negotiate peace terms. His intention was to convince the British that Hitler wanted to avoid further hostilities with them so long as he could have a free hand in eastern Europe. He was jailed as a POW by the British, and Hitler proclaimed him insane and ignored him. He was tried at Nuremberg where he appeared at first to be suffering from loss of memory. Then he produced a remarkable coup by declaring that he had simulated his amnesia as a tactical move, and from then on he would 'respond to the outside world'. He said he would take full responsibility for everything he had done or signed. He was sentenced to life imprisonment, and has been locked away in Spandau prison ever since, for several years as the

Rudolf Hess, Hitler's deputy and one of the strangest figures in the war. Without Hitler's knowledge he flew to Scotland in May 1941 with a plan to negotiate a peace.

only inmate. Efforts by the British, American and French to have him released in his old age have been denied by the Russians, who insist on Hess remaining in jail.

HEWITT, Henry Kent (1887–1972). United States admiral who commanded in a series of American amphibious operations from the 'Torch' landings in North Africa in 1942 to the invasion of southern France in 1944. Hewitt was a bold commander who landed his Western Task Force off Casablanca against the recommendations of meteorologists in London and Washington, relying instead on the assurances of calm weather from his own weather experts on the spot.

It was a decision which greatly aided the campaign in Morocco and Algeria. He was promoted to command of the United States Eighth Fleet, took charge of the landings in Sicily of the Western Task Force, and was then appointed to overall command of naval aspects of the invasion of the Italian mainland at Salerno. In view of his experience of the naval side of amphibious operations he was the natural choice to command the naval force for the invasion of the French Riviera.

HEYDRICH, Reinhardt (1904–42). Leading Nazi, Gestapo chief, and Himmler's (q.v.) deputy, known as 'the hangman'. Heydrich was appointed by Himmler to head the *ss* security service, *Sich-*

Reinhardt Heydrich, 'the hangman', proclaims martial law for the protectorate of Bohemia and Moravia, backed by his state minister Karl Hermann Frank.

erheitsdienst or *SD*. In 1938 the *SD* became the Reich's main intelligence organization, and in 1939 the *SD*, Gestapo, and the *kripo* (criminal police) were unified as the *RSHA* (*Reichssicherheits-Hauptamt*). Heydrich, as its director, therefore held extensive power for Reich security under Himmler. He used his power liberally, and unlike his superior had no compunction about carrying out the more inhuman acts of Nazi policy. Earlier, he had carried out, along with Goebbels (q.v.), the murders of the *SA* during the 'Night of the Long Knives'.

On 23 September 1941 Hitler appointed him vice-protector in Czechoslovakia, where he rapidly confirmed his reputation as a butcher. On 27 May 1942 he was attacked on his way to his headquarters by two Free Czechoslovakian agents, Jans Kubis and Joseph Gabeik, who had been trained in England and parachuted into Czechoslovakia. They opened fire on his car with pistols and rolled a bomb under it. He died from his wounds on 4 June.

The assassins were discovered sheltering in a church along with more than a hundred other resistance men. The *SS* surrounded the church and killed everyone in it. They also eliminated the two villages, Lidice and Lezaki, shooting all the men and some of the women, deporting the remaining women, and either killing the children or lodging them with German families to be brought up as Germans. In those and other reprisals an estimated 3000 people were arrested and 1350 executed.

Heydrich was a clever and cultivated man of considerable accomplishments which included violin-playing and fencing. He was brave enough to revel in flying voluntary sorties with the Luftwaffe fighter pilots, and was shot down over the Russian Front and wounded, though he managed to force-land his plane in Germany. He had originally been a naval officer but was cashiered by Admiral Raeder (q.v.) after a scandal involving the daughter of a dockyard superintendent.

HILL, (Sir) Roderic Maxwell (1894–1954). British air marshal concerned initially with technical development under the ministry of aircraft production. He went to the United States in 1941 and advised American air chiefs on bomber design. He was given his first senior operational command in 1943, with 12 Fighter Group. Promoted soon afterwards to command the air defence of Great Britain, he kept the skies clear of German aircraft during the invasion preparations, and dealt with the v-weapon attacks on London. Hill took personal responsibility for completely redeploying the defences to meet this threat. The Air Ministry disapproved and warned him he would be sacked if the measures failed. Within a few days the new measures, especially moving anti-aircraft guns forward to the coastal belt, produced a large proportion of successful interceptions. On 6 September 1944 the Air Council wrote offering Hill warm congratulations on his imaginative deployment of the defences. From 1944 until the end of the war Hill headed fighter command.

HIMMLER, Heinrich (1900–45). *Reichsführer ss* (the *ss* equivalent of field-marshal) in Hitler's (q.v.) Germany, and the arch-philosopher and architect of the system of Aryan supremacy and subjugation of the Jews and Slavs. Himmler was too young to serve in the first world war, but compensated for his frustrated military ambitions by

joining the Nazi party in 1923. He rapidly rose in the party, and was appointed deputy leader of the ss, whose initial task it was to act as the Führer's bodyguard at meetings. From that time on he held a formidable position as head of the security organs of the party, and was one of the small group of inner followers on whom Hitler relied. He took into his control in the course of the rise of Nazism and the war the entire fabric of the police state, becoming chief of police, chief of the *ss* and Gestapo, chief of the *Waffen ss* which grew into a formidable private army, and head of the intelligence and security services. He was thus a man of extreme power. Allied to this key role of Himmler's at the pinnacle of all the organs of state security was the separate but related strand in his character, which made him without doubt the most influential man in the Nazi machine next only to Hitler himself. This was the philosophy of the racially pure Aryan society. Possibly because of his own physical inadequacies (his small stature and thin-rimmed glasses were hardly in keeping with his own ideals), he idolized the physical prowess and racial purity of the elite young men of the *ss*. He actually cherished the ideal of resurrecting through them the ancient Order of Teutonic Knights, with himself as grand master. To promote and preserve the race he set up *ss* bride schools and invented a special form of marriage for the chosen. Pregnant mothers – married or not mattered little so long as they were about to bear children conceived with racially pure partners – were cared for in special *Lebensborn* (fountain of life) maternity institutions. That was the positive side of his theory, and comparatively harmless. The negative side was infinitely more sinister. To clear the nation of impure elements, that is the 'inferior' Jews, Slavs and Mongoloid people, he set up the concentration camps. There he supervised the extermination of millions of those races, and was responsible for the experi-

Heinrich Himmler (saluting), author of the 'Aryan race' philosophy, and head of the complex machinery of state police control. He evaded coming to trial by swallowing poison.

ments carried out on living subjects, the results of which he followed with dispassionate attention. He also instituted massive programmes of abortion and sterilization. Despite all this he had no stomach for the work personally, and was sickened almost to the point of fainting when he witnessed Jews being shot. Because of his squeamishness he proposed, instead of shooting, the use of gas in chambers disguised as bathrooms, which he declared would be a 'more humane' form of extermination.

Overall, Himmler's racial engineering, by organized breeding of the right kind of people and murder of the wrong kind, was aimed at creating an impregnable European empire of northerners which would in due course dominate the world. This was the basis of Hitler's war policy, and was also the underlying reason why he preferred to come to terms with Britain, or at least not to go to war with a race who were compatible with the ideal, and instead chose to conquer territory in the east and subjugate the 'inferior' Russians. Hitler's was the grand ideal: Himmler was the man who swallowed it, took it up and put it into effect with deadly efficiency. Himmler, who had the mentality of a clerk rather than a leader, kept in the background for most of the war, but exercised a ruthless and merciless authority. He recognized the danger from the professional officers who were not committed Nazis, but they lost their chance of power when they failed to kill Hitler in the plot of 20 July 1944. After that Hitler gave Himmler the additional post of c-in-c home forces, which seriously curtailed the strength of the generals as a potentially independent political force. In April 1945, without first consulting Hitler, Himmler tried to engineer a peace with Britain and America through the Swedish Red Cross leader Count Bernadotte (q.v.). He intended to go on fighting the Russians on the Eastern Front. To his disappointment Count Bernadotte made it clear that the western Allies would not split from Russia at this stage, still less join with the Germans in a war against them. In the last days of the war Hitler finally abandoned him, and Dönitz (q.v.), nominated

by Hitler as president of the Reich, ignored the little police chief. On 23 May 1945 Himmler was captured by British soldiers, and tried to disguise himself as an ordinary soldier. When he was discovered he swallowed a capsule of poison he had managed to conceal, and, despite efforts to save his life and bring him to trial, he died.

HIROHITO (Emperor) (born 1901). Japanese emperor. During the pre-war years Hirohito disapproved of the increasing belligerence in Japanese foreign policy and was personally against the pact with Germany and Italy. However his advisers had always urged him not to become entangled in politics in order to avoid compromising the imperial family. He therefore remained aloof, and did nothing to prevent war. He remained in Tokyo throughout the war, even during the fire raids, and ultimately became convinced of the need for his country to surrender. He then at last made some attempt to assert his authority by ordering the Cabinet to seek terms. Some fanatical groups in Japan made plans to kill or kidnap the emperor to stop the country from surrendering, but these came to nothing. After the war the possibility arose of Hirohito being tried as a war criminal, but MacArthur (q.v.) deemed it inadvisable in the interests of Japan's stability. (*See also* Tojo)

HITLER, Adolf (1889–1945). German dictator. Born in Austria, Adolf Hitler rose from the lowest of origins to lead the most powerful nation in Europe, head its only political party and command its armed forces, with devastating early success but ultimate failure. Despite his early concrete achievements, his ambitions went even further, embracing notions of a thousand-year Reich, some form of world order under his command, and racial determinism, in pursuit of which he was responsible for the extermination of perhaps as many as 6 million Jews and several million Slavs.

After an indifferent start in life as a failed artist and architect, Hitler left Vienna in 1913 and moved to Germany, where he eked out a miserable existence as a down-and-out, and spent some of his time studying political pamphlets in the library

The Führer, Adolf Hitler, leader and inspiration for the bulk of the German people, who carried his country out of the depression to a brief glory as the dominating power in Europe.

A younger Hitler, in his revolutionary days, serves a nominal sentence in Landsberg, a fortress though barely a jail. His ideas had time to ferment during a comfortable imprisonment.

of a men's hostel, where the bulk of his ideas were formed. In August 1914 he joined the German army, served as a despatch runner, and won the Iron Cross for bravery. He was twice wounded and left the army with the rank of corporal. Like millions of other Germans he could not accept the fact of German defeat and resented the humiliation of the Versailles treaty and as a result decided to go into politics. It was in that field that Hitler found his vocation, and the satisfaction of his consuming hunger for political power. Largely by accident he found himself among a few like-minded indivi-

duals bent on restoring the dignity of the German nation by the path of revolution, and saving it from the hands of Bolsheviks and Jews. One of these men, Anton Drexler, formed the German Workers' Party in 1919, with a nominal capital and only forty members. It was in meetings of this party that Hitler discovered his talent for oratory, with impassioned speeches that began to attract thousands to the meetings. He was appointed propaganda officer, and in this role found another natural outlet for his talents. He changed the party name to the National Socialist German Workers'

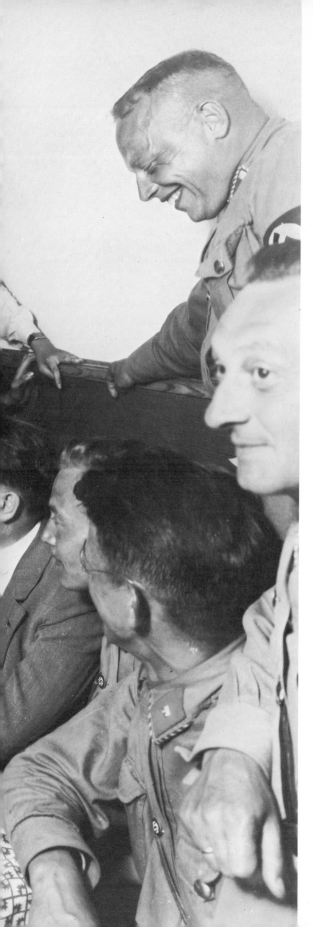

Hitler

Party (*Nationalsozialistische und Deutsche Arbeiterpartei* or NSDAP) which neatly abbreviated to Nazi Party, and in 1921 took over the leadership with title of Führer.

Hitler's work was already paying dividends. His choice of the name for the party was astute, drawing together the dominating strands of German society in the nationalists and socialists, and Hitler himself was recruiting members in vast numbers. He had also boosted his personal power by organizing squads of strong-arm men to keep order at his own meetings and break up the meetings of rival organizations. Out of these squads grew the *Sturmabteilung*, or SA, led by the homosexual bully Ernst Röhm (q.v.). By 1923 Hitler felt his power base sufficiently established to attempt a coup, and on 9 November he and his followers burst into a beer hall in Munich where a meeting was being addressed by the Bavarian ruling group, fired a pistol into the ceiling, and shouted that he was the new head of the provisional German government, with General Erich von Ludendorff as his commander-in-chief. The next morning Hitler and Ludendorff marched through the streets of Munich at the head of a column of 3000 marching supporters, and encountered a thin line of German police. The police opened fire to break up the demonstration, and sixteen of the marchers were left dead in the street. Hitler fled the scene. The outcome of the attempted coup was that Hitler was arrested, tried and sentenced to five years' imprisonment. In fact he served only eight months, all of them in a comfortable room in the Landsberg fortress, where he was allowed visitors, flowers, special food and the freedom of the grounds. It was a productive incarceration. The eight months of reflective tranquillity gave Hitler time to meditate on his ideas and plan his return to political power. He set out details of his scheme in the book *Mein Kampf* (My Struggle), much of it dictated to his amanuensis Rudolf Hess (q.v.). In it he laid out for all to see (though few did) the

Surrounded by youthful fanatics of his embryonic party, Hitler sees his power remorselessly increase.

On the verge of power, Hitler drives in an open car with Field-Marshal Hindenburg, president of the Weimar Republic.

malevolent trend of his thought – his ideas on the superiority of the Aryan race, his anti-semitism, the need for German territory (*Lebensraum*) in the east, the plan to abolish democracy and replace it with dictatorship with Hitler at the head. He also reasoned that although the Nazi party had been outlawed he could rebuild it, integrate it with the state by getting its members elected to the Reichstag, and eventually use it to take over the state himself.

When he left gaol in 1924 Hitler immediately set about pursuing these aims, and by 1932 his was the largest political party in Germany, polling nearly 14 million votes in the election of July that year and securing 230 seats in the Reichstag. Hitler was a political leader of great force and influence, and in the Germany of the early 1930s – wracked by economic disaster, unable to pay the Versailles reparations and by 1932 supporting 5 million un-employed – Hitler represented to the unthinking majority a vision of leadership, hope and stability. In November 1932 Hitler and his party suffered a curious setback when their support at the elections was reduced to 11 million votes and 196 Reichstag seats while the party itself was bank-rupt. In a desperate situation Hitler gambled for the highest stakes. Realizing that he would never come to power on the legitimate vehicle of a majority vote, he fixed up a series of deals with the leading German industrialists, who persuaded the ageing president, Field-Marshal Hindenburg, to declare Hitler chancellor of the German Reich. On 30 January 1933 Hitler became one of the most powerful men in Germany. He still had a long way to go to achieve even his immediate ambitions, but he was moving with a bewildering speed that left his opponents impotent and outmanœuvred. If the industrialists imagined they could submerge Hitler in the Cabinet and use his mass appeal to their own ends, they were mistaken. By July 1933 he had ousted the conservatives, declared that the Nazis were the only permitted political party in Germany, personally taken over the legislative powers of the Reichstag, and abolished the trade unions. On 30 June 1934 he further insulated him-

self from any potential rival threat. Hitler had by now formed his own personal bodyguard in the black-shirted ss (*Schutzstaffel*), who were sworn to absolute loyalty to him personally. On that June night, the 'Night of the Long Knives', members of the ss were detailed by Hitler to murder all his potential rivals, including Ernst Röhm and the members of the sa, two army generals, civil ser-vants, prominent Roman Catholics and the ex-chancellor General Schliecher. Hitler had almost total control, and now enjoyed the support of the army for eliminating their own rivals and making the *Wehrmacht* the only armed force in Germany. One major obstacle remained to Hitler's acquiring complete control, and even that was shortly removed. On 2 August 1934 President Hindenburg died. Rather than go through the pro-cess of finding a new president, Hitler abolished the office and declared himself the new total ruler, with the title Führer of Germany. Soon afterwards he forced the army to swear the oath of allegiance to him personally, and his position was secure.

From then on, for the next four years, Hitler's career was a series of heady successes, each seem-ingly more audacious than the last. Just as he had mesmerized the German people and outwitted his rivals in government, so he mesmerized the rest of the world and outwitted rival political leaders on the international scene. Ignoring any treaty obligations or international opinion, he did pre-cisely what he wanted, carrying his nation from one pinnacle of success to the next, always main-taining an amazing equilibrium and holding his position when he looked certain to fall. Whether he survived by cautious calculation of the chances of failure, or by a reckless gamble that he would simply outrun any opposition, is a matter of con-jecture. But the historical fact is that he succeeded. Early in 1935 he abandoned the Versailles treaty and started to build up his army by conscription to five times the permitted number. He persuaded Britain to allow an increase in the naval building programme. In 1936 he occupied the Rhineland in contravention of the treaty. He also began to build up the Luftwaffe. In February 1938 he dis-

Molotov (left) visits Hitler. The Russo–German non-aggression pact proved to be a convenience, abandoned during 1941 with Hitler's invasion of Russia.

missed sixteen senior generals and personally took command of the armed forces, and a month later marched into Austria. He was to say that if France had then marched against him he and the Third Reich would have fallen. But the failure of the European nations to act only confirmed his confidence. The appeasing attitude of the Allies was verified when Chamberlain and Daladier (qq.v.) signed an agreement with Hitler which gave Germany the Czechoslovakian Sudetenland. In March 1939 Hitler forced the Czechs into formal surrender and ordered his forces to occupy the rest of the country. Czechoslovakia was to be a protec-

torate of Germany. Poland was the next evident target for Hitler's intentions, and Britain and France were both signatories of guarantees protecting Polish integrity. Hitler recognized that a move against Poland could precipitate a European conflict, so he took the precaution of limiting his potential opposition by drawing up a pact of non-aggression with Stalin. Russia received promises of Polish territory in return. On 1 September 1939 Hitler's armies invaded Poland.

The invasion of Poland was a coup which brought a new dimension into warfare – *blitzkrieg* – the sudden shock attack against airfields, communications and military installations, using bomber and fighter aircraft in the first wave followed by fast mobile armour and infantry. Against such military panache defenders conditioned to expect a leisurely attack by infantry were defenceless, and Poland was conquered within hours.

Inevitably, France and Britain declared war on Germany, but even that merely spurred Hitler on to greater ambition. There was a lull through that winter, until in April 1940 the war erupted again with another, similar, explosion of aggression, when Hitler's forces conquered Norway and Denmark, then in May the Low Countries, followed by France itself. Among his Western enemies, only Britain remained. And Hitler stood with his divisions poised for a cross-Channel assault. It was among the most enigmatic episodes of the war. It is arguable that Hitler did not have his heart in the defeat of Britain. Hence he ordered his panzers to stop short of Dunkirk when they could have annihilated the British Expeditionary Force. It is possible, at least, that he admired the British and aimed at setting up a German-dominated Europe running in partnership with the British Empire, and therefore drew back from his attack across the Channel. These theories can never be confirmed, and it may be wiser to rely on the traditional historical interpretation, that the delay in 1940 was a military necessity dictated by the need to secure the air space over the invasion area. For this reason he first ordered Goering's (q.v.) Luftwaffe to clear the skies of the Royal Air Force. The conflict which followed, the Battle of Britain, was Hitler's first setback. The Royal Air Force more than held its own against the Luftwaffe, and when Goering made the mistake of ordering his bombers to attack the civilian populations of the great cities, instead of concentrating on eliminating Britain's air defences, the Royal Air Force was able to survive and deny Hitler air control over the Channel. To this problem of air domination Hitler had no answer. His only course was to abandon or at least postpone the plan to invade Britain, and turn his attention to the east. He would invade Russia. His strategic thinking on this topic had the merit of

being logical, if rather grandiose. He reasoned, according to Halder (q.v.), that with Russia defeated the Japanese strength in the Far East would be increased, which would engage the United States and keep them out of the European war. Without them the British were not an accountable factor, and he could return to complete the invasion of Britain in due course.

For a long time it seemed that Hitler's decision was vindicated. He had predicted a Russian collapse: 'Once I kick the door in,' he had told Jodl (q.v.), 'the whole rotten edifice will come tumbling down.' And so it appeared. Using the same fast armoured techniques that had brought swift victory in the west, he launched his armies in Operation Barbarossa against Russia on a 1000-mile front. The date was 31 June 1941, and within weeks large forces of the Red Army had been over-

Above Hitler skilfully employed his magnetic personality and remarkable oratory to raise crowds to heights of nationalistic fervour. *Overleaf* In the early stages of his power, Hitler devoted much of his energy to addressing massed crowds of his supporters, here the May Day rally in Berlin, 1938.

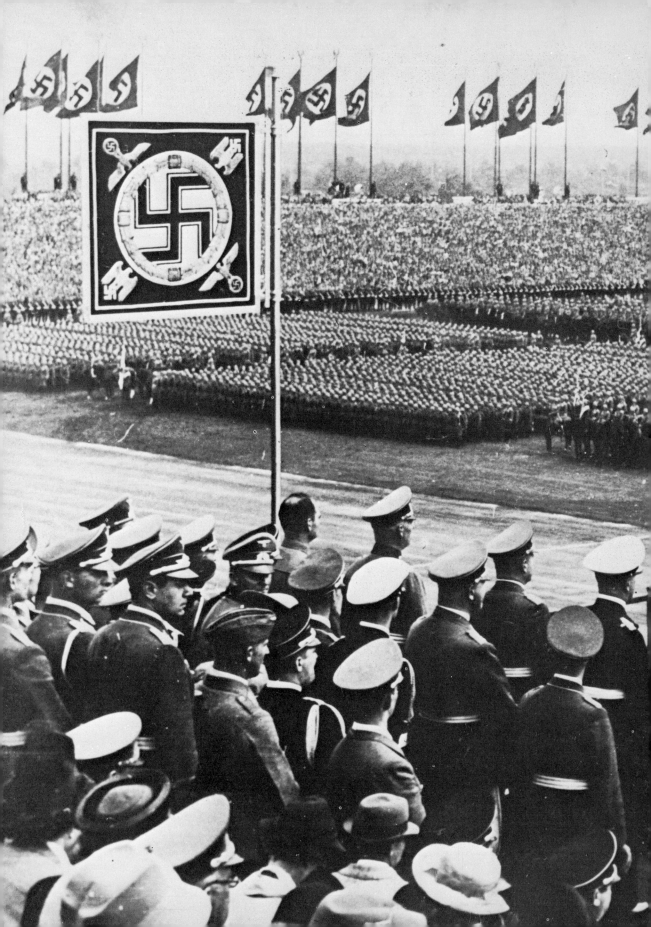

Hitler's aggression pays off, initially. France falls in May 1940, and Hitler dances with delight in the Forest of Compiègne, where the armistice was signed.

whelmed. The Germans had encircled Leningrad, and were within striking distance of Moscow. In the south they were thrusting towards Kiev and the resources of the Ukraine, and Stalingrad was the next target. Only a month after the invasion the *Wehrmacht* had penetrated 300 miles into Russia along a front stretching from Finland to the Black Sea. But in August the problems began to appear. Halder, the army chief of staff, recognized the weakness of such extended lines of communication and also appreciated that the 360 Russian divisions which had been identified, when only 200 had been expected, represented a real threat.

Halder and Brauchitsch (q.v.) tried to persuade Hitler to concentrate the attack on Moscow in the centre. Hitler ordered a pincer movement round Kiev to scoop up the Ukraine, followed by the capture of Leningrad and Stalingrad, the two 'holy cities' of Communism, which he felt would signal the collapse of the Soviet Union. In fact the Soviet Union did not collapse. Hitler had made some serious miscalculations. One was to delay the start of Operation Barbarossa by five weeks to deal with Yugoslavia in April; this increased the likelihood that the offensive would run into the winter, when the weather (Generals January and February, it had been called) would become something of a Russian secret weapon. Another miscalculation was to underestimate the fighting strength of the Russian armies. When the Japanese threat on their eastern frontiers was relieved by the impending attack on Pearl Harbor, which intelligence had led them to expect, they were able to bring up no less than three new armies, eighteen divisions with 1700 tanks and 1500 aircraft, all equipped and trained for winter war. And Hitler had, in the Russian people, an enemy who was stubborn, resilient, tough, resourceful and ample in numbers, as well as generals of the calibre of Zhukov, Timoshenko and Koniev (qq.v.). It was a persistent failing of Hitler that he held his enemies in contempt – the Russians as inferior peasants, the Americans, by illogical contrast, as adventurers who lacked the peasant background which he despised in the Russians. In this case, as in others, Hitler's blind faith that the German armies would prevail could not guarantee victory. They could only win when they fought in the right numbers, with the right equipment, under sound leadership and employing the right strategy and tactics. And in most of these areas during the second half of 1941, they were deficient. Although Hitler could proclaim as late as 3 October that the Soviet Union had been 'struck down and would never rise again', reality was already overtaking his optimism; by 8 December Hitler had at least accepted reality sufficiently to order, in his Führer Directive No. 39, that because of the advent of winter and the difficulty of bringing up supplies, his forces on the Eastern Front should adopt a defensive posture. Nine days later he was admitting that the front would have to be 'shortened in places', a euphemism for withdrawl if not for retreat. But he still forbade his generals to make the tactical withdrawals to prepared defensive positions which they demanded, an attitude which was to become familiar to Hitler's generals, in increasingly hysterical terms, as the war went on. It was at this stage that Hitler reinforced his determination to control his own war machine by dismissing many of his key commanders: Brauchitsch the com-mander-in-chief, Leeb, Bock and Guderian (qq.v.), Hoepner and Rundstedt (qq.v.).

It could not be said that the end of 1941 saw the Germans in retreat. Another year of fighting would follow before the Russians could resume an offensive aimed at recovering their occupied territory. Yet for Hitler the end of that year represented something of a critical point. Once the United States had entered the war against the Axis, the German nation faced enemies of overwhelming potential who, providing their will to pursue the war held out, must ultimately defeat the Axis forces. As Halder, his chief of the army general staff, noted, the myth of the invincibility of the Germany army had been broken. Of course there was no such invincibility. A margin of superior military qualities there may have been, in courage, fighting tradition, organization, officer talent, loyalty. But even German military might was not enough to take on almost the entire world in two concurrent and separate wars. It would take another three and a half years to end the war, but from the winter of 1941 the outcome was inevitable. Hitler continued to adopt the same postures, urging his generals to undreamed-of military accomplishments and raving at his men to stand, fight and die. He would still achieve some remarkable feats, but the balance of force in the world had tipped convincingly against him. As the war went on Hitler's health was visibly deteriorating, and several of the generals who had dealings with him described his maniacal rages, the twitching, outbreaks of sweating and bouts of sultry brooding. His outbursts of fury were most often caused by what he considered to be failure on the part of his troops or reluctance on the part of his generals. It is reasonable to read into this one of the key factors in Hitler's personality, the fact that the only method of operating that he understood was total commitment. In the early days of the war such a commitment was precisely the right military method for the swift conquest of both western and eastern Europe. But after the initial phase of the war it became inappropriate. It was impossible for the generals to maintain the all-out attack which

Hitler

was all Hitler's limited mentality could cope with, and tactical withdrawals, regrouping, pauses for consolidation – all legitimate weapons in the soldier's armoury – Hitler looked on as failure. The consequences of his limited outlook were paralleled in the wider context. Initially his designs held elements of feasibility – the search for territory for an expanded Germany, the attempt to wipe out the humiliation of the Versailles treaty, even the attempt at empire-building by military conquest – all were understandable in the context of the late 1930s. But having achieved domination in western Europe, having entered Russia with a view to its military defeat, what then? Hitler's aims and activities can only be seen as an insane attempt at world domination, insane because it was founded not on any reasoned ideal like communism, but on personal and national aggrandizement. Hitler's wartime career may be judged as the expression of a truly and unprecedentedly megalomaniac mind. Once started on his course for the summit of political power, there was no acceptable limit. He was forced to go on, as he himself said, to victory or defeat. There was no room in his scheme for compromise.

Although the seeds of almost inevitable defeat were contained in virtually everything Hitler attempted after the autumn of 1940, it was not until two years later that the evidence of that defeat started to become clear. In November 1942, after six months of battle around Stalingrad, the Russians amassed thirteen armies and fell upon the Axis forces. The Germans and their Romanian, Slovakian and Italian allies were forced into retreat. The German Sixth Army was cut off and at the end of January 1943 surrendered. In North Africa Montgomery's (q.v.) Eighth Army and the Americans under Eisenhower (q.v.) joined up and in the spring of 1943 defeated the Germans at Tunis. Throughout 1943 Hitler remained on the defensive. In July, as the Allies conquered Sicily and prepared for a landing on the Italian main-

The Pact of Steel is forged. Hitler is seen off from Rome after his visit of 9 May 1938 by King Victor Emmanuel (centre) and Mussolini.

Hitler narrowly avoids death at the hands of opponents within Germany. The shattered remains of his temporary command post at Berchtesgaden testify to a lucky escape.

land, he lost his principal ally, Mussolini (q.v.). In September the Italians signed an armistice and the Allies landed at Salerno. Hitler's actions from that time on began to resemble the desperate throws of a juggler, as he shuffled divisions between fronts to hold off the approaching Russians in the east and Allies in the south and ultimately the west. His worst failing, however, was his total refusal to trust the command of his armies to any of his generals in the field. In the months before the invasion in France, for example, he set up an unworkable arrangement by which both Rundstedt and Rommel (q.v.) held commands, Rundstedt as commander-in-chief west, and Rommel in command of Army Group B, with responsibility for the anti-invasion preparations. The two men were in fundamental disagreement on the organization of the defence, and Hitler refused to give either a clear ruling. Instead he insisted on trying to control even the smallest troop movements from his

remote headquarters at Rastenburg. Rundstedt remarked after the war that the only troops he had been permitted to move were the ones who guarded his headquarters. In the end Hitler lost the confidence of his generals, and shortly after the invasion in July 1944 a number of them, presumably realizing that Germany was heading for inevitable defeat, brought to its climax a plan to kill the Führer, which they hoped would leave the way open for a negotiated agreement with the Allies which might save Germany from destruction and maintain the integrity of German territory. The officer selected to carry out the assassination was Lieutenant-Colonel Klaus von Stauffenberg

Opposite Adolf Hitler. An idealized portrait of the Führer.

Overleaf Hitler visits headquarters at Vinnitsa in the Ukraine during the heady days of late summer 1942. Less cheerful times were shortly to follow on the Eastern Front.

Ein Volk, ein Reich, ein Führer!

(q.v.). He succeeded in carrying the bomb in a brief case into the Führer's headquarters at Rastenburg, and placed it under the table. When it exploded the headquarters were destroyed, but Hitler suffered only superficial injuries. In the retribution that followed nearly 5000 officers and civilians, many of them implicated in the plot by the most tenuous connections, were sought out and executed. The most celebrated among the generals were Kluge (q.v.) and Rommel, both of whom committed suicide by taking poison. Hitler is reported to have watched with cheerful satisfaction film of some of the executions, carried out by hanging with piano wire.

Despite the advance of the Anglo–American armies from the west and the Russians from the east, Hitler's panache and generalship reasserted themselves for one last spectacular campaign in December 1944, when he assembled all the tanks he could muster from new production and the remnants of his retreating armies, and launched them against the Allied line at its weakest point in the west, in the forests of the Ardennes. Showing again the extraordinary insight into his enemies' thinking that had brought his early successes in the war, Hitler reasoned that the Ardennes would be thinly defended and, with the Sixth ss Panzer Army, the Fifth Panzer Army and the Seventh Army, he tried to split the Allied line and reach the North Sea at Antwerp, and by cutting the British off from their supplies, force them to evacuate the continent. The Allies were slow to realize the extent of the German attack, and by Christmas Day the spearheads had penetrated almost as far as the Meuse. After the initial hesitation, and after sustaining heavy casualties, the American First and Third Armies counter-

attacked successfully, and by 18 January had regained all the ground lost a month earlier.

From then on the Allied attacks gathered momentum, and there was a rapid decline in the chances of survival for the Third Reich, and in Hitler's personal position. His health showed further marked deterioration. When adverse news was brought to him his reaction was always the same: General Guderian describes a typical occasion, when reports arrived of the retreat on the Russian front:

His fists raised, his cheeks flushed with rage, his whole body trembling, the man stood there in front of me, beside himself with fury and having lost all self-control. At each outburst Hitler would stride up and down the carpet edge, then suddenly stop before me and hurl his next accusation in my face. He was almost screaming, his eyes seemed to pop out of his head and the veins stood out in his temples.

The Führer had obviously lost the basis of his reason, yet his megalomaniac commitment to either total victory or utter defeat remained intact. He was determined that, if he could not survive, Germany would be destroyed with him. The best of his men had already given their lives: he and his associates would destroy the rest of the nation themselves, for those who remained were the inferior ones. On 19 March 1945 he ordered the destruction of the remaining industry, communications and transport systems. A few of his less extreme supporters managed to frustrate the efforts of the more fanatical Nazis to carry out this order, and the destruction of the fabric of Germany remained the work of the Allied bombers. As the end of April approached, with the Red Army encircling Berlin from the east, the German army defeated in Italy, and the British and American forces on the Elbe, Hitler's physical deterioration and mental decline were almost complete. A close aide who in February had described a senile man in a state of total exhaustion with his head wobbling slightly, his left arm hanging slackly and

Opposite above Stanislaw Mikolajczyk, leader of exiled Poles, and head of the Polish provisional government after the death of General Sikorski. In 1947 he fled to England in the face of the Communist takeover, and subsequently went to the United States.

Below The Axis leadership in Europe. Hitler and Mussolini pay a visit to Marshal Graziani's headquarters.

his hand trembling a good deal, recorded in April that the wobbling of the head and the trembling of the hand increased. There were indications of complete disintegration. In his more optimistic moments Hitler planned to organize the defence of Berlin himself, and hoped to gain something from a clash between the Russian and western Allies – the Bolsheviks and the Anglo-Saxons as he called them. But his predominating mood was one of climacteric despair. On 28 April he made his will. He would, he proclaimed, remain in Berlin, 'and there would choose voluntary death when the residence of the Führer and the Chancellor can no longer be held'. Yet still he could not accept the political and military realities. In a final display of hysterical unreality he blamed the English ruling clique for the war, said that they were the tool of international Jewry, and predicted the glorious rebirth of the Nationalist Socialist movement and the establishment of a united Germany. He appointed Admiral Dönitz (q.v.) as his successor. Himmler (q.v.) and Goering he considered had deserted him when they had recently sought a settlement with the Allies. In the early hours of 29 April Hitler married Eva Braun (q.v.), his companion for the preceding twelve years. It was a fatalistic ceremony with something of the character of a suicide pact, for immediately after it Hitler dictated a second will, a personal document in which he asserted that he and his wife intended to die to avoid the shame of overthrow or capitulation. They wished their bodies to be burned in the place where he had worked daily during his twelve years' service to the German people. The marriage lasted through that day and into the following afternoon, 30 April. By that time, the Russian advance forces were fighting no more than a block away from the *Führerbunker* and Hitler accepted the position as hopeless. According to the best reports available, Eva Braun took poison, and Hitler shot himself through the mouth with a pistol. Aides carried their bodies to the garden of the chancellery, poured petrol over them and burned their remains. No properly authenticated traces of Hitler or Eva Braun were found, and the end of his life thereby only confirmed the mystery which had surrounded him during his life.

How can one summarize Adolf Hitler, his personality and his achievements? In his early years in politics he undoubtedly showed a remarkably accurate and penetrating insight into the functioning of the German ruling establishment, and saw clearly that the key to political power lay in control of the armed forces. In gaining that control for himself he was politically astute, and to this he allied an oratorical skill which has rarely if ever been matched. Despite an utterly unprepossessing appearance he undoubtedly had an abundance of what is now called charisma, expressed in an almost mystical hold over the German people. Indeed in some sense their wholehearted acceptance of his leadership might be considered more reprehensible than Hitler's attempts to exercise it. Perhaps, had his aims been more laudable and acceptable, Hitler's talents would have turned him into one of the great contributors to twentieth-century civilization, instead of one of its near-destroyers. And it was when these aims became too grandiose in relation to his capacity to achieve them that a large proportion of the human race went to war against him and his forces. Those aims were domination of Europe in the west and east, under the rule of a 'pure' Aryan race governing through the German Nazi political system. It is the contradiction between these two sides of the German leader, the brilliant and the absurd, which gives Adolf Hitler such a unique fascination. Ultimately, his career remains one of the most mysteriously unfathomable in history.

HOBART, (Sir) Percy (1885–1957). British pioneer tank theorist. After service in the first world war and later in India, Hobart became convinced that the next war would be won by the tank, and in 1923 he joined the Royal Tank Corps. He rose to be head of the RTC in 1933 and subsequently commander of 1 Tank Brigade in 1934. During that time he was responsible for far-sighted developments in tactics and control. In 1938 he went to Egypt as a major-general, where he raised and trained the 7 Armoured Division.

Major-General Sir Percy Hobart, one of the leading tank pioneers. He devised many of the armoured vehicles which helped the Allies across the Normandy beaches.

General Ho Chi Minh, revolutionary leader who commanded anti-Japanese forces in Indo-China, and rose to the presidency of North Vietnam.

An important aspect of his theory was the formation of independent armoured formations, but his views ran counter to establishment thinking, and he was removed from active service. In 1941 Churchill (q.v.) rescued him from an obscure place as a home guard corporal, and made him commander of the 11 Armoured Division, regretting later that he had not put him in charge of all tank development with a seat on the army council. In 1942 and 1943 Hobart trained the 79 Armoured Division for the Normandy invasion, and was responsible for developing and demonstrating many of the devices, such as the flail tank, which proved so useful in penetrating Axis defences in Normandy. He commanded the division with distinction in north-west Europe. Hobart was a brother-in-law of General Montgomery (q.v.). (*See also* Fuller, Liddell-Hart)

HO CHI MINH (1890–1969). Indo-Chinese general and revolutionary leader. He fought a guerrilla campaign against the Japanese and in 1941 organized his forces into the political movement later called the Viet Minh. He was imprisoned in 1942, but released a year later at the

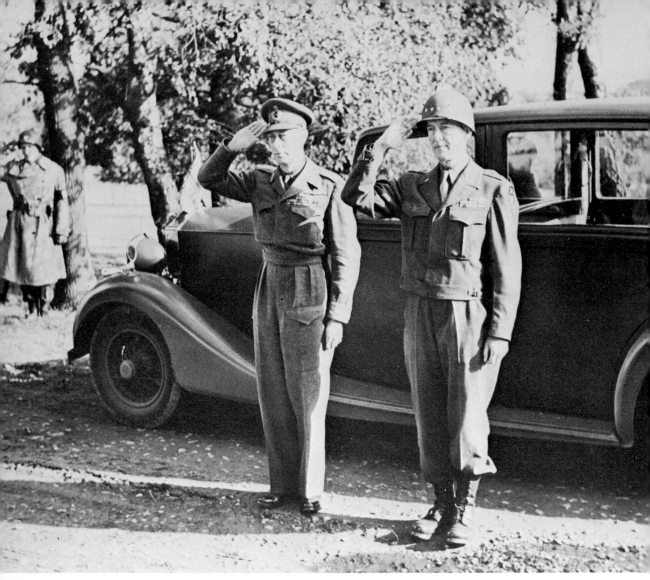

General Courtney Hodges (right), in company with Britain's King George VI. Hodges commanded US First Army from Normandy operations to the entry into Germany.

instigation of the OSS who needed the services of his forces in gathering intelligence about the occupying Japanese. In 1945, when the Japanese surrendered, he rose rapidly to the top in the confused political scene and set up the republic of Viet Nam which took control of the northern half of Indo-China.

HODGES, Courtney Hicks (1887–1966). American general who commanded the US First Army in the European campaign. Early in his career Hodges showed the dedicated professionalism which led him to army command when in 1906

he was forced to leave West Point because he failed geometry. He promptly enlisted as a private and was commissioned a second lieutenant in 1909, only a year behind his former classmates. He served under General Pershing in the punitive Mexican border expedition of 1916–17, and commanded a machine-gun company on the Western Front in the first world war. He rose through a series of staff and command posts to be chief of infantry in the United States army by 1941. He commanded 10 Corps in 1942 and the Third Army in 1943. His most important command was that of the First Army, taking over from General Bradley (q.v.) for the land campaign in Normandy. Under him the First Army achieved a string of credits, in the liberation of Paris, the defeat of the German Ardennes counter-offensive, the first Rhine crossing at Remagen, and the initial meeting with the Russians on the Elbe. Hodges was a brilliant infantry tactician whose achievements and skills were less widely publicized than those of many fellow generals because of his dislike of publicity and his modest bearing.

HOEPNER, Erich (1886–1944). German general and panzer expert who took part in the campaigns in Poland, France and the Soviet Union. As commander of the Fourth Armoured Group he was among the small number of generals who approached within sight of Moscow in December 1941, but was forced to withdraw by the Russian counter-offensive. Hitler (q.v.) flew into a maniacal fury when he heard the news. He dismissed Hoepner for retreating without permission, and publicly humiliated him by denying him the right to wear uniform. Hoepner was involved in several conspiracies against Hitler, including the final plot which culminated in the bomb explosion of 20 July 1944. He was designated to take over as commander-in-chief of home forces if General Fromm proved unreliable. When the coup failed and Fromm remained loyal to Hitler, Hoepner was among those arrested. He chose to go on trial rather than commit suicide, but failed to defend himself adequately and made a poor impression on the court, largely because his abilities were impaired by the brutal treatment he had received at the hands of the Gestapo interrogators. He was hanged by wire suspended from meat hooks at Ploetzensee prison in August 1944.

HOMMA, Masaharu (1887–1946). Japanese general, commander of the Fourteenth Army in the invasion of the Philippines in December 1941. Homma was an unusual Japanese commander in that his interests spread much wider than military affairs, embracing poetry and the arts. Born on 27 November 1887, on Sado Island, into an aristocratic landowning family, he passed with excellent grades in the military academy and the staff college, and travelled to Europe during the first world war as an observer attached to the British army on the Western Front. He subsequently held a variety of appointments, including command of a division and later an army in China. He was serving as commander of the Formosa Army when he was recalled to prepare for the outbreak of war with the Allies.

Homma's individualistic approach to his profession immediately became apparent when he hotly disputed the details of his orders – an almost unthinkable reaction to receiving a command in the normally rigid Japanese army. (Earlier Homma had had the temerity to state publicly that it would be lunacy to go to war against Britain and America.) Nevertheless, once he had clearly established the conditions of his command, his own plan for the invasion of the Philippines proved masterly, and was later described by his opposing commander, General MacArthur (q.v.), as 'a perfect strategic concept'. The first essential to Homma's plan, the neutralization of the American air defences, was accomplished within three days after large numbers of American bombers at Clark Field and fighters at Iba Field were surprised and destroyed on the ground as the result of a defective warning system. Secondly, the defended islands and coastal regions had to be captured so that the airfields could be prepared for the Japanese army's short-range aircraft. These areas were weakly defended and the Fourteenth Army secured them with little opposition. After initial operations beginning on 9 December, the main landings by the bulk of 48 Division began in Lingayen Gulf on 22 December. The Japanese transports met some opposition from B-17 bombers which had survived the earlier air onslaught, and the landing craft were also hampered when they ran ashore and grounded in the soft sand. Homma confessed at his trial after the end of the war: 'If we had been counter-attacked, we would have been helpless.'

But the Americans did not counter-attack. The under-trained Filipino units disintegrated in the face of the Japanese tanks, and Homma soon had some 43,000 men ashore in the main landings. A further 7000 landed with little opposition on the east coast of Luzon, and the capital, Manila, was placed under threat from both sides in the jaws of a classic pincer movement. General MacArthur had decided on 26 December to declare Manila an open city and withdraw according to a long-prepared plan to the Bataan peninsula. Homma's attempts to take the peninsula from the land side were fought off, and the amphibious operations mounted to outflank the defenders also proved unsuccessful. Homma came under severe criticism at imperial headquarters for having let MacArthur

Lieutenant-General Masahara Homma, victor over MacArthur's forces in the Philippines. He was executed for his responsibility for the 'March of Death' of Allied prisoners.

off the hook and allowed him to retreat in good order into Bataan, despite the fact that Homma had specifically secured a written order affirming that the occupation of Manila was the primary objective and permitting him merely to blockade the Bataan peninsula if such a retreat took place. Eventually, however, the main mission was clarified, and Homma went ahead with the problem of wiping out the American and Filipino forces on the Bataan peninsula. On 9 January he dropped leaflets urging MacArthur to surrender, then began the attack. For four days Lieutenant-General Akira Nara's 65 Brigade staged incessant assaults, but each one was repulsed, frequently by accurate artillery gunfire from the Filipinos. Eventually, however, Homma's persistence prevailed, and the defenders of Bataan were forced to fall back on to successive lines. The American and Philippine armies were severely hampered by some 100,000 refugees who had fled with them to the safety of the peninsula, and MacArthur had been forced to cut rations. The troops were also severely depleted by malaria, and their morale was weakened both by the continued retreat and by the failure of promised supply convoys to reach them.

But the Japanese also suffered setbacks: the men were without food themselves, and they too were exhausted. Homma was also deprived of his 48 Division, transferred to the Dutch East Indies, and was left with only 40,000 men. He was also surprised by the strength of the enemy's resistance, which his intelligence had led him to underestimate seriously. On 3 February he halted the attack in order to bring up supplies, and again displayed characteristic individuality in refusing to resume the offensive despite a personal envoy being sent from Field-Marshal Terauchi at Southern Army headquarters. On 8 February the luckless Homma even received a strongly worded note from the emperor himself: 'The Emperor is very concerned about your strategic position. Why are you making no progress?' In response Homma held a prolonged discussion with his fellow officers and ordered his chief of staff to prepare an assessment of the situation, outlining the entrenched

Homma steps ashore at Luzon, 24 December 1941. Nine days earlier he had launched his successful invasion of the Philippines.

position of the defenders and the likelihood of casualties in an attack. He recommended the simple expedient of leaving them where they were until they starved. This report was sent on to Tokyo, where it threw the chief of the general staff, General Sugiyama, into a frenzy. He sacked Homma's chief of staff and thought seriously of ousting Homma, but decided against it. In the end they decided to send Homma the reinforcements he needed. Through February and March, the two exhausted armies faced each other without any serious offensives, while Homma pondered the

dangers of underrating his enemy, and committed to his diary a series of sensitive observations on the conduct of war. Meanwhile, on 10 March the United States government had tacitly acknowledged the loss of the islands when they ordered General MacArthur to leave for Australia.

By the end of March Homma's reinforcements had arrived – 22,000 troops, aircraft which he considered vital to neutralize the US field artillery, and several units of 1 Artillery Corps. These new guns, opening a renewed bombardment on 3 April, annihilated forward defensive positions, and the bombing completely crushed the Allied artillery. Infantry and tanks followed up, and by 7 April the defences were routed. Major-General King (q.v.), the American commander on Bataan, was ready to surrender. Homma now made preparations for the next phase of the Philippines operation, the assault on the fortress island of Corregidor. After a twelve-hour intense artillery bombardment, on 5 May the assault waves set out for the island in landing craft. Losses were severe – two-thirds of the men in the first wave were casualties – and Homma was convinced he had failed. At this point a vigorous counter-attack could have saved Corregidor, at least temporarily. But small groups of the survivors from the assault were assembled by a colonel, and the Japanese took all the inland objectives.

Homma received the surrender of the Philippines from General Wainwright (q.v.) on 10 May. But the campaign had lasted four months, and Homma attracted severe criticism at both army group and imperial headquarters. At the end of August he was recalled and put on the reserve.

He received no further official employment under the existing regime, but remained in touch with government affairs, using his house as an informal meeting place for generals and politicians. In December 1943, after the fall of Tojo (q.v.), he was appointed minister of information by the new prime minister, Koiso.

In September 1945, to his own surprise as much as to that of the Japanese people, Homma was arrested and charged with a long list of atrocities. The alleged offences included having US troops beheaded, allowing prisoners of war as well as sixteen Filipino boys to be bayoneted, shelling the open city of Manila and a field hospital and, most spectacularly, being responsible for the 'March of Death'. This last charge referred to a march made by American and Filipino prisoners from Bataan to central Luzon. The distance was only twenty-five miles, but thousands of the prisoners were too weak through starvation or illness to keep up with the main body, and as they fell out of the lines they were shot or beaten to death by their disorganized and panicky Japanese guards. Reports filtering out about the 'March of Death' horrified and incensed the American public, and when the Americans occupied Japan Homma was called to account. Although he was concerned with the planning for the operation against Corregidor at the time and was therefore unable to supervise the removal of the prisoners of war personally, he was held to be responsible, and on 11 February 1946 was sentenced to be shot. His wife secured a personal interview to plead with General MacArthur, but the sentence was confirmed. It was carried out on 3 April 1946 in the prison yard at Manila.

HOPKINS, Harry Lloyd (1890–1946). American politician and aide to President Roosevelt (q.v.) throughout the second world war. Harry L. Hopkins made his career in social work and was appointed by Roosevelt in 1935 head of works progress administration, with a vast budget (10 million dollars on unemployment relief alone between 1935 and 1938) for a wide variety of construction and social relief projects. He resigned in 1940 through ill-health, but was unable to escape the duties of war. As a personal aide to the president he negotiated with Churchill and Stalin (qq.v.), attended meetings of the joint and combined chiefs of staff, and travelled to all the major conferences. As Roosevelt's closest adviser, Hopkins was thought of suspiciously as an *éminence grise* by some government and military personnel. He was in some ways responsible for Roosevelt's over-optimistic reading of Russia's probable post-war intentions. He also served President Truman (q.v.) briefly in 1945, travelling to Moscow to assure Stalin that US attitudes would not change.

HORTHY, Miklós de Nagybanya (1868–1957). Hungarian statesman and regent of his country from 1920 to 1944. He served in the Austro–Hungarian navy in the first world war, became its commander-in-chief in 1918, and led a national army against the Communist regime in Budapest in 1919, following which in 1920 he was made regent. Siding with Hitler and Mussolini (qq.v.), he ordered the Hungarian army to take part in the invasion of Yugoslavia. He also supported Hitler in the war against the Soviet Union, but in 1943 his relations with the Axis deteriorated. He refused to send further troops against Russia, and in March 1944 requested the withdrawal of Hungarian forces from the Eastern Front. Hitler replied by occupying Hungary, after which Horthy tried, largely without success, to prevent Gestapo persecutions of Hungarian Jews. On 15 October 1944 he drew up a separate peace with the Soviet Union, and was arrested by the Germans. United States forces released him in 1945.

HULL, Cordell (1871–1955). American politician who served as secretary of state under President Roosevelt (q.v.) from 1933 to 1944. Although his most significant work was completed in his early years in office, particularly during America's recovery from the depression, Cordell Hull played an important part in the wartime administration. He was in charge of the negotiations with the Japanese, advocating a conciliatory approach in order to strengthen the Japanese moderates. When this style of negotiation began to fail he took a harder line, and was subsequently criticized for causing the United States to be drawn into a war on two fronts. He visited Moscow in 1943, and helped considerably to improve American–Soviet relations. A man of peace, Hull was probably misplaced in the midst of a world war, but his achievements, including contributing to the creation of the United Nations Organization, were recognized by the award of the 1945 Nobel peace prize.

Cordell Hull, United States secretary of state for much of the war, works on his memoirs in the Bethesda naval hospital.

I

IRONSIDE, Edmund (First Baron Ironside) (1880–1959). British general, holder of the post of CIGS at the beginning of the war. A soldier of vast experience in the Boer war, first world war, and inter-war years, Edmund Ironside met Hitler and Mussolini (qq.v.) at the Germany army manœuvres in 1937, which convinced him that war would come in two to three years. Immediately before the war he was given a variety of innocuous overseas posts, and it appeared that he had missed the chance of senior field command. Then in July 1939 he was recalled to become c-in-c British Expeditionary Force. Gort (q.v.) was then CIGS. By September these appointments had been reversed: Gort was c-in-c BEF and Ironside CIGS, much to his dismay, as he felt this administrative

General Ironside (right), one of Britain's military leaders in the early stages of the war. Despite commendable strategic perception, he was rapidly superseded by men of a younger generation.

post one for which he was not at all equipped. Ironside correctly forecast that Hitler would attack using his army and air force, and that the main German thrust would come through the Ardennes. The government were still wedded to the idea of a trench stalemate with the main battle taking place in Belgium. After the German on-slaught Ironside pressed for an attack to the south against the flank of the German advance, while Gamelin's French forces attacked northwards. In the event the French did not attack, and Gort withdrew the BEF to Dunkirk. Ironside became c-in-c home forces, responsible for preparing the defences against invasion. In 1941 he was removed from office, promoted to field-marshal, and retired. Ironside was the perfect illustration of the danger for an army officer of being too senior at the start of a war, taking the brunt of initial hostili-ties, then being superseded by a younger, fresher generation.

ISMAY, Hastings (1887–1965). Chief of staff to Winston Churchill (q.v.) in his wartime capacity as minister of defence, and one of Churchill's closest aides. Churchill insisted on Ismay sitting on the chiefs of staff committee, which was formed of the heads of the three services. Ismay's real task was to smooth the prime minister's work and run the machinery of the military side of the govern-ment. He recognized the anomaly of his sitting with the chiefs of staff and did not attempt to inter-fere in military decisions beyond his competence, but he remained an influential figure through his close association with Churchill. He was respon-sible for channelling out Churchill's flow of minutes, and in this he was instrumental in remov-ing many potential causes of friction before they could do unnecessary damage. He retired from the army in 1946 with the rank of general, and in 1951 became the first secretary-general of the North Atlantic Treaty Organization.

J

JODL, Alfred (1890–1946). Chief of the operations section of the OKW and Hitler's (q.v.) personal chief of staff throughout the war. The son of a military family and an officer throughout the first world war, Jodl served in the war plans division of the general staff from 1935. When Hitler created the *Oberkommando der Wehrmacht* in 1935 to oversee the political and administrative affairs of the three services, with himself as commander-in-chief, Jodl was appointed chief of the operations section. His job was to keep Hitler informed of military developments and pass Hitler's orders to the operational commands. Since Hitler held a close grip on the armed services Jodl's post was one of great importance, and he became Hitler's closest adviser. By the late stages of the war his position was strong enough for him to issue some instructions to the commanders at the fronts without referring them to Hitler for approval. He was one of the signatories of the German surrender document at the end of the war. When tried as a war criminal at Nuremberg he maintained that he had merely obeyed orders as a soldier. He was convicted and hanged. (*See also* Keitel)

JOYCE, William ('Lord Haw-Haw') (1906–46). British Fascist who broadcast from Germany during the war. Joyce was born in Brooklyn, New York, of Irish parents. He came to England in 1921 where he joined the Conservative party and was expelled over a scandal involving a girl student to whom he was a tutor. He joined the British union of Fascists and made a reputation as a considerable orator. In a confusion of far-right political views, he publicly blamed the coming war on a conspiracy of Jews, Communists *and* capitalists, and in late August 1939 left for Germany. His broadcasts from there were anonymous, and began with the words, 'This is Germany calling.' He was given the name 'Haw-Haw' (later 'Lord Haw-Haw') by the *Daily Express*. His broadcasts were treated with derision by most British people, though others were disturbed by his seemingly accurate intelligence about the situation on the home front.

Joyce was ultimately identified, captured at Flensburg, and brought to Britain for trial at the central criminal court on a charge of treason. He defended himself vigorously on the grounds that he was an American citizen, but as he had held a British passport this defence was dismissed. He was sentenced to death and hanged at Wandsworth prison on 5 January 1946.

JUIN, Alphonse (1888–1967). French general who served first the Vichy government and then the Free French forces. The son of a policeman, who remained proud of his humble origins, Juin passed out first in his class at St Cyr ahead of both de Gaulle and de Tassigny (qq.v.). During the invasion of France he commanded 15 Armoured Division and covered the evacuation from Dunkirk. He was taken prisoner by the Germans, but General Weygand (q.v.) secured his release and he was appointed commander-in-chief of Vichy French forces in North Africa. When the Allies landed in November 1942 he joined forces with de Gaulle and subsequently fought as commander of the French forces in the Italian campaign. He made a reputation both for the toughness of his fighting and for the outspoken nature of his comments on France's post-war government.

Above General Jodl (right), in captivity with Dönitz (centre) and Speer. He was one of Hitler's closest associates. His claim that he was a military officer merely obeying orders did not save him from conviction at Nuremberg.

Right William Joyce – 'Lord Haw-Haw' – is moved by ambulance under armed guard during his captivity in England. He was executed for treachery as the result of his broadcasts from Germany.

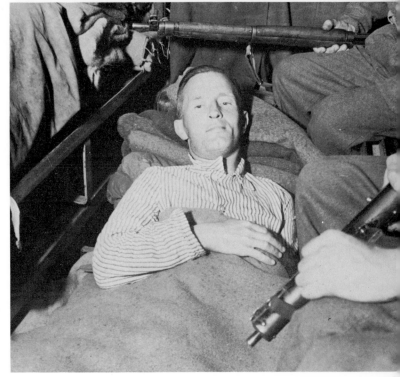

K

KAISER, Henry John (1882–1967). American industrialist responsible for much of the vast wartime munitions and shipping construction in the United States. Kaiser left school at the age of eleven and worked in several jobs before becoming a construction engineer. He was fifty years old before he embarked on 'big business', but in a short time had built three great dams in the western United States. When the war began he had never seen a shipyard, but in an astonishingly short time he had produced massive quantities of shipping. He promised the government nine million tons of shipping in a year, met his promise and reduced the average time for building a cargo ship from 105 days to 46. One ship was finished only five days after the keel was laid. Overall, his yards produced nearly 1500 ships, almost a third of the entire United States wartime construction. He set up, both before and after the war, vast enterprises in half a dozen separate industrial fields, but in terms of the second world war is remembered for his great creative contribution to the industrial capacity of the United States.

KALTENBRUNNER, Ernst (1903–46). Head of the Nazi security services from 1943. An Austrian by birth, Kaltenbrunner worked through the Austrian Nazi party for the union with Germany. He was first security minister in Austria, then chief of ss and police, and in 1943 was appointed by Himmler (q.v.) to succeed Heydrich (q.v.), assassinated in Prague, as chief of the *RSHA*. In that key post he controlled, under Himmler, the security service, the Gestapo, the concentration camps and the extermination squads, and was responsible for administering the 'final solution' of the 'Jewish problem'. He was tried at Nuremberg, found guilty of war crimes and crimes against humanity, and hanged.

KEITEL, Wilhelm (1882–1946). German general and a close adviser of Hitler (q.v.). An experienced artillery officer and staff officer during the first world war, Keitel was chief of staff at the ministry of war in 1938, and Hitler appointed him chief of the *OKW* when he set up that organization in 1938. With Jodl (q.v.), Keitel was involved in all Hitler's strategic decisions, and was one of his close advisers in the later stages of the war when Hitler insisted on running all military affairs personally. Keitel was held in contempt by the generals for his fawning attitude and inability to disagree with Hitler, an attitude characterized by the popular army wordplay on his name – *Lakeitel* (lackey). He was tried at Nuremberg for his part in the war, and hanged.

KESSELRING, Albrecht (1885–1960). German general who served in both the army and the Luftwaffe. He commanded the German air effort in the invasions of Poland and the Low Countries, and was responsible for the bombing attack on Rotterdam, the attack against the British force evacuating from Dunkirk, and the executive direction of the Battle of Britain. It was lost largely because Goering (q.v.), his superior, transferred the attack from RAF targets to the civilian target of London. Kesselring was appointed c-in-c South in December 1941, and technically was Rommel's (q.v.) commander during the battles in North Africa. In 1943 he commanded the campaign in Italy, and was instrumental in holding up the advance of the Allies with a series of highly capable

Field-Marshal Wilhelm Keitel, chief of the supreme command of the German armed forces (OKW). He earned a reputation as one of Hitler's most craven sycophants.

defensive manœuvres. Some commentators, including many among his Allied enemies, judged him to be the most capable of the generals in the west. In March 1945 Hitler (q.v.) sent him to north-west Europe to attempt to halt the Allied advance. It was of course too late for any possible success. Kesselring remained loyal to Hitler to the end, despite urgings from Hitler's opponents within the German armed forces to join in toppling the Führer. He was sentenced to death as a war criminal by a British court in Venice in May 1947 for causing hostages in Italy to be shot – the Ardeatine massacre of March 1944. The sentence

was commuted to life-imprisonment and he was released in October 1952 because of ill-health.

KIMMEL, Husband Edward (1882–1968). United States admiral in command of the Pacific Fleet at the time of the Japanese attack at Pearl Harbor. Ten days after the attack Kimmel was relieved of his post. In January 1942 he and the commander of the Hawaiian department of the army, Lieutenant-General Walter C. Short, faced a board of enquiry and were found guilty of dereliction of duty. They were retired from active service. Kimmel claimed that he had not been adequately warned of the gravity of the international situation, or the impending Japanese attack, and that the aircraft defending Pearl Harbor which were caught on the ground were in any case not under his control. In 1946 the case was heard by a Congressional Investigating Committee which concluded that the errors made by the two men were errors of judgment and not dereliction of duty.

KINCAID, Thomas (1888–1972). United States admiral, commander of the Seventh Fleet in the battles for Leyte Gulf in support of the landings in the Philippines in October 1944. Kincaid was born in Hanover, New Hampshire, and graduated from the United States Naval Academy. As a rear-admiral, he commanded an attack group of cruisers and destroyers in the battle of the Coral Sea in May 1942. In October of that year, in his flagship USS *Enterprise*, he was in tactical command of a group of task forces in the battles for the Solomon Islands, and his ship was damaged in the action known as the battle of the Santa Cruz Islands. On 28 November he was posted to the North Pacific where he commanded US forces in the build-up of bases that led to the recovery of the Aleutian Islands. He returned to the southwest Pacific on 26 November 1943 to take command of the Seventh Fleet and all Allied naval forces in the area. As commander of the Seventh Fleet he took much of the credit for the resounding defeat of the Japanese Southern Force (Admiral Nishimura) in the battle of Surigao Strait (25 October 1944), part of the battle for Leyte Gulf. The battle arose when Admiral Toyoda, commanding, elected to attack the invasion forces approaching Leyte Gulf. His plan broadly was to lure the American carrier fleet to the north by approaching the area with the Northern Force under Admiral Ozawa (q.v.). At the same time his first striking force, sailing from Singapore, would approach from the west and split into two groups, a centre force under Admiral Kurita and a southern force under Admiral Nishimura. A second striking force under Admiral Shima was to follow the southern force. The initial major development was that the American Third Fleet, under Admiral Halsey (q.v.), conformed with the Japanese intentions, leaving Kincaid's Seventh Fleet to deal with the threat from the west. Owing to the ambiguous nature of a signal Kincaid did not know that Halsey had left unguarded the exit from the San Bernadino Strait, towards which Kurita's centre force was heading. On the other hand, his own aircraft had amply supplied him with intelligence about the approach of Nishimura's southern force towards the Surigao Strait. He positioned the bulk of his fleet to guard the exit to the Strait – six old battleships, five heavy and three light cruisers, and twenty-eight destroyers, commanded by Rear-Admiral J.B. Oldendorf. Thirty-nine motor tor-

Admiral Thomas Kincaid, victor over the Japanese Seventh Fleet at Leyte Gulf.

pedo boats were stationed along the Surigao Strait to report the enemy's progress and attack if the opportunity arose. The motor torpedo boats were the first to attack ships of Nishimura's southern force, but only hit one ship. Then Oldendorf ordered successive waves of destroyers into the Strait to attack. Their effect was devastating : all but one of the Japanese destroyers were sunk, and only the flagship *Yamashiro* and the cruiser *Mogami* of the bigger ships were able to continue the fight, and both of those were severely damaged. There still remained the power of the American ships' gunfire, which rained down on the Japanese survivors in an action on 25 October lasting from 3.50 am to 4.09 am. As a result of that action both the *Yamashiro* and *Nishimura* went down. *Mogami* was caught by bombers from a separate task group the following day, and was finally sunk by her own side's torpedoes. Kincaid's concentration on the Japanese southern force, itself the result of mistaken information on the whereabouts of Halsey's Third Fleet, left only weak forces guarding the exit from the San Bernadino Strait, namely sixteen escort carriers and eighteen destroyers and other escort vessels. Against them, early on 25 October, Kurita's centre force emerged from the Strait to threaten the American invasion transports in Leyte Gulf. This consisted of four battleships, six heavy cruisers, two light cruisers and eleven destroyers. In this encounter Kurita, apparently misled by poor visibility in the rain squalls, assumed that he was facing larger ships, and failed to press home the advantage of his overwhelming superiority. The vulnerable American ships were handled with great skill and daring, and at 12.36 that afternoon Kurita broke off the action and made his way back through the San Bernadino Strait. In the other segment of the composite battle of Leyte Gulf Admiral Halsey in the north had encountered Admiral Ozawa's northern force off Cape Engaño and had sunk all four of his carriers and either destroyed or damaged several smaller ships.

The battle for Leyte Gulf, comprising three major and largely separate actions, left the Japanese without a carrier force, and thus virtually ended Japan's ability to assemble a balanced fleet for subsequent naval encounters with the Americans. It stands as one of the most complete Allied victories of the war, and Admiral Kincaid, as commander of the smaller but more heavily involved fleet engaged, deservedly takes much of the credit. He was handicapped by the difficulties of communication with Halsey's Third Fleet, and also by having the command divided equally with Halsey. Equally he benefited from having task force commanders serving under him with great determination and daring – men like Clifton Sprague and Oldendorf. By overcoming the deficiencies and making effective use of his subordinates, he proved himself a thoroughly competent naval commander. He was promoted to the rank of admiral in 1945 and retired from the navy in 1950.

KING, Ernest Joseph (1878–1956). United States admiral who served simultaneously as chief of naval operations and commander-in-chief United States navy. He was the first officer to hold both posts at the same time. Born in Lorain, Ohio, King graduated fourth in his class in the United States Naval Academy in 1901. He served as a midshipman in the Spanish–American war, and was commissioned in 1903. He was promoted rear-admiral in 1933 and became chief of the bureau of aeronautics. In 1941 he was promoted to the rank of admiral, and on 1 February placed in command of the newly formed United States Atlantic Fleet. In 1942 he took up the key posts of chief of naval operations and commander-in-chief, and as the naval representative on the joint chiefs of staff and the combined chiefs of staff committees was closely involved in the strategic direction of the war. His views were at variance with those of the British chiefs of staff committee and his own government in that he was unwilling to accept the necessity of defeating Germany before concentrating on the defeat of Japan. King consistently argued the case for concentrating on the war in the Pacific theatre. His view – a somewhat narrow one even though largely justified by events – was that in the Pacific the powerful American navy would

Admiral Ernest King, United States naval commander-in-chief. He was an ardent advocate of both naval independence and concentration on Pacific operations.

form the predominating arm in the struggle against Japan, and could achieve there the glorious victory which its status warranted. In Europe the war was being fought mainly on land and in the air, and the naval role would be reduced to that of escort, support and transport for amphibious operations. A loyal navy man who thought almost exclusively in naval terms, King fought to avoid this reduction in status. As an American he was also suspicious of British intentions and was determined to avoid the necessity of placing his own country's navy under British control, which he felt

would be an inevitable consequence of concentrating on the war in Europe. The Royal Navy he bluntly declared to be obsolete and inefficient. Roosevelt's insistence on sticking to the 'Germany first' policy overcame King's objections, although King never moderated his view. One outcome was the serious difficulty in finding landing craft for the invasion of Europe. King insisted on retaining the majority of American landing craft in the Pacific, and would agree to assign only 2493 to Overlord out of the 31,123 at his disposal. As a result of this policy Operation Anvil, the invasion of the south of France, intended as a parallel operation, had to be postponed for a month so that all available landing craft could be assigned to Overlord. King's xenophobia also resulted in the British commanders having difficulty in securing intelligence from American sources about the war in the Far East. King is reported to have said: 'What operations are or are not conducted in the Pacific is no affair of the combined chiefs of staff since this theatre is exclusively American.' In 1944, after the capture of the Palau Islands, King became embroiled in further strategic arguments on the best method of attacking Japan. MacArthur (q.v.) pressed for the capture of the Philippines, not least on the moral grounds that the United States had a priority duty to return to the aid of the people of their commonwealth. King, along with Admiral Nimitz (q.v.), advocated campaigns directly against Formosa and then against the bases along the East China coast. In July Roosevelt agreed with MacArthur's plan, and on 1 September ordered him to occupy Leyte, thereby ruling out the King–Nimitz policy. In 1944 King was promoted to the newly created rank of fleet admiral. After the war, he occupied posts as adviser to the secretary of defence and secretary of the navy.

KLEIST, Paul Ludwig Ewald von (1881–1954). German general who took part in the Polish campaign in 1939, and in the battle for France of 1940 commanded an armoured corps which broke through to the Channel coast. In April 1941 he commanded forces which captured Belgrade, then during the Soviet invasion his *Panzergruppe* 1 captured Kiev, and took part in the drive to the Caucasus, but was diverted to the attack on Stalingrad at the end of 1942. Kleist was dismissed by Hitler (q.v.) in 1944, captured by the Americans in 1945 and tried in Yugoslavia for war crimes. He was sentenced to fifteen years' imprisonment, released in 1949, and handed over to the Russians, in whose captivity he died.

KLUGE, Gunther von (1882–1944). German general, whose war career opened as commander-in-chief of the Fourth Army in the Polish invasion. He commanded the same formation in France, after which on 19 July 1940 he was promoted field-marshal, to serve on the Eastern Front. He was in command of the Fourth Army when it became the first German formation to suffer real defeat in the war at Rostov. In the changes that followed Hitler (q.v.) removed several of the exhausted senior commanders, and Kluge found himself, undeservedly, promoted to replace Bock (q.v.) as commander-in-chief of Army Group Centre. His army group had little success during 1942 and into 1943. In fact the period was noted for Kluge's difficult relations with his colleagues. When Guderian (q.v.) returned to the front as inspector-general of armoured forces, Kluge hated him so much that he challenged him to a duel with pistols, and invited Hitler to serve as his second. Hitler treated the proposal with more leniency than it deserved, and merely ordered the two to reconcile their differences. Kluge's drubbing at the hands of the Russians did not impair Hitler's opinion of him, and when in July 1944 the Führer decided to remove Rundstedt (q.v.) in Normandy, he sent Kluge as his replacement in the post of c-in-c West. Kluge was a pliable character, with no great individuality (which perhaps explains his continuing favour in Hitler's eyes), and he went to Normandy determined to put Hitler's orders into effect. He instantly fell out with Rommel (q.v.), who gave him a rapid lesson on why the front was in difficulties. At least Kluge later recognized that Rommel had been right, and supported his views to Hitler. Kluge was also weak enough to obey

Hitler and stage the disastrous Mortain counter-attack, which led to serious losses in the Falaise gap. Kluge himself was out of touch with the battle for twelve hours when Allied aircraft and artillery kept him pinned down in a ditch; because of this absence Hitler felt that Kluge was trying to contact the Allied armies at this time in order to surrender, and he replaced him with Model (q.v.). Kluge by this time knew that the investigators into the bomb attempt on Hitler's life were arresting suspects who would undoubtedly implicate him. He started out for Germany by car on 18 August, stopped for lunch under the shade of a tree and there killed himself by swallowing a capsule of poison.

KNOX, Frank (1874–1944). United States politician and secretary of the navy from July 1940. After an early career as a successful journal-

Secretary of the navy Frank Knox. A former publisher, Knox was a Republican politician who served a Democratic president.

ist and newspaper manager, Knox tried to secure the vice-presidency as a Republican in the 1936 elections, but was defeated. He first declined Roosevelt's (q.v.) invitation to serve as naval secretary in a bipartisan government in 1939, but accepted the post when the invitation was repeated in July of the following year. Although a member of the opposing political party, Knox threw his entire backing behind the wartime policies of the president, and travelled thousands of miles throughout the world to visit naval units wherever they operated. He was among the first men to visit Pearl Harbor after the Japanese attack. He died in office of a heart attack on 28 April 1944.

KOENIG, Pierre (1898–1970). Free French general. After service in Normandy Koenig was in Britain at the time of the armistice in 1940 and immediately opted to support General de Gaulle (q.v.). By 1942 he was commanding 1 Free French Brigade which resisted Rommel's (q.v.) summer offensive at the fort of Bir Hacheim. He rejected Rommel's surrender ultimatum and finally withdrew on 10 June with half his force intact, bringing out several wounded men and Allied prisoners. He not only held up Rommel for two weeks, but did much to eradicate the dishonour of France's disastrous 1940 defeat. He was appointed commander of the FFI, the armed French resistance, and de Gaulle made him governor of Paris after the liberation. After the war he went on to a second, though less distinguished, career in politics.

KONIEV, Ivan Stepanovich (1887–1973). Senior Soviet general who commanded army groups throughout the war from the defence of Moscow in 1941 to the capture of Berlin in 1945. A soldier of peasant origins, he served as an NCO in the tsarist army, joined the Communist party in 1917, and the Red Army in 1918. He passed through a variety of posts and was commander of the Transcaucasian military district at the opening of the war.

Koniev was one of a line of generals who in rapid succession commanded the Western Army Group whose task was to defend Moscow. On 12 September 1941 Koniev took over from Timoshenko,

only to be replaced by Zhukov (q.v.) on 10 October. Stalin (q.v.) blamed Koniev for allowing five armies to be trapped, but Zhukov persuaded Stalin to allow him to keep Koniev as his deputy. Koniev's reputation survived, and he was given command of the Steppe Front for the great offensives of autumn 1943, in which his forces captured Poltava and Kremenchug. Koniev's greatest victories came in the early months of 1944, in the attacks which cut off the German salient at Korsun on the Dnieper. The Steppe Front had been renamed the Second Ukrainian Front, and was positioned on the south side of the German salient. Vatutin's (q.v.) First Ukrainian Front attacked from the north. The closing movements began on 1 February 1944, and the battle, now known as 'the little Stalingrad', resulted in the death of an estimated 55,000 Germans and the capture of 18,000 prisoners, 500 tanks, and 300 aircraft. Koniev then surprised the German armies by immediately going on to the offensive, with his *'blitzkrieg through the mud'*. The Germans did not expect any Russian advance in the terrible conditions in the Ukraine, where the countryside was waterlogged in winter and the roads ran deep with mud. A Russian T-34 tank was virtually the only vehicle that could cope with the conditions. The offensive opened on 5 March with a heavy artillery barrage which forced the Germans to retreat on foot. They destroyed most of their vehicles and armour, and left the remainder to be captured by the Russians.

Koniev commanded the First Ukrainian Front in the great final offensives which began in January 1945, in which his troops over-ran southern Poland. Starting their advance on 12 January, his forces took Cracow on 19 January and reached the Oder on 23 January. On 6 February they crossed the Oder and by April were threatening Berlin from the south. The final moves began on 16 April, and on 25 April Koniev's troops joined up with Zhukov's First Belorussian Front, completing the encirclement of Berlin.

Koniev served as commander of the Russian forces of occupation in Austria, and in 1946 took over from Zhukov as commander-in-chief of

General Ivan Koniev, Soviet commander at the Korsun salient. His aggression in the face of almost impossible conditions brought an unexpected victory.

Soviet ground forces. In 1955 he rose to be commander of all Warsaw Pact forces, and two years later, under Khrushchev's regime, he was instrumental in getting Zhukov dismissed. Koniev was a popular soldier with his troops, and enjoyed a reputation for bravery arising from his guerrilla exploits in Siberia during the civil war, when he commanded an armoured train. He had a fondness for reading, with a preference for the classics.

KRETSCHMER, Otto (born 1912). German U-boat commander, and as captain of U-99 one of the highest scoring U-boat aces in the battle of the Atlantic. In the first eighteen months of war Kretschmer's U-boat sank 267,000 tons of Allied merchant shipping. He was the first commander to sink more than a quarter of a million tons, and his victims included three armed merchant cruisers and a destroyer. The essence of Kretschmer's technique was to penetrate a convoy and launch torpedoes from this close but vulnerable position. On 17 March 1941 he was intercepted, along with Schepke's U-100, by two Royal Navy destroyers, *Walker* and *Vanoc*, during an attack on the convoy HX112. Kretschmer scuttled his boat and was captured with his crew, spending the rest of hostilities as a prisoner of war.

KRUEGER, Walter (1881–1967). Born in Germany, Krueger settled in the United States with his parents in 1889. After a lifetime of army service going back as far as Cuba in 1898, Krueger rose to command the US Third Army at the beginning of the war. He was transferred to the Pacific in 1943 in command of the new Sixth Army forming in Australia, a post which he held through the remainder of the Pacific war, invading New Britain, New Guinea and the Philippines. His Sixth Army was engaged in the occupation of southern Japan in 1945 and 1946, when Krueger retired.

KRUPP. Family name of German industrialists and armaments manufacturers. Dr **GUSTAV KRUPP** (1870–1950), who had assumed the Krupp name on marrying into the family, was considered too senile to stand trial as a war criminal, but was formally indicted for 'promotion of the accession to power of the Nazi conspirators and the consolidation of their control over Germany'. His son, **ALFRED KRUPP von BOHLEN und HALBACH** (born 1907), directed the enterprise from 1942. A central figure in the Nazi war economy, he was responsible for armaments and mining. He moved entire factories from German-occupied territory in the Ukraine, and was responsible for employing 45,000 Russian civilians as forced labour in the factories, together with 120,000 prisoners of war and 6000 other civilians

The armaments tycoon Gustav Krupp. His huge industrial empire was broken up, and he was arrested in 1950 but released on the grounds of ill-health.

Alfred Krupp, on trial at Nuremberg for war crimes.

in the coalmines, ignoring the fact that they were physically below the minimum health standards of German workers. He also located factories near concentration camps, including Auschwitz, because they were 'known sources of labour'. Captured by the Canadians in 1944, Krupp was put on trial at Nuremberg and charged with plundering occupied countries and exploiting forced labour. He received a twelve-year sentence in July 1948, but was released in early 1951. His co-directors were also jailed.

KUZNETSOV, Nikolai Gerasimovich (born 1902). Soviet admiral: commander-in-chief of Soviet naval forces throughout the war. After the war he was responsible for the build-up of a powerful Soviet submarine fleet.

L

LANGSDORFF, Hans (1880–1939). German admiral who commanded the pocket battleship *Graf Spee* at the battle of the River Plate. At the beginning of the war *Graf Spee* operated as a merchant raider in the Atlantic, and by mid-December 1939 had sunk nine ships totalling 50,000 tons. The British sent forces to track down and destroy the ship and on 13 December three cruisers, the *Ajax*, *Achilles* and *Exeter*, brought *Graf Spee* to action near the mouth of the River Plate in Uruguay. Although outgunned they damaged *Graf Spee* and forced Langsdorff to put into Montevideo for repairs. Tense international negotiations followed, the outcome of which was that the authorities at Montevideo, a neutral port, refused permission for the ship to remain there. Langsdorff disembarked 300 prisoners of war and the majority of his crew, and prepared to leave the port, while the population of Montevideo crowded their shoreline cliffs in anticipation of a major action by the Royal Navy against the German ship. Instead Langsdorff and a skeleton crew scuttled their ship in the estuary. Langsdorff left a letter explaining his actions and shot himself.

LAYCOCK, Robert (1907–1968). British general and commando leader, who rose to be chief of combined operations after 1943. Laycock, an officer in the Royal Horse Guards, was serving on the staff of the BEF in France when the war began. He volunteered for the new special service being formed, and found himself commanding one of the first 'commandos' for raiding work, with the rank of lieutenant-colonel. Shortly afterwards he went to the Middle East in charge of a battalion of five commandos known as Layforce, which,

Captain Hans Langsdorff, defeated in the battle of the River Plate, who took his own life rather than surrender his ship to the British.

Left Major-General Robert Laycock, appointed in October 1943 to succeed Mountbatten as chief of combined operations.

Admiral William Leahy, who returned from retirement to serve in the war, became ambassador to Vichy France and later chief of staff to the president.

among other activities, formed the rearguard for the evacuation of Crete. His headquarters were seized by the Germans but he jumped into a tank and drove it at them to escape. He took part in the raid on Rommel's (q.v.) headquarters in November 1941 and was forced to escape into the desert with a sergeant, the two men reaching their own lines after six weeks in German-held territory. He returned to England to train and raise new commandos, and was in many respects their creator as a major force. He took part with them in the landings at Sicily and at Salerno, and had American rangers as well as British troops serving under him. He was a natural successor to Mountbatten (q.v.) as chief of combined operations in 1943, holding the rank of major-general at the early age of thirty-six. He remained chief of combined operations for two years after the war and was subsequently governor of Malta. (*See also* Lovat)

LEAHY, William Daniel (1875–1959). Senior United States admiral and diplomat. Leahy's career stretched back to the Spanish–American war, and included service in the Philippines insurrection and the Boxer rebellion in China. By 1937 he had achieved the post of chief of naval operations and in 1939 retired after forty-two years in the navy, only to begin a new career in diplomacy as governor of Puerto Rico. Roosevelt (q.v.) recalled him in 1940 and appointed him ambassador to Vichy France, where his task was to keep Pétain (q.v.) independent of Germany, and to prevent Morocco and the French fleet falling into German hands. Leahy's reading of the French situation was not entirely accurate. He continued to support the Vichy government and failed to recognize the increasing power of de Gaulle, or the fact that de Gaulle was providing the better instrument for fighting Germany. In 1942 Roosevelt recalled him to be his chief of staff, in which post he was vastly more successful, particularly in reconciling differing Allied points of view. As senior among the joint chiefs of staff Leahy was a close adviser of President Roosevelt and accompanied him to the Allied conferences at Quebec,

Cairo, Teheran and Yalta. He also advised President Truman (q.v.) at the Potsdam conference. He remained chief of staff until March 1949.

LEIGH-MALLORY, (Sir) Trafford (1892–1944). British air marshal, distinguished for his service both in the Battle of Britain and in the invasion of Normandy. He commanded 12 Group of fighter command during the Battle of Britain, covering central and much of northern England. He was severely critical of Park's (q.v.) tactics at 11 Group in south-east England. His own policy was to fly groups of three to seven squadrons as 'wings', which operated with few casualties, and he tried to impress the policy throughout fighter command. His criticism tended to ignore the shorter warning of enemy aircraft that Park was receiving in the south-east. Leigh-Mallory's thesis won general approval amongst the air staff, and he took over 11 Group from Park in December 1940.

Air-Marshal Sir Trafford Leigh-Mallory (left), chief of fighter command from November 1940, who rose to command the Allied Expeditionary Force for the invasion of Europe.

Curtis LeMay, one of the youngest men to hold the
rank of United States general. He served in widely
differing theatres, from daylight raids over Germany to
the atomic bomb attacks on Japan.

Because of this timing, he was able to oversee the return to the offensive, and was the natural choice to head fighter command in November 1942. He was also selected on 15 November 1943 for the key command of the Allied Expeditionary Air Force in Operation Overlord. He developed Britain's fighter control to such a high degree that few aircraft could penetrate the ring during the invasion preparations, and on D-Day itself the invasion forces were not interfered with by the Luftwaffe. For the invasion Leigh-Mallory commanded a total of 9000 RAF and USAF aircraft, which bottled up the Luftwaffe, bombed German road and rail communications, and severely restricted the mobility of potential German reinforcements. Leigh-Mallory's forceful and unswerving approach was directly responsible, against strong opposition, for the policy of bombing rail communications centres within 150 miles of the invasion area. In November 1944 he was appointed to take command of Allied air forces in south-east Asia, but on the way there, on 14 November, his aircraft crashed near Grenoble in bad weather. Leigh-Mallory and his wife were killed. (*See also* Bader, Dowding)

LeMAY, Curtis (born 1906). American air force general, who led bomber raids and organized the Berlin airlift of 1948. An engineering graduate, LeMay worked between the wars in the development of bomber techniques. In 1942 he became the youngest American general at the age of thirty-seven, and led daylight bomber raids on Germany from England making significant improvements in precision bombing. In March 1944 he transferred to the China–Burma–India theatre and organized the B-29 Super Fortress raids of 20 and later 21 bomber squadrons, and subsequently commanded the Twentieth Air Force stationed on Guam, which carried out the atomic bomb raids on Japan. In his post-war career LeMay rose to be air force chief of staff (1961–5) and in 1968 ran unsuccessfully for the vice-presidency with George C. Wallace. His contribution to bomber tactics included developments of pattern bombing and of low-level bombing to inhibit interception.

King Leopold of the Belgians, pictured with his second wife at their home in Switzerland during the post-war period when he waited for the Belgian people's verdict on his return to the country.

LEOPOLD III (King) (born 1901). Belgian king 1934–51, when he abdicated. During the 1930s Leopold remained fiercely neutral, determined not to enter into an Allied alliance against Germany. He made himself c-in-c of the Belgian armed forces in September 1939, and witnessed the defeat of the small Belgian army in May and June 1940. Against much opposition from politicians and soldiers determined to fight on, he surrendered the armed forces on 28 May 1940. He was severely criticized for leaving the flank of the French and British armies exposed. He refused to leave Belgium, despite advice to set up a government-in-exile in London, and was kept in custody in the Laeken palace until 1944, when he was moved to Germany. In September 1944 his Parliament met and approved the decision of the Belgian government in London to ban the king from Belgian soil and appoint his brother as regent. He was brought back in 1950 for one month, but retired again in the face of opposition.

LIDDELL-HART, Basil (1895–1970). English military commentator and tank theorist. Liddell-Hart, who served on the Western Front in the first world war, spoke out during the inter-war years against the lack of modernization in the British army. As early as 1925 he published a book visualizing the future pattern of mechanized war on land and sea and in the air. The War Office in London sanctioned some experiments with tanks, but remained cool and alternately dropped and revived the idea. Liddell-Hart visited France in 1926 and made similar comments on the strength of the French army, which were taken up and developed by the young Captain de Gaulle (q.v.). During the next decade he continued to write widely on the subject of tank development both in the newspapers, including the London *Times*, and in books, but little concrete progress was made. Among the ideas he evolved was the

Basil Liddell-Hart, British military theorist whose ideas influenced German tactics, notably in the use of tanks. His views were less enthusiastically received in his own country.

narrow-front breakthrough followed by the 'expanding torrent', and the brief 'lightning war' which formed the basis of Germany's devastatingly successful *blitzkrieg* attacks in western and eastern Europe. But in Britain the military hierarchy remained obstinate, until in 1937 the tank theory was given new impetus by the arrival at the War Office of Hore-Belisha, who was sympathetic to mechanization. Liddell-Hart served as his adviser, but a year later resigned to be free again to make his views public. Throughout the pre-war period, although the introduction of tanks was resisted in Britain, the German generals read Liddell-Hart's work and, as many of them acknowledged after the war, based much of their technique and strategy on his ideas. Liddell-Hart remained silent during the war in order not to expose his country's weaknesses, and after 1945 spent some months interviewing the leading German generals and analysing their campaigns. (*See also* Fuller, Hobart)

LINDEMANN, Frederick Alexander (Lord Cherwell) (1886–1957). Scientific adviser to Winston Churchill (q.v.). An energetic member of the Oxford University scientific establishment, Lindemann also enjoyed independent means which enabled him to move in high social and political circles. He met Churchill in 1921 and they became lifelong friends. In the mid-1930s he saw the dangers of German air defence, and called for a committee to study the question. The result was the Tizard (q.v.) committee, on which Lindemann served, although he quarrelled with Tizard. After attempting unsuccessfully to increase his influence by entering Parliament he joined Churchill's staff at the Admiralty in 1939 as head of the statistical department. He was made a peer in 1941. From then on he produced a steady and impressive series of achievements, not only in the scientific field, but also as an economist. Churchill relied heavily on his advice, and also on his capacity for boiling down long complicated memoranda to a few succinct lines. Because of his influence 'the Prof' attracted hostility from many opponents. His principal scientific achievements during the

Professor Sir Frederick Lindemann, controversial scientific adviser to Winston Churchill. Rival scientists considered 'the Prof' an adverse influence.

war included hollow-charge bombs, proximity fuses, techniques for bending German navigational radio waves, and the H_2S system of radar navigation. Economically, he produced convincing statistical evidence that radically influenced Air Ministry policy. His uneven wartime career also produced some notable failures, including delaying the introduction of the 'window' device for confusing German radar (he felt it would lead to the Germans also using it) and his denial of the existence of German v-weapons in the face of the evidence.

LIST, Wilhelm (1880–1971). German general who commanded the Fourteenth Army in the attack on Poland and Twelfth Army in the invasion of northern France in 1940. His subordinates included the panzer specialists Kleist (q.v.) at panzer corps level and Guderian (q.v.) as a corps commander. He drew up the agreement with Bulgaria in February 1941 which allowed German forces through that country to attack Greece. List commanded Army Group A in the invasion of the Soviet Union, but he was removed in September 1942 after failing to break through in the Caucasus. He was tried at Nuremberg and sentenced to life imprisonment but released in 1953.

LOVAT, Lord (born Simon Fraser, 1911). British commando leader. After serving as a Guards officer from 1934 to 1937 Lovat commanded the Lovat Scouts, a unit which his father had raised to fight in the Boer war. Churchill (q.v.) suggested that they should form one of the new commandos and as such they served in the Middle East, replacing the original Layforce. In August 1942 he led 4 Commando in the Dieppe raid, when they were the only force to achieve their objectives and withdraw without excessive losses. He commanded 1 Special Service Brigade in the Normandy landings and was wounded, after which he retired from active service. He travelled to Moscow to advise the Russians on river crossings, and impressed Stalin (q.v.), who declared that he liked young warriors like Lovat. He served briefly as an under-secretary at the Foreign Office in Churchill's caretaker government of 1945. (*See also* Laycock)

LUGANSKY, Sergei Danilovich (born 1919). Soviet fighter pilot and air ace. Lugansky commanded fighter squadrons and regiments throughout the war in operations from Finland to the invasion of Germany. He accumulated a personal tally of forty-three kills.

M

MacARTHUR, Douglas (1880–1964). American general and senior commander in the Pacific theatre. Born in the Arsenal army barracks at Little Rock, Arkansas, in 1880, Douglas MacArthur was almost inevitably destined for an army career. His father Colonel Arthur MacArthur was a hero of the American civil war who won the Congressional Medal of Honor with the Twenty-fourth Wisconsin Volunteers. He fought with distinction in the Indian wars, led a brigade in the American intervention in the Philippines, and by 1900 was governor-general of the Philippines. By the time his distinguished father had taken up this appointment Douglas MacArthur was studying at West Point. He passed first in the competitive entrance examination, and entered the academy in 1899. He was eminently successful there, headed the lists in three of his four years, and twice played baseball for the Point. In 1903 he was commissioned as a second lieutenant in the engineers, served briefly in the Philippines after his father had left, and enjoyed a tour of duty as chief of staff to his father when General Arthur MacArthur was sent to report on the Russo–Japanese war. It was there that his lifelong involvement with the Pacific islands began, when he formed the opinion that 'the future and, indeed, the very existence of America [were] irrevocably entwined with Asia and its island outposts'. In the years before the first world war he held a variety of staff and other appointments in Washington, Texas and Mexico, and by the time the United States entered the war he had amassed a wide variety of experience. He joined the Rainbow Division, landed in France in October 1917, and was with the first United States unit to enter the fighting. There he quickly demonstrated that personal courage was among his many soldierly qualities. In February 1918 he led a raiding party through the barbed wire, and was awarded the American Silver Star and the *Croix de Guerre*. These were only the first of many decorations, which in due course included seven Silver Stars, two Distinguished Service Crosses, a Distinguished Service Medal, and a variety of foreign decorations. While his courage was beyond question, there was some doubt about his methods, and an investigation was set up to consider them. He was in the habit of leading an attack from the front, unarmed and carrying no helmet or gasmask. But when the American commander-in-chief General Pershing heard of the investigation he dismissed it with the comment, 'Stop all this nonsense. MacArthur is the greatest leader of troops we have, and I intend to make him a division commander.' After the war MacArthur was appointed superintendent of West Point – the youngest officer ever to hold the post – with the brief of modernizing the institution. Far-sighted enough to see that future wars would be fought by large armies recruited from civilian populations, as opposed to specialized professional armies, MacArthur broadened the outlook of the academy, introducing civilian lecturers, a wide general curriculum, periods of army secondment aimed at eradicating the remote and exclusive outlook of the cadets, and compulsory team games. He also succeeded in doubling the size of the academy. In 1922, at the end of his three-year West Point term, he began the first of two terms of duty

General Douglas MacArthur, commander in the Philippines until the Japanese invasion forced him out in 1942.

in the Philippines, in the first commanding the Manila district with responsibility for the Bataan peninsula, and in the second commanding the American army department. It was then that he consolidated his friendship with Manuel Quezon (q.v.). In 1930 he was back in the United States with the rank of general, to take up the post of chief of staff, again the youngest holder of that office. In the years of the depression, his main difficulty lay in securing enough resources to maintain the size of the army against serious attempts in Congress to make reductions. He also worked to develop a tank strength and other mechanization, and set up the nucleus of an army air corps, but in the circumstances of economic uncertainty, and of American isolationism, the army was not considered a serious priority. MacArthur damaged his reputation when in 1932 he led a detachment against a gathering of first world war veterans who marched peacefully on Washington demanding payment of a bonus promised to them for war service. Riding on horseback at the head of his 600 troops, MacArthur dispersed the marchers with tear gas after some of them had thrown rocks at the troops. Most Americans sympathized with the marchers and MacArthur became a symbol of right-wing repression. Roosevelt (q.v.) became president in 1933, and in 1934 extended the general's term as chief of staff for an extra year. By 1935, aged fifty-five, MacArthur looked set for retirement, with little else open for him to achieve. But his earlier involvement with the Philippines saved him from that fate. He was asked by Quezon to advise on defence, and shortly afterwards, when the Philippines became a commonwealth of the United States, he was asked to take on the job of high commissioner. He declined this civilian appointment, but accepted that of military adviser to the Philippine commonwealth. MacArthur's period of pre-war military involvement with the Philippines was far from successful. Although he correctly anticipated that Japanese expansion in the Pacific was inevitable, he produced only half-hearted defensive measures. The Philippines remained low in the United States' list of priorities, partly through lack of money, partly through political isolationism, and partly because of Roosevelt's belief that the defence of Europe against Nazi Germany was more important than defence against Japan in the Pacific. Continuing neglect of the Philippine defences left the islands totally vulnerable, so that by 1941 panic measures were needed to meet the threat from Japan. On 26 July MacArthur was given command of all the United States forces in the Far East, and the Philippine army was absorbed into the American army.

MacArthur persuaded Washington that the Philippines could be defended against a Japanese attack for up to six months, despite the fact that they were weak in land forces, almost bare of sea-power, and lacking in air cover. After six months reinforcements would be needed if capitulation was to be avoided. The events of late 1941 and early 1942 showed how seriously MacArthur's optimistic judgment had misled him, and called into question his capacity as a strategist. His command ability also failed him in the early hours of the Pacific war, when he allowed the bombing force at Clark Field north of Manila to be caught on the ground by a Japanese strike force, despite ample warning of Japanese hostilities. Eighteen out of thirty-five B-17s were lost, as well as fifty-three fighters and twenty-five other aircraft, and only seven Japanese aircraft were destroyed. As a result of this raid, it has been said that the Philippines were lost in the first hours of the war. MacArthur demanded a fleet attack against Japan, and tried to persuade the chief of staff in Washington, General Marshall (q.v.), to send him 300 fighters and 250 dive-bombers, transported by aircraft carrier. Such reinforcements of course did not exist: the bulk of the Pacific fleet was destroyed at Pearl Harbor, and in any case Washington had no desire to commit any of the few forces they had to a vulnerable Pacific outpost which already looked as good as lost. MacArthur was forced to plan for the invasion with the limited land forces as his only resource, and for this he proposed to declare Manila an open city, and move the newly mobilized Philippines army to the Bataan peninsula. Even these preparations had not been completed when the Japanese Fourteenth Army, commanded by Lieutenant-General Homma (q.v.), attacked on 22 December. The under-strength and ill-trained Philippines army virtually collapsed, and MacArthur began his withdrawal to the Bataan peninsula. Even there he faced difficulties, as more than twice the anticipated 43,000 personnel crowded into the beleaguered fortress and MacArthur was forced to halve the ration allocation. He still maintained, quite unrealistically, that the United States would send supplies and reinforcements. On 10 January Homma invited MacArthur to surrender, which he refused to do. MacArthur actually sent a message to his troops, who by now were staving off a concerted

Japanese attack, stating unrealistically: 'Help is on the way from the United States. Thousands of troops and hundreds of planes are being dispatched. . . . It is imperative that our troops hold until these reinforcements arrive. No further retreat is possible.' By 22 January the Japanese had lost some 1400 casualties and the United States forces had withdrawn behind a shorter and more easily defended line. MacArthur himself was commanding from the island of Corregidor in Manila Bay, where he set up headquarters in a warren of tunnels while everything above ground was destroyed by Japanese shelling. Disdaining a helmet, wearing his soft field-marshal's cap, carrying a walking stick and smoking his corn-cob pipe, MacArthur set a first-rate example of calmness in the face of adversity, emerging frequently to face the shelling and frequently escaping death by a narrow margin. But despite his bravery, leadership and confidence, morale on the Philippines quickly drained, and on 8 February President Quezon asked Roosevelt to declare the Philippines neutral so that he could ask for both American and Japanese withdrawals. Roosevelt urged the Philippines garrison to fight on, but gave MacArthur permission to capitulate when the position became hopeless.

General Marshall in Washington asked MacArthur to evacuate his wife and son by submarine, and Quezon supported the suggestion, but MacArthur declined, declaring that he and his family would share the fate of the garrison. It was not to be. On 22 February, as the Japanese closed the ring round the American forces despite brave and successful efforts to delay them, MacArthur was ordered to Mindanao *en route* to Australia, where he was to take command of Allied forces in the south-west Pacific. His first reaction was to resign his commission and stay with his men, but his staff dissuaded him, and MacArthur agreed to leave when the time was right. On 9 March General Yamashita (q.v.), fresh from his victory in Singapore, took over from General Homma whose attack had lost momentum, and on 12 March MacArthur, his family and some of his staff

boarded torpedo boats and left for Mindanao. When he arrived in Australia MacArthur was asked for a comment on the Philippines situation. He replied: 'The President of the United States ordered me to break through the Japanese lines and proceed from Corregidor to Australia for the purpose, as I understand it, of organizing the American offensive against Japan, a primary object of which is the relief of the Philippines. I came through and I shall return.' Although delivered in a tired and casual mood, MacArthur's words 'I shall return' became a symbol for American determination to return to the offensive and defeat the Japanese in the Pacific.

Throughout the early part of 1942 MacArthur engaged in the familiar round of disagreements with Washington, primarily over supplies and priorities, as MacArthur demanded a 'Japan first' programme, and the government adhered to its policy of defeating Germany in Europe and North Africa. He also alienated his Australian allies by refusing to appoint anyone except Americans, mostly his colleagues from the Philippines, to his staff, and by openly denigrating the qualities of the Australian troops despite their success in holding the Japanese advance in New Guinea. Nevertheless in April 1943 he was confirmed as commander-in-chief of the south-west Pacific area, and pressed on with the build-up of troops and supplies for an offensive in the Solomon Islands and New Guinea. On 8 October 1943 the island-hopping campaign began when marines went ashore at Tulagi and Guadalcanal. From this point on MacArthur's reputation consistently grew. Understanding instinctively the value of good public relations, he succeeded in getting himself promoted as the hero of the south-west Pacific, upstaging the navy despite their success in beating the Japanese at the critical battle of Midway. By the spring of 1943, after MacArthur had served one year as commander-in-chief, the Japanese had been cleared out of Guadalcanal, and were losing decisively in New Guinea. MacArthur was anxious to consolidate America's success, but was still starved of supplies as the European com-

MacArthur, returning to the Philippines in 1944, makes much of wading up the beach.

mitment received the greater priority. By August 1943 he was ready to begin the plan for his dream and declared aim, the reconquest of the Philippines. Even this gave rise to friction, when it was suggested that the conquest of the Philippines should be undertaken by forces from the Pacific Ocean Area commanded by Admiral Nimitz (q.v.). From this point MacArthur became increasingly embroiled in politics, boosting his own interests in pronouncements and press conferences at the expense of the planners in Washington, including the president. He was widely supported in the press, and became a hero in the eyes of the American people. The painful and costly campaign through the islands continued until at last,

by September 1944, MacArthur was able to move his headquarters from Brisbane, Australia, to Hollandia, New Guinea, to plan the attack on the Philippines. At this stage doubts arose as to whether the attack on the Philippines was necessary, or whether it could be bypassed in favour of a direct assault on Japan. Of course MacArthur fought against this notion, having come to regard the capture of the Philippines and the honouring of his pledge 'to return' as a personal mission, almost a crusade. He also presented a cogent case for its capture on purely military grounds. Ultimately MacArthur's view carried, and by this time supplies for amphibious operations were becoming available as the European war drew to a close.

The victorious commander proclaims the liberation of the Philippines, fulfilling his promise to the people – 'I shall return.'

The assault on the Philippines took place in October 1944, and on 20 October MacArthur was able to stride up a beach on Leyte in the wake of the assault troops and make a speech to the Philippine people, which included the words, 'I have returned.' MacArthur still had to battle for permission to take the whole of the group, especially Luzon which both Admiral King (q.v.) and Admiral Nimitz wanted to bypass in favour of an attack on Japan and Formosa respectively. MacArthur's view again prevailed and the landings took place first at Mindoro on 15 December, and then at Luzon on 9 January 1945. The landings themselves met little opposition, as the American invading force was protected by overwhelming air power, but the fighting as the Japanese retreated north into the mountains of Luzon was costly. MacArthur again waded ashore

in the wake of the initial landings on Luzon and was greeted with ecstatic fervour both by the people of the Philippines, who revered him, and by the half-starved prisoners whose camps the Japanese had abandoned. The Japanese still had 50,000 troops on Luzon, and its capture involved a long campaign costing 8500 American lives and lasting until Japan's surrender. After the emotional celebrations which accompanied the liberation of the Philippines, MacArthur played a major part in the remaining campaign to defeat Japan. On the day the Japanese surrendered President Truman (q.v.) appointed him to supreme command of the Pacific theatre, and it was MacArthur who received the Japanese surrender on the USS *Missouri* on 2 September 1945. As supreme commander he became the effective ruler of Japan during the occupation. His career, which had almost ended in retirement before the war, had been resuscitated through the comparative backwater of the Philippines, and MacArthur was now one of the most important personalities in any Allied country. His position at the pinnacle of western power suited him, and there were even greater heights to attain or aim at – as United Nations commander in the Korean war, and in politics. His public disagreements with American policy in Korea led Truman to relieve him of his command in 1951. The attacks on New Guinea and the Philippines during the campaign against Japan had shown MacArthur to be a talented general, but he remained politically naïve and was consistently at odds with his political superiors. It may justifiably be claimed that MacArthur's abilities never quite matched up to his image of himself. He reached towering heights in terms of his personality and popular image. His concrete achievements were less spectacular. (*See also* Wainwright)

McAULIFFE, Anthony Clement (1898–1975). United States general, acting commander of 101 Airborne Division during the battle of the Bulge in 1944. He held the American position at Bastogne, and earned instant fame by rejecting the German surrender ultimatum with the single-word reply 'Nuts!'

McINDOE, (Sir) Archibald (1900–60). New Zealand surgeon who at his hospital in Sussex, England, developed advanced techniques of plastic surgery and skin grafting to repair the damage to thousands of Royal Air Force pilots and air crew burned and disfigured in air combat and crashes. He also worked successfully to restore the morale of his patients and their belief in a useful future, and formed the 'Guinea Pig Club' among men he had treated to aid their recovery and raise funds for their rehabilitation.

MALINOVSKY, Rodion (1898–1967). Soviet general noted for his contribution to the defence of Stalingrad. In the counter-offensive there he commanded the Second Guards Army which absorbed Manstein's (q.v.) attempt to break through to Paulus's (q.v.) encircled Sixth Army,

and then threw Manstein's forces back from the Myshkova river to Zimovniki. Malinovsky had to march his men twenty-five miles or more a day to enter this battle, as they were entirely without supplies of petrol. They went into battle as unsupported infantry and artillery and held the Germans until, with the arrival of fuel on 24 December, tanks and aircraft were able to take part in the fighting, and the Germans were forced into retreat leaving some 16,000 dead behind.

After his success in routing Manstein's forces, Malinovsky was appointed to take command of the Stalingrad Front from Yeremenko (q.v.). It was shortly afterwards renamed the Southern Front. From then on he held a series of high ranks, commanding the South-western Front in the summer 1943 operations in the Ukraine, and Third and Second Ukrainian Fronts in Romania and Hungary in 1944. His Second Ukrainian Front finally took part in the occupation of Slovakia and Austria in 1945. His final wartime post was as commander of the Baikal Front in the brief conflict with the Japanese Kwantung Army in 1945. An intelligent and professional general who deserved to attain his high rank at an exceptionally early age, Malinovsky continued to serve after the war in a variety of important posts, including a period as Soviet defence minister from 1957.

MANNERHEIM, (Baron) Carl Gustaf Emil (1867–1951). Finnish general. After a career as a cavalry officer Mannerheim led the army of the newly independent Finland against Soviet-backed Communists in 1918, and after a victorious campaign was made regent of Finland. He declared the country a republic in 1919, but was defeated in the ensuing elections and retired. He was recalled to become chairman of the council of national defence, and in 1933 decided to fortify the Karelian Isthmus with the Mannerheim Line. He took command of his country's armies against the Russian invasion of 30 November 1939, at the age of seventy-two. The Mannerheim Line broke and he was forced to accept terms on 12 March 1940. In June 1941 on the second outbreak of war with Russia he again commanded the Finnish army.

Hitler (q.v.) visited him on 4 June 1942 to enlist Finnish aid for an attack on Leningrad and an assault on the Allied supply convoys to the Soviet Union. Mannerheim refused to commit his forces to either cause. He became president of the Finnish republic on 1 August 1944 and in September signed the armistice with the Soviet Union. He retired to Switzerland in March 1946.

MANSTEIN, Erich von Lewinski (1887–1973). German general, considered by many to be the most talented and able of all the German generals. Born Lewinski but adopted by the family whose name he took, Manstein joined the army and was commissioned before the first world war. He rapidly impressed all his superiors and rose to be head of the operations section of the general staff by 1935. In 1936 he was deputy to Beck (q.v.), the chief of staff, but was removed when Hitler (q.v.) sacked Beck and his colleagues in the army staff (OKH) and increased the importance of his own Nazi-dominated all-services staff, the OKW. Manstein was sent to command a division in Silesia, but just before the outbreak of war was made chief of staff to Rundstedt (q.v.) in the Polish invasion. Afterwards he and Rundstedt were transferred to the Western Front and without doubt it was Manstein who invented the idea of the armoured breakthrough in the Ardennes which brought about France's defeat. But Manstein's brilliance was already beginning to disturb the orthodox hierarchy and in January 1940 he was despatched to command 38 Infantry Corps, theoretically out of the way and unconnected with the armour. He responded by breaking through the French lines along the Somme and his corps was the first to cross the Seine, on 10 June. He was appointed to command the landing forces in the invasion of England. When that was called off he was placed in command of 56 Panzer Corps in East Prussia. There in the invasion of Russia he produced another breakthrough, and pushed his force on

Carl Mannerheim (front), Finland's greatest wartime figure as both soldier and statesman. He led his country's armies in the winter war with the Soviet Union.

200 miles in four days to reach the Dvina. He was held up from taking Leningrad, but mounted a further spectacular drive in mid-July to take Ilmen. In September 1941 Manstein was promoted to command the Eleventh Army which invaded the Crimea, besieged Sebastopol, and took the city in July 1942 after 250 days of siege, denying the Russian Black Sea Fleet their main base. After this, with something of a reputation for breaking sieges, he was moved north to take over the assault on Leningrad, but before he got there he was diverted to Stalingrad to become c-in-c Army Group Don, with the task of rescuing the beleaguered Sixth Army. He arrived there too late, and those forces which were not captured were thrown into retreat. However, Manstein organized the retreating forces and prevented the Russians from crossing the Dnieper.

His technique, which he naturally found it extremely difficult to 'sell' to Hitler, was to avoid the costly attrition of an unyielding resistance (for which he recognized the Germans had not sufficient numbers of troops) and instead roll with the Russian punch, allowing them deep penetrations which he could cut off with flank attacks using the manœuvrability of the panzer forces. He did this with devastating effectiveness in February and March 1943, and in a brilliant counter-offensive (Germany's last successful advance in the east) he threw the Russians back to the Donets and captured Kharkov. In the summer of 1943, commanding Army Group South, he proposed a series of alternative moves to defeat the Russians, including a pincer movement against the Kursk salient at the earliest moment before the Russians could organize themselves, and a tactical withdrawal in the face of the next Russian advance followed by an attack against its flanks from the Kiev region. Hitler rejected Manstein's suggestions as too risky, and instead forced on Manstein a pincer movement at a later date. By then the Russians were prepared and the defeat was all the heavier. The Russian counterstroke was more than the Germans could contain and, although Manstein conducted a skilful withdrawal to the Polish

General Erich Manstein (right) meets General Antonescu, the Romanian dictator.

frontier, Hitler was not satisfied. He considered stubborn resistance over every inch of ground the only fit tactic for German troops, and lost patience both with Manstein's brilliant manœuvring, and with his increasing tendency to stand up to the Führer, even to the point of telling Hitler to his face in open conference that some of his ideas were nonsense. In March 1944 Manstein was dismissed.

MARSEILLE, Hans Joachim (1919–42). Leading German fighter ace who served in the North African theatre. Marseille, a Berliner, had a reputation for indiscipline on the ground and dashing bravery in action. He arrived in North Africa in the spring of 1941 and joined the squadron 3/JG27, completing his journey to his base at Gazala in a chauffeur-driven car borrowed from an army general, after his aircraft had force-landed with engine failure. Once he began combat flying he quickly began to shoot down British planes,

using the dangerous tactic of flying aggressively straight into their formations, but also displaying exceptional gunnery and total mastery of the skill of deflection shooting. On 24 September 1941 he shot down five aircraft in a single day. By June 1942 he had taken command of his squadron, and flying his familiar yellow Messerschmitt, '14', he continued to accumulate 'kills' including seventeen claimed on 1 September. By 26 September 1942 his personal tally (so far as the claimed victories can be considered authentic) had reached 158. Then four days later his engine caught fire during a patrol, and he baled out after turning his aircraft upside down. His parachute failed to open and he was killed. Injuries indicated that his chest had struck the tail-plane. Aged only twenty-two when he died, Marseille had been awarded a series of decorations, including the Diamonds of the Knight's Cross.

General George C. Marshall, chairman of the United States joint chiefs of staff, and Roosevelt's indispensable military aide throughout the war.

MARSHALL, George Catlett (1880–1959). United States general and army chief of staff. Born in Uniontown, Pennsylvania, George Marshall always intended to become a soldier, and in 1897 entered the Virginia military institute, graduating in 1901. He joined the infantry, and in 1902 was commissioned as a second lieutenant. His first tour of duty was in the Philippines, after which he returned to the United States and in 1908 was appointed instructor at the army staff college. He saw further service in the Philippines, and in 1917 went to France with the American Expeditionary Force. By the end of the war he had risen to the post of chief of staff of 8 Corps. After the war he served in China, and as assistant commander at the infantry school. In 1938 he was made chief of the war plans division, and later that year became deputy chief of staff. In 1939 he was promoted to the rank of general and became chief of staff, an appointment which he held throughout the second world war. General Marshall was without doubt the greatest master of logistics of all time. Under his guidance the United States army expanded from a small, ill-equipped force of less than a third of a million men into a vast army with the most lavish equipment the world had ever seen. By the end of the war he had put more than eight million men into service. Marshall was a member of the combined chiefs of staff committee which determined strategy, and was a dominant figure at all the major international conferences, from Washington in 1941 to the vital discussions which determined the course of the war and its aftermath at Teheran in 1943, Quebec in 1944, and Malta, Yalta and Potsdam in 1945. Marshall was criticized after Pearl Harbor for failing to warn against the possibility of a Japanese strike at the American Pacific base, but he regained the confidence of President Roosevelt, and subsequently of President Truman (qq.v.). He was a remote, even enigmatic figure, but proved a reasonable and reliable though determined colleague both to his own generals and to the Allies. Because he never held high office in the field in any of the great land campaigns of the second world war, General George Marshall remains a less glamorous personality than some of the more colourful generals who directed the battles on the ground. Nevertheless his contribution to the success of the Allies in the war was inestimable. He was the master of organization, and therefore a key figure in a war in which material and supply were critical factors. He was also expert in the art of man-management, unfailingly appointing the right men for all the important posts. For example he recognized General Bradley's (q.v.) abilities as a commander and appointed him to command the Twelfth US Army Group after the Normandy invasion. But his clear-sighted appreciation of General Patton's (q.v.) dashing approach to armoured warfare led him to appoint Patton to command the Third Army for the key expansion phase into northern France. One of the basic tenets of Marshall's military

Marshall visits the American sector of the Normandy beach-head together with Admiral Ernest J. King, 1944.

outlook was that an officer should be appointed to the job for which he was most suitable, with no thought for personal feelings, and regardless of how useful he might be in his present post. He made only one exception to this rule – himself. Although Marshall thought he should take command of the Normandy invasion himself, President Roosevelt felt that he could not do without him in Washington. Marshall therefore remained in staff work, and ended the war a relatively obscure general compared with some of his subordinates. Retiring as chief of staff in 1945, he served as ambassador to China for two years, then returned to become secretary of state in 1947 and 1948, when he was responsible for the European recovery programme, more familiarly known as the Marshall plan. He was secretary of defence 1950–1, and was awarded the Nobel peace prize in 1953.

MARTEL, (Sir) Giffard (1889–1958). British general, engineering expert and tank pioneer. Martel's introduction to the tank came in 1916 when he was sent home from the trenches to design a training ground for the new tanks in preparation in Norfolk. He wrote a paper in 1916 forecasting the creation of 'tank armies' operating like ships at sea in fleets. His forecast was not precisely fulfilled, but was a useful early visionary concept. After the war he remained in the Royal Engineers, where he designed the Martel box girder bridge for use by tanks. He also invented a variety of military devices, often at his own expense and in his

Lieutenant-General Giffard Martel talks with men of his 1940–42 command, the Royal Armoured Corps.

private mobile workshop, including a one-man light tank, a bridge of rafts which was developed and used in Normandy in 1944, and another bridge of wooden crates. He commanded 50 Motorized Division in France in 1940, which counter-attacked Rommel's (q.v.) division and almost halted it. Later that year he was appointed commander of the Royal Armoured Corps in preference to Hobart (q.v.), the other candidate. The two men, formerly friends, soon disagreed on tank policy. Martel was removed from his post in September 1942 and later sent as head of the British military mission to Moscow. He retired in 1945. Martel's contribution to the theoretical side of tank tactics was not great, but his technical ingenuity and originality were considerable, and

should not be underestimated because of his over-enthusiastic ideas on the role of the new weapon. He was also all-services boxing champion at his weight, and was known for his practice of amusing himself in the first world war by dodging about an area under shellfire predicting where the shells would fall.

MASARYK, Jan (1886–1948). Czechoslovakian leader who became foreign minister in the government-in-exile in London. Masaryk was in London as his country's ambassador at the time of the German invasion. He became an important figure through his broadcasts to his fellow countrymen at home. In July 1940, when the provisional government under Benes (q.v.) was recognized, Masaryk became foreign minister. He remained in that post after the liberation of his country in 1945, and through the period of the Communist take-over in 1948. However he died shortly afterwards, apparently having thrown himself out of a window at the Foreign Office.

MERRILL, Frank (1903–1955). American general who commanded the raiding force known as 'Merrill's Marauders', which operated against the Japanese in the jungles of northern Burma in 1944. In many ways the counterpart of Wingate's (q.v.) Chindit force, they marched into the jungle from Ledo in February 1944, and after moving several hundred miles behind Japanese lines carried out a series of skirmishes and ambushes. Although exhausted, half-starved, and reduced by fever, the Marauders captured the airfield at Myit-kyina from the Japanese, and made possible the opening of the road from India to China. Merrill became the deputy commander of the United States forces in the China–India–Burma theatre, and later chief of staff of Tenth Army in Okinawa.

MIKOLAJCZYK, Stanislaw (1901–66). Polish leader who worked unsuccessfully to preserve the independence of Poland. Born of peasant stock, Mikolajczyk fought in the army against the German invasion of 1939, and escaped through Hungary to France. He travelled to England, and became deputy to General Sikorski (q.v.) as leader of the government-in-exile, and succeeded him on his death in 1943. He tried to establish a democratic Poland with good relations with the Soviet Union, but in June 1945 he was forced to abandon this ideal and joined the Russian-backed provisional government as minister of agriculture and vice-premier. Even then he was attacked and forced to flee the country two years later to avoid arrest and possible death. He settled in the United States after being branded a traitor and banished from Poland for life. (*See also* Smigly-Rydz)

MITCHELL, Reginald (1895–1937). Designer of the Spitfire fighter aircraft which formed the basis of Britain's victory in the Battle of Britain.

MITSCHER, Marc (1887–1947). American naval commander who served with distinction throughout the campaigns in the Pacific theatre,

Dr Jan Masaryk, Czechoslovakian politician and foreign minister in the government-in-exile in London, visits the Foreign Office in Whitehall during the Czech crisis, 12 September 1938.

General Frank Merrill, dressed and equipped for the jungle fighting which made him famous as the leader of the guerrilla fighters, 'Merrill's Marauders'.

notably as commander of the famous Fast Carrier Task Force. A native of Hillsboro, Wisconsin, Mitscher graduated from the United States naval academy in 1910. He was among the first naval officers to take up aviation, and in fact became the thirty-second to qualify for his wings, which he received in 1915.

In October 1941 he took command of the aircraft carrier *Hornet*, from which, on 18 April 1942, sixteen B-25 Mitchells took off for the Doolittle (q.v.) raid, the first air raid of the war against Japan. Mitscher's principal contribution during 1943 was as commander of the air forces in the Solomon Islands. In January 1944 he took command of the Fast Carrier Task Force, which covered the American landings in the Marshall Islands, and neutralized Truk on 17 and 18 February, making it unusable for Japanese planes. During 19–21 June 1944 he commanded the American fleet at the battle of the Philippine Sea. He was criticized for not flying night searches after dusk on 19 June, which some commentators felt

might have led to greater damage to the enemy fleet on the following day. His main justification was the desire to give his exhausted fliers a chance to rest after their daylight missions. It was on 20 June at 3.40 pm that he located his quarry, the Japanese First Mobile Fleet commanded by Vice-Admiral Ozawa (q.v.). Mitscher then launched a vigorous attack, flying 216 aircraft off his ten carriers in only ten minutes. Although hampered by gathering darkness, his planes shot down 65 of Ozawa's aircraft, and damaged several ships. The American planes then had to land in darkness. Mitscher contravened established practice, and deliberately ignored the threat from submarines, by lighting up his ships for the recovery. Nevertheless the night landings on the carrier decks remained a problem; almost half the aircraft landed on the wrong carriers, and eighty were lost, although most of the baled-out pilots were picked up by the force's destroyers. Mitscher's victory restored American control of the Philippine Sea. In 1945, carrier planes from Mitscher's force

Vice-Admiral Marc Mitscher aboard his ship USS *Lexington* at the battle of Saipan in the Marianas. The long-peaked cap became his trade-mark.

attacked the powerful battleship *Yamato* in the East China Sea. This magnificent ship represented new standards of battleship design, carrying nine 18·1-inch guns with a range of twenty-two and a half miles. But the carrier-borne air strike had abruptly rendered the battleship out of date, and in an hour and a quarter on the afternoon of 7 April Mitscher's aircraft flew wave after wave against the ship, pounding it to a shambles, until it sank with 2488 officers and men at 2.23 pm. Mitscher, the pioneer aviator, had demonstrated in the last months of the war that the naval air arm, in which he had placed his faith, had achieved irreversible supremacy over the battleship. No more battleships were subsequently built. Vice-Admiral Mitscher was well liked in the United States, partly because his weathered features and familiar long-peaked baseball cap made excellent photographic material for the press. At the same time

his quiet gentle manner, and determination to save pilots' lives by energetic rescue operations, made him popular with the navy.

MODEL, Walther (1891–1945). German general, and one of Hitler's (q.v.) favourite commanders. He picked up the nickname 'the Führer's fireman' from his ability to solve other people's problems. In the years before the war he served in the war ministry in training and technical roles, and came to Hitler's notice through his energy and lack of conservatism. He commanded 4 Corps in the Polish invasion and the Sixteenth Army in the French campaign. In Operation Barbarossa he commanded 3 Panzer Division with great energy and panache, and made a reputation for his ruthless offensive aggression. By the winter of 1941–2 he had risen to command of the Ninth Army, and by that time he was having to develop a comparable ability in the area of defensive tac-

Walther Model (left), promoted to field marshal after victories on the eastern front, was a firm favourite with the Führer, partly because of his blunt and unsophisticated manner.

tics. He was a strong influence on Hitler in the offensive against the Kursk salient, when he persuaded Hitler to delay the attack in order to build up stronger forces. Unfortunately the delay also enabled the Russians to build up their defence and the Germans lost heavily. He went on to command Army Group North in 1943 and Army Group South in 1944, then in June of that year was moved yet again to stem the Russian summer offensive as commander of Army Group Centre. After the July 1944 bomb plot on Hitler's life he was sent to take over the Western Front, where he was instrumental in holding back the offensive of the western Allies, with successes at Arnhem and in the Ruhr pocket, when he held up eighteen American divisions for nearly three weeks. He was extremely effective in scraping together reserves for spoiling attacks. Model was one of the middle-class officers with whom Hitler liked to deal in pre-

ference to the old guard of Prussian aristocratic officers. He had a talent for ignoring Hitler's orders and doing what he thought right, and what he thought the troops were capable of. At times he went further, and stood up to Hitler to argue over orders with which he disagreed. Preferring to die rather than surrender, he shot himself in the ruins of the Ruhr on 21 April 1945. It was an unnecessary death for an honourable and stainless soldier.

MOLOTOV, Vyacheslav (born 1890). Soviet foreign minister who worked closely with Stalin (q.v.) throughout the war and took over many of his responsibilities when Stalin's health began to fail in the late stages. In view of Stalin's reluctance to leave the Kremlin, Molotov was entrusted with all the major dealings with foreign powers. On 9 November 1940 he went to Berlin where Hitler (q.v.) suggested a four-power pact between Ger-

Stalin's foreign minister, Molotov (centre, in fur hat), sees off Winston Churchill and his party after the Yalta conference.

many, Russia, Italy and Japan. Stalin agreed, so long as German troops were withdrawn from Finland. On 13 April 1941 Molotov signed the neutrality and non-aggression pact with Hitler.

When the German invasion of Russia caused an abrupt change in foreign policy in the Soviet Union, Molotov went on missions to London and Washington, and on 26 May drew up the Anglo–Soviet 20-year alliance. He also obtained assurances, subscribed to mainly by Roosevelt (q.v.), that an invasion would be made by the western Allies against Germany in Europe in 1942. It was left to Churchill (q.v.) who travelled to Moscow in August 1942, to tell the Russians that such an invasion was not possible.

Molotov was a member of the five-man state defence committee with Stalin, Voroshilov, Beria and Malenkov, and attended all the major wartime conferences.

Apart from his solid work in pursuing Soviet interests throughout the war, Molotov was remarkable as possibly the most inscrutable major figure of any combatant nation, and he produced a variety of mainly mystified judgments from those who met him. At the foreign ministers' conference of 1943 Eden (q.v.) was impressed by his grasp of affairs. Churchill described him as a man of outstanding ability and cold-blooded ruthlessness who never displayed an inch of flexibility. The British ambassador reported that in conference with Molotov it was necessary to say exactly what you meant, neither more nor less, and repeat it over and over again in the same words before he understood what you meant. It was reported that the niceties of normal diplomacy were lost on Molotov, and that he was an ice-cool, stern, unyielding diplomat. Perhaps Stalin's judgment was the most cryptic. When someone observed to him that Molotov was brainy, he replied that Molotov was indeed a man with brains, but that his brains were stupid.

MONNET, Jean (born 1888). French economist and politician. In 1939 Monnet was concerned with the purchase of aircraft from the United States. In 1940 he was among the architects of the proposal for the Anglo–French union espoused by Churchill (q.v.) but rejected by the French government. He went to Washington, after France surrendered, as a diplomat for Britain. There he saw and warned about America's lack of preparedness for war, and was closely concerned with the programme to increase American war production – the so-called victory programme. In 1944 he became minister of commerce in de Gaulle's (q.v.) provisional government, and presided over France's post-war economic development and the establishment of the common market (EEC).

MONTGOMERY, Bernard Law (First Viscount Montgomery of Alamein) (1887–1976). British general, senior battle commander in the British army from August 1942 until the end of the war. Montgomery ranks as probably the most controversial British general of all time, and whenever the war is seriously discussed his name evokes passionate and partisan emotions. His opponents vilify him as a ponderous, over-cautious commander, an unpleasant individual. His supporters acclaim him as the general who took hold of a shattered Eighth Army on the verge of defeat, and by a process of solid professional skill and inspired leadership transformed it into an invincible war machine, before going on to command with the same qualities the Allied forces in the invasion of Europe and the British Army Group in the drive against the German homeland.

Born in Kensington, the fourth child of a clergyman, Montgomery was taken at the age of two to Tasmania, where his father was appointed bishop. He returned with his family to London in 1901 and was entered as a day boy at St Paul's School, Hammersmith. The school was doubly important in his military career. While at school he entered – almost inadvertently – the 'army class', which opened up to him for the first time a military career, and he returned to St Paul's to set up his headquarters there in the planning stage for the invasion.

Sandhurst was a natural choice after school, and his time there was notable more for his extrovert escapades than for any distinction in his studies.

Bernard Law Montgomery, one of the longest serving and most successful of western field generals. He made his name in the desert as chief of Eighth Army, and headed Twenty-first Army Group up to the end of the war. Montgomery lectured students as early as 1926 on the need for commanders to wear a distinctive hat.

He did however excel at sports, and after some set-backs in mid-term decided to apply himself to his work, with the result that in 1908 he passed out thirty-sixth of a hundred and fifty cadets. This was too low in the list to join the Indian army, as he had hoped, and he therefore joined the Royal Warwickshire Regiment.

The First Battalion of that regiment was garrisoned in India and he served there until 1912, when he returned to England. Then in August 1914, along with thousands of other officers in the British army, he was abruptly thrown into the holocaust of the first world war. He crossed the Channel on 23 August, and went into battle during the following night. He fought until 23 October, when he took a bullet in the chest from a German sniper. His life was saved by another man who came to his aid, was shot, and fell dead over Montgomery, taking several more bullets aimed at them. He was brought in after lying there for several hours and assumed to be dead, until he weakly signalled his plight to a doctor. The result was that his life was saved and he was taken unconscious to hospital in England, promoted to captain and awarded the DSO. He returned to France in 1916, served on the Somme, and became a staff officer with his corps. After the war he served with the occupation forces in Germany, completed a course at Staff College, and was posted to Ireland during the conflict with Sinn Fein.

It was during this period of his life, the end of the first world war and its aftermath, that much of Montgomery's character and outlook on military life were formed. He had seen, both in combat and as a staff officer, the appalling waste of life in the trenches, and the attitudes among higher echelons that regarded men as fodder for hopeless attacks regardless of the individual value of a soldier's life. From this experience he came to several profound conclusions which he applied with undiminished faith during the rest of his military career. One was the need for a plan: precisely organized and followed to the last possible detail. A second was his elevation to the top rank in importance of the soldier's morale, which he developed both by his insistence on putting the soldier serving with him in the picture, so that every man knew what he was fighting for and how his effort would fit into the wider battle, and by making himself seen by as many soldiers as possible and establishing a personal contact with them, in direct contrast to the remoteness of the senior commanders of the first world war. A third was his devotion to training. He set out to ensure that every man serving under him was extensively trained; and this, added to his insistence on having his soldiers well-equipped, led to his refusal to begin a battle prematurely, for which he was much criticized. The troops on the other hand revered him because they knew that their lives were not being wasted carelessly or needlessly. Overall, Montgomery's developing outlook amounted to a simple feature of his life – an almost unique devotion to the profession of soldiering, to the exclusion of practically all else. He had set out, as

he said, to 'dedicate himself to his profession, to master its details, and put all else aside'.

One of his most significant appointments during the inter-war period came in 1930, when he was appointed secretary of the committee in the War Office appointed to rewrite the army manual on infantry training. The job illustrated clearly Montgomery's approach to a problem. He sat down, virtually ignored the committee and set out his own views on infantry training. And when three members of the committee challenged his rights to this individual approach he proposed they should be disbanded so that he could get on with the job unimpeded. It was an illustration not merely of his supreme self-confidence, but of his single-minded refusal to be burdened by peripheral details which might distract him from the central task.

Later in 1930, Montgomery rose to command his own regiment, the Royal Warwickshires, and was responsible for keeping the peace in the early Arab–Jewish conflict in Palestine. He subsequently served again in India, and by the eve of war, in 1939, had taken command of 3 Division, one of the few forces in a state of combat readiness, serving as part of General Wavell's (q.v.) Southern Command and due to form part of the BEF for operations in France.

He had also during these years been married and widowed. The death of his wife left him devastated for a time, but following his recovery he devoted himself with even greater single-minded determination to the business of soldiering.

Under Montgomery, 3 Division was one of the divisions concerned with the BEF on the evacuation from Dunkirk. On 1 June 1940, Montgomery found himself back in Britain, and shortly afterwards under orders to re-embark for France. Then France fell, and Britain faced the threat of invasion. Montgomery was promoted to take over 5 Corps covering Dorset and Hampshire against the threat of invasion. There he put into effect his

Back from Dunkirk and playing a key role in anti-invasion measures as c-in-c south-eastern command, Montgomery inspects his troops.

own scheme for defending against an amphibious attack. He insisted on abandoning the concept of a defence on the beaches, as he recognized that a concentrated and well-organized enemy would punch through weak linear defence and fan out into open country beyond. Montgomery insisted on forming a mobile counter-attacking force from his well-trained troops, finding transport for them by commandeering the double-decker buses which were still, unbelievably, being used to amuse holiday-makers with pleasure trips along the front at Brighton.

He also, again, proved his eccentricity – his egocentricity even – by questioning and even countermanding orders from his Southern Command superior, General Auchinleck (q.v.), by going over Auchinleck's head with requests to the War Office, and by arranging the transfer to his corps, from other Southern Command units, of officers he wanted working under him. This abrasive self-confidence made him many enemies but did nothing to hinder his career: as others were moved up the promotion ladder or were moved out of posts of importance, Montgomery emerged as one of the few officers of outstanding ability and experience, and by December 1941 he had risen to head of South-east Command, with the rank of lieutenant-general.

In this capacity he was responsible not only for commanding Britain's most important anti-invasion forces, but also for planning the army side of the Dieppe raid, which was staged from his area. For a time it was one of the great controversies in Montgomery's career. It was one of his decisions to stage the raid without a preliminary bombardment. On the other hand, it should be recorded that the landing force had already been embarked and disembarked because of bad weather, after which Montgomery wrote to the commander-in-chief home forces urging that the raid should be cancelled 'for all time'. It was not. Montgomery had by then moved on to his next command, and the raid on 19 August 1942 went ahead with severe losses. Montgomery, as the originator of the plan, incurred much of the blame.

It was a blot on his otherwise stainless military record, but was soon lost in the successes of his subsequent command. The route by which Montgomery arrived at the climax of his career, command of Eighth Army in North Africa, was complicated. When Winston Churchill (q.v.) flew to Cairo on 3 August 1942 he had it in mind to remove Auchinleck who was then commanding both the Middle East theatre and Eighth Army, and appoint to these two posts Generals Alexander and Gott (qq.v.) respectively. Brooke (q.v.), the CIGS, dissuaded him, on the grounds that Gott was exhausted, and suggested that Montgomery would be the better choice to command Eighth Army.

Churchill then responded by hiving off part of the Middle East and setting up a separate command based on Persia and Iraq. Alexander would then command the North African theatre, newly named 'Near East Command'. He decided to ignore much good advice (including Gott's own) and put Gott in command of Eighth Army. Montgomery was to take over from Alexander command of the British component, First Army, in the Torch landings in north-west Africa. Then, on 7 August, General Gott's aircraft was shot down and he was killed. Montgomery came back into the picture, was appointed to command Eighth Army, and thus stepped on to the stage as the man responsible for bringing about the defeat of Rommel (q.v.).

It was at this point, his first command of an army in the field, that the serious controversies about Montgomery began to emerge, along with the bitter and lasting disputes about the quality of his generalship. The one fact which is beyond dispute is that Montgomery arrived on the scene at a favourable point in the Mediterranean war. His predecessor Auchinleck had brought Rommel to a standstill in the first encounter at El Alamein and Rommel had recognized that his opportunity for an offensive had gone. At the same time, while Rommel was being starved of supplies and reinforcements, Eighth Army was beginning to receive a steady flow of men and material which in a few months would give Montgomery a pre-

Wearing his Australian bush hat, a precursor of the famous black beret, Montgomery meets Brigadier Katsotas, commander of the Greek brigade in Eighth Army, August 1942.

ponderance of roughly two-to-one in tanks, men and air power, and even more in guns. At last, in addition, the British could count on superiority in quality, as new equipment became available from a geared-up American industry to replace the outdated material with which they started the war.

But perhaps the greatest area of contention arose over Montgomery's approach to the war. Once he had seen the state of the Eighth Army he had inherited (he considered it so demoralized and unorganized that he 'seized control' of Eighth Army on 13 August, two days before the transfer was officially due to take place), he set out deliberately to impose his personality on his force. It may

seem trivial, but in that process one of his most significant tools was his hat. He changed his general's peaked cap first for an Australian slouch hat, subsequently for the beret, which became his trademark. Some officers have expressed themselves horrified at the commander's obsessive concern with his hat instead of with his plans: Montgomery's concern was with getting himself known to the men. As he said: 'This beret is worth two divisions.' Also, since he considered remoteness from the men a failing in modern commanders, he drove out in his jeep daily to visit as many units as he could, making short incisive speeches on the 'we're going to hit 'em for six' theme.

In the desert, Montgomery developed a unique style of command, devoting himself to building up morale, leaving planning details to his staff.

His constant visiting of his units meant that Montgomery was not in close operational control of his army, but he was content to leave that to his chief of staff, Francis de Guingand (q.v.). He laid down the broad plan, and made the men under him responsible for working out the details, through the chief of staff. Senior commanders had access to him if they wished, but were obliged to state their business in ten minutes, and he would not discuss details with them. Montgomery considered it more important to get a proper ration of sleep in the caravan which he brought up to headquarters, to devote a certain time morning and evening to quietly thinking about the prob-

lems facing him, and to spend the bulk of his remaining time out among the men building up their morale for the coming battle.

It was the epitome of egocentricity, in the sense that Montgomery knew instinctively that much of the coming battles would depend on the projection of his own personality. In this he was quite ruthless, and his ruthlessness extended into the fighting of the first of his battles with the Afrika Korps. At Alam Halfa he took over a force that was dug-in in positions laid down by Auchinleck, and inherited a plan worked out under Auchinleck's regime. Montgomery adopted it, and presented it quite coldly as 'my plan'. It was of course no part of

Montgomery's brief to promote the interests of the deposed generals whom he and his selected colleagues replaced, only to win the battles, but it is this merciless refusal to acknowledge his debt to them, either at the time or after the war, which has so antagonized his critics and opponents. The battle of Alam Halfa took place, closely according to the pattern predicted by Dorman-Smith (q.v., Auchinleck's chief of staff) in his appreciation of 27 July, nearly three weeks before Montgomery arrived in the Middle East. Montgomery also angered his critics by claiming to have invented an armoured formation – a *corps de chasse*, which he called his panzer army. His predecessor had planned a new formation of a different kind – mixed armour, artillery and infantry. But Montgomery did not believe that the training of a formation wholly alien to British tradition could be accomplished in time, and elected to keep the tanks as a separate formation to be used as a striking force while the infantry was used as a vice in which the Afrika Korps would be pinned. In fact O'Connor (q.v.) had already used such a formation in 1940.

The Alam Halfa battle which was Montgomery's initiation into desert warfare began on 31 August with an advance by Panzer Armee Afrika. They were held up by 22 Armoured Brigade and, although they attacked again on 1 September, they made no progress. Rommel acknowledged his defeat and called off the attack.

Montgomery again defied his critics, this time by passing up the opportunity to counter-attack. He stated that he was going to 'loose the Eighth Army headlong into the enemy' but in fact he put off further offensive operations until late in October. Churchill had no alternative but to accept: after all he had only just put Alexander and Montgomery in command.

The attack at El Alamein began on 23 October, and again occasioned the fiercest criticism for Montgomery's mishandling of the armour, at great cost in tanks, against the advice of his armoured commanders. The battle lasted for twelve days of fierce fighting. Then Montgomery

was able to begin the pursuit, and gradually bore back the Axis forces: Tobruk, Benghazi, El Agheila, Tripoli. It was April before the Axis was defeated in North Africa, and then it required the aid of the troops approaching from the Torch landings in Algeria to accomplish it. Whatever else it was, Montgomery's North African campaign was not notable for its flair in tactical handling. In fact Rommel continued to attract approval from later commentators for the brilliance of his handling of his meagre forces in retreat.

Montgomery, on the other hand, had operated exactly as he said he would and exactly in keeping with his philosophy of war. He forced relentlessly onwards, spurning individual brilliance of any kind. As he had said when he arrived in North Africa: 'No more manœuvres – we will fight a battle.' And, 'This will be an *army* fight.' It was a measure of his dedication to the principle of mass force applied to eliminate risks. Whether it was right or not is still a matter of conjecture and debate. Perhaps the most appropriate comment is that of an Axis general, who declared, 'After Montgomery arrived war ceased to be a game.'

The North African campaign cemented Montgomery's reputation for all time, even if it was based more on the impact of his personality than the acknowledged quality of his generalship. But he still had two years of war to go, and other major campaigns to fight – Sicily, Italy and Europe.

In Sicily Montgomery came up against a new variation of the problem caused by his prickly personality. For the first time he had to accommodate himself to a reduction in his own role and work alongside an ally. Unfortunately it was General Patton (q.v.), whose own sense of his place at the centre of affairs was as strong as Montgomery's. The result was almost inevitably a clash. Patton's troops were assigned a minor role both in the invasion of the island and in the subsequent fighting. In the end Patton enjoyed his triumph in taking the town of Messina before Eighth Army. But Montgomery's real problem in Sicily was not so much learning to live with the other generals, as accepting that his own role would be proportionally reduced as the American forces took an increasingly important role in the war. Until now Montgomery had been answerable only to Churchill and his theatre commander Alexander, who imposed little restraint on him. Now he was forced to work under a new command structure, with Eisenhower (q.v.) as commander, Alexander as his deputy, and Roosevelt (q.v.) and Churchill jointly determining the Allied strategy above them. Montgomery was no longer in a position to fight

the war on his own terms, and for a general who had been elevated from relative obscurity to the status of international saviour in the course of nine months it was difficult. His difficulties were further increased in the campaign in Italy. There the parallel American general was Mark Clark (q.v.) who commanded the landing at Salerno shortly after Montgomery's forces had landed at Reggio. The misunderstandings and quarrels continued as Montgomery's forces were accused of

Montgomery entertains Churchill in Tripoli on 8 February 1943 after the tide had turned in the North African theatre.

moving ponderously towards a link-up with Clark's, and the American press portrayed Clark's Fifth Army as carrying the worst of the fighting. Montgomery made the problem even worse by refusing to receive General Clark at his Eighth Army tactical headquarters when the link-up was finally made.

But perhaps worse than this mixture of favourable publicity at home and hostile comment overseas was the fact that in Italy Montgomery came close to suffering a real military failure. His army was given the task of fighting up the eastern side of the Italian peninsula while Clark's fought in the west towards Rome. Montgomery himself pressed for a single combined assault, but his advice was ignored. And as the fighting progressed, and the weather changed with the onset of winter in late 1943, the Italian campaign began to look interminable. Overall, the Italian campaign is significant in Montgomery's career not so much for the fighting, although Eighth Army kept up the advance despite the appalling conditions, as for Montgomery's own fierce criticism of the strategic command, most seriously because he thought there was no overall plan. However, shortly after his forces had crossed the Sangro, and just as they were about to assault successfully the German Gustav Line, Montgomery was whisked out of the intractable Italian campaign to take over a vital part in the vastly more important assault in northern Europe, the cross-Channel invasion.

His introduction to this operation was characteristic. After saying farewell to his colleagues in Eighth Army he flew to Marrakesh where Churchill was recovering from an illness. Churchill showed him a plan and asked for his comments on it. It was New Year's Day 1944. After staying up half the night reading the document, Montgomery went back to Churchill the next day and told the prime minister that he could not comment on the plan since he had not had a chance to study it properly, and had not been able to consult the air and naval commanders. In any case, he pointed out, he was not the prime minister's military adviser. But Churchill pressed him, and Montgo-

mery, after underlining again his reservations about not being given time to study the plan and consult the appropriate people in detail, promptly pointed out that it would not do and would have to be dramatically revised. It was not an operation of war, he declared. The front was too narrow and the command structure was wrong. In fact when the invasion took place six months later it conformed closely to Montgomery's instant analysis, with a landing by three divisions of British Second Army (British and Canadian forces) to the west of the river Orne, and two American divisions of United States First Army on the western flank of the invasion area.

During the campaign in Europe he again caused frictions and problems on a personal level. There is strong if circumstantial evidence that some of his fellow generals anticipated the possibility of trouble in this area. When the decisions to choose the commanding generals were made, Montgomery was by no means high on the list. In the early planning Brooke (q.v.) was expected to take on overall command, but Churchill dropped him in favour of an American. Marshall (q.v.), the natural American choice, was needed in Washington by Roosevelt, and Eisenhower was therefore selected. The pick of the lower jobs then went to Britons. Tedder (q.v.) became Eisenhower's deputy, and Eisenhower, although he wanted the British to choose the land force commander without pressure from him, let it be known that he could work well with Alexander. Churchill also favoured Alexander, but Brooke persuaded them that Montgomery was the man to command the land forces.

From then on Montgomery reverted to the kind of role he had played with Eighth Army. Having laid down the overall plan, he left the details to his talented and loyal chief of staff de Guingand and the rest of the staff, and went off to build up the morale and fighting spirit of the armies. He had a personal train in which he travelled at night to leave the days available for meeting the troops. The train even carried its own road cars so that Montgomery could move independently away from the railways. He saw something like a million men in this way, inspiring them with the same simple message of faith in the battle, and perhaps more important boosting their morale by assuring them that their lives would not be thrown away needlessly: he promised the men that he would not send them into an attack without adequate air and artillery support, and he would never launch an operation prematurely. Against the usual accusations levelled at Montgomery as a ponderous, over-cautious setpiece battle commander must be set this declared concern for men's lives, expressed in his determination to set out his plan for a campaign and stick to it. To Montgomery that was the essence of good generalship; to judge him according to different criteria might, in view of the fact that he won his battles with almost boring consistency, be considered irrelevant.

As for the plan itself, Montgomery has been fairly universally condemned on two counts: firstly for failing to meet the 'phase-lines' for the various dates after the invasion; secondly for getting caught up in the battles around Caen, which was among the objectives for D-Day. With regard to the first criticism, it should be remembered that Montgomery himself only laid down one major objective for a specified day – D+90 for the arrival in Paris: the Allies got there eleven days earlier. In regard to the second it must be remembered that the war was being fought against an active and still powerful enemy, in many respects still one of the most formidable military forces ever assembled. And although Caen was perhaps a ridiculously over-optimistic target for D-Day, it was defended by 21 Panzer Division, and could hardly, therefore, be expected to fall like a ripe apple. In the last analysis Montgomery recognized, like other percipient generals, and unlike many hindsight commentators, that it is useless to plan too far ahead and in too much detail: such plans are certain to be confounded by events. He therefore evolved a plan to draw the German armour on to the anvil of the British at the eastern flank of the battlefront around Caen, while preparing for an American breakout on the western flank around

St Lô. And after the inevitable battles of attrition, and a build-up whose slowness began to worry almost everybody except Montgomery, including Eisenhower and Churchill, that is precisely what happened, with a free-running rampage in the succeeding weeks which left the Allies in command of Brittany, cost the Germans heavily in the Falaise pocket, and sent British and American forces racing on past the Seine into the Low Countries well ahead of schedule.

There were problems of course, which Montgomery seemingly dealt with by a policy of lofty detachment. At times during the Normandy battle he was in danger of being removed from his post. He survived, at least temporarily, but the damage to his relations with his superiors was too great to leave him unscathed. Having made the successful lodgment and established the Allies as the overwhelming masters of the Germans in western Europe, Montgomery felt with some justification that he should remain in command of the Allied land forces for the thrust into Germany. But the Americans had no desire to see Montgomery snatch all the glory as the conqueror of Nazi Germany. A new post-invasion command structure was set up, with two new army groups, and Eisenhower was persuaded to implement his planned intention to take over direct command of the land forces for the post-invasion phase. Effectively this demoted Montgomery to command of one British and one Canadian army. There were also in the field by this time four United States armies and one French army. Montgomery's role in the direction of the war was thereby dramatically reduced. His natural vision of himself at the pinnacle of the military pyramid however remained unimpaired, and this led inevitably to the last of his great wartime conflicts.

In the great strategic debate in 1944 and 1945 Montgomery maintained that the way to beat Germany in the shortest possible time was by halting the Allied effort on the right and concentrating all resources on a single thrust on the left through Belgium, into the Ruhr, and on to Berlin. While in command of the Allied land forces he had in

In Normandy, his most difficult battle, Montgomery failed to convey his intentions to colleagues and critics alike. Here he receives King George VI at the beach-head.

fact ordered Bradley (q.v.) to halt outside Paris. When Eisenhower took command of the land forces on 31 August 1944 Montgomery ceased to exercise strategic control of the battle. And Eisenhower's view was that a single thrust would expose long and vulnerable flanks to German counterattack, and would send Allied forces too far in advance of supply ports. He favoured the broad front strategy with an advance by all the Allied forces engaged. There was a tense interview between Montgomery and Eisenhower, after which Montgomery was forced to back down. However, he soon returned to the attack, and wrote to Eisenhower stressing his opinion that the broad-front strategy would produce no quick advance, and would give the Germans time to reorganize,

Montgomery reads the terms of surrender to grim-looking admirals Wagner (left) and Friedeburg on 4 May 1945.

thereby prolonging the war. He urged the supreme commander to put the land forces back under the control of a single man subordinate to Eisenhower. Eisenhower, he suggested, had a separate task to perform which was too concerned with international political matters for him to be able to concentrate on the battle on the ground. It appeared at first to be a typical attempt by Montgomery to boost his own role, except that Montgomery ended his letter (and a number of others which followed) by suggesting that if he himself was not suitable for the post of commander-in-chief in the field, Bradley should have the job, and he would be willing to serve under him. It was a demonstration that on this occasion at least Montgomery was willing, indeed anxious, to put personal considera-

tions below the winning of the war in the order of importance.

Eisenhower ignored this offer, and continued with his broad-front strategy, and Montgomery accepted that he had no alternative but to obey orders.

Yet the bitterness between the Allies flared up again, this time after the battle of the Ardennes. In this instance Eisenhower, reluctantly but unavoidably, put two American armies north of the German salient under the temporary control of Montgomery. The public and press were naturally inclined to see this as a case of the Americans not being able to cope with the German counterattack, and Montgomery being brought in to help the Americans out of a tricky situation. It was a view which Montgomery did nothing to attempt to dispel. The Americans, especially Bradley, were understandably incensed, but the order stood. Then Montgomery added further fuel to the argument by urging Eisenhower yet again to reorganize the command, and by stating bluntly that if Eisenhower gave him US Ninth Army, he would take the Ruhr. This was too much for Eisenhower, who banged his fist on the table during a meeting with Montgomery's chief of staff de Guingand, and declared that one of them would have to go, and London and Washington could decide which. This abrupt outburst finally brought Montgomery to heel. He sent an abject telegram to Eisenhower accepting his authority, and from then on behaved impeccably.

He also, incidentally, won his point. Eisenhower reorganized the command structure as Montgomery had recommended, and put Ninth Army under his control.

Relations between the two generals, and between the Allies, were restored, and remained so until the end of the war and after. The differences were accepted by both sides as minor divergences of opinion arising out of the tensions of the battle, and as having no particular consequences in the overall context of the war.

How then can the historian summarize Montgomery? At times he appears to be a simple phenomenon in military terms, a straightforward general devoid of any subtlety, and therefore easy to interpret. But other of his actions appear so incomprehensible as to deny any simple explanation, and his achievements are complicated by his very inconsistency.

In personal terms, almost any adjective can be applied to Montgomery, and most of them have been. He has been seen as simple, single-minded, pigheaded, cruel, callous, politically naïve, embarrassing, disagreeable.... But he was also a hero to millions of ordinary people, not only in his own country but throughout the Allied world. And the reason lies not in the complications of his own unfathomable personality, but in the simple fact of his military career: he was the senior and most ex-

perienced fighting general on the Allied side in the war, and the one, in Britain at least, best known for his cheerful commitment to victory. He refused to be defeated. Seen in those terms, his massive popular esteem was understandable. He was simply a winner.

One can only come to a compromise in attempting to assess Montgomery as a general. Perhaps the most illuminating comment on his fighting capacity is his own judgment. Asked to name the three greatest commanders in history he replied that the other two were Alexander the Great and Napoleon. The trouble with Montgomery is that you could never be sure that he was joking.

MORGAN, Frederick (1894–1967). British general who carried out much of the early planning for the amphibious invasion of occupied Europe which ultimately developed into Operation Overlord of D-Day 1944. After serving at Dunkirk and as a division and corps commander in Britain Morgan was appointed chief of staff to the supreme commander in March 1943. Known from then on by the title COSSAC, he set up headquarters in St James's Square, London, and rarely moved from his office, even sleeping beside his desk, until the plans were fulfilled. Initially he faced the problem of having no supreme commander yet appointed, and few resources to rely on, in view of other commitments in the Pacific and Mediterranean theatres. Among his plans was the idea for using artificial harbours – 'mulberries' – to solve the early supply problem to the beach-head. Morgan's role changed when Eisenhower (q.v.) was appointed supreme commander for the invasion early in 1944, and a more elaborate planning hierarchy set up under him. The result was a vast alteration in the scope of the landings and related planning for them. This nevertheless did not detract from Morgan's contribution in settling the basis of the plan in advance of any concrete prospects of its fulfilment. When Eisenhower arrived as supreme commander Morgan became deputy chief of staff at his headquarters.

MORGENTHAU, Henry (1891–1967). United States secretary to the Treasury from 1934 to

Roosevelt's long-serving Treasury secretary Henry Morgenthau (right) signs an aid agreement for China with T. V. Soong, China's foreign minister.

1945. Although his chosen profession was farming, and he was too shy to be successful in a campaign for political election, Morgenthau was selected by Roosevelt (q.v.) to lead the Treasury through the New Deal and the recovery from the depression. Working closely with Roosevelt he devised financial policies which led to the strengthening of the United States economy, particularly in building up massive gold reserves. His policies were complicated by the advent of war. He regarded defensive strength as vital, and was prepared to tax heavily and spend lavishly to bring about the defeat of his country's enemies. Morgenthau was a key figure in devising the Lend-Lease agreement for the supply of war material to Britain. In 1943 he took part in the Breton Woods conference in New Hampshire which formulated

plans for post-war reconstruction. His least successful enterprise was the plan to turn Germany into an agricultural economy after the war, as he believed that it was Germany's industrial capacity which had led to the two world wars. Churchill (q.v.) and Roosevelt had both signed the document supporting this idea, but later more judicious thoughts prevailed and led to its rejection by President Truman (q.v.). As a result of his disagreement with this pastoralization policy, Truman refused to take Henry Morgenthau to the Potsdam conference, and Morgenthau promptly resigned. He spent much of his retirement editing and publishing his voluminous letters and diaries, and the transcripts he kept of every conversation and meeting during his eleven years at the Treasury. **MORSHEAD, (Sir) Leslie** (1889–1959).

Australian general. Originally a schoolmaster, he joined the army in 1914 and served in Gallipoli and France. He took up business life after the first world war, but retained his interest in the army as a battalion commander in the citizen military forces. He was appointed commander of 18 Brigade on the outbreak of war and of the 9 Australian Division in February 1941. The division was sent to Cyrenaica, and he commanded the troops besieged in Tobruk during the eastward advance of the Afrika Korps. Rapidly developing a reputation as a tough and able commander of tough and able troops, he fought with his division at the second battle of El Alamein, and then commanded 1 Australian Corps in the amphibious operations against Borneo.

MOUNTBATTEN, Louis (Earl Mountbatten) (born 1900). British admiral who rose from the rank of captain in command of a destroyer at the beginning of the war to be supreme Allied commander South-east Asia at its end. Mountbatten was born into an aristocratic family and was related to most of the royal households of Europe. His father, Prince Louis of Battenberg, served throughout his life in the Royal Navy, and at the outbreak of the first world war held the office of first sea lord, the senior naval post in Britain. Then in the hysterical wave of anti-German feeling that spread throughout Britain Prince Louis was hounded out of office because of his own German ancestry. The young Louis Mountbatten, then a sea cadet in training for the Royal Navy, remained determined to succeed in the face of this slur on his family's reputation. As a young sailor he specialized in signals, being astute enough to recognize that in the future the success of the navy would depend largely on the quality of its communications.

Shortly before the outbreak of the second world war Mountbatten was appointed to command the Fifth Destroyer Flotilla, and on 23 August he took over his newly commissioned ship HMS *Kelly*. After completing the commissioning and storing of the destroyer in three hectic days (three months is the normal time) Mountbatten was quickly into

action in an encounter with a German submarine which the *Kelly* claimed she sank. In December 1939 the first serious damage to the *Kelly* occurred when she was ordered to hunt for submarines which had blown up four ships in the mouth of the Tyne. In the course of the search the ship collided with a mine which exploded under the stern, but she was able to limp back to port. From then on the *Kelly* was frequently in action. At the end of April 1940 the ship was torpedoed in the North Sea and limped back towards Scapa Flow in serious danger of sinking. In a night of increasingly rough seas Mountbatten was forced to transfer the entire ship's company to other destroyers while under fire from German aircraft, in order to reduce the topweight and avoid a capsize. He was also ordered to scuttle her to release his escorting ships for other duties, but he refused to do so, claiming that the *Kelly* had enough ammunition to look after herself without escorts. Eventually they made port, where the builders were astonished that she had survived. Mountbatten remained in service in the other ships in the flotilla, and consolidated his reputation for skilled seamanship, daring and considerable luck. Repairs to HMS *Kelly* were completed in November 1940, and the Fifth Destroyer Flotilla was ordered to the Mediterranean. In May 1941 the flotilla was ordered to aid the Allied forces in Crete, and on that mission they were attacked by a force of Stuka dive-bombers. *Kelly* was sunk, and Mountbatten narrowly escaped drowning. He was picked up by the *Kipling* and this ship also was attacked and damaged, but finally reached Alexandria.

Mountbatten was next appointed to command the aircraft carrier *Illustrious*, then being repaired in the United States, but before it was ready to sail he was recalled personally by the prime minister Churchill (q.v.), to take up the post of adviser on combined operations. He tried to decline the appointment, but Churchill, who considered that Mountbatten's eventful war career ideally fitted him for the post, challenged him with lacking a sense of glory: if he stayed where he was he would achieve little except being sunk 'in a big-

Lord Mountbatten (centre), then chief of combined operations, with Montgomery in Sicily in 1943.

ger and more expensive ship'. A programme of raids at the end of 1941 and early in 1942 kept the combined operations organization busy, and included commando expeditions to Norway on 26 December 1941, Bruneval in February, and St Nazaire in March. But most of Mountbatten's attention in the early weeks was devoted to recruiting men for the organization, and persuading officers in all three services, but notably the Royal Navy, that combined operations was worth having at all.

Significant changes began to arise as a result of the entry into the war of the United States of America in December 1941. Churchill had hinted to Mountbatten on his appointment that although raiding and sustaining an offensive spirit were the first tasks, he should not lose sight of the main and

ultimate aim, the invasion of France. Now American planners were quickly drawn into the discussion on the eventual amphibious assault on France, and Mountbatten's position as head of combined operations became one of great importance. In March this importance was recognized when Mountbatten's title was amended from 'adviser on' to 'chief of' combined operations; he was also given the acting rank of vice-admiral in the Royal Navy, as well as lieutenant-general in

Opposite The Quebec conference, August 1943. Roosevelt and Field-Marshal Dill (seated) pose for pictures with Churchill and Canadian premier Mackenzie King.

Overleaf The Allied leadership for Operation Overlord, the invasion of northern France. From the left are Bradley, Ramsay, Tedder, Eisenhower, Montgomery, Leigh-Mallory, and Bedell-Smith.

the army and air marshal in the Royal Air Force. And he became a full member of the chiefs of staff committee. Then in August came the Dieppe raid. It was a conspicuous failure, in which 3336 men were lost out of the 5000 engaged. The details of the raid have been argued about ever since, but there is universal agreement that it provided invaluable experience for the planning of the assault in Normandy in 1944. By a clear chain of consequences, therefore, Mountbatten played a key role in the success of that invasion. The political and military leaders of Britain and America recognized this when they wrote to Mountbatten one week after D-Day in 1944, saying that they had visited the beach-head, sailing through vast fleets, and watching the landing craft pouring men and equipment ashore in the build-up. They realized, they wrote, that the success of the venture had its origins in the developments effected by Mountbatten and his staff at combined operations. This remarkable tribute was signed by Arnold, Marshall, King, Brooke, Smuts and Churchill (qq.v.).

But a year before this event Mountbatten had been transferred to another theatre of war, as supreme commander South-east Asia. His appointment was again the result of Churchill's intervention, after the prime minister had observed that 'there is no doubt of the need of a young and vigorous mind in this lethargic and stagnant Indian scene'. The Japanese were in control of Burma, and there seemed little likelihood of a major Allied offensive being mounted in the theatre. Mountbatten arrived in India on 7 October 1943 and found himself at the centre of a complicated military command structure which included Field-Marshal Wavell (q.v.) as viceroy of India, General Auchinleck (q.v.) as commander-in-chief India, and the American general Stilwell (q.v.) as deputy supreme commander, holding a complicated variety of other military and political posts. There was also General Chiang Kai-shek (q.v.), the Chinese leader whom Mountbatten was

Field-Marshal Erwin Rommel, 'the desert fox', pays one of his frequent visits to his men in the desert.

to describe as 'the worst headache I had to cope with'. Moreover Mountbatten had serving under him three British service chiefs, of whom the naval one was senior in rank to Mountbatten. Then there was Orde Wingate (q.v.), who had separate orders from Britain to carry out his long-range penetration operations aimed at cutting communications behind Japanese lines. Equally disturbing to the new supremo was the morale of the troops, which had sunk to a low level after their defeat by the Japanese. They were suffering badly from the high incidence of tropical disease, and because of their low standing in the list of priorities they had taken to calling themselves the 'forgotten army'.

Mountbatten went on a tour of as many units as possible, trying to restore their belief in themselves and in the part they were playing in the war. Aside from these difficulties, Mountbatten's main problem was to obtain agreement on the specific aims for his south-east Asia forces. Churchill's inclination was to press for an attack on Sumatra, bypassing the Japanese armies in Burma which would be dealt with at a later date, but amphibious operations were rendered impossible by the withdrawal of landing craft. The Americans were pressing for an attack in northern Burma by the spring of 1944, aimed at establishing overland communications with China. Chiang Kai-shek himself condemned such a plan on the grounds that unless the Allies controlled the Indian Ocean the Japanese could retake all lost territory. In the end Mountbatten's role was reduced to four strictly limited operations, by Stilwell in the north, 4 Corps on the Central Front, Wingate behind the Japanese lines, and 15 Corps in the Arakan. In January Mountbatten sent a mission to London and Washington to present his views, but found that he could get no agreed orders on operations. Stilwell also sent a separate mission, the result of which was a widely circulated accusation that Mountbatten had acted feebly in Burma, and a demand that the British should support Stilwell's operations in northern Burma. The American chiefs of staff wrote to the British chiefs of staff recommending as much. Roosevelt (q.v.) added his weight to the argument when on 25 February he wrote to Winston Churchill urging an all-out drive in Burma. A month later, on 24 March, the Americans promised to provide 100 transport aircraft a month for four months beginning in July. It seemed that the Americans were prepared to back the British supreme commander when his own political leaders were not. In the event, the prospects of an offensive in Burma were wiped out when the Japanese took the initiative in their 1944

summer offensive, which opened on 15 March. Far from bringing a vigorous new offensive spirit to the theatre, Mountbatten was forced into taking desperate measures to prevent the Burma Front from disintegrating. Throughout April and into May the offensive of Mutaguchi's (q.v.) Fifteenth Army threatened to break Slim's (q.v.) Fourteenth Army. But eventually the Japanese supply position deteriorated, the Allies improved theirs, and the Fifteenth Army, fought to a standstill in early July, was forced into a retreat. From then on the

April 1945: a victory in Asia is in sight. Mountbatten, sent to Asia to revitalize a badly run-down theatre, gives one of his innumerable talks to the men, at the Royal Naval Transit Camp, Colombo, Ceylon.

Allies took and held the initiative, and by June 1945 had completed the re-conquest of Burma. Mountbatten took the salute at a victory parade in Rangoon. From that time on, Mountbatten's main task was the re-conquest of Malaya, and he planned a massive amphibious operation involving 250,000 troops sailing from five bases including Bombay, 2000 miles from the Malayan coast. In fact the invasion was unopposed because of the Japanese surrender following the dropping of the two atomic bombs. Mountbatten signed the surrender document for the Allies at the formal ceremony in Singapore's municipal buildings on 12 September.

After the war Mountbatten's career was characterized by both the diversity and varying stature of succeeding occupations. Initially he was concerned with the problems of repatriating 750,000 Japanese prisoners of war, and rehabilitating the Allied prisoners. He was subsequently involved in the diplomatic problems associated with the rise of nationalism in Asia and the end of colonialism, notably in Singapore, Indo-China, Indonesia and India. He became viceroy of India, and presided over the partition of the sub-continent. In 1947–8 he served as governor-general of the new India. Some critics held Mountbatten to be responsible for the disorders which followed partition, and he was widely criticized in Britain. On his return home in 1948, he asked to go back to the navy, and was given a relatively minor post as commander of the first cruiser squadron in the Mediterranean, with the rank of rear-admiral. He was subsequently made fourth sea lord, commander-in-chief Mediterranean, and c-in-c Allied forces in the Mediterranean. Eventually he rose to be first sea lord in 1955, and in 1959 chief of the defence staff.

MURPHY, Audie (1924–1971). United States soldier who won more decorations for bravery than any other serving man. He was awarded the Medal of Honor during the battle in the Colmar pocket in January 1945, along with twenty-seven other decorations. After the war he made a successful career as a film actor.

First-Lieutenant Audie Murphy, America's most decorated soldier ever, and at the age of twenty the holder of every award for courage in the US Army. He is photographed after receiving the highest award, the Congressional Medal of Honor, together with the Legion of Merit.

MUSSOLINI, Benito (1883–1945). Italian dictator and war-leader. Widely considered the most ludicrous and comic of the major wartime figures, of whom little of merit can be said. His only real achievement lay in the economic improvements of his pre-war career which are customary in dictatorships but almost invariably won at the expense of repression and inhuman treatment of opponents. Mussolini was born in Dovia, the son of the village blacksmith and schoolmistress. After a school career distinguished for its rebellion against authority, he went to Switzerland in 1902 to escape from Italian poverty, and earned a meagre living labouring. He crossed the authori-

216

ties there by indulging in revolutionary propagandism, was expelled, and returned to Italy to complete his obligatory military service in 1904. 1908 saw him editing a socialist paper in Austria, from where he was also expelled. From then on Mussolini's life ran an archetypal course through the turmoil of revolutionary politics – left-wing journalism, prison for inciting riots, struggle against socialist moderates, more journalism, persistent quarrelling with the authorities, and then the war. The first world war gave Mussolini an excellent opportunity to add the requisite decoration to his list, that of an honourable wound, though he subsequently glossed over the fact that he received it in an accident at bombing practice. After the war it was again the familiar pattern, a series of attacks against both progressive democracy and the establishment, which prospered in the unstable economic atmosphere of the 1920s. Having started the Fascist movement in 1919, two years later he secured election to parliament, and by tough measures, including armed attacks on strikers and a march on Rome, he emerged as the only man strong enough to restore stability, and in 1922 was invited to form a government. On 3 January 1925 he converted his position to that of dictator, with the title Il Duce. From then on the strength of his own position steadily increased as he tightened his grip on potential opposition, stifling the trades unions, abolishing the right to strike and setting up tribunals to try political crimes. He also fixed the exchange rate of the lira, set up an industrial reconstruction institute, and drained the Pontine marshes to produce 200,000 acres of new farmland. This mixed record of harsh repression and imaginative reconstruction was not enough for Mussolini. Conquest and expansion were vital to sustain him in his concept of his own position, and in 1935 he invaded and conquered Ethiopia. Then in 1936 he sent troops to aid Franco's rebellion in the Spanish civil war, and in 1939 invaded Albania. On 22 May 1939 he signed

the Pact of Steel with Hitler (q.v.), although he felt that war had come too soon and at first proclaimed a policy of non-belligerency. By 22 June 1940, however, after the collapse of France and with the defeat of Britain apparently imminent, there seemed little profit in such a course and Mussolini declared war on France and Britain. His campaign in the Alps against the French was easily held in check, but the influence of the Italian navy in the Mediterranean proved a serious threat to Allied shipping. Britain had to reinforce her armies in North Africa by the long sea route round the Cape. But the main consequence of the Italian declaration was the overwhelming superiority of forces Mussolini could bring to bear in North Africa: 200,000 in Eritrea and Abyssinia, and even

An official portrait from 1923 shows Mussolini determined and resolute, and on the way to dictatorial power.

'We must prepare for war not tomorrow, but today', says Mussolini. With King Victor Emmanuel he supervises army manœuvres on 26 August 1934.

more in Cyrenaica under Marshal Graziani (q.v.) facing the small British contingent guarding Egypt. In the last months of 1940 and early in 1941 Graziani's armies were routed by the numerically inferior troops of General O'Connor (q.v.). The remnants of the Italian army, and incidentally of Mussolini's prestige, were saved by the British decision to divert Wavell (q.v.) to the aid of Greece, from where they were soon ejected by a strong German force. Equally unimpressive was the Italian performance in Ethiopia, where the commander, the Duke of Aosta (q.v.), surrendered a total of 230,000 Italian troops on 19 May 1941. From then on Mussolini proved to be something of a liability to the Axis. But despite his dependence on German help, his faith in himself remained unimpaired, and when Rommel's (q.v.) advance of May 1942 took the Afrika Korps to the Egyptian border, Mussolini flew into Derna, with a white charger following in the next aircraft for his triumphal ride through the streets of Cairo.

In the course of the next year, Mussolini's power gradually declined as his grasp of reality became less secure. He continued, nominally, to exercise

Mussolini settles down to earnest discussion with Hitler in the Führer's private train. The Pact of Steel proved an embarrassment to the Germans.

supreme command in North Africa, but it was an impatient Rommel who testily pointed out the impossibility of conforming to his directives. His real test came after the battle for Sicily, which was defended by 195,000 Italian troops and 60,000 German. The failure of the Axis forces to hold the island meant the conquest of the first Axis home territory. And the threat to the Italian mainland from powerful American and British forces was evident. In Rome, discontent with Mussolini was growing, and even among his closest staff there were men who wanted to see him removed. His new chief of staff, General Ambrosio, and the Duke of Acquarone, a minister of court, were anxious to end Fascism and restore the king. But it was on the former military leader, Marshal Badoglio (q.v.), that the burden fell of carrying out the dangerous process of removing Il Duce. In concert with the king, Badoglio and his associates hatched a plot to arrest him. At the same time the Fascist grand council insisted that Mussolini call a meeting, aimed at reviving their party's fortunes. Events were obviously running out of Mussolini's control. When he entertained Hitler at Rimini on 19 July 1943 his new chief of staff urged him to tell Hitler that Italy could fight no longer. Mussolini could not bring himself to do so. But the surest sign of the weakness of the dictator's position was that he could not even stifle his own opposition any longer, and on 22 July a leading Fascist, Dino Grandi, told Mussolini that he would propose, at the meeting of the grand council to be held two days later, that he intended to call for the restoration of the king as commander-in-chief of the armed forces, and the formation of a national government. Mussolini turned up to argue his case at the grand council, and a nine-hour debate followed, a heated affair which eventually faded to a quiet ending. Mussolini, as he confessed in his memoirs, still had not got the picture, and after spending the morning in his office went to see the king at five o'clock that afternoon. It was the king who told him that his end had come. Mussolini made a blustering protest, but the audience was over. Outside the king's villa, a captain of the

Carabinieri approached Mussolini and told him he was being offered 'protection'. Whatever name it carried, this spelled the end of his political power; he was taken away and two days later sent to the Island of Ponza. After twenty-one years of leadership, Mussolini's power was ended, but the last two scenes in his tragi-comedy had still to be played.

On 12 September, four days after the announcement of the armistice in Italy, Hitler laid on a force of ninety parachutists led by Captain Otto Skorzeny (q.v.) to snatch Mussolini from his latest confinement in a hotel 6500 feet up in the Abruzzi mountains. In a raid of great daring and efficiency, they crash-landed by glider, burst into Mussolini's room, and flew him away in a Storch light aircraft. He was taken eventually to Hitler's headquarters for a reunion of the two Axis leaders in Europe, and the Führer, determined not to accept without a fight the desertion of Italy from the Axis, set up a rival government to the new Badoglio regime, in which Mussolini was proclaimed head of the new Fascist Socialist republic. Mussolini lasted for another eighteen months, until 28 April 1945. Three days earlier, with the British and American forces advancing relentlessly through northern Italy, the Italian partisans had staged an uprising and were attacking the German troops with enthusiasm and surprising efficiency. Mussolini, a shadow of his former commanding self, attempted to escape by hiding in the back of a German lorry, in a convoy of retreating Germans, wearing a German soldier's uniform and taking with him his mistress Clara Petacci. A group of partisans intercepted the convoy and searched the lorry, and one astonished political commissar recognized Il Duce. Mussolini and Clara were taken to a nearby farmhouse. They might have been safe but for the bitterness of a small Communist caucus within the partisan movement. They discovered the hiding-place, and sent a Communist member of the volunteer freedom corps to eliminate the former dictator, principally to keep him out of the hands of the Allies and prevent a war crimes trial. The man, Walter Audisio, burst into the couple's bedroom, and told them, 'Hurry, I have come to rescue you.' They followed him and were taken in his car down the road. He stopped, ordered them out, and made them stand against a wall. Clara, by all accounts, screamed in protest and tried to shield her lover's body from the bullets. Audisio shot them both. Their bodies were flung into a removal van with those of fifteen other leading Fascists, and taken into Milan. There on the following day the two mutilated corpses were hung upside down from the girders of a partly built garage in the Piazzale Loreto. The public humiliation was an ignominious end which not even Mussolini can have deserved to suffer at the hands of his own countrymen. (*See also* Ciano)

MUTAGUCHI, Renya (born 1888). Japanese general, commander of the Fifteenth Army in Burma in the 1944 drive against Imphal, which ended in defeat for his army and his removal in disgrace from its command. Mutaguchi, the son of a well-to-do family which had fallen on hard times, enrolled at the military academy in 1908. After spells at staff college as both student and instructor he became embroiled, as did most of his fellow officers, in the political movements of the 1930s. He joined first the Cherry Society and later the Imperial Way. After the abortive coup staged by members of the Imperial Way in 1936, Mutaguchi was posted to Peking for his suspected complicity. There he played a leading role in engineering the 'Peking Incident' which led directly to war with China. For the uncompromising toughness he showed then he was singled out for rapid promotion by Tojo (q.v.), war minister and later prime minister. As a lieutenant-general in 1942, he commanded the 18 Division in the attack on Malaya, and was threatening the town of Singapore when the British commanders decided to surrender. In March 1943 he took command of the Fifteenth Army in Burma. The Burma Area Army was planning an offensive against Assam and India, primarily as a defensive measure to secure control of the Imphal plain and the mountainous passes between Assam and Burma, thereby forestalling an Allied offensive for the 1944 dry season. For Mutaguchi it was much more: his proposal was that holding attacks should be staged in the north by Honda's Thirty-third Army and in the Arakan to the south by Sakurai's Twenty-eighth Army. Mutaguchi's army would then advance in the centre and capture the vital town of Imphal. From there, he privately speculated to himself, the way would be open for an advance on India, where he was assured the people were ripe for revolution and straining to overthrow the British and welcome the Japanese as liberators. He saw himself riding into Delhi on a white horse. As a result of Mutaguchi's wistful vision the 1944 advance has taken the name of 'the march on Delhi', although the concept was not subscribed to either by the Burma Area Army or by imperial headquarters in Tokyo.

When the time came for the offensive, Mutaguchi began to engage in a series of disputes with his senior commanders, including the BAA commander-in-chief General Kawabe, and with his juniors, most notably the 33 Division commander Lieutenant-General Yanagida, who turned out to be dilatory and lacking in resolution. Despite the customary Japanese problem of securing supplies, Mutaguchi went on with his plans. The battle was due to start on 15 March, and despite dire warnings from his staff Mutaguchi was confident. He even ordered aircraft to be ready to fly in the army's geisha girls and prostitutes ten days after D-Day. He was not even perturbed by reports that Orde Wingate's (q.v.) second Chindit operation had begun, with Allied forces now operating in the jungle behind his own lines. Mutaguchi was warned by his air experts that in view of Wingate's operation and Allied air attacks the Japanese supply system could be badly disrupted. They recommended that he should call off the Imphal offensive until Wingate's forces had been wiped out. Mutaguchi refused. At first the operation went well. In four days his army, advancing in nine large columns, stood within thirty-six miles of Imphal. Then the hold-ups began. Yanagida failed to sustain his attack on Imphal from the

south, and at the same time the Allies brought in reinforcements from India. They also held the advantage which time and again proved decisive – air domination. By 10 April Mutaguchi was despairing of completing the capture of Imphal. To the north General Sato's 31 Division had done particularly well: his forward patrols had invested Kohima, and the way lay open to push on forty miles and capture the Allied base at Dimapur, the railhead and storage depot where enormous quantities of food, fuel, ammunition and vehicles awaited capture. Mutaguchi called BAA for air cover to protect Sato's advance, but Kawabe turned him down with the remark that Dimapur was not within the Fifteenth Army's strategic objectives. During the next few weeks the setbacks for the Fifteenth Army continued. By 18 April a counter-attack ordered by General Slim (q.v.) had relieved the garrison at Kohima, Sato's division was becoming starved of supplies, and Wingate's long-range penetration groups were beginning to exert an influence. In one operation they ambushed twenty transport companies and intercepted vital ammunition and supplies intended for the divisions attacking Imphal.

The keys to the battle, as usual, were proving to be not the courage of the men or tactical skill of the generals, but the steady flow of supplies, the availability of reinforcements, and command of the air space. At this stage in the battle the Allies had all three; Mutaguchi had none. In May, as the rains came and made campaigning even more difficult, Mutaguchi sent out increasingly hysterical orders calling for greater efforts from the troops: 'If your hands are broken fight with your feet. If your hands and feet are broken use your teeth. If there is no breath left in your body, fight with your spirit. Lack of weapons is no excuse for defeat.' At the same time he alienated his fellow officers with orders which were little more than insults. In the end Lieutenant-General Sato ignored him and ordered his beaten and starving men to withdraw from Kohima. And when Mutaguchi threatened him with a court-martial Sato's reply was simple: 'Go ahead. I'll bring you down with me.'

Then Sato bluntly told Mutaguchi that the tactical ability of his Fifteenth Army staff was below that of cadets. Eventually, during July, the British Fourteenth Army reached the Chindwin. On 8 July Mutaguchi was ordered by the Burma Area Army to withdraw. Two-thirds of his entire army strength was lost, and the remainder was in no condition to fight. After this failure, Mutaguchi lay for some time under the threat of court-martial, but fortunately for him imperial headquarters had no desire to air the causes of the Burma failure in public. In December he was simply relieved of his army command.

Mutaguchi was in many ways a simple man, probably too simple to fit successfully into the complex patterns of warfare that emerged between 1941 and 1945. He was aggressive beyond measure, a fighting man of phenomenal personal bravery in the tradition of the Japanese *samurai* warrior. But the lesson of Mutaguchi's career (which he personally never learned) was that for a soldier in high command blind aggression divorced from political skill was useless. When he used that aggression to impose his ideas on his chiefs, bludgeoning them into an attack on Imphal which they never really wanted, he should not have been surprised when they left him isolated. A similar dominance of aggression over discretion had almost cost the panzer leaders their success in 1940, and nearly destroyed General Patton in 1944. The difference in Mutaguchi's case was that his colleagues would not come to his rescue. As Mutaguchi found to his cost, the essential quality of a modern army commander is to fit accurately into the overall strategic pattern. The code of *bushido* and the cry of *banzai* were not enough.

N

NEURATH, Konstantin von (1873–1956). German diplomat who served as protector of occupied Czechoslovakia, 1939–41. An experienced and intelligent diplomat, he served in a variety of posts and was foreign minister 1932–8, when Hitler (q.v.) dismissed him after Neurath had opposed Hitler's aggressive policies. He was made protector of Czechoslovakia in 1939, but was too easy-going for Hitler, who dismissed him in 1941 and replaced him with the infamous Heydrich (q.v.). He was put on trial at Nuremberg after the war and sentenced to fifteen years' imprisonment.

Konstantin von Neurath, enjoying the pinnacle of his career as a dipolomat on a visit to London with his wife.

1945, and a transformed Neurath faces trial at Nuremberg. A fifteen-year sentence consigned him to Spandau.

Fleet-Admiral Chester Nimitz signs the Japanese surrender document aboard USS Missouri, backed by General MacArthur, Admiral Halsey and Rear-Admiral Forrest Sherman.

NIMITZ, Chester William (1885–1966). Senior American admiral of the Pacific theatre. After a career which encompassed a wide variety of seagoing commands, Chester Nimitz was serving as chief of the Bureau of Navigation when Pearl Harbor brought the United States to war. Ten days later Roosevelt (q.v.) selected him in preference to twenty-eight senior admirals to take command of the United States Pacific Fleet. In 1942 he took overall control of Allied forces in the Pacific Ocean and Central Pacific Commands, in parallel with General MacArthur's (q.v.) Southwest Pacific Command. His greatest operational achievement was without doubt the battle of Midway. With knowledge of Japanese naval codes provided by his intelligence services he was able to assemble a large fleet to counter the planned Japanese offensive at Midway, with land-based aircraft from Midway and Hawaii to support the ships. He directed the battle from his land HQ at Pearl Harbor, and severely defeated Admiral Yamamoto's (q.v.) fleet, sinking four Japanese carriers, a cruiser and a destroyer. Midway spelled the end of Japan's chance of dominating in the Pacific, and from then on Nimitz completely undermined Japan's capacity to wage war. He was a signatory of the Japanese surrender document aboard the USS *Missouri* in September 1945.

O

O'CONNOR, (Sir) Richard Nugent (born 1889). British general who as commander of the Western Desert Force in 1940 and 1941 defeated the Italian forces in North Africa. The desert campaign began in earnest in September 1940, when Mussolini ordered Marshal Graziani (qq.v.) to advance against Egypt. After sixty miles of progress, at Sidi Barrani he dug in and prepared to move to the next objective – Mersah Matruh. To defeat the Italians O'Connor devised a plan which is widely acknowledged to have been daring, original and highly imaginative. It called for his small force of 36,000 men to penetrate the group of Italian desert camps, then attack each one in the rear. After a risky approach march through the desert O'Connor's force attacked at dawn on 9 December 1940, and caught the Italians by surprise. In a series of attacks during the next three days they employed tanks to great effect, and also benefited from a mobile and aggressive style of command from O'Connor himself. By the night of 11 December 1940 the Western Desert Force had captured 38,000 prisoners and seventy-three tanks. It was an annihilating victory.

Following that battle, O'Connor was ordered to attack the fortress of Bardia in the Gulf of Sallum. He received the 6 Australian Division as replacement for the 4 Indian Division, and ordered them to attack the perimeter and clear lines for the tanks of the 7 Armoured Division to enter the fortress. The attack took place on 3 January 1941, and after heavy fighting, for which the Italians have received scant credit in terms of their wartime reputation, the Australian infantry and British tanks took the town. The tally of victory this time included 40,000 Italian casualties, 128 tanks and considerable transport.

O'Connor next persuaded his commander-in-chief, Wavell (q.v.), to attack Tobruk. In a similar assault to that at Bardia, with the Australians advancing behind an artillery barrage, O'Connor's force attacked on 21 January and took the town that day with 25,000 prisoners and more artillery and armour. With a driving determination to keep the demoralized Italian army on the run, O'Connor ranged energetically round his units in the field. His first intention was to attack Benghazi. Then, when he learned that the Italian divisions were evacuating Benghazi, he decided to make for the coast to the south in order to cut them off. The thrust to the coast turned into a furious race, which O'Connor's force narrowly won, trapping the bulk of the Italian force at Beda Fomm. In fighting that lasted from 5 to 7 February, the British prevented the Italians from breaking out and completely destroyed the Italian Tenth Army, taking a further 20,000 prisoners, 120 tanks, 216 guns, and 1500 trucks.

O'Connor pressed for a further advance into Tripolitania, but by this time Wavell had been ordered by Churchill (q.v.) to prepare for an operation in Greece. O'Connor's force was therefore broken up just at the climax of a brilliantly successful campaign, and within grasp of further opportunities which could have dramatically altered the subsequent course of the war. O'Connor himself became GOC Egypt.

On 12 February a new factor entered the picture, when General Erwin Rommel (q.v.) arrived at Tripoli, and his small force began to ad-

General Richard O'Connor (far right), victor over the Italian armies in the desert, a prisoner of the Afrika Korps, and after his escape a corps commander in the Normandy battles.

vance virtually unhindered across ground recently captured by O'Connor. O'Connor was sent out from Egypt to supervise the work of General Neame, now commanding British troops in Cyrenaica. On 6 April Neame and O'Connor were in a car when they ran into a German unit operating behind British lines, and both were captured. When Italy capitulated O'Connor escaped from prison camp with Neame and another senior officer and in 1944 returned to active service as

commander of 8 Corps under General Montgomery (q.v.) in the Normandy invasion.

A small, slight man, O'Connor gave the impression of being always alert, taut and keyed up, while at the same time showing considerable sensitivity and intellect. Far from content to run battles from his command headquarters, he moved restlessly among his troops, urging his subordinates to greater efforts, especially in pursuit of a disconcerted enemy.

Above The atomic bomb explodes over an ocean test area. *Below* The 'little boy' version of the bomb, as dropped on Hiroshima : dimensions are 28 inches diameter, 120 inches length, 900 pounds weight. Robert Oppenheimer was the scientist in charge of its development.

OPPENHEIMER, Julius Robert (1904–67). American physicist closely associated with the creation of the atomic bomb. In 1943 he was appointed head of the laboratories at Los Alamos, New Mexico, where the atomic bomb was designed and built. After the war he pressed unsuccessfully for international control of atomic weapons.

OZAWA, Jisaburo (1886–1966). Japanese naval commander in the two most important conflicts of the latter part of the Pacific war, the battle of the Philippine Sea and the battle for Leyte Gulf. Ozawa commanded the First Mobile Fleet, attempting to prevent the American invasion of the Marianas which began in June 1944. His forces consisted of three main groups: the main carrier force of three fleet carriers with cruisers and destroyers, Admiral Kurita's main battle fleet of four battleships with light carriers, cruisers and destroyers, and a reserve carrier force consisting of two fleet carriers and one light carrier, one battleship, and cruisers and destroyers under the command of Admiral Joshima. The plan under which Ozawa was operating at the time of the Marianas invasion aimed at halting the American advance across the Pacific by intercepting the American carrier forces and trapping them between Ozawa's carrier fleet and land-based aircraft. As the American invasion of the Marianas began at Saipan on the morning of 15 June, Ozawa's carrier force sailed out of the San Bernadino Strait into the Philippine Sea for what Ozawa's signal described as 'the decisive operation'. Their approach had already been detected by American submarines, and Admiral Spruance (q.v.) in command of the US Fifth Fleet prepared to meet them. He cancelled the planned landings on Guam, and stood off the transports far to the east for safety. But he failed to locate the approaching Japanese fleet until the morning of 19 June. By then Ozawa's own reconnaissance planes had located the US Fifth Fleet, and he ordered the first of four heavy air strikes to be flown off the carriers. From then on the battle was a chapter of disaster for Ozawa. The alternative part of his plan proved impossible to operate, as the shore-based aircraft in the Marianas had already been annihilated, though he did not know it, by aircraft from Admiral Mitscher's (q.v.) fast carrier force. Then shortly after Ozawa had flown off the aircraft from his own carrier *Taiho* it received a torpedo hit from the US submarine *Albacore*, and sank. Ozawa was rescued. Later that morning another fleet carrier, *Shokaku*, was also torpedoed and sunk. The aircraft themselves received a drubbing at the hands of the Americans, and in what came to be known as 'the great Marianas turkey shoot' 218 Japanese aircraft were lost, having destroyed only twenty-

Vice-Admiral Jisaburo Ozawa, whose fleet was unfortunately sacrificed in the battle for Leyte Gulf when used to lure away Halsey's ships.

nine American aircraft. Late the following afternoon the remainder of Ozawa's fleet was spotted by US reconnaissance planes, and Mitscher launched yet another strike, even though it would mean relanding the aircraft in the dark. This strike resulted in the sinking of another fleet carrier, *Hiyo*, and damage to Ozawa's new flag carrier *Zuikaku*, as well as the carrier *Junyo* and four other major ships.

The battle was a decisive defeat for the Japanese leaving the Americans in full control of the Philippine Sea, with the way open to the complete invasion of the Marianas. Ozawa offered to resign his command, and in fact shortly after this battle the government of Hideki Tojo resigned. Ozawa was not dismissed, but was placed in command of the northern force of the Japanese combined fleet. In October 1944 he was operating as the 'bait' in a trap designed to lure the US Fast Carrier Task Force away from the Philippines. It was a suicidal mission, and whether his own fleet survived or not was deemed immaterial, providing he gave the other forces the chance to destroy the American Philippines invasion fleet. He sailed from the Inland Sea in Japan on 20 October, deliberately intending that his presence should become known to the American commander Admiral Halsey (q.v.) at the earliest possible moment. It was ironic that the American submarines which normally patrolled the area had been withdrawn. Also, although the Americans had clear reports of the other Japanese forces sailing from Borneo (Kurita's centre force making for the San Bernadino Strait, and Nishimura's southern force making for the Surigao Strait), Halsey failed to send out reconnaissance to the north, and Ozawa's fleet was allowed to come right into range of the Ameri-

can fleet. After a succession of reconnaissance failures which in other circumstances could have cost them dear, the Americans at last sighted Ozawa's carriers at 3.40 pm on 24 October. Halsey again misread the development of the battle, and convinced himself that Ozawa's force was the main component of the Japanese fleet. By midnight that night, therefore, he assembled the whole of his available fleet to strike at Ozawa's somewhat pathetic force.

Halsey's pursuit of Ozawa continued despite a succession of appeals from the American commander in Leyte Gulf, Admiral Kincaid (q.v.), pleading with Halsey to come south to his aid. At 11.15 pm on 25 October Halsey did so, having sunk one of Ozawa's light carriers, *Chitose*, and damaged three other carriers. Halsey did, however, leave Admiral Mitscher in command of two groups of the Fast Carrier Striking Force, which inflicted a series of fatal wounds on Ozawa's fleet. His losses included the fleet carrier *Zuikaku*, the light carrier *Zuikho*, the carrier *Chiyoda*, and the light cruiser *Tama*. In losing heavily, Ozawa had completed his mission admirably.

P

PAGET, Bernard (1887–1961). British general who served with distinction in Norway and later commanded home forces in preparation for the liberation of occupied Europe. He commanded 18 Division when the Germans invaded Norway and took over the British force halfway through the attempt to reoccupy Trondheim. Three days later, after heavy fighting without artillery, transport or air cover, he was ordered to withdraw, which he did with great skill in the face of heavy attacks. On his return to Britain he became chief of staff of home forces, and later commander-in-chief. In June 1943 he was selected to command Twenty-first Army Group preparing for the invasion of Normandy. He made great strides in the training of troops, establishing battle schools which introduced new training systems, including the preparation of troops for battle with the use of live ammunition in exercises. He appeared almost certain to command British forces in the invasion, but at the end of 1943 he was passed over in favour of Montgomery (q.v.), who had experience of commanding large armies in the field. Paget bore the disappointment, and was sent to the Middle East as commander-in-chief. By that time there were no major operations in the theatre, and he therefore ended the war without having been employed in the key commands which his early experience and performance in Norway had promised.

PAPAGOS, Alexandros (1883–1955). Greek general who became prime minister of his country from 1950–55. A career soldier, Papagos rose to be minister of war by 1935, and chief of staff by 1936. He was commander-in-chief of his country's

General Alexander Papagos, Greek soldier and politician who spent most of the war as a prisoner in Germany but returned to achieve political power in post-war Greece.

forces at the time of the Italian invasion in October 1940. He conducted a defensive campaign but still succeeded in driving the Italians back out of his country into Albania. In April 1941, when the Germans mounted an invasion, he was less successful, and as his defences collapsed his own surviving troops and the British force sent to defend the country were forced to withdraw. Papagos was interned by the new regime led by Tsolacoglou, and taken to Germany as a hostage. He was released in 1945 from the Dachau concentration camp by the advancing Americans. In 1950 he headed the Greek Rally political party which subsequently achieved office. He died while serving as prime minister.

PAPANDREOU, George (1888–1968). Greek liberal leader and political figure who rose to be prime minister of his country. After serving a number of terms of imprisonment and exile for his opposition both to the monarchy and to dictatorships, in 1942 Papandreou was again imprisoned, this time by the occupying Italian forces. Released in 1944, he fled to the Middle East and was proclaimed by the British as prime minister of the Greek government-in-exile. In October of the same year he returned to a liberated Greece but was deposed as prime minister by General Plastiras. He was re-elected twenty years later in 1964, but was forced to resign after a year.

PAPEN, Franz von (1879–1969). Leading German political figure in the 1930s, and vice-chancellor in Hitler's (q.v.) first cabinet. Papen had held the post of chancellor in the second half of 1932, and worked to bring the Nazis into the government. Hindenburg made him vice-president when he nominated Hitler president, but Papen proved too moderate for the hard-core Nazis, and was forced from office. He served in a number of diplomatic posts, and was ambassador to Turkey during the later war years. He was tried at Nuremberg but acquitted, although he was jailed in 1947 by a German court.

PARK, Keith (1892–1975). Royal Air Force commander, a New Zealander by birth. He commanded 11 Group of fighter command during the Battle of Britain, his aircraft being responsible for covering the airfields in south-eastern England and the approaches to London. Acknowledged as one of the brilliant air marshals of the war, he organized his squadrons with great skill to frustrate the Luftwaffe attacks, despite shortage of pilots and their great fatigue, which he dealt with by insisting on periods of rest and training even at the height of the battle. His handling of the

Air-Marshal Keith Park, removed from 11 Group command after the Battle of Britain to take over as air c-in-c Mediterranean. Here he visits bomb armourers during the campaign against the Axis in Tunisia.

battle and his sending up of separate squadrons were the subject of an enquiry arising out of criticism by Leigh-Mallory (q.v.), commanding the neighbouring 12 Group, who had much success flying his fighters in wings of three or more squadrons. The issue was not formally settled, but in November 1940 Park was replaced by Leigh-Mallory and given a 'rest' period commanding a flying training group. In 1941 he was appointed air officer commanding at Allied HQ Egypt, and in July 1942 AOC Malta. This was a second key role in the war, as with increasing resources he organized the growing offensive against Axis Mediterranean convoys, and provided British air support for the Torch landings in North Africa, and the Sicily and Italy operations. In January 1944 he took over air command of the Middle East, and a year later became air c-in-c South-east Asia Command, providing air support for General Slim's (q.v.) operations to retake Burma. He rose to the rank of air marshal. (*See also* Bader, Dowding)

Lieutenant-General Alexander Patch, commander of the US Seventh Army, and a veteran of operations in both Pacific and European theatres.

PATCH, Alexander (1889–1945). United States army officer who served in the Pacific and in the invasion of southern France. After service in the first world war Patch held a variety of posts, many of them concerned with troop training. He commanded the infantry replacement centre at Camp Croft in 1941, but was sent into field service in 1942 to command the United States forces in New Caledonia. He moved to Guadalcanal in December 1942 commanding the army units who replaced the marines. In February 1943 the island was cleared and he returned to Washington to take over 4 Corps. In March 1944 he received his first army command – the Seventh Army, replacing General Patton (q.v.) – and in August that year it carried out the invasion of southern France. Within a month it had linked up with the Third Army driving eastwards after the Normandy invasion. In June 1945 Patch returned to the United States to command the Fourth Army. A modest, quiet and scholarly man, Patch epitomized the

American officer of the old, traditional school. (*See also* Devers)

PATTON, George Smith (1885–1945). United States general. A colourful personality and vigorous armoured commander, Patton was one of the most controversial generals of the second world war. He was born in San Marino, California, the child of wealthy ranch-owners, and throughout his youth Patton was familiar with the local 'high-class' society. He attended no formal school until he was twelve, but was well educated at home, mainly by his father, who concentrated on the classics and the literature of the Bible. Patton passed into West Point military academy, where he was eminently successful both as a cadet and as an athlete. He graduated in 1909. Patton first saw service in Mexico in 1916 as aide to General Pershing on the expedition to capture the bandit-general Pancho Villa. He failed to find Villa, but distinguished himself in a fierce local fire-fight which launched his reputation for courage and élan. In 1917 he served in France, first on Pershing's staff, later as one of the officers bringing the embryo tank corps into combat condition. The tanks were briefly in action in August and September 1918, and in the second engagement Patton was severely wounded leading a heroic but hopeless charge against the German lines. The armistice was agreed almost at the moment Patton discharged himself from hospital, and he was unable to return to active fighting. In the army reductions that followed the war he reverted from his new rank of colonel to his peacetime rank of captain, then, as a major, began two decades of service in a variety of unexciting tasks while he enjoyed the pleasures available to a wealthy American who could afford horses, yachts and cars.

It was through the patronage of General Marshall (q.v.) that Patton achieved his most significant posting, when in 1940 Marshall embarked on a controversial modernization of the American army. He singled out Patton to command a brigade of the newly formed 2 Armoured Division, and Patton embarked enthusiastically on a training and working-up programme for his unit of the new

tank arm, drawing studiously on the writings of Guderian, Fuller, Liddell-Hart and de Gaulle (qq.v.), the early tank enthusiasts. His career advanced again when Marshall chose him to command the land forces for the American invasion in North Africa, Operation Torch. In the end Patton's role was reduced to command of one of the three task forces which took part in the operation. There was considerable resistance from the Vichy French forces based in Africa, but within three days, under the threat of the bombardment of Casablanca, Patton had secured the surrender of the French troops in Morocco. Patton's next combat appointment was the result of Rommel's (q.v.) arrival in Africa, when 2 Corps took the brunt of the German advance in Tunisia, and was badly mauled at Kasserine Pass. General Eisenhower (q.v.) was compelled to relieve the commanding general, Fredendhall, and replaced him with Patton. Within days of his arrival on 7 March 1943, Patton transformed the corps. He fined troops for slovenly dress, tightened up discipline, and made every man aware that a tough regime had begun. In a short time he had brought his inexperienced and 'soft' corps to a new standard of soldierly bearing. In the battles that followed the corps distinguished itself and vindicated Patton's methods by holding off a substantial counter-attack by fifty tanks of the 10 Panzer Division on 23 March. On 14 April Eisenhower promoted Patton. He gave command of 2 Corps to General Bradley (q.v.), until then Patton's deputy, while Patton was appointed to command the Seventh Army and plan for the invasion of Sicily.

Patton was, with Eisenhower and Bradley, one of a triumvirate of key generals who introduced the American armed forces into the war in the west, and who would remain the leading military figures, apart from Marshall in Washington, until the end of hostilities. In Operation Husky the American and British armies would be fighting alongside each other, and Patton found it difficult

General Patton the tank commander takes a bearing. No Allied general took up the new tank warfare with more enthusiasm or panache.

to adapt to his new role as an ally. He was of course not the only general to find this difficult. There were radical differences in personality, style of generalship and military philosophy, and these quickly became apparent in the Sicily operation. The role of Patton's Seventh Army, as a subordinate force to the experienced British Eighth Army under General Montgomery (q.v.), came into dispute in the planning stages. Patton, despite his opposition to it, accepted the plan laid down by the British commander-in-chief General Alexander (q.v.) for the Eighth Army to make the direct drive for Messina while the Seventh penetrated the centre of the island on the British left flank. The landings began on 10 July 1943, and when the British attack slowed down around Mount Etna, Patton on 17 July secured permission for a vigorous exploitation towards Palermo in the north-west of the island, with a subsequent turn eastwards for a campaign along the north coast. The Seventh Army captured Palermo in a spectacular campaign covering 100 miles in only three days, in which the Seventh Army's estimate of enemy casualties was 6000 killed or wounded, 44,000 prisoners, sixty-seven guns captured and 190 aircraft destroyed. The dash for Palermo had demonstrated Patton's vigour and aggression as an army commander, but it threw into doubt his capacity for strategic thinking. It was a theatrical gesture, which gave him the undoubted pleasure of being able to enter the historic city as conqueror. But it tended to neglect the main point of the attack on Sicily, the destruction of the maximum number of Axis forces on the island and the prevention of their withdrawal to mainland Italy. This failure to understand that the real targets were in the east of the island, especially at Messina, may have contributed to Patton's being overlooked in 1944 in favour of his subordinate Bradley when an army group commander was selected for the Normandy invasion. Patton's reputation also suffered as the result of two seemingly trivial, but in their implications far-reaching, incidents shortly after the capture of Palermo. On two separate occasions, during visits to field hospitals to talk

Patton (left) moves in on the war, sailing in USS *Augusta* with Admiral Kent Hewitt for the North African invasion, 9 November 1942.

to his wounded soldiers, Patton encountered men who claimed their nerves could not stand the war. While he thought a physical wound represented the height of honour in battle, Patton had no concept of shell shock or battle fatigue, and considered these men guilty of cowardice. So he lost his temper, slapped them across the face, and tried to have them discharged and sent back to the front. The incidents might have been confined to a small circle except for one member of the press. Although other correspondents had agreed not to file the story, the radio reporter Drew Pearson brought the issue out into the open. Patton had undoubtedly felt justified, as the commander in the field in the middle of a campaign, in slapping the faces of a couple of whimpering men to restore their battle sharpness and protect the morale of the other troops, both those wounded and those so far unhurt. Yet Eisenhower considered this behaviour unacceptable and ordered Patton to apologize publicly to the units concerned. The slapping incidents have been widely viewed since the war as the reason for the reduction in Patton's place in the command structure. It is much more likely, however, that the real reason lay in the shrewd and accurate assessment of his proper talents on the part of his superiors – Eisenhower, and more especially Marshall. Marshall, as accomplished in the

The United States leadership in North Africa. Patton served under Eisenhower, except for a brief interval following the Sicily scandal, from Tunisia to the war's end.

skills of man-management as any general in history, saw that Patton's ability lay in his tactical aggression, and did not hesitate to appoint him when a swift armoured breakthrough was required in Brittany, while at the same time he realized that problems of strategy and planning would be safer in the intellectual care of General Bradley.

Meanwhile Patton went on with his Sicily campaign. On 17 August his 3 Division under General Truscott beat the tanks of the Eighth Army into Messina. But from then on until the end of 1943 he was left kicking his heels in Sicily, unable to take part in the invasion of Italy in the autumn. Then in January 1944 he was ordered to London,

and given command of the Third Army for operations in Europe. Unfortunately for Patton the Third Army was not due to be activated until well after D-Day. For the vital invasion he was still without a command. In the critical pre-invasion period, indeed, he was employed more for his propaganda value than for his command ability, as head of an entirely non-existent force, 'Army Group Patton'. This was a mythical formation aimed at deluding the Germans into believing that the armoured commander they feared most was about to lead an invasion in the Pas de Calais. It was hardly to Patton's satisfaction that he was the key factor in a ruse, even if it was largely success-

Patton, hand on his cherished ivory-handled Colt 45 revolver, imposed new standards of discipline and aggression on the US forces in North Africa.

ful. Patton spent the first half of 1944 building up his Third Army in England, waiting for it to become active at an indeterminate stage between D+15 and D+60. He went over to France on 6 July 1944, but still had to wait impatiently, while Montgomery, as overall commander of land forces, and Bradley, as commander of the First Army, worked to break out of the Normandy bridgehead. Meanwhile Patton stamped around Normandy like an impotent tourist, convinced

that his plan for an armoured breakthrough could end the deadlock and set the Allies off on an advance across Brittany and subsequently towards Paris. In fact the breakout was made across the St Lô road by Bradley's troops well before Patton's Third Army was activated. It took place on 25 July, when units of General Collins's (q.v.) 7 Corps crossed the St Lô–Périers road, and within two days were rampaging southwards down the Cotentin peninsula against scanty German opposition. General Bradley, who was due to become Twelfth Army Group commander over both the Third and First US Armies, realized that the time to activate the Third Army had almost arrived, and in the meantime asked Patton to supervise General Middleton's 8 Corps, which would transfer from the First to the Third Army when the overall change was made. It was a modest gesture to General Patton, but at least it got him an active command in the war, albeit a small one. And he made the best of it. He withdrew his infantry spearheads and replaced them with two armoured divisions, the 4 Armoured under Major-General John S. Wood, and the 6 Armoured under Major General Robert W. Grow. Within days they had taken Coutances, and were making for Avranches, which they secured by the end of July. Most of the German defences had fled in disordered panic at the unexpected approach of the Americans. The way to Brittany lay open.

The Third Army at last came into the picture on 1 August, with the task of advancing in four separate directions into Brittany to secure the ports of St Malo and Brest and take the remainder of the peninsula. Patton sent the 6 Armoured Division off with dramatically simple orders to its commander, Grow, to 'Take Brest'. They were to bypass pockets of resistance and ignore the threat to their flanks. The gains in territory were dramatic, but the problems of communication, supply and protection for the flanks of the extended armoured thrusts were such that even the dynamic General Wood, the 4 Armoured Division's commander, pleaded for reinforcements from the 8 Corps commander, Middleton, who in turn complained to the army group commander, Bradley, about the threat to his corps' flanks. Bradley responded by sending in reinforcements. As it turned out, the port of Brest took until the third week in September to capture and cost some 10,000 American casualties, while the ports of Lorient and St Nazaire remained in German hands until they surrendered at the end of the war. Patton's style of warfare at this stage was highly suitable for occupying territory against dispersed and meagre opposition, but could well have led to disaster against more concentrated German forces. By this time it was rapidly becoming recognized that the campaign in Brittany was something of a sideshow. Originally conceived as a kind of enlarged beach-head offering ample port facilities and room to build up forces for a concerted campaign to the east and north-east towards Germany, Brittany was now rapidly taking second place in Allied thinking, as the possibility of rapid gains in France and the Low Countries promised port facilities closer to where they were needed. Brittany would soon become unnecessary as a territorial base. By the beginning of September Patton at last received his orders to put the Third Army on the offensive for a drive eastwards, clearing Lorraine and advancing towards Saarbrücken, subsequently crossing the Rhine between Mainz and Mannheim. During this phase, from September to November 1944, Patton was dogged by ill-luck, reverses, depression and difficult relations with his fellow commanders. During September and October, for example, his forces failed twice to break into the fortress of Metz, largely because Patton's generalship failed him, and he neglected to concentrate his considerable forces for a decisive attack, in contrast to his performance at Avranches. Despite considerable superiority over the German Fifth Panzer Army commanded by Field-Marshal Hasso von Manteuffel, Patton attacked instead on a broad front, and failed to make the breakthrough. Patton's reputation declined, but the opportunity to redeem it came in December when Hitler (q.v.) assembled a force of three armies, two of them armoured, for an attack against the centre

of the American Twelfth Army Group through the Ardennes forest. Patton's impending advance on the Saar was abruptly called off. He was quick to respond to the challenge of the German attack – he left orders with his staff to prepare for a move to the north in any one of three directions, then set off to Verdun for a conference on 19 December with Eisenhower. Brimming with confidence at this new opportunity, he urged the supreme commander: 'Hell, let's have the guts to let the sons of bitches go all the way to Paris. Then we'll really cut them off and chew them up.' Equally, he astonished his sceptical fellow commanders by assuring them that he was ready to attack northwards with three divisions as early as 22 December. This was a considerable feat involving disengaging his army from their attack towards the Saar, turning his advance units from east to north, and sending them on a mission which had not yet even been selected. It was a peak in Patton's career, showing tactical perception, forward thinking, and an infrequently recognized talent for delegation – a vital component in good leadership. The immediate result of the counter-moves against Hitler's Ardennes offensive was the revival of Patton's reputation, although less emotional post-war reappraisal has judged that Patton's success, although spectacular, was less important than the four battles fought by General Hodges's (q.v.) First Army on the northern flank of the salient. At the end of January Patton again found himself at the centre of the command controversy when he received orders for the next stage in the campaign. The main thrust was to be carried out by units of Montgomery's Twenty-first Army Group in the north. Patton's Third Army was ordered to pursue 'active defence'. Patton insisted that if his army had to go on the defensive at this stage, he wished to be relieved of his command. Bradley therefore allowed Patton the greatest possible freedom of interpretation of that order, and Patton, borrowing the 10 Armoured Division from the Allied reserve, set about clearing the Saar–Moselle triangle. Then on 3 March the First and Third Armies were both given the order they had waited for, to prepare for the advance to the Rhine. Again covering vast distances at unprecedented speeds, the Third Army raced to the Rhine on a 100-mile front from Koblenz to Mannheim, killing 37,000 Germans and capturing a further 82,000 on the way. Aiming at yet another coup, by taking the Rhine 'on the run', Patton pushed troops of the 5 Infantry Division and tanks across the river south of Mainz without the benefit of air support or artillery. Patton made much of his achievement in beating Montgomery's heavily publicized and more elaborately prepared crossing in the north. Exploiting their bridgehead, Patton's divisions raced rapidly across Germany against ever-weakening opposition. Yet even in the last days of the war, when the fighting was going so heavily in his favour, Patton could still not avoid the taint of bad publicity, even scandal. In one incident he sent troops to rescue the famous Lippizaner stallions and bring them to rejoin the mares in Vienna. More seriously, he detached a 300-man task force to liberate the prisoners of war held in camp at Hammelburg, well behind the German lines. The task force commander Captain Abe Baum, most of his men, and the freed prisoners who were fit to walk were cut off by the Germans and captured. The raid proved abortive and costly. It was later discovered that Patton's own son-in-law was a prisoner there. Patton's Third Army, half a million strong by now, continued their rapid exploitations across southern Germany and were seeking permission to enter Prague when the war ended on 9 May 1945. Patton's only remaining ambition was to stay in combat, and he looked forward to a command in the Pacific theatre; even a division would have contented him. Instead General Marshall made him governor of Bavaria, a political appointment for which he was conspicuously unsuited. During the immediate post-war period his outspoken pronouncements in favour of the German people and against the Russian allies, and his objections to some practical aspects of de-Nazification, embarrassed and dismayed his superiors. He was relieved of command of the Third Army, and began an unhappy period of semi-retirement. Two months later, at the age of sixty, his jeep collided with an army truck and he died from his injuries eleven days later, on 21 December.

In the course of the battles in Africa, Sicily and Europe Patton had become one of the two or three best-known generals in the war. He had no equal for aggressive drive, determination to win battles and inspirational leadership. He was an incomparable field commander, and achieved several great tactical triumphs. He was, on the other hand, no great strategist, and had little organizational skill or patience with administration, both essential for success in a modern mechanized army. He needed firm guidance and control from his superiors to keep his objectives in line with the overall Allied effort, but given that guidance his contribution to the Allied efforts was considerable. He was, in addition, the Allied general the Germans respected above all others.

PAULUS, Friedrich von (1890–1957). German general who commanded the Sixth Army which was defeated at Stalingrad and surrendered on 31 January 1943. Paulus served as chief of staff to Tenth Army in the campaigns in Poland and northern France. He was given his first and much-wanted operational command as head of Sixth Army for the campaign against Stalingrad, which opened on 28 June. By mid-October his forces reached Stalingrad, but became bogged down in fierce house-to-house fighting. By November, when he had not received the reinforcements or supplies he needed, he asked Hitler (q.v.) for permission to withdraw. Hitler refused, and a Soviet counter-offensive beginning on 19 November led to the encirclement of his army within four days. Attempts to break out failed and on 31 January 1943 Paulus, with fifteen generals and the remnants of twenty divisions, surrendered. Paulus refused to join the 'free Germany' committee set up by Seydlitz among prisoners of war in the Soviet Union, but did so when he learned of the plot on Hitler's life of 20 July 1944. He was called as a witness at the Nuremberg trials in 1946, but was kept in prison by the Russians until 1953.

Field-Marshal Friedrich von Paulus, defeated at Stalingrad, and held prisoner by the Russians long after the war's end.

PERCIVAL, Arthur Ernest (1887–1966). British general commanding in Malaya at the time of the Japanese invasion. Percival is remembered mainly, though unfairly, not as the man who commanded the retreat in Malaya and defence of Singapore, but as the general who personally surrendered the troops under his command to the Japanese General Yamashita (q.v.). Percival was one of the most unfortunate generals of the war.

He was given an important job but not supplied with the tools to carry it out, and when the job could not be done it was of course Percival who had to take the blame.

He was one of the most promising British soldiers in the years before the war. Although a rather colourless personality, unimposing in appearance and not endowed with the charisma which later commanders either possessed or were

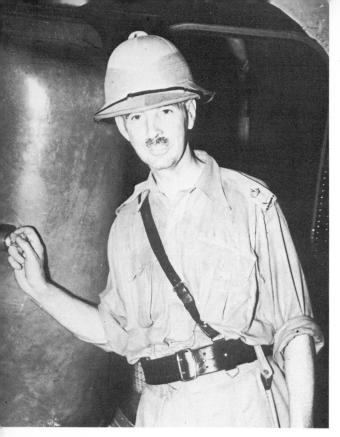

Lieutenant-General Arthur Percival, forced to surrender Singapore by the advance of Yamashita's troops and lack of support for his own forces.

amounted to only 158 out-of-date aircraft, compared with Japan's 560 planes. There was no fleet in the Far East, and the ill-conceived attempt to remedy that defect by sending the *Prince of Wales* and the *Repulse* was destined to end in their loss two days after the invasion. There were no British tanks, while the Japanese had 211, and the Allied troops were a mixture of British, Australian, Indian and Malayan units, most of whom lacked jungle training and were badly equipped. Britain, the Middle East and Russia all had prior calls on the necessary equipment.

In the event, there was little Percival could do except try to delay the Japanese advance and wait for reinforcements. Although 18 Division and two brigades of 17 Division and other units were sent out, they marched straight into captivity. By the night of 8 February 1942 the Japanese were ready to cross to Singapore Island. By 15 February they were in a dominant position, with their air forces holding complete air command. The Allies were short of ammunition and food, were hampered by the large numbers of refugees who had crowded into Singapore town, and faced the prospect of having their water supplies cut off by Japanese artillery. Percival was left with no alternative to surrender. On the morning of 15 February the British flew a flag from the radio station. They followed it with a car driving out from Singapore town bearing a flag of truce. At two o'clock that afternoon Yamashita was informed, but he insisted on seeing the British commander in person. The truce party went back to the city, and later that afternoon General Percival marched out with two staff officers, one of them carrying a white flag, to face General Yamashita. The negotiations, if they could so be called, took place in a room at the Ford factory. After establishing that the Allies held no Japanese prisoners, the Japanese presented Percival with a surrender document. He asked to be allowed to answer it the next morning. Yamashita apparently grew angry, though whether with Percival or with his interpreter is now unclear. At any rate, he insisted on a yes-or-no answer from Percival. Percival is reported to have

able to manufacture, he was nevertheless a man of iron courage and evident strength of character. A brave leader of troops at all levels in the first world war (he had two DSOs and an MC to his credit), he was later a student and instructor at the staff college, both of which occupations he filled with great distinction. He was so highly thought of by his superiors that progress to chief of the imperial general staff was considered inevitable.

As a colonel, Percival had been sent to Malaya to study its defence in 1936, and the plan he produced was closely similar to the one ultimately adopted. After service in France at the beginning of the war, he returned to Malaya in March 1941 as GOC, with accelerated promotion to lieutenant-general. When the Japanese invasion began on 7 December the defences lacked resources in every department, to such an extent that even the British chiefs of staff accepted that Malaya could not be held by the forces available. The air cover turned pale and replied: 'Yes.' It was the end of Allied resistance in Malaya, and Percival marched into captivity at the head of some 130,000 troops.

Percival spent four years as a POW until, with Japan's defeat, he was liberated and brought to Tokyo with the captured American commander in the Philippines, General Wainwright (q.v.). At MacArthur's (q.v.) personal instigation, the two men witnessed the signing of the Japanese surrender document on the battleship *Missouri*.

PÉTAIN, Henri Philippe (1856–1951). French general and statesman who led the Vichy French government. At the age of sixty Pétain became a national hero when he stopped the German advance at the battle of Verdun in 1916. He was appointed commander-in-chief in 1917, and rapidly restored morale in the weakened French army. During the 1920s he was responsible for the construction of the fixed defences, the Maginot Line, which proved disastrously easy for the German panzers to outflank in 1940. His prestige was quite enough to silence the calls of generals like de Gaulle (q.v.) for mechanized forces operating a mobile defence. Pétain retired in 1931 and briefly served as war minister in 1934. Later he became the central figure in the right wing of French politics, around whom advocates of authoritarianism could gather. In May 1940 he was recalled from his post as ambassador in Spain to become vice-premier, and when France was on the point of defeat in June 1940 he was asked by the president, Albert Lebrun, to form a government and negotiate a peace with Germany. On 22 June the armistice was signed. Under it France was divided into a German-occupied zone in the north and west, including the Atlantic coastline, and an unoccupied zone in the south with the Mediterranean coast. The French fleet was to remain intact, but the army would be reduced into a law-and-order force of 100,000 men. Pétain became head of the new government in the south, which was set up on 10 July 1940 at Vichy. The political stance of the Vichy government, and hence that of Pétain, remained confused. Some members were in favour of open alliance with the Axis and

Henri Pétain sits out the post-war period on the island of Yeu, where he was imprisoned while awaiting trial in 1945.

going to war with Britain, hoping that France would emerge on the winning side. Pétain was equivocal; he appeared anxious to avoid war with Britain and dismissed its leading advocate Laval, although he was forced by the Germans to take him back in April 1942. Pétain's principal aim appeared to be merely to keep France safe from the ravages of war as suffered in 1914–18. The picture changed dramatically in November 1942 when the Allies invaded North Africa and Germany responded by occupying the Vichy zone. Pétain's friends urged him to leave France, but he refused. As a result he became, unfairly, associated with the whole-hearted collaborationists who retained office during the later years of the war. On 20 August 1944 the retreating Nazis arrested him and took him to Germany. He voluntarily returned to France in April 1945, and was arrested by de Gaulle's provisional government. He was tried for treason, convicted and sentenced to military degradation and death. De Gaulle himself commuted the sentence to life imprisonment, and Pétain died six years later. Opinions on Pétain's role in French history are still divided, as they were in France during the course of his trial. Some see him as the arch-traitor. His right-wing admirers still consider him the hero who sacrificed everything after 1940 to save France from suffering as she had in the preceding war. (*See also* Reynaud)

PHILLIPS, (Sir) Tom Spencer Vaughan (1888–1941). British admiral. After a distinguished early career at sea and in naval staff posts, Tom Phillips was appointed vice-chief of the naval staff shortly before the outbreak of the second world war. He became estranged from Churchill (q.v.) (originally first lord of the admiralty and then prime minister) over policy, and in October 1941 was sent to the Far East as c-in-c Eastern Fleet. He sailed in the new battleship *Prince of Wales*. On the way they were joined by the old battle cruiser *Repulse*. A third ship due to join them, the

Admiral Tom Phillips, British sailor sent out to Malaya with the ill-fated Force Z, the *Prince of Wales* and the *Repulse*. Devoid of air cover, both ships were sunk, and Phillips was lost with them.

aircraft carrier *Indomitable*, was not ready in time after repairs. It was an ill-fated expedition from the start, as Jan Smuts (q.v.) prophetically warned when the ships put in at South Africa during the voyage. The *Prince of Wales* and *Repulse* arrived at Singapore on 2 December, and on 8 December the Japanese began their invasion of Malaya. Phillips without doubt recognized the danger of attempting to interfere with the invasion while he was devoid of air cover, and while the Japanese had strong land-based air forces available. Nevertheless, having asked for fighter cover from Singapore, he set out to the north. On 9 December he learned that the fighters would not be available, and when he knew that his ships were sighted by Japanese reconnaissance aircraft, he decided to return to Singapore. The next morning they were located by a substantial force of Japanese aircraft sent to search for them, and both ships were sunk by bombs or torpedoes. Phillips was among the 47 officers and 793 men killed. 2081 men were saved by the accompanying destroyers.

PIUS XII (Pope) (1867–1958). Pope during the second world war. Born Eugenio Maria Giuseppe Pacelli in Rome, he became pope on 2 March 1939. Throughout the war he maintained a public posture of serene independence, despite urgings from both sides to declare in their favour. The Allies wanted him to condemn Nazi Germany, especially with regard to the persecution of the Jews; the Axis sought his blessing on their invasion of Soviet Russia as a holy crusade against Communism. He maintained his policy of international neutrality, in the hope that the Vatican could be effective in the role of peacemaker. The argument over Pius XII's failure to condemn the oppression of occupied peoples has never been resolved, and the issue has been clouded by the fact that he was an archbishop in Munich and Berlin from 1917 to 1929, during which period he developed a love of Germany and a hatred of Communism, which he thought the enemy of Christianity. It must be said in his favour that in practical terms he did much to aid refugees, fleeing Jews and escaping Allies, frequently hiding them

Pope Pius XII. His apparently equivocal attitudes to
Nazi Germany aroused controversy and disapproval.

Air-Marshal Sir Charles Portal, Britain's chief of the air
staff.

in Vatican property, and he organized a committee
to supply relief to war victims in several countries.

POPSKI (real name **Vladimir Peniakoff**)
(1897–1951). Leader of a small force of commando-style troops in North Africa and Italy.
Popski, born in Belgium of Russian parents,
studied at Cambridge and became a businessman
in Egypt in the 1920s. He offered his services to
the British on the outbreak of war, and because
of his command of several languages, especially
Arabic, he was commissioned and posted to the
Libyan Arab Force. Although he raised a colourful
band of warriors, they were never large enough to
cause serious damage to Axis forces, and some of
the detractors of such independent units have even
suggested that 'Popski's private army' was a
greater inconvenience to the Allies than to their
enemy.

**PORTAL, Charles (First Viscount Portal of
Hungerford)** (1893–1971). British air marshal
and chief of the war staff for most of the war. From
April to October 1940 Portal was head of bomber

command. On 25 October he was made chief of
the air staff, and was therefore responsible for
British air policy throughout the war. His early
directives included an indication of faith in the
bombing policy, when he called for militarily significant targets to be selected – power stations, oil
refineries, or aircraft factories – but wanted them in
populated areas where the attacks would be profit-
able even if the bombs missed their precise objectives, and the destruction would 'demonstrate to
the enemy the power and severity of the air bombardment'. In December 1940 this policy was
extended further, with the beginning of area
bombing, starting at the town of Mannheim.
Among Portal's main contributions was his popularity with his American opposite numbers. They
liked and trusted him, and perhaps more impor-
tantly respected his grasp of strategy and detailed
knowledge of the RAF. He was therefore a key
figure in the Casablanca, Washington, and Quebec
conferences in 1943 which determined Allied strategy. Portal was a quietly spoken man, but was

Captain Gunther Prien (left), captain of U-47, comes home to a hero's welcome after sinking the *Royal Oak* at Scapa Flow. Greeting him are admirals Schlachtschiffe (centre) and Raeder.

unshakeable in his outlook and impressive for his total honesty.

POUND, (Sir) Dudley (1877–1943). Senior British admiral and naval administrator during the first four years of the war. Pound was born in the Isle of Wight, fell in love with the navy at an early age, and enjoyed a long and distinguished naval career. His chief joy, especially when he was c-in-c Mediterranean, was to be out on the bridge of a ship improving the standard of the fleet in manœuvres. But shortly before his intended retirement at the age of sixty-two he was recalled to a job he liked less as first sea lord, with the rank of admiral of the fleet. He enjoyed a chequered career in that post, which was inevitable in view of the uneven history of the navy itself, from which his own service was inseparable. His setbacks included the loss of the *Prince of Wales* and *Repulse*, and the escape through the Channel of the *Scharnhorst* and *Gneisenau*. His credits included the gradual securing of the Mediterranean in extensive naval operations, and most notably the defeat of the U-boats, for which purpose he created

Western Approaches Command. He travelled with Churchill (q.v.) to several conferences, and at Washington in September 1943 told Churchill that he could not go on because of ill-health. He died a few weeks later on 21 October.

PRIEN, Gunther (1908–41). German U-boat captain. As commander of U-47 in October 1939 Prien was ordered by Dönitz (q.v.) to carry out an attack on the British fleet anchored at Scapa Flow. In fact the bulk of the fleet had moved to the Scottish west coast, but the *Royal Oak* and other vessels were still there. Prien skilfully navigated past the blockships in one of the narrow entrances, and at 1.30 am on 14 October torpedoed and sank the *Royal Oak*, before escaping through the same shallow tidal passage. Prien's brilliant exploit was a severe shock to British morale after only six weeks of war, and he became a hero in Germany. He went on to command in the battle of the Atlantic and at Narvik, and was almost certainly killed on 8 March 1941 when U-47 was chased and sunk by the British destroyer *Wolverine*.

Q

QUEZON, Manuel (1878–1944). President of the Philippines. On his election to the presidency in 1935 Quezon declared himself also chairman of the Council of National Defence, effectively commander of his country's armed forces. He was elected for a second term in November 1941, and moved to the island of Corregidor when the Japanese captured Luzon. In March 1942 he left the island first for Australia, and then for Washington, where he remained confident that his people would ultimately achieve victory. He did not live to see his country liberated, but died on 1 August 1944. (*See also* MacArthur)

QUISLING, Vidkun (1887–1945). Norwegian Nazi leader. His name gave a new word to the English language – a quisling – to describe a political leader serving a foreign occupation power in his own country, and therefore a traitor. Quisling approached Hitler (q.v.) before the war with a proposal for a *coup d'état* in Norway. Hitler preferred to invade, and Quisling set himself up as ruler of conquered Norway. His regime lasted only a week as few Norwegians would work with him. He remained head of the *Samling*, the only permitted political party, but even the Germans ignored him and from September 1940 to February 1942 he was deprived of all his powers. Then the Germans restored him nominally to office as minister president, but without any authority. He surrendered to Norwegian police in May 1945, was tried for treason, and was executed on 24 November that year.

Vidkun Quisling (centre), the Norwegian politician briefly in charge of his country's government after the invasion. Effectively rejected by both his own people and the occupying Germans, his achievements never matched his ambitions.

R

RAEDER, Erich (1876–1960). German admiral, commander-in-chief of the German navy until 1943. Raeder joined the navy in 1894 and became an officer three years later. He served in the first world war in a variety of posts and rose to be chief of the naval staff in 1928. Hitler (q.v.) made him commander-in-chief in 1935 when he denounced the Versailles treaty and began to rearm. Raeder was responsible for the rapid expansion of the navy. He was an aggressive advocate of avoiding war on two fronts and defeating Britain before invading Russia, although he pressed Hitler not to invade Britain until the RAF had been knocked out. He also urged Hitler to concentrate on severing Britain's sea communications, and forced through the policy of unrestricted U-boat warfare. At Nuremberg he was sentenced to ten years in prison for war crimes.

RAMSAY, (Sir) Bertram Home (1883–1945). British admiral credited with the evacuation of the

Admiral Raeder, c-in-c of the German Imperial Navy (second from left), meets Hitler with other service chiefs: on Raeder's left, Brauchitsch, Keitel and Himmler.

Admiral Sir Bertram Ramsay (left), commander-in-chief of Allied naval forces for the Normandy invasion, visits the beach-head with King George VI in June 1944. It was Ramsay who had organized the Dunkirk evacuation.

British Expeditionary Force from Dunkirk in 1940. Ramsay's long naval career, beginning at the age of fifteen, encompassed a vast variety of service in almost every part of the world, both in land battles (with the navy brigade) and at sea. He was also experienced as a staff officer. The most significant part of this wealth of early experience with regard to the second world war was a tour from 1915 to the end of the war with the Dover patrol, which made him familiar with conditions in the English Channel. By 1938, after a disagreement with a commanding officer three years earlier, Ramsay had been taken off the active list, promoted to the rank of vice-admiral, and retired. However in August 1939, on the eve of war, he was recalled as the man with the right experience and appointed flag-officer-in-charge at Dover. He was responsible for keeping the Channel clear of German submarines, and for taking the BEF across to France safely, along with a variety of other tasks. He was also of course responsible for bringing the BEF back home when France collapsed. He mounted the operation, including the passage of the small private boats to lift the men off the beaches, and 338, 226 men were brought back to Britain from the harbour and beaches of Dunkirk.

During the next two years Ramsay was in the front line of the war, facing the initial impact of the threatened German invasion, and, once that threat receded, being responsible for the control of the Channel with the Germans then holding the opposite shore. In April 1942, as defensive preparations gave way to planning for the offensive, Ramsay was appointed to work with Eisenhower (q.v.), first in the Torch invasion of North Africa as deputy naval c-in-c, then in Sicily as naval commander for Montgomery's (q.v.) British landings. He was recalled to England during the planning stages of the invasion of Normandy, and appointed c-in-c Allied naval expeditionary force with promotion to the rank of admiral. Although less spectacular or enshrined in folklore than the Dunkirk evacuation, the D-Day landings and subsequent buildup were Ramsay's supreme achievement. Much of the time in the post-D-Day period he

spent at sea supervising the operation off the invasion beaches. On 2 January 1945, while still conducting the vital naval side of the drive through north-west Europe, he set out from an airfield near Paris to fly to Brussels, and was killed when his plane crashed on take-off.

REYNAUD, Paul (1878–1966). Prime minister of France at the time of the German invasion in June 1940. In the years before the war Reynaud had warned, as Churchill (q.v.) had done in England, of the dangers of the rise of Nazism, and had called for the creation of a strong armoured force of professional soldiers, in addition to the conscripted army, along the lines advocated by de Gaulle (q.v.), then a little-known colonel. Reynaud was minister of finance from November

Paul Reynaud, French premier, at the height of the crisis of the summer of 1940. He survived concentration camp internment to return to political life in the post-war era.

1938 to March 1940, when he took over from Daladier (q.v.) as premier. He was unable to form a strong government, and made the mistake of including Pétain and Weygand (qq.v.) in his team, which led directly to the decision to capitulate. On 6 September he was arrested by the Vichy government, brought to trial with other opponents of the French surrender, including Blum (q.v.) and Daladier, and sentenced to life imprisonment. The Germans took custody of him from 20 November 1942 and he was kept in Oranienburg concentration camp before being returned by them to the Vichy government in July 1944 and liberated by the Americans on 4 May 1945. He returned to politics after the war and occupied ministerial rank in the Fifth Republic from 1958.

RIBBENTROP, Joachim von (1893–1946). German foreign minister immediately before and during the second world war. The son of an officer, Ribbentrop was educated in Switzerland and Britain and worked in America and Canada, an international background which impressed Hitler (q.v.) when Ribbentrop joined the Nazi party in 1932 so much that the Führer made him adviser for foreign affairs. In 1936 he was sent as ambassador to London, where he naturally supported Britain's appeasement policies. He returned to Germany in 1938 to become foreign minister. He was disliked by almost everybody. The Reich banker Schacht (q.v.) described him as vain and incompetent. Ciano (q.v.) said he was vain, frivolous and loquacious, and Mussolini (q.v.) remarked that you only had to look at his head to see that he had a small brain. He was put on trial at Nuremberg and hanged.

RIDGWAY, Matthew Bunker (born 1895). American airborne commander. At the beginning of the war Ridgway held the rank of lieutenant-colonel and served until 1942 in the war plans division of the War Department. He was then appointed assistant commander and shortly afterwards commander of the 82 Division, which he led in the invasions of Sicily in 1943 and Normandy in 1944. In August 1944 he took command of 18 Airborne Corps which was credited with a total

Joachim von Ribbentrop, German foreign minister. Elegant but of doubtful competence, Ribbentrop was a long-serving member of Hitler's entourage.

General Matthew Bunker Ridgway, commander of 82 Airborne Division for the Normandy invasion, and of 18 Airborne Corps during Hitler's Ardennes offensive. At the time of the photograph he was United States commander in Korea.

of 500,000 captured Germans in operations up to the end of the war. He led the corps in helping to block the German counter-offensive in the Ardennes. In 1945 he briefly had a command in the Philippines, which was cut short by the Japanese surrender. After the war he rose to top army commands in Korea and at NATO, and in 1953 became chief of staff.

RITCHIE, Neil Methuen (born 1897). British general who commanded the Eighth Army in the North African desert in the period of its greatest setbacks. The majority of Ritchie's experience had been in staff posts. He had served as brigadier-general-staff to Brooke (q.v.) in 2 Corps in 1939 and 1940, and as Auchinleck's (q.v.) BGS at Southern Command during the period of preparations against the German invasion in 1940. He followed Auchinleck to the Middle East and at the end of November 1941 was deputy chief of the general staff at Middle East Command. He was therefore the only feasible choice, though because of his lack of experience of field command not the ideal one, to take over the Eighth Army when Cunningham (q.v.) was forced to give up through fatigue. Auchinleck knew that he had thrown Ritchie into the battle in the most severely difficult circumstances, and he therefore intended Ritchie's appointment to be temporary. In the meantime Auchinleck stayed in effective command of the battle, with Ritchie as nominal head of the army.

Ritchie took over at a point when both the Axis and the British had fought themselves to a virtual standstill. He was fortunate in being able to convert the temporary stalemate into an immediate victory. Rommel (q.v.) and his panzers were denied supplies, and the Germans were forced to retreat with heavy losses first to Gazala and then to El Agheila, leaving the British in command of Cyrenaica.

After this early victory it would have been difficult to remove Ritchie, and his temporary appointment became permanent. An unshakeable optimist, Ritchie prepared for an advance, and neglected to build up the defences at Gazala, so that when Rommel, supplied with tank reinforcements, began his own advance on 21 January 1942, the Eighth Army was almost overwhelmed. Ritchie lost control of the battle, and by 4 February the British were back in Gazala. Rommel's own advance stopped only because his supplies ran out yet again. Auchinleck sent his confidant, Brigadier Dorman-Smith (q.v.), to report on the condition of the Eighth Army, and Dorman-Smith recommended that Ritchie should be removed.

General Neil Ritchie (in beret), formerly Eighth Army commander under Auchinleck, receives a visit from Eisenhower (centre) and Dempsey while serving as a corps commander in Normandy.

Auchinleck turned down that advice on the grounds that sacking two commanders in three months would be bad for morale. Still under Ritchie, therefore, the Eighth Army prepared for the new round of battles, and between February and May 1942 built up fixed defences around Gazala and Tobruk. Auchinleck himself wrote from Cairo advising Ritchie to keep his armour concentrated to deal with Rommel's anticipated advance. However Ritchie ignored him, distri-

buted his armour, and was forced to commit it piecemeal. When Rommel began his advance on 26 May 1942, the Eighth Army had no real idea of how to stop him. They were confused and badly handled, and the commanders were inclined to disbelieve their own intelligence. The German advance was so rapid that one British corps commander, General Messervy, was captured twice during the battle and twice escaped. The outcome of the battle was the loss of the fortress of Bir

Hacheim, the siege and eventual loss of Tobruk, and an unimpeded advance by Rommel's forces as far as Mersah Matruh. It was on 25 June 1942 that Auchinleck came to appreciate his error in leaving Ritchie in command of the Eighth Army, and personally came up to Ritchie's headquarters to take over the command himself. Somewhat surprisingly, Ritchie survived this debacle. Although Auchinleck recommended that Ritchie was not suitable for an army command, he remained confident of his soldierly qualities and Ritchie survived

to become, in 1944, a corps commander in Europe under Montgomery (q.v.).

RÖHM, Ernst (1887–1934). An early associate of Hitler (q.v.) in the embryo Nazi party. Röhm had been Hitler's commanding officer in the years immediately after the war. When Hitler came to head the party Röhm commanded the group of strong-arm men who formed Hitler's bodyguard and kept order at meetings, throwing out hecklers and beating up opponents. They wore a para-military uniform – brown shirts – and called themselves the

Ernst Röhm. His work as head of the SA made him a serious threat to Hitler. He was therefore despatched in the great purge of the 'Night of the Long Knives'.

Sturmabteilung or *SA*: literally the 'storm section'. Hitler recognized in the following years that the strong *SA* were a potential threat, and on 30 June 1934 he had Röhm and a large number of his *SA* murdered by his new personal bodyguard, the blackshirted *SS* (*Schutzstaffeln*, literally protection squads) commanded by Himmler (q.v.). The best evidence indicates that after Röhm's arrest a small group of officers led by Sepp Dietrich (q.v.) went to his cell to force him to commit suicide. When he refused, a Colonel Michael Lippert and/or an *SS* officer called Theodore Eicke shot him through the head. The military chiefs were delighted to see the disintegration of the *SA*, and Hitler from then on enjoyed the generals' support behind the protective screen of his own loyal and growing private army.

ROKOSSOVSKY, Konstantin Konstantinovich (1896–1968). Soviet general, noted for his part in the victories over the German armies at Stalingrad and Kursk. Twice decorated with the title of Hero of the Soviet Union, Rokossovsky had equally strong connections with Poland, being the son of a Polish father and a Russian mother. He was orphaned at the age of fourteen and earned his living as a construction worker. In 1914 he was drafted into the tsarist army and at the end of that year had become a cavalry sergeant. He joined the Red Army in 1917 and entered the party in 1919. He rose to command of a cavalry division by 1930, and a corps by 1936.

In 1937 he was arrested in the political purge of the Red Army, beaten and thrown into jail, nominally for neglecting the supply of his corps. He was released and rehabilitated in March 1940 and given command of 5 Cavalry Corps. He commanded 9 Mechanized Corps in the Ukraine in June 1941, and in the battle for Moscow in 1941–2 held command of the Sixteenth Army. He commanded the Briansk Front in July–September 1942, and the Don Front in the battle for Stalingrad at the end of that year. It was Rokossovsky who offered surrender terms to General Paulus (q.v.) on 8 January 1943 (they were rejected) before launching the encircling movements two days later which isolated and finally crushed the German Sixth Army. In July 1943 he was in command of the Central Front which absorbed and then defeated the German offensive in the Kursk salient. He commanded the First Belorussian Front in the advance towards Warsaw, but was stopped by Stalin (q.v.) outside the city. The Russians were severely criticized for not aiding the Warsaw uprising, but Rokossovsky justifed their restraint on the grounds of military caution, stating that his troops were exhausted and were in fact thrown back by the Germans. He described the Warsaw uprising as a 'political stunt' by the Polish underground. In 1945, in the last phase of the offensive which brought an end to the war in eastern Europe, Rokossovsky was replaced by Zhukov (q.v.) as commander of the First Belorussian Front, and transferred to command of the Second Belorussian Front. Stalin's aim in making this change appears to have been to give Zhukov the distinction of capturing Berlin, but in the event Rokossovsky's forces, along with those of Koniev (q.v.) and Zhukov, did participate in the attack on Berlin. Rokossovsky returned to Moscow and led the Red Army in the victory parade in Red Square reviewed by Stalin, when Soviet troops flung down captured enemy flags at the foot of the Lenin mausoleum, a re-enactment of the ceremony in which Napoleon's flags were thrown down before Tsar Alexander I.

After the war Rokossovsky became involved with the military affairs of Poland, serving as deputy minister of defence from 1956 to 1962, when he returned to become inspector general for the Soviet Ministry of Defence.

An interesting sidelight on Rokossovsky's character – and Stalin's – emerges from the story of a planning meeting in May 1944. Rokossovsky told Stalin that he planned to break through the enemy's defences in two sectors. Stalin argued that a single effort in one sector would be advisable. Rokossovsky, unlike almost all the other generals, was prepared to stick to his point, and insisted that two attacks would be better. Stalin told him: 'Go out and think it over again.' Rokossovsky, whose

254

experience of political imprisonment had not intimidated him but had merely tempered his nerve, went into the next room, but could not bring himself to give advice contrary to his beliefs. He went back in and again told Stalin: 'Two blows are more advisable, Comrade Stalin.' Stalin argued for the single blow, but Rokossovsky still argued against. There was an empty silence. Then Stalin said: 'Go out and think it over again. Don't be stubborn, Rokossovsky.' For a second time Rokossovsky went out. Molotov (q.v.) and Malenkov both followed him and warned him gravely about disagreeing with Stalin. Malenkov told him sternly: 'Agree. That's all there is to it.' When they went in again Stalin asked him yet again. Rokossovsky again told him that two blows were better. 'But which of them should be primary, in your opinion?' 'They should both be primary,' Rokossovsky replied. Then the silence set in. It was the silence, Rokossovsky knew, that normally preceded outbursts of rage in those conferences. But after a long pause Stalin said: 'Can it be that two blows are really better?' And he agreed with Rokossovsky's plan. It was one of several illustrations that those who held their ground with Stalin could sometimes achieve success.

ROMMEL, Erwin (1891–1944). German general, widely considered one of the most able commanders in the war, both by his enemies in the battles of North Africa and by post-war commentators. Rommel was born at Heidenheim, near Ulm, the son of a schoolmaster – a bourgeois background which contrasted with the aristocratic origins of most of his fellow German generals. He joined the infantry in 1910 as a cadet, and was commissioned in 1912 as a second lieutenant in the 124 Infantry Regiment. Rommel showed his talent for soldiering in the first world war as a platoon, company and battle group commander. He was brave, decisive, energetic and full of initiative and

Marshal Rokossovsky (right) entertains Montgomery at his headquarters on 10 May 1945. He was described by Montgomery in favourable terms: 'Rokossovsky was an imposing figure, tall, very good-looking, and well-dressed; I understand he was a bachelor and was much admired by ladies.'

imagination. By penetrating deep into enemy-held territory, he frequently took prisoner large groups of soldiers, both Romanians and Italians, often by surprise and force of personality rather than by military strength. He was awarded the coveted *Pour le Mérite*. He returned to peacetime soldiering in 1918 as one of the corps of officers allowed to Germany by the restrictive terms of the Versailles treaty.

He rose by stages to the rank of colonel, and made the acquaintance of Hitler (q.v.) as commander of the Führer's bodyguard during the entry into the Sudetenland and during the Polish campaign of 1939. There Rommel first witnessed the startling power of the tank in modern warfare, and when the opportunity arose he requested command of an armoured division. His request was granted, and it was as commander of the 7 Panzer Division that he began his combat in the second world war in the invasion of Belgium in May 1940. His first campaign was notable for the speed of the advance, and in this Rommel displayed exactly the same panache that had made him so successful as an infantry officer. Although not a tank pioneer himself, Rommel instinctively hit on the most effective use of the tank. He employed his leading armour on a narrow front, punching through any opposition and fanning out through the breach into lightly defended rear areas, where the confusion caused by the sudden appearance of the tanks was as damaging to enemy morale and organization as their actual firepower. Rommel was usually at the front, frequently under fire, and always in position to give decisive leadership to his junior officers. In fact he was often so far ahead of the mass of his division that he did not even know where they were. This tactic of racing forward at times extended a dangerously narrow salient far into enemy rear areas, leaving vulnerable flanks which the French could have attacked to serious effect had they been quicker to react. But Rommel's nerve held; as his instincts rightly told him, confidence and mobility were superior in the circumstances to static defence, however highly organized. His division reached the

Left General Rommel, never a fanatical Nazi but certainly an enthusiastic Hitler supporter in the early days, and at the beginning of the war commander of the Führer's bodyguard.

Below The victor in northern France. Rommel's division captures the British 51 Highland Division at St Valery-en-Caux. Major-General Victor Fortune and other British officers are taken prisoner.

Channel, and Rommel's part in the campaign ended on 19 June when the French garrison at Cherbourg surrendered. Rommel's success appealed to the Führer. Hitler found him easier to get on with than the aristocratic officers of the traditional Prussian school, and rewarded him with a series of promotions which would rapidly take him to the highest level. Rommel in return enjoyed Hitler's attention, and betrayed in his letters to his wife an almost naïve glee at being singled out for small gestures of personal appreciation: 'The Führer greeted me with the words, "Rommel, we were very worried about you during the attack." His whole face was radiant and I had to accompany him afterwards. I was the only divisional commander who did.'

In February 1941, recently promoted lieutenant-general, Rommel was posted to North Africa to command the German forces in Libya, specifically to assist the Italians and block the British advance on Tripoli. From then until May 1943 when the Afrika Korps was defeated, Rommel was the dominant Axis figure in North Africa. In the highly mobile tactical battles fought over the narrow strip of desert stretching for some 600 miles between El Agheila in the west and El Alamein in the east, Rommel's style of warfare achieved its full expression. In those deserts the tank was king: battle lines were seldom strictly drawn, except in a defensive sense in front of the Axis and British bases respectively, and infantry had comparatively little scope. There were few airfields and no great numbers of aircraft to impair the tanks' mobility. The only outside factor of any great influence was supply, and in that Rommel suffered a permanent disability. The high command in Berlin, notably Hitler's personal aides Keitel and Jodl and the chief of staff Halder (qq.v.), were throughout the course of the North African campaigns preoccupied mainly with the Russian front and, although they congratulated Rommel on his victories, they never thought his campaign important enough to send him the supplies which could have secured victory in North Africa. It was therefore as something of a sideshow that Rommel conducted his campaigns in the desert. He began with a phase of domination from March to November 1941, beginning with a campaign in March–June in which he pushed the British out of Cyrenaica and beat them at Sollum, leaving only Tobruk as a British-held fortress which continued to threaten his lines of communication. As a result of Rommel's success in these operations Churchill (q.v.) sacked the British commander Wavell (q.v.) and replaced him with General Auchinleck (q.v.). In November the war flared up again, when Auchinleck and Rommel planned offensives which began almost simultaneously. The battle which followed was fast, furious and confused, and both sides lost large numbers of tanks. During the early part of the battle the Afrika Korps held the initiative. British confidence dwindled, and was only revived when Auchinleck arrived to take personal command of the Eighth Army. Rommel himself again went out in the desert in a command vehicle, and for four days was lost, out of contact with his staff and behind the British lines. Eventually the British prevailed and, although he mounted several desperate counter-attacks, Rommel was forced to concede defeat and agree, however reluctantly, to the withdrawal which his staff recommended. By 11 January 1942 the Afrika Korps were back behind the defensive lines at El Agheila, having lost 300 tanks and 33,000 men, compared with British losses of 278 tanks and 17,000 men. They did not stay there long. On 21 January, having taken delivery of fifty-five new tanks, Rommel mounted an ambitious attack which proved to be the start of the run of his greatest triumph. The British commander at this stage realized that his hold on Libya was tenuous, and ordered the defences to be strengthened way back at El Alamein, as it turned out wisely. Rommel's January attack carried the Afrika Korps through to Benghazi, but it was only the prelude to the startlingly successful campaigns of the summer. On 26 May Rommel attacked the British defences at Gazala, the start of the battle which ended in the fall of Tobruk. Again Rommel's idiosyncratic style of command was evident. He was personally under

Rommel, briefly employed in Italy, talks with Field-Marshal Albrecht Kesselring, who had organized Germany's stubborn defence of Italy.

the prepared positions at El Alamein. There, in a long and wearying campaign beginning with the first battle of El Alamein, the Afrika Korps was fought to a standstill. Rommel was sick and exhausted, but at the height of his fame. After the seizure of Tobruk, Hitler had given him the rank of field-marshal, and the German propaganda machine, hungry for compensations for the setbacks on the Russian front, had begun to elevate him to the rank of an invincible hero. The British had also taken this view. Churchill thundered at his military chiefs: 'Rommel, Rommel, what else matters but beating him?' And Auchinleck had written to his commanders early on urging them not to let their troops think of Rommel as a magician or superman. The notion was in fact somewhat dispelled in the autumn of 1942, which brought the turning point in the North African war. Rommel's advance from El Agheila to El Alamein looked to the British war staff in London like a comprehensive defeat, and as usual the commander paid the price. Auchinleck's brilliance in halting the Afrika Korps at El Alamein went unrecognized, and Churchill dismissed him. General Alexander (q.v.) was appointed to command in the Middle East, with General Montgomery (q.v.) (the second choice for the post) as Eighth Army commander. They took over on 15 August 1942. Although British success in the summer 1942 battles was credited to these two commanders, especially Montgomery, the real key was that of supplies. The British were not seriously engaged elsewhere, and their forces were receiving the best material available. The German effort in North Africa was on the other hand less important than their massive commitment in Russia. Rommel tried to persuade his superiors in Berlin that with proper support he could take the Suez Canal, drive through the Middle East, bring Turkey into the war on the Axis side, and link up with the Russian front in the Caucasus. But this strategic vision remained an ephemeral ideal, and he was starved of resources. He was also increasingly ill from a stomach ailment, and his whole demeanour from this time on began to betray increasing pessimism.

fire almost continuously, and always in the thick of the fighting. He came close to being captured, and was frequently out of contact with his staff. Nevertheless his presence with the front-line troops and his almost infallible knack of turning up at the critical points in the battle again exerted a decisive influence, and in the peculiar open conditions of the North African theatre were more telling than the most effective orthodox style of command functioning well behind the front. Tobruk fell on 21 June. Large and valuable quantities of British stores and arms fell into Axis hands; and the British retreated in some chaos to

He left North Africa, both to visit Berlin and to recover his health on leave, early in October. Hitler decided then to transfer Rommel to an Army Group command in the Ukraine. But when Rommel's replacement, Stumme, died of a heart attack, and the British attacked out of their positions at El Alamein, Hitler recalled Rommel from his hospital bed and asked him to return to Africa. The battle was unusual for North Africa in that it was fought from prepared positions, in contrast to the earlier mobile and fluid desert battles. British air supremacy and the Africa Korps' fuel shortages had changed the picture. Rommel arrived back in North Africa on 25 October, two days after the battle started, but he was too late to influence it. With the margin of British material superiority growing as German losses mounted, he could do little except plan for withdrawal. By November the British had made the decisive breakthrough and the Afrika Korps were in their final retreat. Although the British advance was deliberate, cautious, even ponderous, it was the right advance in the circumstances. It prevented Rommel bringing to bear his mobile flair, and it gradually forced the Afrika Korps back along the North African coast. On 8 November the Anglo–American force had landed in Operation Torch, and Rommel was realistic enough to recognize that this spelled the end of his chances. He even flew to Germany to recommend to Hitler that North Africa should be abandoned and the Afrika Korps saved to fight in Italy. Rommel brought his forces back behind the fortifications of the Mareth Line in Tunisia towards the end of January 1943, then on 14 February executed his last great coup, halting the American advance at the battle of the Kasserine Pass. In March, with the British threatening the Mareth Line, he flew to Germany yet again to try to save his troops by withdrawal. Hitler refused, and although Rommel's forces were doomed, it took until 13 May to force the Afrika Korps to surrender. By that time Rommel was no longer concerned in the theatre. Hitler first sent him on sick leave, then pulled him out of Africa. When his 200,000 troops went into captivity Rommel was in

Berlin where Hitler decorated him and told him that they should have listened to him earlier. For most of the rest of 1943 Rommel held appointments in Italy, outside the mainstream of the war. Then in November he was sent to northern France with the mission of inspecting the defences against the invasion which even Hitler now recognized the western Allies would eventually attempt. It was one of the most difficult periods in his career. In Africa he had held total control over the Axis forces in an entire theatre of the war. Now he had no specific command responsibilities. Rundstedt (q.v.), brought out of retirement to take on the job, was commander-in-chief West, although even he had to refer every major decision to Berlin. At first the two field-marshals, in their different ways the two most revered figures in the army, held each other in wary respect. But Rommel eventually complained to Berlin about the ineffective nature of his job, and was given a specific appointment as commander of Army Group B, the likely invasion area. Rundstedt was his superior. Paradoxically this clarification of the command structure highlighted the problem, as Rommel disagreed with Rundstedt's concept of the best form of defence. Rundstedt insisted on maintaining a powerful mobile armoured reserve, prepared to move against the invading force wherever it attempted to land. Rommel, in a further paradox, had no faith in the usefulness of a mobile reserve. For a general who had made his reputation in the mobile tank warfare of the western desert, it is ironic that he instantly abandoned the technique of which he was the acknowledged master. He reasoned that Allied air superiority would neutralize the mobility of an armoured reserve and, if they secured a foothold, the Allies would be able to build up a bridgehead and ultimately break out. The only way to stop them was to prevent them landing at all, and the defence would therefore have to be undertaken by whatever troops were on the spot. This meant, in effect, a thin line, with all available troops pressed into the forward areas, and the armour spread out along the coastline, virtually piecemeal. The

Rommel, late on the scene and starved of resources, found himself responsible for more than 3000 miles of coastline where the Allies might invade. Here he visits the northern extremity, where anti-invasion obstacles protect the coast of Denmark.

dispute was never clearly resolved. But nothing could stop Rommel preparing the ground defences in his own way, and in the months preceding the invasion he produced a new display of the old energy, scurrying up and down the coastline, visiting the forward units, helping to site the guns and troop emplacements, discussing plans with the unit commanders, and devising a variety of physical obstacles – tetrahedrons, concrete spikes, stakes, traps – anything that would hold a landing craft or take the bottom out of a boat, even a vast network of wire strung from poles to impede paratroops, widely known as 'Rommel's asparagus'. He also laid 4 million mines in the invasion area,

a massive threefold increase on those required by his predecessors. Whether Rommel's plan or Rundstedt's was the correct one is of course impossible to say, since the Allied invasion in any event succeeded, but the total air domination over Normandy both before the invasion and during the period of the build-up indicates that Rommel's reasoning showed a clearer grasp of reality than any other German general's at the time. In fact Rommel was away from his post when the invasion took place in June 1944. It was another paradox of Rommel's career: as on a number of occasions in North Africa, the general who insisted on fighting alongside his troops had again missed the critical opening phase of the battle which he himself had planned for. This time he was once more in Berlin reporting to the Führer. Within two weeks of the invasion his estimation of the dominance of the air space by the Allies had been proved so accurate that he was back in Berlin advising Hitler that the invasion could not be contained. He and Rundstedt together recommended that Hitler should 'draw the proper conclusion from this situation' – in effect that he should concede northern France to the Allies. Hitler's response was the sack for Rundstedt, and one of the now customary orders to Rommel for the troops to 'stand fast'. Rommel was by now thoroughly disillusioned with Hitler, and was becoming loosely enmeshed with one of the number of groups which recognized Germany's inability to win the war and were plotting to remove Hitler as a prelude to attempting to negotiate a peace with the Allies, at least in the west. How far Rommel's involvement went is unclear, but plans were conceived for him to take over the presidency of Germany on Hitler's removal. The opportunity never arrived. On 17 July Rommel's staff car was strafed by a British aircraft and crashed, and Rommel suffered severe injuries including a fractured skull. He was not expected to recover, but quickly did so, and on 8 August he went home to convalesce. But by that time the end of his life was ordained by other means. On 20 July a group of plotters had attempted to assassinate Hitler when Count Klaus von Stauffenberg (q.v.) placed a bomb under the table in the Führer's headquarters at Berchtesgaden. In the aftermath of the failure of that attempt, one of the principal figures in Rommel's circle, Stulpnagel, uttered Rommel's name when he was recovering from his own suicide attempt. From this and possibly other intelligence traces Rommel was implicated in the plot. The investigations continued until mid-October as Rommel spent the weeks quietly at home. Then on 14 October two investigating generals arrived at Rommel's house at Herrlingen, to keep an appointment made the previous day. They offered Rommel the choice of taking poison, or of being

tried by a people's court for complicity in the assassination attempt. Rommel had no fears of a public trial, but felt certain that he would be murdered on the way to Berlin. Besides, he had been promised (for what the promise was worth) that his family would be honourably treated if he took the poison. Given no time for reflection, he made a rapid decision, took his leave of a tearful wife and his son, and quickly left with the two generals in their car. After a few minutes one of the generals ordered the car to stop, and there Rommel swallowed the poison. He died quickly in the back seat of the car. The fiction was maintained that Rommel died of wounds received in France, and he was given an elaborate funeral with full military honours near his home at Ulm before his body was cremated. Rommel's reputation in Germany therefore remained untarnished for the remainder of the war, and in the decades since has not suffered from the iconoclasm directed at most of the other participants. He has been accused of acting recklessly in conducting his campaigns invariably from the centre of battle, thereby causing two separate problems: both risking capture, injury or death from enemy fire, which would hardly have enhanced his control, and not being able to see the entire picture of the developing battle. Rommel's own writings give a convincing and lengthy answer to such criticisms. He was the first to visualize the novel nature of mobile tank warfare in the early battles in the desert, that they are more like sea battles than orthodox land campaigns fought for territory. He recognized where the key to desert generalship lay, and wrote: 'In motorized warfare speed of operation and quick reaction of the command were the decisive factors ... the commander-in-chief must frequently busy himself in the front line.' It was only when Montgomery, enjoying the advantages of better supply and air domination (which Rommel himself predicted would be decisive), refused to fight such mobile armoured warfare that Rommel's generalship was really mastered. Perhaps his greatest quality was his flexibility: his ability to read the precise phase in the development of warfare at

Rommel was never a good headquarters general: the soldiering he liked best was out in the field – or the desert – among his men. He was frequently out of touch with his own staff.

which he stood, and adjust his methods accordingly. He is also remembered as a general who remained close to his men in battle. He made his presence felt by his habit of turning up, in his command vehicle or just on foot, to see for himself what was happening at the front. He could discuss with his young officers, NCOs and the men themselves the details of their own jobs, although he warned of the dangers of simulating a feeling for the troops, because the ordinary soldier had a good nose for a fake. Like his adversary Montgomery, he understood instinctively the value of being easily recognized, and rarely appeared without his peaked cap and goggles, themselves a simple trophy of a victorious battle. Above all, Rommel

was a soldier's soldier – brave, straightforward and trustworthy.

ROOSEVELT, Franklin Delano (1882–1945). President of the United States 1933–45, and probably the most influential wartime figure on the Allied side. Among the other two claimants to that distinction, Stalin and Churchill (qq.v.), the former was forced to wait until the western Allies were ready to make their moves, while the British prime minister, despite his strategic influence and persuasive powers, was obliged to grant precedence to the view of the president whenever a divergence of opinion occurred. As Churchill himself observed, he was conscious that he was only his country's political chief; Roosevelt was also the

American president Franklin Delano Roosevelt returns in triumph to the White House after his third inaugural, 20 January 1941.

head of state, and occupied a position equivalent to that of Churchill and King George VI combined. From this commanding and dominating position Roosevelt determined, almost personally, the strategic direction of the war. He and Churchill were of course liberally supplied with advice and information from the combined chiefs of staff but, as several of their close associates have acknowledged, it was Roosevelt and Churchill who laid down the strategic plans which it was the task of the professional servicemen to carry out. And when Churchill and Roosevelt disagreed in their deliberations, it was invariably Roosevelt's view that prevailed. With the ultimate victory dependent on American material and manpower, it could hardly have been otherwise.

The details of Roosevelt's career before the war are well known and do not warrant a place here. In brief, however, it must be said that even if the war had never occurred, or if he had been removed from office at its beginning, Franklin D. Roosevelt would still have earned a place as one of America's great presidents. The child of one of the aristocratic families of the republic, he was born on the family estate at Hyde Park, NY. He was educated by private tutors and at an exclusive preparatory school in Groton, Conn., before going on to Harvard and Columbia University Law School. He entered politics as a form of social service, and in 1910, at the age of twenty-nine, ran for the Democratic party in the election for the New York Senate, and won. In 1913 he was appointed assistant secretary of the navy, and although he lost in the 1914 elections to the United States senate, he remained in his navy post, became familiar with military leaders on the world stage, and at the war's end was one of the most famous figures in the United States. There followed, at the age of thirty-nine, the attack of poliomyelitis which left him barely able to stand for the rest of his life, and the narrowly successful election to the office of governor of New York. In the presidential election of November 1932 he proved his capacity to overcome physical disability with an election tour of thirty-eight states in which he campaigned on the promise of a 'new deal' to lead the nation out of the depression, and was elected to the first of his administrations.

His first impact on the nation's affairs was drastic and imaginative. He halted the financial panic by closing the banks, allowing only those which could be shown to be sound to reopen. He called Congress into special session to pass a mass of legislation aimed at alleviating the problems of the depression. That session gave the new concept of the 'hundred days' to the language of politics. He inaugurated his practice of 'fireside chats', designed to inform the American public of his policies through the medium of radio. Above all he managed, through communicating his own bravery and faith in the future, to restore the faith and courage of the American people. With his far-reaching and radical programme of new legislation, Roosevelt almost single-handedly led the United States out of its recession, rescuing the economy and saving the business-orientated civilization of the New World. When he ran again in the presidential election of 1936, seeking a mandate to continue to fight, there was barely any opposition and he won the greatest landslide victory in American history.

In the last years before the outbreak of war in Europe, Roosevelt's popularity suffered a serious decline, partly over his battles to reform the Supreme Court, partly because his reductions in public spending led to a minor recession, and partly because the end of the worst phase of the depression had released the more conservative of opponents from their fears and enabled them to express their opposition to Roosevelt's reforms, which many of them condemned as Communism. In the congressional elections of 1938 the Republican candidates almost doubled their representation in the house, and it appeared that Roosevelt's fortunes were approaching the decline customary towards the end of a president's second term.

But in 1939 and 1940 Roosevelt's vision turned away from these troublesome domestic difficulties as war approached, and arrived, in Europe. During the second half of the 1930s public opinion in

Roosevelt

America leaned heavily towards the policy of isolationism, and as early as 1935 Congress had passed the Neutrality Act banning the provision of arms to all nations at war. But in 1937 Roosevelt took the brave step of deciding to reform public opinion (and incidentally contradict Congress) by publicly opposing the neutrality laws. He told the nation: 'There is no escape through mere isolation or neutrality.' The response was a deluge of hostility and antagonism – a demonstration of his disparity with public opinion which left him slightly bewildered. Nevertheless he fought on, and in January 1939 tried to secure the repeal of the neutrality laws to give 'all aid short of war' to nations opposing the Axis. The Senate did not agree, and there is no doubt that Hitler (q.v.) was thereby encouraged in his adventures in Czechoslovakia and Poland. When war broke out in September 1939 Roosevelt delivered another of his fireside chats, underlining to the American people the fact that events in Europe seriously influenced their own future. His personal campaign to educate the nation paid off, and in November 1939 Congress repealed the Neutrality Act to allow the policy of 'cash and carry', by which Allied nations could have American arms so long as they could transport them away themselves. 1940, as Roosevelt himself observed, 'witnessed a great change in the attitude of the American people'. His own attempts to sway public opinion were reinforced by the facts – the overrunning of Denmark and Norway (declared neutrals like the United States) and the overwhelming of France, reputedly the best-armed nation in the world. The realization came to the United States people that a Nazi-dominated Europe would not leave them unaffected, and isolationism declined, to be replaced initially by committed sympathy for the Allied cause. In the light of this change of heart, the 1940 elections arrived at precisely the right moment for Roosevelt. The Democratic party nominated him for an unprecedented third term and, campaigning on a promise to try to keep the country out of the war, Roosevelt again won decisively, carrying thirty-eight of the forty-eight states with 449 electoral votes, com-

Roosevelt enjoys a moment of relaxation in the months before his country is drawn into the war. His task is to pitch the opening ball of the 1941 baseball season at the Griffith Stadium, Washington DC, 20 May 1941.

pared with his opponent Wendell L. Willkie's 82.

1941 was a difficult year for Roosevelt. Both public and political opinion were split between earnest attempts to avoid provoking either Germany or Japan to go to war against the United States, and the contrary view that a declaration of war against Hitler was the straight answer to U-boat sinkings of American ships in the Atlantic. Roosevelt steered a course roughly down the middle. He set out to supply to Britain, and from September 1941 also to Russia, what he described as 'all aid short of war', which meant arms and ancillary equipment. The device which made this possible was Lend-Lease, one of Roosevelt's most inspired inventions. The president felt the Lend-Lease Act to be one of the most important issues of the period. If it failed, he maintained, it would mean that Britain would have to fight the Nazis alone, and few people doubted the outcome of that struggle. The probable consequence was a western Europe dominated by Germany, controlling the Atlantic and facing, a menacingly short distance away, the eastern seaboard of the United States. If he succeeded in getting the Lend-Lease Act passed, on the other hand, he would have stilled much of the isolationist voice. Again he set out to bring public opinion round to agreeing with him, on this occasion with a persuasive and picturesque analogy in which he likened the passage of the Lend-Lease Act to lending your neighbour your garden hose when his house is on fire. All you asked was that he gave you the hose back when he had put out the fire, or, if it was damaged, that he replaced it. The bill was passed on 11 March 1941, and by an amusing coincidence the first list of supplies to go to Britain included an item of 9000 feet of fire hose.

Roosevelt was not entirely right, however, in his judgment of the effect of the passing of the act on American opinion. In fact large quantities of the shipping carrying Lend-Lease supplies across the Atlantic were sunk, which dismayed the American public and tended to strengthen support for the 'America firsters'. Nobody, after all, wanted to see so much public money going down into the depths of the Atlantic. On the other hand, the sinkings gave rise to further pressure for an outright declaration of war. The secretary of war himself, Henry Stimson (q.v.), advocated the use of American ships and planes on convoy duties, which would inevitably have forced the United States into more active belligerency. But President Roosevelt remained constant as ever on the middle course. He limited his measures to ordering the transfer of American ships from the Pacific Fleet to the Atlantic.

By September the United States had moved closer to war, when further sinking of American ships prompted Roosevelt to press Congress for amendments to the Neutrality Act in order to adopt a 'shoot on sight' policy. In October two further attacks on US ships took place, on the *Kearny* on 17 October and the *Reuben James* on 31 October. Congress agreed with his request on 14 November, after Roosevelt had again led public opinion forward with an aggressive declaration of his position: 'That determination of ours not to take it lying down has been expressed in the orders to the American Navy to shoot on sight. Those orders stand. . . .' History has tended to gloss over this period of uncompromising hostility without the declaration of war, and taken the attack on Pearl Harbor as the beginning of the American involvement. Technically such a view is accurate, although with Roosevelt determining policy, merchant ships already armed, and German U-boats regularly sinking American destroyers, it is doubtful whether a declaration of war by the United States against Hitler could have been delayed long into 1942.

Roosevelt in fact wanted to avoid war with Japan, and was prepared to sustain protracted negotiations to delay involvement in the Pacific. He saw clearly that war in the Far East was precisely what Hitler wanted as a means of impeding the flow of American war material to Britain and Russia. The attack on Pearl Harbor on 7 December was therefore greeted with varying emotions by the major warring nations. It played into Hitler's hands. Churchill greeted it with undisguised delight,

Roosevelt brings the United States into the war at last, with a resolution by both houses of Congress declaring a state of war with Germany and Italy.

since it brought the United States directly into the war, and he could at last be confident, however long it took, of ultimate victory. To Roosevelt it was something of an inconvenience. Most seriously, it threw up a new set of problems in the form of arguments which would never die down, about which enemy to deal with first. Although many Americans, particularly of course those on the west coast, advocated all-out war against the Japanese, Roosevelt stayed firmly committed to the Germany-first approach. This policy was based on several powerful arguments – that an early concentration of forces against Japan was impossible because of the sea distances involved and the absence of airfields and naval staging areas; that only in Europe could the air support for war be provided and the build-up of combined British and American forces be achieved; and, most important, that the economic and scientific resources of Germany were strong enough for them to develop new weapons which might defeat the Allies unless Germany were defeated first. In 1942, which was mainly a year of painstaking planning for Roosevelt, this argument would not rest. When the British declared their opposition to attempting an invasion of France in that year, and called instead for the invasion of North Africa to fight against Rommel (q.v.), several of Roosevelt's advisers were hostile to the suggestion. If the British were not prepared to take part in a direct attack against Germany, they said, then American resources could profitably be diverted to the Pacific Ocean. It was General Marshall (q.v.), the army chief of staff, who signed the memorandum which said so, although he had the backing of the naval chief of staff, Admiral King (q.v.), who remained throughout an ardent advocate of the Japan-first policy. Roosevelt dismissed their demands with a peremptory note, stating that this was precisely what Hitler hoped for after Pearl Harbor, that it would only occupy troops in fighting in a lot of islands whose occupation would not affect the world situation this year or next, and that it would not help Russia or the Near East. 'Therefore it is disapproved as of the present.' It was a measure of the president's confidence in his judgment on political and strategic issues that he could dominate his senior advisers so completely. It also underlined the wisdom of coupling the president's office with that of commander-in-chief of the armed forces, at least when the two were held by a figure of Roosevelt's competence.

The early months of 1942 brought little other than setbacks for the Allies. The Japanese conquests had taken them as far as Borneo, New Britain, New Guinea and the Solomon Islands; they had taken Malaya and Singapore, sunk the *Prince of Wales* and the *Repulse*, and were besieging General MacArthur's (q.v.) forces in the Philippines. In North Africa the German forces were on the offensive and winning, and in the Atlantic the

U-boats were sinking Allied shipping at a faster rate than it was being replaced. Roosevelt's predominant task at this time was settling the strategic plan against Hitler, so far as it was possible, and by 1 April he had endorsed the scheme for Operation Roundup, the original plan for a cross-Channel invasion in the spring of 1943, supported by the vital Operation Bolero, the build-up of strength in Britain for that invasion.

But this was all superseded by the German successes in North Africa. Churchill knew that the cross-Channel invasion was out of the question for 1942, and sought Roosevelt's agreement to the invasion of North Africa. Roosevelt himself had consistently been sympathetic to such a move as an effective means of keeping German forces occupied and relieving pressure on the Russian front. By 25 July Operation Torch had been agreed, and Roosevelt wrote to Churchill that he felt the preceding week had represented a turning point in the whole war, 'and that we are now on our way shoulder to shoulder'. After the invasion of North Africa by the Anglo–American forces in Torch had taken place, the continuing need for strategic discussions led Roosevelt to make the first of his many journeys to Allied conferences in foreign countries. His original desire was to bring Stalin to a conference with himself and Churchill, but the Russian leader pleaded that he was preoccupied with the war on the Eastern Front, and could not attend. The main decision made at the Casablanca conference was to mount the attack on Sicily as the next move against the Axis. But the conference has become perhaps more famous for the origination of the term 'unconditional surrender' applied to the Axis powers in the second world war. Roosevelt's son has asserted that the term was invented by Roosevelt, uttered at a dinner, and approved by Churchill. Witnesses have alleged that the first time it was used in public was by Roosevelt at his press conference of 24 January 1943. Churchill asserts in his history of the war, with the evidence of the documents, that the phrase was used in his report to the War Cabinet of 20 January. The War Cabinet's concern was not

Despite his disability, the result of poliomyelitis, Roosevelt was energetic in promoting the war effort at home. Heavily flanked by secret service bodyguards, he visits the Douglas Aircraft Corporation at Long Beach, California, 25 September 1942.

about the phrase itself but about whether it should be applied to Italy, which they did not favour. Overall the phrase was not considered important enough to appear in the official communiqué approved by the two leaders after the conference, and Churchill records his surprise at hearing Roosevelt use the term at his press conference. The controversy never died down, and persisted until well after the war when the Allies confronted the problems of rebuilding Germany. Perhaps the most interesting sidelight on the problem is Roosevelt's uncharacteristic error in telling the press a long, 'folksy' story about the origin of the term. It was, he explained, used by General Ulysses Grant to General Robert E. Lee, when Lee was forced to surrender at Appomattox Court House in 1865. It was a good story, enhanced by Roosevelt's telling of it. In fact the scene was Fort Donelson, the surrendering general was S.B. Buckner, and the date was 1862.

In May 1943 Roosevelt met Churchill at the Trident conference in Washington. There the

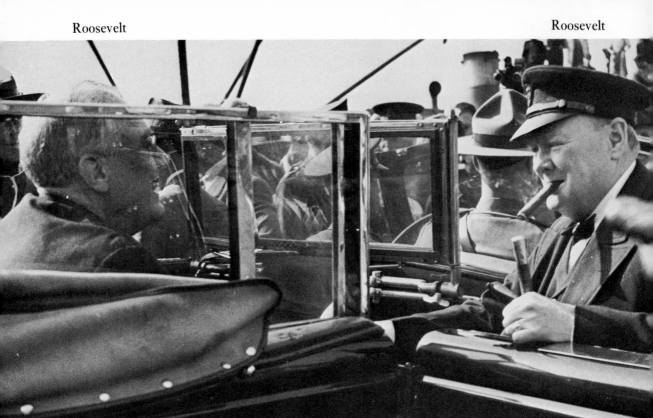

Roosevelt meets Churchill for the conference in Quebec, August 1943.

target date of 1 May 1944 was agreed for the cross-Channel invasion. In August the two leaders met again in Quebec for the Quadrant conference, where it was agreed to support the Normandy invasion with landings in southern France. It was also decided that the supreme command in Overlord should be held by an American. After these conferences, when the Allies were rapidly coming within sight of victory, Roosevelt began to concern himself to a great extent with the problems that would emerge at the end of the war, both at home and overseas. This aspect of his leadership is often

overlooked, but it is a measure of his farsightedness that even as early as October 1943, when the war was only just turning in favour of the Allies, he was considering the economic difficulties that would follow the end of hostilities. His measures included setting up a demobilization office, establishing a programme of education for troops returning home after the war, and initiating the body (Office of Foreign Relief and Rehabilitation Operations) which would deal with shortage of food and shelter in liberated countries. December 1943 brought about the meeting which Roosevelt had so long worked towards between himself, Churchill and Stalin. Teheran was the only location which Stalin would agree to visit, although Roosevelt thought the journey hard and unnecessarily difficult, and feared that the time spent out of Washington would complicate his dealing with domestic matters. When Stalin proved adamant Roosevelt agreed on Teheran, and it was there that he struck up the relationship with Stalin which proved to be one of his few failures of judgment in the course of the war. We 'got along fine', he told the press after the conference. And he genuinely felt that he understood the Russian leader. He later tried to reassure a worried Churchill that he could handle Uncle Joe, but he completely misread Stalin's intentions and outlook. The one concession which he did wring out of Stalin at Teheran, and which he took home to the United States with a sense of triumph, was an assurance that the Russians would declare war on the Japanese eventually. Stalin was equally insistent that the two western powers should state categorically when they were going to open the second front in Europe. Churchill was the figure whose nose was bloodied on this occasion. He still talked about alternative operations against the 'soft underbelly' of occupied Europe. But Roosevelt was as keen as Stalin on seeing Operation Overlord take place. Stalin also pressed Roosevelt to name the commander for Overlord. The name of General Marshall was widely canvassed for this post, and Roosevelt at that time appeared to accept that the task of leading the most important campaign of the war would go to the senior American general. Roosevelt, however, declined to name the commander, and when the time came he decided he could not manage without Marshall in the post of chief of staff in Washington. He nominated Eisenhower (q.v.) instead.

His other main achievement, or so it appeared at the time, lay in the Declaration of Teheran, which was signed by Stalin as well as the western powers. Seen from the point of view of hindsight as unrealistically idealistic, it seemed at the time a genuine step towards securing world peace: it

declared the dedication of the signatory nations to the elimination of tyranny and slavery, oppression and intolerance, and welcomed all nations who aligned themselves with that aim 'into a world family of democratic nations'. In the light of this declaration Teheran was regarded as the peak of Roosevelt's career in terms of his contribution to international diplomacy. No doubt it was not his responsibility that Stalin failed to honour the terms of the agreement. It was certainly Roosevelt's responsibility – and an indication of the one myopic facet of his outlook – that he sustained his naïve optimism about the goodwill of the Russians long after Churchill had voiced his fears about Russian intentions.

In one other important way Teheran was the climax of Roosevelt's career. He arrived home tired and suffering from a cough, and close observers detected the first signs of the deterioration in his health. The unity which the nation had shown during the early years of the war proved, during the early months of 1944, to be rather fragile, and much of Roosevelt's attention was taken up with his differences with Congress. Nevertheless in July he accepted the nomination as Democratic candidate for the presidential election. He wanted to retire, while at the same time he also wanted to see the job through until the end of the war. Harry S. Truman (q.v.) was selected as his vice-presidential candidate. The Republicans campaigned on the protest that nobody could remain president for sixteen years, and that in any case Roosevelt was in poor health. The Democratic reply maintained that the nation should 'not change horses in midstream'. Roosevelt defeated Dewey by the familiar wide margin. He began his fourth term in poor health. Photographs taken in his last year show the transformation that had taken place during the war, from a confident man at the peak of maturity (except of course for his disability) to a pallid figure of advanced age. He had been troubled by colds for twelve months, and had lost fifteen pounds in weight. The election campaign itself, which he had been forced to undertake to silence persistent charges that his health was not

Roosevelt confers with Churchill, Chiang Kai-shek and Madame Chiang.

up to another term, left him exhausted. However he soon recovered his old enthusiasm and threw himself into the three main problems of his last administration: keeping up the nation's will to fight when the war was apparently as good as won; fighting for his vision of the new America when the boys came home; and striving for international agreement on the means of securing peace after the war. In pursuit of this last aim he travelled in February 1945 to Yalta, the Black Sea resort in the Crimea, for his final conference as one of the 'Big Three'. Again he took the chair, being both head of state, which neither Churchill nor Stalin were,

and head of the three nations, as even Stalin acknowledged. Because of the strains on his health, Roosevelt was given accommodation in the Livadia Palace, where the plenary sessions of the conference were held. Yalta was widely considered the high point of co-operation and unity among the three major powers, although again this view took little account of the extent of Roosevelt's error in accepting at face value Stalin's own intentions. So far as the military side of the conference was concerned, there was agreement on the measures for dealing with Germany after that nation was defeated, including occupation by the four powers, the end of Nazism, punishment of war criminals, reparations and the end of German militarism. Of this last phenomenon Roosevelt, who was shocked by seeing at first hand the effect of the war in Europe, observed bitterly: 'I know that there is not room enough on earth for both German militarism and Christian decency.' His enemies criticized Roosevelt severely for making too many concessions to Stalin. These involved the return of several Russian rights which were lost in the 1904 war with Japan, in return for which the Russians agreed to join in the war against Japan two to three months after Germany's surrender. The fact was that at the time of the Yalta conference there was no indication that the atomic bomb would be developed and tested successfully within a few months, nor that the conventional bombing raids would reduce Japanese military and industrial capacity, and civilian morale, to the point where a surrender was likely. At the time of the conference the war in the Pacific was beginning to falter, and the invasion of the Japanese homeland was being planned for November 1945. The military experts were coming up with estimates of a million more American lives that would be lost before Japan was defeated, and it therefore seemed reasonable at the time that Roosevelt should press for Russian support with every means at his disposal, including concessions that later developments showed to be unnecessary.

In the two months that were left to him Roosevelt did at least begin to see the truth of Stalin's attitude, and to appreciate the extent of Russian indifference to honouring the terms of the agreements. He cabled Stalin on 1 April, expressing disappointment at the lack of progress in carrying out the political decisions reached at Yalta. And on 12 April he referred in a message to Churchill to 'the general Soviet problem', and advocated firmness in dealing with it. Certainly he was disappointed at the changing Russian position, after having worked so hard to secure co-operation among the three major Allies. But this, like the closing of the war itself, was a problem he did not live to deal with. On 12 April he was at Warm Springs,

Georgia, working at his desk while having his portrait painted. Suddenly he fell over in his chair, and whispered: 'I have a terrific headache.' He died a few hours later, without regaining consciousness, of a cerebral haemorrhage. The last words he ever wrote have become something of an epitaph for this colossal American leader in war and peace: 'The only limit to our realization of tomorrow will be our doubts of today. Let us move forward with strong and active faith.'

ROSENBERG, Alfred (1893–1946). Nazi minister for the occupied eastern territories. Born in Estonia of German parentage, Rosenberg studied architecture in Moscow, but fled to Ger-

Alfred Isidore Rosenberg, Nazi polemicist and author of the standard account of Nazi racial and political beliefs.

273

many after the revolution in 1917, where he joined the Nazi party two years later. He was an important figure in the early days of the party, as editor of its newspaper the *Völkischer Beobachter*. He became deputy leader but resigned in 1924, then came back to prominence when he was elected to the Reichstag in 1930. He became head of the party foreign affairs department in 1933, with responsibility for the Nazi parties in other countries. Appointed minister for occupied eastern territories in 1941, he was responsible for organizing conquered countries, notably the Soviet Union, in the way most beneficial to Germany. He was remarkably tolerant in his policies, favouring semi-independent regimes in occupied countries, and arguing against the brutal oppression advocated and practised by some of his Nazi colleagues. But his influence was too weak to have any serious effect. He was also a leading party ideologist and wrote the important Nazi bible on racial and political beliefs, *The Myth of the Twentieth Century*. He was tried as a war criminal at Nuremberg and hanged.

RUDEL, Hans-Ulrich (born 1916). German fighter ace who flew on the Russian front and accumulated a massive total of 519 Russian tanks destroyed. He flew more than 2530 sorties, outnumbering the missions of any other pilot of any country during the war. His achievements led in January 1945 to the creation and minting of a special decoration for him alone, the Golden Oak Leaves of the Knight's Cross.

RUNDSTEDT, Karl Rudolf Gerd von (1875–1953). One of the most senior and respected German generals, who served with distinction in top field commands from the German invasion of Poland in 1939 to the Allied invasion of Normandy, when he held the post of commander-in-chief West. In the invasion of Poland, as commander-in-chief Army Group South, his masterly contribution was to judge accurately, and contrary to the views of German supreme command, that by 8 September the Poles had not retreated across the Vistula. He was therefore able to outflank the central Polish forces, locate his own army behind them, and thereby prevent them from reaching the river. The German attack then became, in the classic manner, a tactical defence, as they merely had to hold their area to prevent the Polish withdrawal. Against Rundstedt's defence the Poles had no chance of success. In the invasion of France and the Low Countries in May 1940, Rundstedt commanded Army Group A, with the task of carrying out the secondary attack through the Ardennes. In fact this part of the assault emerged as of vital importance. The French considered the Ardennes impassable and Rundstedt's armoured thrust, with Kleist (q.v.) commanding the three panzer corps, outflanked the Allied armies and threatened to cut them off in the Dunkirk–St Omer region. It looked certain that Rundstedt would annihilate the British Expeditionary Force. Then Rundstedt received a telephone call from the Führer's headquarters: 'Your further operations in the Dunkirk area. Pass on the order to Kleist's tank group not to cross the line of the St Omer Canal.' Rundstedt was astonished: 'You cannot be serious. Our panzer formations are on their way to the town.' 'They are not to cross the canal. It is an order from the Führer personally.' Hitler (q.v.) held up the tanks for three days, and enabled the British Expeditionary Force to escape from the beaches and harbour at Dunkirk. After this successful command Rundstedt was appointed to command the major part of the invasion of England. That enterprise never took place, but was halted in favour of the invasion of Russia, for which he was transferred to the Eastern Front to command Army Group South. Again his farsighted strategic grasp brought remarkable success. Despite limited tank strength, his armies over-ran the Crimea and the Donetz basin, and his advanced units reached as far as Rostov on the river Don. There they were thrown back by Russian counter-attacks. Rundstedt, recognizing the exhaustion of his troops, asked permission to pull back to the Mius river. Hitler, still smarting from his failure to take Moscow to the north, characteristically refused to permit any form of tactical withdrawal, and Rundstedt thereupon asked to be relieved of his com-

Field-Marshal Gerd von Rundstedt (right), senior German general brought out of retirement by Hitler to serve as c-in-c West, in nominal charge of the anti-invasion preparations.

mand. It was the end of November 1941. He was replaced by Reichenau. Rundstedt went into an honourable retirement, and avoided any responsibility for the defeats at the hands of the Soviet armies in 1942 and 1943. He was recalled in July 1942 to become commander-in-chief West, in northern France, with responsibility for the anti-invasion preparations. It was a difficult and in some ways anomalous position to hold, and Rund-

stedt, now an officer of massive stature and dignity, with the enviable record of never having lost a battle, held it as the 'Grand Old Man' of the German army. All major decisions had to be referred to Hitler, and, as Rundstedt observed, the only troop formation he was permitted to move was the guard at the gate of his headquarters. His position was made doubly difficult when the German armies were beaten out of Africa, and Hitler sent Rommel (q.v.) to France to take on executive responsibility for the anti-invasion preparations in northern France as commander of Army Group B. There were thus two field-marshals with the same job.

Rundstedt's strategy was based on the concept of a mobile defence. He reasoned that with the limited forces at his disposal he could not be expected to man the entire coastline along a front of some 3000 miles. Moreover, as the general who had outflanked the static French defences in 1940 he was not willing to repeat their errors, and insisted that there would be no 'Maginot spirit' in the German defences. His solution to the problem was to assemble a strong mobile reserve, ready to be brought into action wherever the invading Allies landed. Rommel's view was that the mobility necessary to make such a force effective would be impeded by Allied air superiority. Instead he insisted on a system of thin but consistent defence all along the likely invasion area, aiming to throw the Allies back into the sea before they could establish a beach-head. Neither plan worked. The Allies landed and established their beach-head in Normandy, and on 17 June Rundstedt and Rommel both travelled to Hitler's little-used command post in the west at Soissons to try to persuade Hitler to permit a withdrawal to a new line out of range of naval gunfire. Hitler of course refused and sent them back to the front with a promise that a new weapon was on the way, the flying bomb, which would win the war for them. On 1 July, after counter-attacks had made no significant impression on the Allied forces, Rundstedt telephoned Hitler's headquarters to report these setbacks. When the *Wehrmacht* chief Keitel (q.v.) asked him what they could do, Rundstedt told him: 'Make peace, you fools. What else can you do?' Keitel of course told Hitler, who wrote a polite note to Rundstedt telling him that Kluge (q.v.) was to replace him.

As a senior general of impeccable character without any post, Rundstedt was ideally placed to help in clearing up after the attempt on Hitler's life on 20 July 1944. He presided over the court of honour which expelled from the army the generals implicated in the assassination attempt, before handing them over to the people's court for trial and subsequent execution. Then on 5 September, after the fall of Antwerp, Rundstedt was recalled yet again to take over the post of commander-in-chief West. His task was to hold the Allied advance in Europe, by fighting for time so that the preparation of the West Wall could be completed – specifically by holding the line of the Albert Canal–Meuse–Upper Moselle. Such were his orders from the Führer, and such was the Führer's distance from reality that by the time Rundstedt took over the Allies had already secured bridgeheads over the Albert Canal and the Meuse. So when Rundstedt told Hitler that it would take him six weeks to prepare the West Wall, and requested all available tanks to be sent forward to reinforce his lines, it was a plea uttered with little hope or expectation of a favourable response. The Allies, he estimated, already had twenty times as many tanks as the Germans, and there was no source of reserves from which Hitler could suddenly produce the 2000 required to make good the deficiency. Nevertheless, by sending such tanks as were available to the Moselle, Rundstedt had succeeded, by 17 September 1944, in halting the Allied advance and stabilizing the defence line. He held the position throughout October and November and into December, so that Hitler, with renewed cheerfulness, was able to promise a new military triumph at Christmas. At the same time the Allies gloomily faced the possibility of the stalemate being extended, partly owing to the weather, right through the winter.

Hitler's 'military triumph' turned out to be the Ardennes offensive. Rundstedt objected to the plan, but Hitler, true to character, over-rode his senior military commander and sent him detailed orders for the attack, endorsed with the words, in his own handwriting: 'Not to be amended.'

When the Ardennes offensive failed, Rundstedt recommended taking up a new defensive line. Again Hitler dismissed his recommendation, saying that only a renewed offensive would enable them to turn the war in the west to success. The result was yet another attempt to reach the Meuse, which also ended in failure. The truth was that Rundstedt, then aged sixty-nine, was totally circumscribed by the Führer. While still capable of taking sound strategic decisions, he had not the steel left in his soul to insist on carrying them out in defiance of Hitler's irrational ravings. Perhaps too long a period of subservience, including one previous dismissal and his earlier resignation, together with the cloud hanging over the German army after the July plot, had drained him of his independence. Then when the 9 Armoured Division of the US First Army took the bridge at Remagen and crossed the Rhine, Hitler removed him yet again and replaced him with Kesselring (q.v.), whose tenacious defence in Italy made him as well qualified as any general to hold back the Allied advance. Rundstedt briefly became a prisoner of war after the German surrender.

Wise and strategically sound, Rundstedt was a towering figure among the German generals. Aloof, aristocratic and a natural exponent of the old-fashioned Prussian military values, he has been criticized as too hidebound to exploit the techniques of modern warfare in the manner of some of the more innovative and ingenious generals. Nevertheless, although not noted himself as a modernist, he was sufficiently flexible to recognize the merits of the new forms of armoured warfare and allow his junior officers freedom to exploit them, to known devastating effect. He can hardly be faulted for excess conservatism.

S

Dr Hjalmar Schacht, Danish banker who became Hitler's financial wizard. He was acquitted at the Nuremberg trials and went on to further successes.

SAUCKEL, Ernst (1894–1946). Chief of the Nazi party's labour allocation organization from 1942. Sauckel was responsible for forcibly deporting 5 million people from their homes in occupied territories to work as slave labour in Germany. He ruled that they should be exploited as much as possible for the lowest possible expenditure. He was tried and convicted at Nuremberg and hanged.

SCHACHT, Hjalmar (1877–1970). German economics expert: president of the Reichsbank 1924–9, and again 1933–9. The son of a Dane, Schacht was brought up in America but returned to Germany for his university studies. He entered banking, showed a genius for finance, and quickly made a fortune. He was appointed currency commissioner in 1923 with the task of halting inflation and stabilizing the currency. After his first spell as Reichsbank president he supported Hitler (q.v.), used his skill to finance German rearmament, and became president of the Reichsbank again in 1933 and minister of economics in 1935. He resigned from the ministry, unable to work with Goering as economic overseer, and Hitler dismissed him from the bank after further policy disagreements in 1939. He lived in obscure privacy until 1944 when he was implicated in the bomb plot on Hitler's life, though nothing was proved against him. The Allies arrested him and tried him at Nuremberg on charges of conspiracy to cause the war and crimes against peace. He was confident of his innocence throughout the trial and was acquitted. After the war he made a second fortune and advised several developing countries on their economies.

The leading German figures stand trial at Nuremberg. Baldur von Schirach is speaking. The other defendants are: (back row from the left) Raeder, Sauckel, Jodl, Papen, Seyss-Inquart, Speer, Neurath and Fritzshe; (front row) Goering, Hess, Ribbentrop, Keitel, Kaltenbrunner, Rosenberg, Frank, Frick, Streicher, Funk, Schacht.

SCHIRACH, Baldur von (1907–74). Head of the Hitler Youth movement and governor of Vienna. The son of an aristocratic German father and American mother, Schirach was a leading figure in student politics, and in 1933 Hitler (q.v.) made him Reich youth leader, in which post he drew all the German youth movements under his control, including the boy scouts. He served in France in 1940 as an infantry officer, and was later made governor of Vienna with the task of bringing the troublesome and potentially rebellious Austrians under strict Nazi control. He was found guilty of war crimes at the Nuremberg trial, hav-

ing been implicated in the deportation of Jews from Vienna. He was sentenced to twenty years' imprisonment, and released from Spandau in 1966.

SEYSS-INQUART, Arthur (1892–1946). Nazi Reich commissioner in the Netherlands. Born in Moravia, at that time Austrian territory but later Czechoslovakian, Seyss-Inquart studied law at Vienna and was a leading worker through the Austrian parliament for union of Austria with Germany. He was a Nazi sympathizer from early on and Hitler (q.v.) appointed him minister of the interior and in 1938 chancellor. He forced the law through parliament which made Austria a German province, and Hitler rewarded him with the post of governor. When the war began he became briefly deputy governor of Poland, and then moved to the Netherlands. There, as Reich commissioner, he was responsible for recruiting labour for deportation to Germany and for rounding up Dutch Jews. He was tried as a war criminal at Nuremberg and hanged.

SHAPOSHNIKOV, Boris Mikhailovich (1882–1945). Soviet general: chief of the general staff during the first two years of the war against Germany. The son of a minor civil servant, Shaposhnikov secured a commission in the imperial Russian army, passed out of the Moscow military school and the staff college, and held mainly staff posts on the Caucasian Front in the first world war. He joined the Red Army in 1918 and, although he did not become a party member until 1930, was highly influential in the planning and theory of Soviet military affairs. He wrote extensively, arguing in his book *The Brain of the Army* (1927–9) in favour of the integration of military and party leadership. He also delivered a notable series of lectures during his term as principal of the Frunze military academy from 1932 to 1937. Both Stalin and Molotov (qq.v.) reputedly attended his lectures.

Shaposhnikov became chief of the general staff in 1937, and was instrumental in planning both the Polish invasion and the Finnish war after the

Marshal Boris Shaposhnikov (second from left), chief of the Soviet general staff until 1942, and a respected Soviet military theorist.

debacle of the early defeats. He also played a great part in the defence planning against the German invasion. Except for a period of leave through ill-health from August 1940 to February 1941, he remained chief of staff until his heart condition finally forced his retirement in November 1942. Even then he retained considerable influence, running the Soviet Union's important military research and planning organization, the historical administration section of the Defence Commissariat. Shaposhnikov was a highly professional and intellectual soldier, and has been described as Stalin's mentor in military matters.

SHTEMENKO, S.M. (born 1901). Soviet general who served as deputy chief of operations under Antonov (q.v.), and held several important planning posts. He rose to be chief of operations and deputy chief of the general staff in 1943. After the war he suffered a measure of disgrace under Khrushchev's de-Stalinization, but was rehabilitated and became chief of the Warsaw Pact forces in 1968.

SIKORSKI, Vladislav (1881–1943). Polish leader, head of the government-in-exile in London and c-in-c of the Free Polish Forces. When the Germans and Russians invaded his country in 1939 Sikorski went to Paris, where he built up a force from among the Polish miners in France, amounting to a strength of 100,000 men by the time France fell in 1940. He then moved to England to lead the Polish expatriates there. In 1941, when Russia was at war with Germany, he signed an agreement with Stalin (q.v.) ending the state of war between Russia and Poland and repudiating the partition of his country. It was also agreed to form a Polish army from among the Poles in Russia to fight against Nazi Germany under Russian command. But one other question remained the subject of disagreement and dissension: the liberation of all the Poles who had been imprisoned by the Russians after their entry into east Poland in 1939. Stalin agreed to the amnesty for the Polish prisoners, but Sikorski continued to assert that it had not been carried out. Sikorski claimed that the occupants of three camps had not been released,

General Vladislav Sikorski flies into London from Paris for consultations with the British government, 14 November 1939. His stay in Britain became more permanent in the following year, when he took over as head of the government-in-exile.

nor had anything been heard of them since the spring of 1940. At the end of November 1941 Sikorski went to Moscow and challenged Stalin over the whereabouts of the released Poles, Stalin could give only unsatisfactory excuses, claiming that the men had been released, but had fled, or that officials had made mistakes. Early in 1943 Sikorski produced evidence that virtually the entire Polish officer corps had been murdered by the NKVD, the Russian secret service, and buried in the Katyn forest. A Russian committee appointed to enquire into the deaths of the Polish prisoners alleged that they had been murdered by the Germans during the advance of July 1941. Sikorski refused to accept this explanation, and continued to charge the Soviet government with the crime, disrupting relations between the Poles and Russians to such an extent that the fragile co-operation between the Allies was threatened. Churchill (q.v.) lost patience with Sikorski and told him in March 1943 that they had got to beat Hitler (q.v.) and this was no time for quarrels and charges. Three months later, on 4 July 1943, Sikorski was killed when his aircraft crashed as he was taking off from Gibraltar. (*See also* Mikolajczyk, Smigly-Rydz)

SIMONDS, Guy (1903–74). Canadian general. A young, aggressive and versatile commander who had valuable experience leading the 1 Canadian Infantry Division in Sicily and the 5 Canadian Armoured Division in Italy before he took on his most important command, as head of Canadian 2 Corps in the Normandy invasion. Although only forty-one he already had a reputation as a military innovator, a perfectionist, and a ruthless authoritarian. He displayed his originality in breaking the German anti-tank screen south of Caen in August 1944. He devised a plan of attack never before

used, sending four tightly packed columns of tanks at night to penetrate German forward lines without any preliminary bombardment. The infantry were to follow in armoured vehicles, then leave them to attack the German rear areas on foot. A bomber attack on both sides of the advance was to provide flank cover. At night and in clouds of dust navigation was a real problem, and some tanks got lost, but the formation penetrated the German lines and made several German units panic. Simonds's highly novel plan almost produced a breakthrough on the eastern flank of the beach-head. It was only through lack of experience among his forces that it stopped narrowly short of total success. Simonds went on to command successfully through the Pas de Calais, the Scheldt campaign, and into northern Germany, taking over the Canadian First Army during Crerar's (q.v.) absence.

SKORZENY, Otto (1908–75). German soldier, one of the few exponents of commando-style war-

Otto Skorzeny's commando force escorts Mussolini to an aircraft after rescuing him from imprisonment in a lightning raid on Gran Sasso.

fare his country produced. Rejected by the Luftwaffe because he was too old, Skorzeny started the war as an *ss* soldier and served in France, Holland and Russia. He was invalided home and after a period with little to do was asked to set up a unit for commando training. He studied British methods and after some desultory attempts was ready by 1943 for his first major enterprise, when Hitler (q.v.) asked him to rescue Mussolini (q.v.). Skorzeny laid on a difficult and enterprising raid, landing his force by glider on 12 September on a small plateau in the Abruzzi mountains. The startled garrison of 250 guards surrendered to Skorzeny's ninety men with few casualties, and he took off with Mussolini in a Storch light aircraft. In 1944 he organized a campaign in support of the Ardennes offensive in which his men were disguised as American troops and operated behind Allied lines, causing some considerable confusion and spy mania. Several of them were discovered and shot. Skorzeny was tried at Nuremberg as a war criminal and acquitted.

SLIM, William Joseph (First Viscount Slim) (1891–1970). British general who defeated two Japanese armies in the Burma campaign. Widely considered to be one of the best of Britain's commanders, and by at least one authority to be the best general of any nation in the second world war. William Slim, who was born in Birmingham, was too poor to achieve his ambition of becoming a regular officer, which in his youth required a private income. However after he left school to join a local industrial concern he succeeded in joining the Birmingham University officer cadet corps, even though he was not a student. When the first world war required an influx of officers, he obtained a commission in the Royal Warwickshire Regiment, and served at the Dardanelles, where he was severely wounded by a bullet which passed through his body close to his spine. He also served in Mesopotamia. After the war he joined the 1 Battalion Sixth Gurkha Rifles and served with the Indian army on the north-west frontier. He entered the staff college at Quetta in 1926, passsed out top, and was selected as an instructor for the British

staff college at Camberley in 1934. Three years later he was selected to study at the Imperial Defence College, which marked him as an officer destined for the highest rank. On completing that course he returned to India, where he quickly achieved command of 10 Indian Infantry Brigade, and it was in that post that he entered the second world war. The brigade was sent to fight against the Italians in the Sudan and Eritrea in 1940, and served in Syria and Iraq in 1941.

In March 1942 Slim was appointed to command of Burcorps, the combined 1 and 17 Burma Divisions, whose task was to hold northern Burma following the Japanese capture of Rangoon. The plan failed, and between his arrival and the end of May the corps suffered a steady series of misfortunes, culminating in the retreat from Burma. They had been compelled to withdraw 1000 miles in two months, and had lost 13,000 men and most of their tanks and transport. The survivors who arrived in Imphal were a ragged and emaciated band. Slim handed over command of Burcorps in Imphal, and took command of 15 Corps, which was being raised near Calcutta to protect against a possible sea or land invasion of Bengal. The problems were enormous, as the Allied difficulties in other theatres in the early months of 1942 allowed small priority to be given to the Burma–India problem. There was no air cover, poor intelligence and communications, and few heavy weapons. Slim's main contribution at this stage, and it was extraordinarily far-reaching, lay in his transformation of the attitudes of the men in that theatre. He fundamentally changed the morale of his shattered and demoralized forces, and taught them to believe in themselves. He did so mainly by revising their approach to the jungle, and improving their fighting techniques. Basing his lesson on his own experience of the Burma retreat, he put the men through intensive acclimatization and training programmes, teaching them to move silently, use cover, gather intelligence, set up ambushes and live successfully when away from their bases for extended periods. He emphasized the need for aggressive patrolling to regain the

General William Slim: dour, professional and undemonstrative. But it was his 'forgotten' Fourteenth Army that defeated the Japanese in Burma.

initiative from the enemy, and restored their offensive spirit. He taught them that the jungle was not a hostile environment, but an ideal fighting terrain which could be turned to advantage for concealment and protection. He revised old-fashioned attitudes regarding front lines, and persuaded the men that having Japanese forces to their rear was not the defeat they imagined: in fact it was the Japanese who were surrounded, not they themselves. And he taught them that jungle warfare was not a question of holding an extended front, but of dominating strongholds, well supplied by air, with mobile reserves ready to counter-attack Japanese moves against them. He also brought home the simple truth that there were no non-combatants in jungle warfare, and that every unit, including field hospitals and headquarters, was responsible for its own defence. The result was an end to the myth of Japanese invincibility in jungle fighting, and the beginnings of the emergence of a hard, mobile, highly trained force confident in its ability to take on and defeat the Japanese.

This period of preparation occupied almost the whole of 1943, during which time there were further setbacks, particularly in the Arakan region. On 16 November 1943 the scene changed radically when a new command structure came into effect. Louis, Lord Mountbatten (q.v.) became supreme commander of the South-east Asia Command, and a new army was formed to replace the demoralized Eastern Army. Mountbatten appointed Slim to command the Fourteenth Army. Slim again devoted himself to training and preparation, especially to improving morale and fitness. Medical attention was a high priority, aimed at minimizing the effects of tropical disease. Slim introduced drugs to prevent malaria, and sacked any unit commander whose men were found in spot checks to be taking the ordained measures at less than a ninety-five per cent rate. He also ordered field hospitals to be pushed up to immediately behind fighting lines, to reduce the time taken to return sick men to their units, and assure them that if they were wounded or ill they could be hospitalized within a few hours. Not least among Slim's

achievements during this phase was to get himself known, liked and trusted by his men. He visited as many units as he could, and dealt directly with the greatest possible number of subordinate commanders. He talked directly to the men, with none of the superior detachment they had come to expect from some of their generals. They got to know him as a firm and fair commander, and derived confidence and aggression from his square jaw, burly figure and resolute approach to war.

In the area of strategy Slim's main difficulty was to secure a clear directive from London on his exact tasks. At the Teheran conference in November 1943 the western Allies agreed to devote their main efforts to conquering Germany in Europe, in return for Stalin's (q.v.) agreement to declare war on Japan as soon as that was accomplished. The immediate result was that half of the landing craft in the Burma theatre had to be withdrawn for use in Europe. This made planned amphibious operations impossible, and forced Slim to accept that the main effort to destroy the Japanese armies in Burma would be on land. He was left with a series of limited operations, by 15 Corps in the Arakan, 4 Corps to the River Chindwin, and Wingate's (q.v.) proposed long-range penetration operation by the Chindits. The Japanese also were planning a new offensive, in the Arakan and on Imphal, aimed at securing Burma from invasion by the British. It began in the Arakan, when General Hanaya's 55 Division penetrated the left flank of the British 7 Division and by 4 February 1944 was in a position in strength threatening the rear of the 7 Division. Initially it looked as if Slim and his commanders had been taken by surprise, despite their extensive preparatory work, particularly as the Japanese attacks had scattered the 7 Division headquarters into the jungle. But in due course Slim's preparations were vindicated. Using his mobile reserves, on 5 February he sent the 26 Division to aid the 7 Division, and on 10 February committed the 35 Division. With resolute defence from the 7 Division itself, the Japanese attack was halted. Slim's Fourteenth Army had won its first major battle

Slim offers his views, usually laconic, always reliable, in a press interview during victorious days in Burma.

with the Japanese, and the Arakan campaign emerged as a turning point of the war in Burma.

It was clear to Slim and the British planners that the next Japanese blow would fall soon after the Arakan offensive, and intelligence indicated that it would be against 4 Corps in the Imphal plain. Slim elected to concentrate his divisions only when the Japanese disclosed their intentions, pull-ing back the 17 Division from their forward posi-tions around Tiddim and the 20 Division from Kuntaung only when the Japanese had committed forces against those positions. There were dis-advantages, most seriously the loss of morale that would follow a withdrawal. But the advantages – shorter lines of communication, easier air support and greater tank mobility – made this course the best choice. Slim also approved the long-range penetration enterprise organized by General Wingate to land his Chindits 100–150 miles east of Imphal. Operation Thursday began on the night of 5 March. The predicted Japanese offensive began on 7 March, and for about a month they held a distinct initiative. General Mutaguchi (q.v.) launched attacks by his Fifteenth Army against the 17 and 20 Divisions in their exposed positions, aiming to compel Slim to commit his reserves. He would then destroy the bulk of the Allied force and have Imphal at his mercy, rendering a British invasion of Burma impossible. Slim acknowledged that he made a mistake in delaying the withdrawal of the 17 Division from 7 March, when the first Japanese troops were sighted, until 13 March. The division was cut off, and two brigades had to be sent to aid their withdrawal. In the event they fought their way out, and inflicted severe casualties on the Japanese. Slim was also able to fly in another reserve, the 5 Division, which again amply vindicated Slim's foresight and thorough preparation in the co-operation he had developed between the air and army organizations.

By 4 April 4 Corps had all its divisions concentrated in the Imphal plain. The problem of supplying this besieged garrison was acute, but the supreme commander insisted on retaining air squadrons which were required elsewhere, and by June intense efforts had solved the supply problem. The battles for Imphal and Kohima lasted from mid-April until early June. The Japanese launched fierce attacks by three divisions, but made no real impression on 4 Corps positions, and sustained heavy casualties. Unable to solve their own supply problems, and with the onset of the monsoons adding to their difficulties, Mutaguchi's Fifteenth Army was forced into retreat. It was a further three weeks before the Kohima–Imphal road was opened and the siege relieved, but there was no further doubt about the balance of advantage. The Japanese had suffered their greatest-ever land defeat, and the British were in a position to re-enter Burma. The pursuit of the Japanese began on 7 August 1944, but the main element in the operation, crossing the Chindwin and advancing towards Mandalay, could not get under way until December, when bridgeheads were established over the river and the Kalewa bridge, until then the longest Bailey bridge ever built, was in place. The main advance beyond the Chindwin began on 4 December, but doubts immediately arose about whether the Japanese were preparing to defend or were crossing the next river obstacle, the Irrawaddy. Slim rapidly produced a new plan to deal with this problem, which is acknowledged as the master strategical stroke of the Burma war. He ordered 33 Corps to attack Mandalay from the north, giving the Japanese the impression that Mandalay was the only target of his Fourteenth Army. At the same time he ordered 4 Corps to march by a little-used and difficult route to the south of Mandalay, cross the Irrawaddy, and attack the vital Japanese supply pivot of Meiktila. The moves by 4 Corps took place in January 1945 and were almost completely concealed from the Japanese by extensive deception measures. From 12 February for a week the crossing took place at several points along the front. The fighting that followed was among the fiercest of the war, but on 1 March the 17 Division captured Meiktila, which was only lightly held by administrative and hospital units. The Japanese realized the importance of this thrust of Slim's, and launched heavy counter-attacks by the Fifteenth Army, with General Honda himself taking charge. The fighting went on for the rest of March, but in the open country around Meiktila the British had the advantage of mobility with armour. They also had air superiority, and when it came to hand-to-hand fighting, the British and Indian troops of 4 Corps proved themselves the equals of the Japanese. By 1 April both the Fifteenth and Thirty-third Japanese armies were in disarray. There remained only the pursuit of the fleeing Japanese, and the bid to capture Rangoon before the onset of the monsoon. This was accomplished by a land advance from the north in concert with seaborne landings on 3 May.

Apart from tidying up the remnants of Japanese

Slim receives his knighthood, 1 January 1945, from Field-Marshal Wavell, acting on behalf of the king as viceroy of India.

resistance, General Slim had accomplished the recapture of Burma. He had done so by a rare combination of great administrative competence, and flexibility and flair in old-fashioned generalship. Slim had enjoyed the lowest priority of any major theatre of war, and was consistently starved of both fighting forces and war material. He had also in the early days of the war suffered a series of setbacks which might have caused other generals to accept defeat. But William Slim retained his determination, and communicated his courage and resolution to his men. Because of their training and confidence, and because of their trust in Slim himself, his men were prepared to fight battles as hard and as bloody as any in the war.

Perhaps a measure of Slim's greatness is that while almost every other major leader of the second world war, however brilliant his reputation, has some detractors, virtually no one has levelled serious criticism at Slim. And his supreme commander in the South-east Asia Command, Lord Mountbatten, has gone so far as to bestow on Slim the ultimate accolade of being the finest general of the second world war.

SMIGLY-RYDZ, Edward (1886–1943). Polish leader at the time of the German invasion. He directed the futile defences against the German *blitzkrieg* and, after two weeks of ineffective resistance, recommended falling back to the south-east corner of Poland to continue the fight, while

Marine Lieutenant-General Holland Smith (standing) shows two distinguished naval colleagues, admirals King (left) and Nimitz, around the newly secured island of Saipan, 17 July 1944.

waiting for help to arrive from the British and French, both of whom had declared war in Poland's favour. When the Russians also invaded Poland on 17 September Smigly-Rydz fled to Romania where he was interned. Sikorski (q.v.), who took over the leadership of the exiled Poles from his base in Paris, dismissed Smigly-Rydz as c-in-c. In 1941 Smigly-Rydz escaped back to Poland and helped organize the resistance. Nothing is known of him after 1943, and it is assumed that he was killed in action in the streets of Warsaw. (*See also* Mikolajczyk)

SMITH, Holland McTyeire (1882–1967). United States marine corps general who served as commander of the Fleet Marine Force in the Pacific, and devised or influenced many of the techniques which were used in the island conquests. 'Howling Mad' Smith, as he was nicknamed, trained many of the army and navy units engaged in the recapture of the Aleutian Islands Kiska and Attu. He commanded the invading troops for the operations in the Gilbert and Marshall Islands, the Marianas and the Volcano Islands, from Tarawa to Iwo Jima. Smith was largely responsible for the refinement of the amphibious landing technique, combining accurately timed co-ordination of the landing forces with preliminary naval and air bombardment.

SMITH, Ian (born 1919). Rhodesian fighter pilot. Ian Smith joined the RAF in 1941 and suffered severe injuries to the right side of his face and leg in a crash in North Africa. The extensive facial damage was repaired by plastic surgery. He returned to flying with 237 Rhodesian Squadron, baled out in northern Italy in June 1944 after being hit by flak, and fought with Italian partisans. He crossed the Alps to rejoin the Allies and fought with 130 Squadron for the rest of the war. Ian Smith became prime minister of Rhodesia in 1964 and on 11 November 1965 unilaterally declared his country's independence from Britain.

SMUTS, Jan Christian (1870–1950). South African statesman, friend and adviser to Winston Churchill (q.v.), and holder of the rank of field-marshal in the British army. After fighting against the British in the Boer war, Smuts became reconciled with the former enemy, and worked for the union of the South African colonies. When the Union of South Africa was formed in 1910 he was appointed minister of the interior. He led South African forces against the Germans in the first world war, and in 1919 became prime minister of South Africa. He was defeated in an election in 1924, served a period in a coalition government from 1933, and in 1939 returned to the premiership on the platform of helping Britain fight Nazi Germany, as opposed to remaining neutral. From that time on he was a close confidant of his friend of long standing, Winston Churchill. Under Smuts's leadership South African forces played a significant part in the Allied war effort. Smuts was promoted to the rank of field-marshal in the British army in 1941. Among his most notable contributions was his advice to Churchill on the changes in command in the Middle East in August 1942. After the war he was active in promoting the organization of the United Nations at San Francisco.

SOMERVILLE, Sir James (1882–1949). British admiral who commanded the important Force H stationed at Gibraltar during the early part of the war. In 1938 Somerville was compulsorily retired after an illness, but was recalled on the outbreak of war and worked in connection with the development of radar. During the evacuation from Dunkirk he volunteered to serve under Admiral Ramsay (q.v.), and helped organize the shipping to withdraw the British troops. Sent to Gibraltar after the fall of France, he was in charge of the negotiations through which the British government tried to eliminate the French fleet as a factor in potential German strength. The alternatives offered to the French were to join the British and fight the Germans, hand over the ships to the British for the course of the war, or sail to the West Indies where they would be free from potential German takeover. These choices were rejected, although Churchill (q.v.) later expressed doubts that the last offer, of sailing to the West Indies, was properly put. Somerville, who found the entire business distressing, was nevertheless under strict orders from the British government, and at 5.54 pm on 3 July 1940 opened fire on the French fleet at Oran, and subsequently at other ports. The French fleet was almost completely destroyed and the action, described by Churchill as 'this mournful episode', removed the French navy from calculations of possible German strength. In the following months Force H was fully occupied in escorting Mediterranean convoys, engaging the Italian fleet, and seeking out and destroying the *Bismarck* in the Atlantic. In March 1942 Somerville was appointed to command of the Eastern Fleet, guarding against Japanese expansion in the Indian Ocean. His final wartime post, from October 1944, was as the British naval representative in Washington.

SORGE, Richard (1895–1944). Russian spy working in Tokyo who warned of Japan's intention to attack the United States. He was also able to give Russia precise information, in May 1941, of Germany's plan to attack Russia without any ultimatum or declaration of war. He even gave the date as 20 June or two or three days after that. He was ignored, and the invasion began on 22 June with the Russians ill-prepared. After this it was important to discover whether Japan's rapid military build-up would be launched against Russia, forcing her into war on two fronts, or against the

Above Field-Marshal Smuts (right), the South African elder statesman and soldier, visits the Normandy beach-head with Churchill and Brooke.

Right Admiral Sir James Somerville (left) aboard HMS *Warspite*, in company with Captain G. N. Oliver. Somerville carried out the order to destroy the French fleet.

United States and Britain. At the end of August he was able to tell the Soviet Union, through contacts close to the Japanese cabinet, that there would be no Japanese attack against Soviet Russia that year. On 18 October 1941 Japanese police uncovered Sorge's ring. He was arrested, held in prison until 7 November 1944, then hanged.

SPAAK, Paul Henri (1899–1972). Belgian socialist politician and wartime foreign minister in the Belgian government-in-exile in London. Before the war Spaak favoured neutrality for Belgium, and refused to allow Allied forces into his country, though when Germany invaded he called on Britain and France to meet their obligations. He repudiated King Leopold's (q.v.) surrender, but later retracted his accusation. He arrived in London via Spain, and in 1944 returned to Belgium. He worked for the Benelux customs union which was set up in 1948, the United Nations Organization, of which be became president, and NATO, in which he served as secretary-general.

SPAATZ, Carl (1891–1974). Senior United States air force officer, who commanded United States strategic air forces in both Europe and the Pacific. Carl Spaatz served as a combat flier in France in the first world war and between the wars held a variety of staff and command posts. In 1940 he headed the air corps plans division, and in 1941 became chief of the air staff. Eisenhower (q.v.) chose him as his air adviser for North Africa in December 1942, and in 1943 he became deputy commander of the Allied air forces in that theatre, following which he served as commander of the north-west Africa air forces during the Sicily operation. In January 1944 he was promoted commander-in-chief of the US strategic air force in the United Kingdom and Fifteenth Air Force in Italy. He was responsible for organizing the massive bombing campaign against Germany, when he concentrated on knocking out the synthetic fuel plants and oil refineries. As D-Day came closer the task changed to attacks on rail communications, and his forces thereby made a major contribution

Lieutenant-General Carl Spaatz, commander of United States strategic air forces. He carried overall responsibility for the air offensive against Germany from Britain and the Mediterranean.

to the defeat of Nazi Germany with over one-and-a-half million tons of bombs dropped.

In July 1945, after the defeat of Germany, Spaatz moved to the Far East in the equivalent post as commander-in-chief of the US strategic air force operating against Japan, where his forces included Eighth and Twentieth Air Forces, and he was responsible for the operations which dropped atomic bombs on Hiroshima and Nagasaki.

On 1946 he became the first chief of staff of the newly independent United States Air Force.

Opposite An Axis cartoon attacks the Allied leaders. Churchill, Roosevelt and Stalin are depicted as a decadent trio of comedy characters at the time of the Teheran conference of November 1943.

Overleaf Prime minister Churchill and his senior military adviser, Field-Marshal Brooke, visit Montgomery's caravan headquarters in Normandy six days after D-Day.

J. Carlos

"*The more we are together . . . .*"

Albert Speer (second from left), Hitler's architect and a talented industrial organizer. He listens as the Mayor of Nuremberg explains to Hitler the plans for the new Nazi Congress buildings in the city, 4 May 1939.

SPEER, Albert (born 1905). Reich minister for armaments and war production in the Nazi government. An architect by profession, Speer joined the Nazi party in 1932, and Hitler (q.v.) made him his personal architect in 1934. He designed the new Reich chancellery in Berlin, and the party palace at Nuremberg. Although only thirty-six years old, and without experience in large-scale industry, he was appointed head of the Todt (q.v.) organization in 1942 with responsibility for state construction, and armaments minister. He proved a talented administrator, and rapidly expanded the war production capacity, so much that output increased in 1943 and 1944 despite the massive Allied bombing attacks on Ger-

The last meeting of the 'Big Three'. Churchill, Roosevelt and Stalin confer at Yalta in February 1945. Churchill and Roosevelt were soon to disappear from the scene.

man industry. He became disenchanted with Hitler, and contemplated taking steps to remove the Führer by passing gas into his bunker through a ventilator. But he recognized that the German people still believed in Hitler and dropped the idea. Instead he contented himself with attempting to protect German industry from destruction. He was tried as a war criminal at Nuremberg. There he was the most rational of the defendants, and accepted responsibility as a member of the government which had started a world catastrophe. He was convicted of war crimes and crimes against humanity, and sentenced to twenty years' imprisonment. He was released in 1965.

SPERRLE, Hugo (1885–1953). German air commander who led the Condor Legion in the Spanish civil war and was promoted commander-in-chief of the German Third Air Force in 1940. He commanded all the air forces in North Africa

General Hugo Sperrle, German air force chief who commanded the Condor Legion in Spain, and led Air Fleet 3 in the anti-invasion measures. He was acquitted of war crimes.

in support of the Afrika Korps, and was made head of all the air forces in western Europe defending against the Allied invasion of Normandy. He was tried at the end of the war but was acquitted of all war crimes both by the Allies in the Nuremberg trials and by a German de-Nazification court.

SPRUANCE, Raymond Ames (1886–1969). American admiral who served in the Pacific theatre and was widely considered one of the most talented naval commanders of the war. On the outbreak of the war with Japan Spruance was sent to the Pacific to command a cruiser division. In June 1942 he was in command of a task force which inflicted a severe defeat on the Japanese navy at the battle of Midway. In 1943 he took command of the Gilbert Islands operations in which he landed marines on the Makin and Tarawa atolls. In January 1944 he headed Central Pacific Command, and organized a series of amphibious operations from the Marshall Islands on 30–31 January, to Iwo Jima and Okinawa. In April 1944 he was also named commander of the US Fifth Fleet. In November 1944 he succeeded Nimitz (q.v.) as c-in-c Pacific Fleet. A calm, scholarly, quiet man, he was of an unusual temperament in the US Pacific navy hierarchy, but no less successful for that.

STALIN, Joseph (1879–1953). Soviet dictator and supreme commander. The man who ruled the Soviet Union for three decades, led his country through the worst dangers of the German invasion, and took it through the burden of fighting the major part of the war against Nazi Germany, to victory and eventual domination of eastern Europe, was born Iosif Vissarionovich Dzhugashvili, the son of a shoemaker in Georgia. He was educated at the local school at Gori, and entered the theological seminary at Tiflis with a view to becoming a priest. But he rebelled with hatred against the brutal authority of the seminary's regime and against the religious ideas it embodied. In 1899, by now a member of the Russian Socialist Revolutionary party, he was expelled. From then on for the next eighteen years the young rebel led the life of an underground revolutionary. His quarrels with the tsarist regime began in 1901 when he helped organize demonstrations. In 1902 he was arrested, and between then and 1917 escaped and was recaptured four times. When the party split in 1903 into Bolshevik and Menshevik factions, Stalin followed Lenin and the Bolsheviks. He was turned down for army service in the first world war on medical grounds, and in 1917, when the tsar fell and the prisons were opened, he returned in triumph from his exile in Siberia. By March 1922 he had achieved the position of general secretary of the Bolshevik party, and when Lenin died in January 1924 Stalin was ready to take over completely. His one remaining opponent of significance was Leon Trotsky, and by astute moves he outflanked Trotsky's supporters, expelled him from the party in 1927, and banished him to exile in 1929. Trotsky was assassinated in Mexico City in 1940, and it is now widely accepted that Stalin's secret police were responsible.

In many ways, the key year in Stalin's early career was 1928. The grain shortage of that year, which threatened starvation among the masses and their disillusionment with the Communists, demanded the kind of nerve and ruthlessness which Stalin alone possessed. He ordered the collectivization of the farms and instituted a five-year industrialization plan which he forced through without regard for the effect on human lives. Like Hitler (q.v.), Stalin approached the national economic problem with total commitment, and once he had embarked on this course the only possible consequences were complete failure, or success at any cost. And the real cost lay in the vast damage to the Russian peasant classes, who resisted collectivization and industrialization and suffered starvation, deportation and death in their millions. Stalin later told Churchill (q.v.) that the five-year plan had been a 'terrible struggle'. This process was followed in the 1930s by the purges, in which thousands of Stalin's enemies, potential enemies and imagined enemies were arrested. Some of them were exposed at three great show trials in Moscow and executed or jailed. Others were summarily murdered without the formality of a trial. By these methods Stalin succeeded in establishing his position as undisputed and immovable dictator of Soviet Russia, but the damage he did in removing from the scene the intelligentsia who could have led the military and economic recovery of the Soviet Union was incalculable. The year 1939 was crucial for Stalin in the field of foreign policy. As Germany, Italy and Japan sought to extend their territories by military conquest in various parts of the world, Stalin searched for some form of political alliance which would avert the danger of Soviet Russia being drawn into an exhausting war. When Britain and France declared their intention to guarantee Poland's territorial integrity, Stalin was more than willing to listen to approaches from the British which sought to create a British–French–

Soviet alliance agreeing mutual military aid in the event of German aggression in the Baltic or Black Sea states. At the same time he was equally willing to listen to overtures from the German foreign minister Ribbentrop (q.v.) suggesting closer relations between Germany and the Soviet Union. Stalin skilfully manipulated these two strands of policy, and as the negotiations drew on through 1939 the British and French commitment remained lukewarm, and a pact between Germany and Russia offered the better prospects for Russian security. In fact it was Hitler who forced the issue to settlement. With the invasion of Poland imminent, he was anxious to avoid being drawn into war with the Soviet Union and possibly the western powers at the same time. Despite British protests, the Russo–German non-aggression pact was signed on 23 August 1939. Its terms, which were to last for ten years with the option of a further five, not only protected the signing parties from war with each other, but carved Poland into specified German and Russian areas, and in a secret clause established designated spheres of influence: Russia to have Finland, Latvia and Estonia, Germany to control Lithuania. War was by that time inevitable. Hitler had mobilized the German forces and on 1 September they invaded Poland. By 8 September they had reached Warsaw. The Soviet armies were far from ready for this lightning invasion, but on 18 September they also crossed the Polish border and occupied their assigned area. This double invasion was followed on 27 and 28 September by a further conference at the Kremlin to work out the exact line of demarcation between the two forces. In October and November Stalin tried to secure his country's western frontiers by attempting to persuade Finland to cede territory in the Gulf of Finland in exchange for less strategically significant territory in the north of the country. The Russian desire for these territorial concessions arose from the fact that the second largest city in the Soviet Union, Leningrad, was only twenty miles from the Finish frontier, and could come under threat from the Gulf of Finland should either Britain or Germany

Joseph Stalin (left), Soviet dictator and supreme commander, with Voroshilov, his chief of staff.

decide to send in naval forces. After protracted negotiations the talks broke down. A Russian attack looked unavoidable and the Finnish army was mobilized. On 30 November Russian troops crossed the frontier, and the remarkable Russo–Finnish war – the 'winter war' – had begun. It was as surprising to Stalin as it was to the rest of the world that his armies were so decisively beaten in the early stages of the war, as the ingenious Finns took advantage of the terrain, the climate and their mobility to inflict severe losses on Russia's ponderous army. But Finland was forced to fight with no help from the western Allies, beyond a handful of British bombers and volunteer soldiers, and no help from the Germans, who cautiously

observed the terms of their non-aggression pact with Russia. By the end of February the strength of the Soviet forces proved more than the Finns could hold, and they were forced to sue for peace. The terms imposed by Stalin were less severe than anticipated, although they included not only the original demands over which the war began, but the annexation of the port of Viborg and the whole of the Karelian isthmus. However, Finland was at least able to retain its independence and national identity.

In the summer of 1940, Russia's position was transformed by German conquests in Scandinavia and western Europe, and by Germany's failure to complete the invasion of Britain. Stalin had originally been pleased that Germany was preoccupied with the fighting in the west, but his pleasure gave way to concern as the situation stabilized. And his alarm increased when the Germans sent troops into Romania and into Finland, ostensibly as a precaution against an imagined threat from the British. Stalin sent Molotov (q.v.) to Berlin to challenge the Germans on these issues, and Molotov's cold questioning caused Hitler to squirm in his search for excuses for these contraventions of their mutual pact. The talks produced nothing, and on 25 November Stalin officially demanded that German troops should be withdrawn from Finland and Romania, and that Germany should recognize Soviet domination in the Balkans. Three weeks later, on 18 December, Hitler ordered plans to be drawn up for an invasion of Soviet Russia, to be completed by 15 May 1941. Throughout the early months of 1941 Stalin received persistent warnings from several quarters that Germany was on the point of making war with the Soviet Union. But wherever these reports originated, whether from Churchill or from Roosevelt (q.v.) or from his own intelligence services, Stalin refused to take them seriously. In April he made several gestures of friendship towards German diplomats, apparently still in complete ignorance of what was about to happen, and it was only in May that he began to accept that war was probable. During this period his principal precaution was to order his troops to avoid all incidents which might provoke Germany to hostility: if he had to face war with Hitler, he recognized at least that the longer it was postponed the better. Even so, along with Molotov he still believed that persistent reports of a breakdown in relations with Germany were misguided. By 21 June 1941 he was at last fully awake to the reality. He personally ordered the anti-aircraft defences of Moscow to be brought up to seventy-five per cent combat readiness, and ordered Timoshenko and Zhukov (qq.v.) to put their troops on full combat alert. If this failure in his appreciation of the true military and diplomatic situation was an indication of the low calibre of Stalin's thinking, then his reaction to the German

invasion provided confirmation of his flimsy and inadequate statesmanship. After the attack, which took place on 22 June 1941, Stalin lapsed into something approaching a state of shock. He disappeared from public and political view for several days, remained locked in his study, and showed distinct signs of mental disturbance. When he emerged, at the instigation of members of the *Politburo*, it was to make a speech to the Soviet people exhorting them to battle against the invaders. He also had several of his generals shot for the failure of the defence on the Western and North-western Fronts, including the army group commander General Pavlov. He then reorganized the army commands. The Western Front, defend-

Stalin takes up an equivocal position over Japan, signing the Soviet–Japanese neutrality pact on 13 April 1941, with Japanese foreign minister Yosuke Matsuoka.

ing Moscow itself, was given to Timoshenko; the North-western, defending in the area of the Baltic and Leningrad, was taken over by Voroshilov; and the South-western, covering the Ukraine, by Budenny (q.v.). Zhukov was given a roving commission, with the task of supervising any front where he was needed. In August Stalin made himself supreme commander of all the Soviet armed forces. After he had recovered his poise, Stalin began to exert again the familiar iron control over his country. The need for firm control led him to admit in a broadcast that 'the war had greatly curtailed and in some cases stopped the peaceful building of socialism'. From then until the end of the year he presided over a surge of national determination similar to that which had sustained Britain through the summer of 1940. Although vast areas of the Soviet Union were over-run by the German armies, the people drew on amazing reserves of courage and effort, supplying recruits for the armed forces, producing armaments in vast quantities and helping with a brilliantly organized wholesale evacuation of war industry to the safety of the east. Against efforts like that, and with the size of Russian reserves in manpower and territory, the German invasion was doomed to failure, however far into the Soviet Union the armies penetrated. On 6 and 7 November, when the battle for Moscow was being fought, Stalin made two speeches, the first to party workers and armed forces celebrating the anniversary of the revolution, the second in Red Square to soldiers on the way to the front. Both speeches were filled with heroic rhetoric similar to Churchill's inspiring words to the British people in 1940:

> The world is looking upon you as the power who will destroy the German invading hordes. The enslaved people are looking to you as their liberators. ... The war you are waging is a war of liberation, a just war. ... Death to the German invaders. Long live our glorious country, its freedom and independence. Under the banner of Lenin – onward to victory.

These speeches greatly boosted the morale of the

Russian people. Like others who had suffered the insult of an invasion of their homeland, they were eager for leadership and receptive to inspiration. And Stalin offered it to them. In foreign policy, Stalin's main concern during these months was to persuade the British to open a second front in Europe. In his requests for foreign help his approach was completely unrealistic. When Harry Hopkins (q.v.), President Roosevelt's representative, had visited Moscow in July 1941, Stalin had said that he would welcome American troops, fighting under American command, on any part of the Russian front. Hopkins had been obliged to tell Stalin that he had come to Moscow to discuss questions of supply only, though he promised to pass the request on to Roosevelt. In September Stalin urged upon Churchill a diversion in the Balkans and later called for a landing by twenty-five to thirty British divisions either in Persia for use on the southern front, or at Archangel. As Churchill later recorded, it was incredible that Stalin could have committed himself to such absurdities, and it was hopeless to argue with a man thinking in terms of utter unreality. In 1942 Stalin decided to press the opening of a second front on the western Allies with even more vigour. His first step was to send Molotov to Britain and America. In Washington the Russian foreign minister persuaded the Americans to issue a joint communiqué asserting that full agreement had been reached on 'the urgent task of creating a second front in Europe in 1942'. The wording was such as to allow a variety of interpretations, and the Russians took it as a firm undertaking. When the events in North Africa made the opening of such a front impossible, Churchill was obliged to travel to Moscow to put matters right with Stalin in August 1942. At the start of this meeting, Stalin gave the prime minister a hard time. When Churchill declared bluntly that the invasion of Europe was impossible in 1942, Stalin accused him of breaking a solemn promise made in the spring by the British and American leaders. When Churchill took out a map and listed various reasons why the invasion of Europe was impossible, Stalin asked if the British were afraid of the Germans. And when Churchill assured him that the operation would take place in 1943, Stalin asked haughtily where the guarantee was that this promise would not also be broken. The tone and balance of this meeting, which until now had some of the characteristics of a headmaster's interview with a recalcitrant pupil, changed when Churchill introduced the plan for the invasion of north-west Africa – Operation Torch. Here Churchill brought in his favourite simile, the 'soft under-belly' theory. He actually drew a picture of a crocodile, to show how the western Allies would attack the soft belly while the Russians dealt with the hard snout. Stalin showed only moderate en-thusiasm at first, but after a few critical remarks suddenly appeared to wake up. He outlined four separate reasons why he saw that Operation Torch was strategically sound: it would hit Rommel in the back, it would overawe Spain, it would bring the French and Germans into conflict in France, and it would expose Italy to the whole brunt of the war. Churchill records that he was 'deeply impressed with Stalin's remarkable statement', which showed 'the Russian Dictator's swift and complete mastery of a problem hitherto novel to him'. According to Churchill very few people alive could have comprehended in so few minutes the reasons which they had been wrestling with for months: 'He saw it all in a flash.' Field-Marshal Brooke (q.v.) in his memoirs came to a similar flattering conclusion about Stalin's abilities. He rapidly appreciated the fact that Stalin had a mili-tary brain of the very highest calibre. Brooke's judgment was that Stalin never once in any of his statements made any strategic error, nor did he ever fail to appreciate all the implications of a situation with a quick and unerring eye. Harry Hopkins was a third important figure to be impressed by Stalin. He said it was like talking to a perfectly co-ordinated machine, an intelligent machine. It is difficult to argue with the views of such authoritative observers who all saw Stalin at first hand. Equally, it is impossible to suppress reservations about Stalin's strategic perception.

His failure at the beginning to accept the likeli-hood of the German invasion leaves him open to severe condemnation. His insistence on the premature opening of the second front betrayed a savage lack of understanding of the situation, and was elsewhere described by Churchill as absurd and unrealistic. Even at their first meeting in Moscow it took Churchill two 'bleak and sombre' hours to overcome Stalin's misapprehensions about the possibilities of the second front in 1942. The question must be asked: was Stalin not a mere 'passive strategist', able to follow the implications of an argument when it was put to him forcibly and clearly, but falling far short of any claims to be considered a master of creative strategy? And was not Russia's victory over the Germans in the war in eastern Europe the result of strength rather than guile, an outcome of being ready to accept enormous losses of territory, weapons, and, above all, people without being forced into surrender, and still have enough left to wear down the Ger-mans by attrition? After that first meeting Stalin agreed to see Churchill again at eleven o'clock the next night. Because of his hostile reception Chur-chill had already warned Molotov that 'Stalin would make a great mistake to treat us roughly when we have come so far'. But this evidently did not impede Stalin. That night there took place what Churchill described as 'a most unpleasant discussion'. Stalin taunted Churchill for two hours, asking when the British were going to start fighting, and were they going to look on while the Russians did the work? When Stalin eventually accused Churchill of a breach of faith in not launch-ing the second front in Europe, Churchill lost his temper, or at least feigned doing so. He thumped the table, and told Stalin that he had come all this way and had expected the hand of comradeship. Churchill's outburst evidently impressed Stalin, who broke out in a broad grin and said that, although he could not understand what Churchill was saying ... 'by God I like your spirit'. After that the discussion resumed in a less tense atmos-phere. Obviously the Moscow meeting was turning into a struggle between two forceful personalities rather than a considered discussion of strategic matters. And Churchill ultimately managed to come out on top. It happened the next night when, after a lavish banquet, some incident caused Churchill to walk away after being photographed with Stalin, and he refused to talk to the Russian leader even when Stalin joined Churchill at his table. Churchill got up, said goodbye, shook hands and hurried out of the room. Stalin, who normally never hurried anywhere, virtually trotted after Churchill to keep up with him, and accompanied him to the door of the Kremlin Grand Palace, an action without precedent in Soviet history. There was one more meeting the following night. This took place after Stalin had refused to see Churchill during the day, sending messages that he was 'out walking'. The meeting developed into a visit to Stalin's own quarters for drinks, followed by dinner, and the proceedings lasted altogether from 7 pm until 3.30 the next morning. Churchill took off at 5.30, with the exhausted Molotov obediently turning out at the airport on Stalin's orders to see the prime minister off. At the end of this difficult and important session, the honours were about even. Stalin had been able to gauge the strength of the British leader, and was reassured about the benefits that would arise from Operation Torch. They parted on friendly terms.

Apart from their views of his strategic grasp, the visitors were left with one other important impression of Stalin. This was his command over his subordinates, who jumped when he told them to, and lived in awe and fear of the dictator. The only exception was Marshal Zhukov, who came almost to dominate Stalin, at least after the battle for Moscow, and to whom Stalin willingly deferred in military matters. On 27 August 1942 Zhukov was appointed deputy supreme commander. Stalin's main concern during the remainder of 1942 was the battle for Stalingrad, the city which Hitler prized above all others in Russia. During October and November the Germans launched massive attacks, and fought their way into the suburbs. Then Stalin ordered equally large attacks, aimed at cutting off Paulus's (q.v.) army. Hitler replied

by committing Manstein's (q.v.) reserves to relieve Paulus, and the Russians in turn responded by defeating Manstein first and then turning to deal with Paulus. By the end of December 1942 Manstein's army had been flung back 120 miles from Stalingrad, and by the end of January Paulus also had been defeated. German losses were 30,000 killed and 90,000 prisoners, including Paulus himself. Stalingrad proved the turning point both in the war in eastern Europe and in Stalin's fortunes.

The Russian people quickly realized that their armies had the measure of the Germans, and that they would eventually win the war, however long it took and however severe their losses in doing it. Stalin, who until the end of 1942 had by no means held a firm grip on the Russian people, began to gain a position of total ascendancy. Elements of idolatry appeared in the Soviet press, most notably in constant references to 'Stalinist' military strategy, and 'Stalin's military genius'. There was little credit for Zhukov, Vasilevsky (q.v.) and other generals who had been directly responsible for the victory. It was the beginning of the cult of personality, confirmed in March 1943 when Stalin took on the title of Marshal of the Soviet Union, and the Praesidium of the Supreme Soviet acclaimed him 'the greatest strategist of all times and of all peoples'. His position was further enhanced after the battle of the Kursk salient at the end of July 1943. Here Hitler attempted to recover his position prior to Stalingrad in a great counter-offensive, and when it failed it was clear that the tide had turned. In Moscow the Kursk victory was celebrated with parades and a 120-gun salute. The Russians were well aware that they were now certain to win the war. This knowledge gave Stalin a major psychological advantage in his dealings with the western Allies. Although he had warned his people early in 1943 against the over-optimistic view that the war could be won by the Russians alone, he now recognized that in his dealings with the Allies he was negotiating from a position of strength. The Russians were still bearing the brunt of the fighting. They had absorbed the German invasion and had thrown

The presentation of the massive Sword of Stalingrad to the Soviet leader. It was a tribute to the defenders of Stalingrad from King George VI and the British people, represented here by Churchill.

back the German armies in their great victories of Stalingrad and Kursk. The British and Americans on the other hand were still engaged in the southern Mediterranean and there was no prospect of their opening the much vaunted second front in Europe. Stalin still needed the Allies, if only as a threat to keep twenty-five German divisions facing the English Channel in a defensive posture. But he recognized that the Allies equally needed

him. It was therefore with renewed confidence that Stalin pursued his dealings with the west during 1943, and his approach led to sour relations. In February he was able to complain yet again that the western Allies were not playing their part as they did not envisage opening the second front until August-September. He called for it to be opened much earlier. In March the British suspended the supply convoys via the northern route because of the difficulties of providing escorts, and in April they decided they could not be resumed until autumn, when the long summer daylight gave way to darkness. By October the U-boats were again destroying large quantities of Allied shipping, making a clear convoy commitment impossible. Churchill wrote to Stalin that they proposed to reopen the supply route and sail a series of four convoys from November to February. 'But', he stated, 'I must put it on record that this is no contract or bargain, but rather a declaration of our solemn and earnest resolve.' Stalin wrote back an acid reply. Churchill's communication, he said, was

> neither an obligation nor an agreement, but only a statement, which the British side can at any moment renounce regardless of any influence it may have on the Soviet armies at the front. Supplies from the British Government to the USSR, armaments and other military goods, cannot be considered otherwise than as an obligation. . . .

There was also an angry exchange about the conditions of British servicemen working in northern Russia. Churchill found this message from Stalin offensive, and assumed that it was written not by Stalin himself but by the Soviet machine which 'is quite convinced it can get everything by bullying'. In fact he officially refused to receive the message, and handed it back to the Russian ambassador in London. The diplomatic Anthony Eden (q.v.) was left to tidy up the pieces at the foreign ministers' conference in Moscow. He succeeded in soothing Stalin's anger. One other important aim of the foreign ministers' conference was to prepare for a summit meeting, the first between Roosevelt and Stalin. Even in the matter of choosing the location, Stalin again showed himself to be inflexible and implacable: when they were negotiating from a position of strength, the Russian leadership showed that they were prepared to give nothing away. Stalin took the view that, since he was still concerned with running the major part of the fighting with Hitler's Germany, he was not prepared to go to the west: 'Let the West come to

us,' he said. Roosevelt also was unwilling to travel far outside his own country, because of the difficulty of receiving papers from Congress within the specified time. Stalin dismissed Roosevelt's view contemptuously, remarking that a delay of two or three days in the delivery of state papers was not vital, but a false military step was not a grammatical error which could later be corrected. The venue at last agreed was Teheran. Again the proceedings were marked by an extraordinary degree of acrimony among the Allies, particularly between Churchill and Stalin. Roosevelt went to Teheran determined to get along with the Russian leader, and studiously avoided private meetings with Churchill so that Stalin would not feel the western leaders were 'fixing things' behind his back. On the other hand Roosevelt had no reservations about holding private conversations with Stalin. The two were staying at the same embassy, and Churchill understandably felt aggrieved by this offhand treatment. Roosevelt formed the impression that he could 'handle Uncle Joe', as he persisted in calling Stalin, and from that time on refused to listen to Churchill's warnings of hostile Russian attitudes. Churchill's feeling of isolation was aggravated by the behaviour of Stalin and Roosevelt at dinner after the second plenary session. Roosevelt began by teasing Churchill, much to Churchill's annoyance, about his Britishness, his cigars, his habits, about John Bull. Stalin was vastly amused, and for the first time in three days broke out in hearty laughter. From that time on, Roosevelt recorded, their relations were personal. The ice was broken and they 'talked like men and brothers'. Stalin joined in teasing Churchill, and Churchill took it in good part until Stalin started to discuss the punishment to be meted out to the Germans after the war. Stalin suggested that the German general staff must be liquidated, and the 50,000 officers and technicians on whom the army depended should be rounded up and shot. Churchill replied that the British Parliament and public would not tolerate mass executions. They would turn violently against those responsible for this butchery. And the Soviets must be under no delusion on this point. Stalin repeated sternly: 'Fifty thousand must be shot.' Churchill said he would rather be taken out into the garden there and then and be shot himself than sully his own and his country's honour by such infamy. President Roosevelt, trying to show the whole matter up as a joke, intervened to suggest a compromise, that only 49,000 should be shot. Eden gesticulated to Churchill to indicate that they were not serious. Then President Roosevelt's son Elliot stood up at the end of the table and made a speech saying that the United States army would, he was sure, support Marshal Stalin's plan. At this Churchill, who considered Elliot Roosevelt's remarks an intrusion, got up from the table and went to an adjoining room, which was in semi-darkness. Stalin, accompanied by Molotov, followed him, clapped his hands on Churchill's shoulders from behind, and assured him that they were only playing. 'Stalin has a very captivating manner when he chooses to use it, and I never saw him so to such an extent as at this moment,' wrote Churchill. But he was still not fully convinced that there was no serious intent lurking behind Stalin's remarks. It all demonstrated, the British ambassador later remarked, what piffle great men sometimes talk. A further interesting insight into the Russian character in general, and Stalin's own enigmatic and inscrutable nature in particular, is provided by Sir Alan Brooke, the British chief of the imperial general staff. At the dinner on 30 November, at which Churchill insisted on being host since it was his sixty-ninth birthday, there were the usual customary speeches and toasts which characterized these occasions. At one point in the evening President Roosevelt made a speech proposing the health of General Brooke, in which he referred sentimentally to General Brooke's father, whom his own father had met at Hyde Park, and made further flattering remarks. Stalin then got to his feet and insisted on finishing the toast, but turned it into an attack on Brooke. He accused Brooke of failing to show real feelings of friendship towards the Red Army, and of lacking a true appreciation of its fine qualities and said that he hoped Brooke

would in future show greater comradeship towards the soldiers of the Red Army. Brooke was surprised by these remarks, but he had seen enough of Stalin to know that if he accepted such insults he would lose any respect Stalin had for him, and that the insults would continue in the future. So he got to his feet to reply, thanked Roosevelt for his kind remarks, and turned on Stalin. He was, he said, surprised that Stalin had found it necessary to raise entirely unfounded accusations against him. Then he produced a complicated analogy to the need for deception in war, and said that Stalin had been deluded by Brooke's own use of deception, and had failed to observe those feelings of true friendship which Brooke had for the Red Army. While this was being translated Stalin retained his inscrutable expression, until at the end he turned to Churchill and said: 'I like that man. He rings true, I must have a talk with him afterwards.' In the ante-room where they went after dinner Brooke returned to the attack, and told Stalin again that he was surprised and grieved that the Russian had found it necessary to raise such accusations against him. Stalin shook Brooke by the hand and said through his interpreter: 'The best friendships are those founded on misunderstandings.' From that point on there was a new warmth in their relationship, and Stalin's confidence in Brooke was established on a foundation of respect and goodwill which was never to be shaken. Brooke had instinctively hit on the Russian inclination to apply the test of intimidation, and had discovered that the only successful response was a refusal to be intimidated: in fact a show of strength.

As the rising tide of victory developed during 1944, Stalin's principal concerns, like those of the other leaders, lay in the field of foreign policy, particularly post-war politics. Although after the invasion of France Churchill was able to say: 'Stalin is more friendly these days. The invasion and the number of prisoners taken by us have sent us up in his eyes,' it was obvious to the western Allies (though less so to Roosevelt) that Russia's principal foreign policy objective was to gain the greatest possible Russian advantage. Stalin was clearly not prepared to see two and a half years of fighting and 5 million dead wasted in a return to the *status quo ante bellum*. The greatest and most central of these problems was Poland, over which the Russians and the western Allies seriously disagreed. Stalin was continually irritated by Churchill's persistent complaints about the Polish problem, and in August 1944 their relationship was severely strained over the Polish uprising. At the end of July the Red Army had reached the Vistula and stood within sight of Warsaw. By this time, a pro-Stalinist government had been formed behind the Russian lines in Lublin, and they declared the rival Polish government, the government-in-exile in London, to be illegal. Within Warsaw, the Polish underground fighters were planning to stage an uprising to coincide with the Russian attack, and its timing was left to the judgment of the underground leader, General Bor-Komorowski (q.v.). On the afternoon of 1 August 1944, when he saw the Red Army approaching the city, he gave the order for the uprising. But there was no advance by the Red Army. On Stalin's orders the Russian commander Rokossovsky (q.v.) stayed put, and the fighters in the city were left to fight alone. Stalin received repeated protests and calls for aid from Churchill, Roosevelt, Bor and Mikolajczyk (q.v.), the new leader of the London Poles. On 16 August he replied to Churchill that the Warsaw action was a reckless and terrible gamble, taking a heavy toll of the population, which would not have occurred had the Poles told Soviet headquarters about their action and kept in contact with them. Of course it suited Stalin's purpose perfectly to see the anti-Nazis in Warsaw virtually commit suicide, and some 200,000 Poles, one-fifth of the total population, died in the uprising. When the Russians entered the city three months later they found it devastated, with the buildings lying in rubble and the streets littered with corpses. And when on 9 October 1944 Churchill went to Moscow to discuss Poland and other political questions, Stalin refused to concede any points to the London Poles.

The Lublin national liberation committee under Bierut complied perfectly with the Soviet line, and received wholehearted Soviet backing. The Polish question also proved a source of contention when de Gaulle (q.v.) discovered, as Brooke had done, the key to success in negotiating with the Russian leader. De Gaulle's visit was aimed at concluding a non-aggression pact with the Soviet Union, but the Russians insisted as a condition that the French should recognize the Lublin Polish government. De Gaulle was prepared to have certain dealings with the Lublin Communist leaders, but declared that they did not represent independent Poland. For this reason he firmly refused to ratify the pact, and went back to the French embassy. Two hours later a message arrived saying that the Russians had dropped the condition about recognition for the Lublin Poles, and the treaty was ready for signing. De Gaulle was also one of a number of visitors to Stalin's headquarters – politicians, diplomats and military personnel – who were unfavourably impressed when they observed Stalin's method of dealing with his subordinate commanders. He treated all of them with total ruthlessness, barking orders at them, calling them to him and sending them away like trained dogs, and frequently threatening to have them shot or hanged if they failed to carry out their duty. Several of the western visitors were sickened by this display of blind authority on the part of Stalin, and servile obedience on the part of the men who worked close to him. Stalin's particular brand of diplomacy, a combination of wheedling charm and cynical indifference, was most in evidence at the Yalta conference in February 1945. Again Stalin was intransigent in choosing the meeting place, insisting on holding the conference on Russian soil. The meeting was arranged to settle post-war policy, in particular to set up a united nations organization. The discussions highlighted the difference between the lofty idealism of the western Allies and the calculated nationalism of the Russians. Stalin agreed, for example, to the inclusion of France as one of the powers that would occupy Germany after the war,

Stalin, accompanied by several of his ministers, including Bulganin, Beria, Malenkov, Molotov, Kaganovich and Zhdanov.

but he ensured that France's territory should be taken out of the blocks designated for occupation by the British and Americans. He also secured far-reaching concessions in the Far East to be implemented after the defeat of the Japanese, and in return the Russians undertook to declare war on Japan at the earliest possible moment. It only became apparent after the war that such agreements were designed solely to promote Russian interests. In the final battles, Russian interests came out well on top. At this stage Roosevelt made his one great misjudgment of the war, in opting to deal with Stalin on a friendly and trusting basis. And as his health rapidly declined, until his death

on 12 April, the direction of the war effort in Washington fell increasingly into the hands of the military, notably General Marshall (q.v.), who planned with little regard for the political consequences. As a result the Allies left Berlin to the Russians, approaching from the east, and concentrated on attempting to defeat the Germans in the field, most ludicrously swinging to the south-east to attack the 'southern redoubt' which Allied intelligence had mistakenly come to believe in. Stalin was delighted with the Americans. When Eisenhower (q.v.) wrote to tell him that the Allies were intending to bypass Berlin, Stalin hastily agreed that the city 'lost its former strategic

Stalin takes up the key position over Berlin, flanked by the other Allied leaders Truman and Churchill, as German refugees return to occupied Berlin during the summer of 1945.

importance'. Then he proceeded to devote no fewer than three army groups to its capture, with results which have continued to shape the course of European history ever since, producing one of the most sensitive spots in twentieth-century politics. Stalin's last great contribution to the war was at the last of the 'Big Three' conferences, at Potsdam. Again it was Stalin's choice of venue, held in recently liberated territory now held by Russia. But curiously, Stalin did not secure the ad-

vantages at this meeting that he was accustomed to expect. The most important of his failures was to abandon the Soviet occupation of Vienna, which in due course ensured an independent Austria. On the other hand he succeeded in consolidating Soviet control over East Germany, Poland, Romania, Bulgaria and Hungary. But perhaps his greatest triumph was a symbolic one. When Churchill returned to England to learn of his government's rejection by the British people in the election of 1945, he was replaced by Clement Attlee (q.v.). Stalin was therefore the only one of the Big Three to survive as his country's leader from the beginning of the war until its end. He had secured for his country more real influence than any observer could have imagined, and consolidated a Soviet empire which has outlasted not only the rapidly declining British empire, but also the pervading American influence in world affairs. He had developed his country from a backward peasant nation which almost fell to Nazi Germany, into one of the two major powers in the world. And he had done so by a process of unyielding stubbornness, uncompromising nationalism and utter indifference to world opinion. These qualities continued to predominate in Stalin's post-war policy, when he brought down the familiar iron curtain across central Europe. Stalin continued to develop his country's interests under the same firm control until his death in 1953.

STANGL, Franz (1908–71). Austrian commandant of Treblinka concentration camp during 1942 and 1943, after which he was transferred to Italy to organize the campaign against the partisans. Stangl was captured by the Americans in 1945 but escaped to Brazil. In 1967 he was tracked down working at the Volkswagen factory and extradited to West Germany, where he was tried for the murder of 400,000 Jews and sentenced to life imprisonment.

STARK, Harold Raynsford (1880–1972). United States admiral, chief of naval operations from August 1939 to 1942, and as such the architect of the vital development of American naval strength in the period before the war. Recognizing the inadequacy of previous naval policy which had relied on the British and French navies to contain the German threat, Stark went to Congress in June 1940, when German domination of Europe was imminent, to ask for a sum of four billion dollars over the normal appropriation to build a 'two-ocean navy'. It was clear that it would take two years to repair the deficiencies arising from the pre-war neutrality policy. Meanwhile, Stark and the United States government had to contain the

Admiral Harold Stark, chief of naval operations, and an energetic advocate of the massive build-up of naval strength to meet the growing threat from Germany and Japan.

threat of further German expansion as well as possible. Among the measures instituted by Stark were the introduction of convoys for merchant shipping supplying American bases overseas, and the organization of escorts to protect merchant shipping carrying Lend-Lease supplies in the western half of the Atlantic. At the end of 1941 it was Stark who put the navy on a war footing in the face of deteriorating relations with Japan. In 1942 Stark was sent to London as commander of naval forces in Europe, where he was also naval adviser to the United States embassy, and was responsible for establishing bases for the United States naval forces engaged in the invasion of Europe.

STAUFFENBERG, (Graf) Klaus Schenk von (1907–44).

German officer and key figure in the bomb plot on Hitler's (q.v.) life of 20 July 1944. Stauffenberg was a staff officer who had served in the Polish campaign, and in western Europe and North Africa. He was a capable staff officer, and a handsome, debonair character who made no secret of his contempt for Hitler. His life almost came to an end on 7 April 1943 when he was wounded in Tunisia in an attack by fighter aircraft. He lost his right arm, two fingers from his left hand, and his right eye. His left eye was damaged but saved. As he lay in hospital recovering he remarked to his wife that he 'had to do something to save Germany'. When he recovered he was sent to work in the supply section of the reserve army at the German War Office, where he encountered like-minded opponents of Hitler and joined them in the conspiracy. Shortly afterwards, in June 1944, he was promoted to the rank of colonel and made chief of staff to General Fromm, the head of the reserve army, which gave him access to Hitler's headquarters. The arrival of D-Day made it essential, in the opinion of Stauffenberg and the other plotters, to stage the attempt on Hitler's life as soon as possible. Stauffenberg, as the only man with access to Hitler, volunteered. They arranged to kill Hitler, Goering and Himmler (qq.v.) together at Berchtesgaden on 11 July, but as he was alone at the headquarters they called off that attempt. The same thing happened on 15 July and the plan was again postponed.

Finally they decided to go ahead even if Hitler was alone, and Stauffenberg's next opportunity arose at a staff conference at Rastenburg, Hitler's headquarters – the 'wolf's lair' – in East Prussia. Stauffenberg arrived by plane from Berlin, met Keitel (q.v.), the Führer's aide, and excused himself to fetch his cap and belt. While alone momentarily he reached into his briefcase with a pair of tweezers and broke a capsule of acid which began eating into some wire. Then, carrying the case, he followed Keitel into the map room where Hitler and his chiefs stood around a table. The bomb was set so that in ten minutes the wire

Colonel Klaus Schenk von Stauffenberg, shot after his attempt to assassinate Hitler at Berchtesgaden on 20 July 1944.

would disintegrate, activate the firing pin and detonate the bomb. Inside the map room Stauffenberg put the briefcase down unobtrusively against the table support, and after a few moments left the room saying that he had to take a telephone call from Berlin. Nobody took much notice. Stauffenberg walked out into the fresh air, got into the staff car, and made his way to the exit, bluffing his way with iron nerve and extraordinary luck through two checkpoints after the explosion had taken place. But what happened inside the map room was not as Stauffenberg had thought. An officer apparently moved the briefcase round to the other side of the plinth which supported the table, away from Hitler, and at the moment the bomb went off Hitler was leaning over the heavy oak table top, which saved him from the full force of the explosion. Furthermore the conference was being held, because of reconstruction, in a wooden hut instead of the usual concrete bunker. The result was that the full force of the blast was dissipated instead of being contained. Four men were killed, but Hitler was not among them; he suffered only minor injuries. Stauffenberg saw the explosion and took off in his plane for Berlin firmly believing that the Führer was dead, and that the next task was to set up the planned alternative government and make peace with the Allies, saving Germany from the destruction that otherwise faced it. Between 12.42 pm, when the explosion took place, and early evening the conspirators made half-hearted attempts to put their *coup d'état* into effect, but they were not well prepared, and they still had no definite confirmation that Hitler was either alive or dead. Then at 6.45 pm a broadcast told them that Hitler had survived. General Fromm, the reserve army commander and Stauffenberg's boss, then became a key figure in the episode. He had refused to join the *coup d'état*, and Stauffenberg had arrested him. But he was carelessly guarded, and managed to alert a group of his staff who, loyal to the regime, armed themselves, went upstairs, and arrested Stauffenberg and several of his associates after an exchange of gunfire. Stauffenberg was injured in the struggle. Fromm immediately formed a court-martial and straight away tried the men he considered to be traitors. Whether his aim was to save them from the Gestapo, or to prevent the Gestapo questioning them and implicating him, is not clear. In the event, the business was completed just before the Gestapo arrived. Stauffenberg and three other men were taken downstairs into the courtyard, stood up against the wall in the light of army vehicles and shot.

STETTINIUS, Edward (1900–49). American businessman and administrator, and secretary of state from 1943. Stettinius was appointed chairman of the War Resources Board in 1939, and a year later became a member of the Defence Advisory Commission with responsibility for war materials. He was made America's Lend-Lease administrator, a key post in the organizational backing of the Allied war, and later worked to organize the Dumbarton Oaks conference which led to the setting up of the United Nations Organization. His part in the war was somewhat overshadowed by Roosevelt's (q.v.) own close personal grip on foreign affairs, but he was a competent and successful administrator.

STILWELL, Joseph (1883–1946). A tough and resourceful American general who probably held the most frustrating post of all the leading commanders in the second world war. His main difficulty stemmed from his dealings with Chiang Kai-shek (q.v.), whom he considered untrustworthy and guilty of duplicity. Stilwell presented to the world a brusque, bristling personality. He was consistently rude to people and frequently ill-tempered. But as Slim (q.v.) recorded, if he liked and respected a person, in private he was tolerant, straightforward and utterly reliable. The likelihood is that Stilwell made some conscious effort to cultivate an abrasive personality and live up to his nickname, 'Vinegar Joe'. He also kept a diary of his war experiences, and his comments on the political machinations which he was unable to avoid are among the most illuminating writings to emerge from the war. On Japan's entry into the war Stilwell was commanding 3 Corps in California. He was soon removed from that posting and appointed chief of staff to Chiang Kai-shek with the task of equipping and training thirty Chinese divisions; he also became commander of all American forces in the China–India–Burma theatre, and took up his appointments on 23 January 1942. A few days earlier Japan had begun the invasion of Burma. Stilwell worked energetically to organize the defence of Burma, but could get no clear co-operation from Chiang Kai-shek, and suffered serious obstruction from the Chinese General Tu, who also claimed to command the Chinese Fifth and Sixth Armies. Stilwell considered that Tu had refused to commit his troops through cowardice, but it is more likely that Tu was under orders from Chiang who wanted the Americans to defeat Japan while he saved his forces and supplies to deal with the threat from Mao Tse-tung, in the north. Stilwell considered resigning, and flew to Chungking for a showdown with Chiang, after which he decided to stay on.

Lieutenant-General 'Vinegar Joe' Stilwell, in unfamiliar best dress uniform, arrives in England for conferences, 1943. He was uncomfortable in political and diplomatic circles, but a successful trainer of troops and a lively field-commander.

Nevertheless the Allied forces could not hold the Japanese advance. Stilwell was in Lashio when that town fell, and he set out for Myitkyina over 100 miles to the north. In fact the Japanese cut off Myitkyina, and Stilwell only reached Indaw. There he made contact with an American doctor and a group of fifty nurses, and decided that the only escape route was on foot over the hills, westwards into the Chindwin valley, and on to Imphal in Assam. They set out in trucks, but abandoned them on 6 May and continued a hard journey through the jungle on foot. Stilwell's notes complain of the breakdown of many in the party through poor physique. On 10 May they reached the Chindwin, bought rafts, and poled their way down the river. Then they took to the jungle on foot again, in appalling conditions. The monsoons arrived and made conditions even worse, but the rain also stopped the Japanese advance. After travelling 140 miles in twenty days, Stilwell's party reached Imphal. Stilwell was warmly commended in both China and America for his part in the Burma retreat. With the Japanese in control of Burma by the end of May, Stilwell devoted himself for the remainder of that year to building up and training a Chinese force in India. After the front-line fighting he found the world of political intrigue uncomfortable, with a difficult position in the centre of political dealings between President Roosevelt and his chief of staff General Marshall (qq.v.) on the one hand, and Chiang Kai-shek and his politically astute wife Madame Chiang on the other, with the whole picture complicated by the intervention of the Chinese ambassador in Washington, T.V. Soong, who was also Madame Chiang's brother. In August 1942 Stilwell was able to escape the political atmosphere of the luxurious house provided for him in Chungking and return to the business of training the Chinese divisions. Stilwell was almost alone in believing that the Chinese soldier, properly trained and equipped, would prove as courageous and efficient as any other. But to carry out this training he had to establish separate headquarters as far apart as Chungking in China and New Delhi in India, as

Stilwell holds a briefing for war correspondents following operations by Brigadier-General Frank Merrill (smoking pipe) and his 'Marauders'.

well as a command post at Ramgarh where the Chinese in India were based. By his energetic driving, when everybody else seemed to have lost faith in the Chinese, he not only succeeded in securing facilities for their training but also in arranging for 13,000 of them to be flown in from China, in planes of Major-General Claire Chennault's (q.v.) China Air Task Force, returning from supply trips over the mountains between China and Assam. By the end of 1942 the aggressive Stilwell had not only proved that he could train the Chinese as good soldiers, but was pressing for a spring offensive.

He received a great deal of opposition in this aim, and also came into conflict with the other important American commander in the region, Claire-Chennault, who put forward an alternative plan for an air offensive which he claimed would finish the war in six months. Several key figures, including Madame Chiang, sided with Chennault, and Chiang himself backed it as a way of winning the war without serious Chinese participation. The air plan was given the go-ahead at the Trident conference in Washington in May 1943 and began in July, but quickly ran out of momentum as Stilwell had predicted. In August 1943 Stilwell's position improved when at the Quadrant conference in Quebec a new command structure was established. A new South-east Asia Command was set up with Admiral Lord Louis Mountbatten (q.v.) as supreme commander and Stilwell as his deputy. It did not, however, cover India. Nor did it cover China, where Stilwell remained chief of staff to Chiang and commander of all American troops in the China–India–Burma theatre. Stilwell reflected on the confusion: 'a Chinese puzzle with Wavell, Auk, Mountbatten, Peanut [his nickname for Chiang], Alexander and me all interwoven and mixed beyond recognition'. For a short time Stilwell's relations with Chiang and Madame Chiang reached an encouraging level of cordiality, but when discussions on future strategy were resumed at the Cairo conference of November 1943 Chiang's duplicity and vacillation reached new levels. This appalled Stilwell so much that he virtually abandoned his staff post in China for a time and joined the ground troops he had trained in operations in northern Burma against the Japanese. His leadership on the ground proved electric, and convinced the Chinese troops taking part that they could fight and beat the Japanese. But where Stilwell was not in evidence the usual laxity and inertia prevailed. His problems continued throughout the battles in Burma of 1944, as he put all his aggressive drive and energy into forcing the Chinese to fight, and struggled to overcome the political difficulties. The only senior commander he could come to terms with was Slim: at one stage Mountbatten asked for Stilwell's removal on the grounds of insubordination. Stilwell's part in the ground battles culminated in the attack on Myitkyina in May, described by Stilwell himself as 'sink or swim'. A mixed Chinese and American force known as Galahad made a long march in great secrecy (Stilwell had told only Slim of his plan, and had kept it from even his divisional commanders to ensure security) and took the Myitkyina airfield. But the Japanese heavily reinforced the defences in the town itself. The Allied force was reduced by illness and exhaustion, and

by the end of May 2000 troops were evacuated, while the condition of the remainder was low. Stilwell reported 'only 12 men left in 2 Battalion of Galahad. Galahad is just shot.' But the Japanese finally withdrew, and on 3 August the Americans and Chinese took over. Stilwell received recognition for his efforts in his promotion to four-star general, a rank held only by Marshall, MacArthur, Arnold and Eisenhower (qq.v.). In the face of serious setbacks in east China in the Japanese offensive of the summer of 1944, both Mountbatten and Marshall came to the view that to avert catastrophe Stilwell should take over complete command of the Chinese armies. On 6 July Roosevelt endorsed this view and sent a note to Chiang, who at first appeared to accept the proposal. In fact this was the beginning of the end of any co-operation between Stilwell and the Chinese leader. Chiang attempted to establish the principle that the Chinese should have control of the Lend-Lease supplies coming from America and there was bitter argument on this point. The issue complicated Stilwell's position, and in September 1944, while negotiations were still going on about the details of Stilwell's appointment to the Chinese command, Roosevelt sent a note to Chiang taking an uncompromisingly firm line. He warned Chiang that they were faced with possibly catastrophic consequences in east China, and Stilwell had not yet been placed in command of the Chinese forces. For several days there was no reply, until Chiang finally sent a letter to the president complaining bitterly about Stilwell, claiming that Stilwell would not obey his orders and asking for his dismissal. Roosevelt himself made no reply to this note for several weeks, and then on 18 October agreed to recall Stilwell. Washington felt that they could not afford to lose the support of Chiang and China.

Stilwell arrived back in Washington on 2 November 1944 to a cold reception. He was warned off making his views on the Chinese question public. From July to September 1945 he held command of the Tenth Army in Okinawa, and received the surrender of 105,000 Japanese in the Ryukyu Islands. By this time Stilwell was old for

Above Stilwell takes a meal at a field-kitchen at Sarkan, Burma.

Overleaf General Stilwell makes his way in style through terrain difficulties in Burma. His diaries reveal a tough fighting man struggling in the political jungles of the Far East. The real jungle was more to his liking.

a fighting soldier, weary and humiliated by his dismissal. Years of frustration in one of the most difficult jobs of the war, and the hard life of active campaigning in the jungle, had broken him. He spent a short time working on his papers, but died in 1946 before he could finish preparing them for publication. Although he is remembered largely for his prickly, tough-talking personality, an image which he maintained to the last, his writings show him to be a sensitive man with thoughtful, questioning views on matters such as honour, leadership, courage and character. It is difficult to judge Stilwell's capacity as a military man. He was without doubt one of the bravest and most aggressive of second world war leaders, and one of the most single-minded in pursuit of objectives. Doubts arise over whether these objectives were the right ones, as Stilwell failed in most cases to place his own objectives in the wider context of the war. In terms of his dealings with fellow Allied commanders, that was where his difficulties stemmed from. In his dealings with the Chinese, which were the dominating factor in his war career, it is doubtful whether any other commander would have had greater success, or would even have lasted as long as Stilwell did. In that Stilwell was a victim of fate.

STIMSON, Henry Lewis (1867–1950). American statesman, and secretary for war in President Roosevelt's (q.v.) wartime administration. Already over seventy when the war began, Stimson was nevertheless an energetic and forward-looking administrator. Part of his policy was to provide the maximum possible help to Britain in the Atlantic battle and he fought for the repeal of the Neutrality Act. He was an ardent advocate of defeating Germany before Japan, and urged Churchill (q.v.) to plan for a European invasion in 1943. Churchill eventually managed to convince him of its impossibility. Stimson was heavily engaged in the atomic bomb policy, and gave the project his complete support. He was able to tell Truman (q.v.) at the Potsdam conference in 1945 that the device was ready for use. He resigned shortly after Japan's surrender.

STIRLING, David (born 1915). British com-

Lieutenant-Colonel David Stirling, founder of the SAS, the adventurous desert raiding force which, he once claimed, destroyed more aircraft in North Africa than the RAF.

mando officer, originator of the Special Air Service (SAS) which carried out raids behind Axis lines in the North African desert. Stirling conceived the idea of a desert raiding force in July 1941, and was given permission to develop it by General Ritchie (q.v.), then deputy chief of staff of Middle East Command and later Eighth Army commander. The SAS worked in close concert with the Long Range Desert Group, formed a year earlier as a reconnaissance unit. The efforts of Stirling and his small unit have been belittled in post-war years, mainly because of the British prejudice against 'private armies' which orthodox opinion condemns as drawing too heavily on scarce resources while attracting an excessive share of the glamour and applause. In many cases such criticisms were justified, but in this instance should be modified by two considerations. Firstly Rommel (q.v.) himself declared that Stirling's commandos had caused the Afrika Korps more damage than any other British unit, and even German radio began to talk of the exploits of the 'phantom major'. Secondly the Special Air Service, although trained for a different role as a clandestine reconnaissance regiment, is still in being in the British army and is widely considered one of the army's elite formations. Stirling himself was captured while on an operation in January 1943. He escaped four times from an Italian prison camp and was ultimately sent to Colditz.

STREICHER, Julius (1885–1946). Early member of the Nazi party and a principal author of its anti-semitic views. He proclaimed himself 'Jew-baiter number one', and was a perverse and sadistic individual who seldom appeared in public without a whip. Streicher became a schoolteacher, and served as an officer in the first world war, but soon concentrated on his anti-Jewish activity, founding a small party of his own to promote his views until he merged it with the Nazi party in 1921. He was dismissed from teaching after taking part in the Munich putsch and from then on devoted himself to Nazi work. He owned and edited the newspaper *Der Stürmer*, and rose to be a member of the Reichstag by 1933. Streicher proved too corrupt even for Hitler's (q.v.) Nazi party, and was dismissed in 1940 after being found guilty by a Nazi party commission of misappropriating Jewish property. He lived throughout the war on his farm and was found guilty at the

Julius Streicher, one of the original perpetrators of the Nazi code of anti-semitism. His early photographs portray Streicher as he saw himself – harsh and uncompromising.

Nuremberg war crimes trial of crimes against humanity. He maintained his aggressive hatred of Jews to the last, claiming the trial was a 'triumph of world Jewry'. He was hanged.

T

TASSIGNY, Jean de Lattre de (1889–1952). French general, one of the few who emerged with his reputation intact from the French defeat. He was active against the German occupation forces and the Vichy French, and was jailed for ten years for speaking against the German occupation in 1942. He escaped in 1943 and the RAF flew him to England. He commanded French forces in North Africa, and went on to head the First Army in the invasion of the south of France. A tough professional officer with an understanding of modern war, Tassigny did much to eradicate the shame of France's defeat in 1940.

TAYLOR, Maxwell Davenport (born 1901). American general and airborne leader. Taylor commanded airborne troops in Sicily and Italy, and carried out a mission into Rome to discuss the prospects of Italian surrender with the Rome authorities in 1943, evading capture by the Germans in the city. He commanded the 101 Airborne Division in the invasion of Normandy and subsequent operations in north-west Europe.

TEDDER, Arthur William (1890–1967). British air commander and deputy to General Eisenhower (q.v.) as supreme commander for Allied operations in north-west Europe. Having joined the Royal Flying Corps in 1915 Tedder served in France and Egypt, and remained in the Royal Air Force between the wars, rising to command the air force in the Far East in 1936. He was recalled in 1938 to become director-general of research and development at the Air Ministry, and when the war began was engaged briefly in aircraft production. He was appointed deputy air commander-in-chief, and later commander-in-chief Middle East, and worked in close co-operation with the land campaigns of Wavell, Auchinleck and Alexander (qq.v.). He evolved the technique of obliterating enemy defences along a corridor in advance of the ground troops, the so-called 'Tedder carpet'. In November 1942, shortly after his forces had played a part in the advance from El Alamein, he returned to Britain as vice-chief of the air staff. Soon afterwards, in February 1943, he was sent once more to the Mediterranean as air commander-in-chief, serving under General Eisenhower's overall command, and controlling all the air forces in the Mediterranean theatre.

Among Tedder's notable contributions was to hold together the air component when several land and sea commanders were keen to hive off various elements. His policy of attacking land communications, particularly railways, behind enemy lines, was employed to great effect in Sicily and the invasion of Italy and subsequent operations there. In December 1943 he came to Europe as deputy supreme commander under General Eisenhower, and employed the same technique of attacking rail communications which made it almost impossible for the German defenders to move reinforcements, and thus helped to secure the Allied beach-head. After the invasion, Tedder was critical of what he considered to be Montgomery's (q.v.) slowness in advancing with his armour in the Caen region.

Tedder was appreciated for his clear-sighted grasp of wide strategic issues, while at the same time retaining the common touch. He seldom lectured the troops, but preferred to sit down with a group of young officers on the grass of an airfield and ask them, 'What do you want to know?'

Air Chief-Marshal Sir Arthur Tedder (right), deputy supreme commander for Operation Overlord, goes ashore in a *dukw* shortly after D-Day, with a keen eye on the air component.

Timoshenko took part in the Soviet occupation of Poland in 1939, and commanded Karelian troops in the war against Finland in 1940. He was people's commissar for defence between July 1940 and July 1941, when two weeks after the outbreak of war with Germany Stalin took over that top post himself. Timoshenko was assigned the all-important field command as chief of the Western Front, which covered the approaches to Moscow, but he was removed from that post in September, after which first Koniev and then Zhukov (qq.v.) took over the Moscow defence. Timoshenko was sent to command the South-western Front. There he could not prevent the encirclement of Kiev, and he narrowly escaped capture himself, leaving Kiev with Khrushchev and Budenny (q.v.) in an aircraft. Two months later, on 19 November, the German armies were still advancing and captured Rostov, the so-called gate to the Caucasus. The Soviet high command considered this city so important that even with the battle for Moscow raging, they ordered its recapture. Timoshenko was given reinforcements, and ten days later took Rostov and pushed back the German front line thirty miles. It was Russia's first major victory of the war.

Shortly afterwards Timoshenko was pulled out of front-line command to occupy advisory posts close to Stalin at the Kremlin. After the German advance had been halted, Timoshenko was the main figure who recommended Stalin to mount an immediate general counter-offensive while the enemy was still off balance, against the advice of Zhukov. Later Stalin came to rely less on Timoshenko for advice and more on the recently promoted (though not appreciably younger) generals such as Zhukov.

TITO (real name **Josip Broz**) (born 1892). Yugoslavian Communist statesman and wartime guerrilla leader. After fighting in the first world war and the Russian civil war, Tito became a member of the Communist party of Yugoslavia in 1920, and was jailed for five years in 1928 for his political activities. He enjoyed Stalinist support during the 1930s, and after his rivals had been murdered he became secretary-general of the Yugoslav Com-

Marshal Semyon Timoshenko, at first one of Stalin's favourites, later ignored in favour of a new generation of advisers.

TIMOSHENKO, Semyon Konstantinovich (1895–1970). One of the older guard of Soviet officers and a close adviser to Stalin (q.v.). An NCO in the tsarist army in the first world war, Timoshenko rose rapidly through the ranks of the cavalry in the inter-war years, and also completed several courses at the military-political academy, after which he occupied several high military offices culminating in the post of commander of three successive military districts between 1937 and 1940.

munist party. His basic aim was to reconcile the diverse factions in Yugoslavia and preserve the country's unity, established only in 1918. When Axis forces invaded in 1941 he set the party on a course of guerrilla activity operating under the name 'partisans'. His main rival for control was the anti-Communist and anti-Fascist Colonel Draža Mihajlović, leading the Četniks and enjoying the support of the exiled King Peter II in London. Initially the guerrillas achieved significant successes against the Germans and defeated them in Serbia, but clashes between the two factions allowed the Germans to regain control. Tito expanded his guerrilla force into a massive national liberation army, and succeeded in unifying the diversity of religious and ethnic groups under the Communist banner on the way. His military activity was almost without parallel in the European war. He led his weakened forces from the mountains, came close to capture several times, alternately took the offensive and went into retreat, and tied up large occupying forces for the duration of the war. By 1943 he had won the support of the Allies, who saw him as the genuine leader of Yugoslavia, while Mihajlović led with less energy and sided with the Axis. (The conflict between them led to civil war and Mihajlović was tried and executed in 1946.) In December 1943 the Allies recognized Tito's government and he began to receive substantial aid from Britain and the United States. In the course of the next year they fought the Germans into retreat, and on 20 October Tito led his forces into Belgrade, accompanied by Soviet troops. He declared the country a republic on 29 November 1945, and refused, despite British pressure, to restore the monarchy. Although a lifelong Communist, Tito retained his country's independence throughout the post-war years, much to the annoyance of the Soviet Union. The key to his success was not his devotion to the Communist cause but his ardent nationalism, which both during and after the war was a key factor in preserving Yugoslavia's unity and integrity.

TIZARD, (Sir) Henry (1885–1959). British scientist concerned with air defence develop-

Marshal Tito, Yugoslavian guerrilla leader who won Allied support in preference to his rival Mihajlović.

ments. In the course of a long and distinguished scientific career, Tizard became in 1933 chairman of the aeronautics research sub-committee, and from them on was concerned with air defence problems. He was made chairman of an Air Ministry committee to consider how scientific invention could aid air defence. He quarrelled with Lindemann (q.v.) and resigned most of his committee posts. However he remained involved in radar research, and in 1936 instituted trials at Biggin Hill which led directly to the development of

Sir Henry Tizard (left), one of Britain's most important scientists and a key figure in the development of radar. His committee found itself at odds with Professor Lindemann and Tizard's influence declined.

the fighter station which played a vital part in the Battle of Britain. He also inspired and supported research into airborne radar which proved invaluable. In 1940 he led a scientific mission to Canada and the USA which vastly enhanced transatlantic co-operation on scientific research in military matters. In 1942 he partially returned to academic life as president of Magdalen College, Oxford. His importance in the war effort was reduced as Churchill (q.v.) preferred the advice of Tizard's antagonist Lindemann.

TODT, Fritz (1891–1942). German civil engineer responsible for the bulk of major construction work in connection with Germany's war effort. He became a member of the Nazi party almost at its beginning, and built Germany's *Autobahn* system. He constructed the German defence fortifications known as the West Wall, or Siegfried Line, using a vast army of slave labour and several divisions of troops, under the mighty umbrella of the 'Todt organization' which Hitler (q.v.) authorized him to set up. His men built a chain of concrete submarine bases on the French Atlantic coast, and converted the rail system in occupied Russia to German gauge. He was made minister of armaments in 1940, and was promoted major-general in recognition of his work. He was killed in 1942 when his aircraft crashed on take-off.

TOGO, Shigenori (1882–1950). Japanese statesman who served as ambassador in Berlin during 1937 and 1938, and in Moscow from 1938 to 1940. In 1941 he became foreign minister in Tojo's (q.v.) cabinet. He was sentenced to twenty years' imprisonment for his part in the war and died in gaol.

TOJO, Hideki (1884–1948). Japanese general, politician, and virtual wartime military dictator. Tojo was born in Tokyo, the eldest son in a family with *samurai* antecedents. He graduated in 1915 from the military academy and spent three years from 1919 to 1922 in Europe. By 1936, after service in a series of staff and command posts, he became chief of staff to the Kwantung army in Manchuria. He led two brigades in the war with China, and helped bring Inner Mongolia under Japanese control. In 1938 he was appointed vice-minister for war, and built up Japan's armed strength to be ready to fight a war on two fronts with China and Russia. In 1940 he became war minister in Konoye's government, and was largely responsible for signing the tripartite pact with Germany and Italy. However Japan did not, as Hitler and Mussolini (qq.v.) wanted, go to war against Russia. Instead they pursued a policy of southward expansion. And when the United States imposed its embargo on exports to Japan, Tojo pressed for war. Konoye resigned, and Tojo became prime minister in October 1941. Hirohito's (q.v.) mandate was to wipe the slate clean

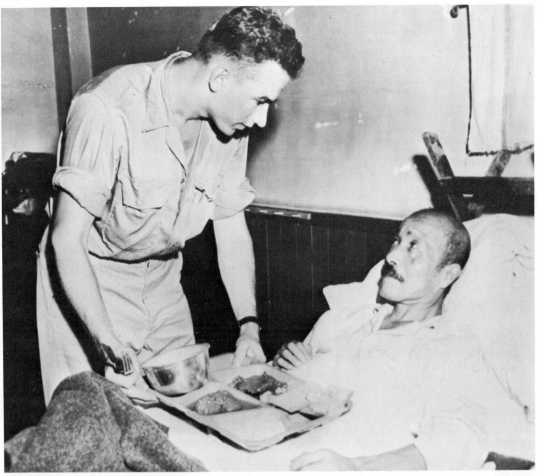

Hideki Tojo receives a meal in a United States army field hospital. He was wounded attempting suicide on 11 September 1945, but recovered to stand trial.

and work for peace, but Tojo ignored this and decided on war, since he was dedicated to establishing 'a new stable order in East Asia'. As Japan enjoyed phenomenal successes in the early stages of the war Tojo accrued more and more power, as a general, prime minister, war minister and chief of staff. However, Japan's setbacks from the battle of Midway onwards reduced his influence. By 1944, with the Americans in the Marianas within bombing range of Tokyo, his ministers and army colleagues forced him to resign his cabinet on 9 July. On 11 September 1945, when General MacArthur (q.v.) had ordered his arrest for trial as a war criminal, Tojo shot himself in the chest. The bullet did not kill him and he was revived.

Proceedings against him began in May 1946 and lasted for two years. Tojo accepted responsibility for the policies of his nation and government, but maintained they were legitimate self-defence. He was found guilty of war crimes and hanged on 23 December 1948. Known as 'the razor' because of his ruthless approach, Tojo's sanguine optimism was undoubtedly to blame for forcing Japan into a war which they ultimately had not the resources to win.

'TOKYO ROSE' (real name **Iva D'Aquino**) (born 1916). An American born to Japanese parents, 'Tokyo Rose' broadcast to American forces on behalf of Japan. Her seductive voice was employed to undermine the GIS' morale by

327

Tokyo Rose, one of many propaganda weapons. Her seductive messages were designed to undermine American soldiers' morale.

Marshal of the RAF Lord Trenchard, the 'father of the Royal Air Force'. He fought with great determination to keep the young service independent.

inferring that their women were being unfaithful to them, and urging them to go home. After the war she was tried for treason, sentenced to ten years' imprisonment and fined 10,000 dollars. She subsequently settled in Chicago.

TRENCHARD, Hugh (Lord Trenchard) (1873–1956). British air marshal, universally known, though he did not like the term, as the 'father of the Royal Air Force'. Trenchard started service life as a soldier, although his school career and academic grounding were so inadequate as nearly to fail him for entry. He served in India and South Africa, Nigeria and Ireland. In 1912, aged thirty-nine and on the point of retiring from the army to modest obscurity, he bought himself flying lessons, passed and joined the staff of the central flying school of the newly formed Royal Flying Corps. From then on he developed, trained and organized the new air wing with passionate faith in its future. He served in France, sending

his air arm in support of land forces and on bombing raids into Germany. Churchill (q.v.), as war and air minister, asked Trenchard to return to the post of chief of the air staff in 1919, and between then and 1929 he developed the Royal Air Force, and preserved its independence from the other services, on the basis that an effective air arm should be the spearhead of national defence. He retired to a highly active civilian life in 1929 but returned to the RAF in 1939 at the age of sixty-six. His legendary esteem, universal respect and unparalleled detailed knowledge of the RAF made him a valuable figurehead and roving ambassador. The sobriquet 'father of the Royal Air Force' probably belittles him. His visionary concepts were the origin of all independent air forces.

TRUMAN, Harry S. (1884–1972). United States president who came to office on the death of Roosevelt (q.v.) on 12 April 1945. He was most noted, in terms of his brief service during the last

Harry S. Truman (centre), United States president, who took over from Franklin D. Roosevelt for the last months of the war, makes up the 'Big Three' at the Potsdam conference, July 1945.

months of the second world war, for his decision to drop the atomic bombs on Hiroshima and Nagasaki. Before his accession to the office of president Harry S. Truman's career was notably unspectacular. Brought up in Independence, Missouri, he worked as a bank clerk and on the family farm, and engaged in a few largely unsuccessful small business ventures. In the first world war he served as a battery commander in the 129 Field Artillery in France, of which he remained endearingly proud, and in 1934 was elected to the United States Senate, where he served diligently for ten years until he was nominated as vice-presidential candidate for Roosevelt's fourth term in 1944. He thus fell into that area of politics which must constitute the most glaring deficiency in United States government in these violent and uncertain times. He could become chief executive, and more significantly in the wartime context also commander-in-chief of the armed forces, in an instant: yet he was totally unfamiliar with the job and completely ignorant of the detailed directions of the war in which he could find himself overnight taking decisions of global importance. Truman recognized this problem when he told journalists: 'Boys, if you ever pray, pray for me now.' When Franklin D. Roosevelt died, Truman had served only eighty-two days as vice-president, and did not know that the Manhattan project (the development of the atomic bomb) was in an advanced state. He was quickly briefed on the subject, and then had to decide whether to drop the bomb.

Post-war argument has centred not so much on how effective the bomb was at the time, but on the ethics of staging the nuclear explosion. Truman stressed repeatedly after the war, and was irritated that earnest analysts could not bring themselves to believe him, that he saw the problem in purely military terms. For him the atomic bomb was simply a devastating new weapon, powerful enough to force Japan into surrender and shorten the war, while at the same time, he was assured, saving thousands of American lives. One of Truman's less publicized decisions was to cancel a plan to launch remotely controlled aircraft packed with explosives against industrial targets in Germany. The project would no doubt have proved effective in terms of destruction and cost effectiveness, but Truman responded favourably to Churchill's (q.v.) pleading that the project could well invoke retaliation against British cities. The only major wartime conference which Truman attended was Potsdam. It was there that he received news of the successful testing of the atomic bomb, and on his way home he issued the order for it to be used against Hiroshima on 6 August.

V

VANDEGRIFT, Alexander (1887–1973). United States marine corps general who commanded the marines at Guadalcanal in the Solomons in the first major amphibious operation against Japanese-occupied territory in August 1942. In this area of operations, in which there was no substantial experience, Vandegrift evolved a successful technique employing concentrated fire power, and held the beach-head until army forces arrived to take over in December. He went on to command the marines in the landing at Bougainville in November 1943, and in January 1944 took over command of the United States Marine Corps.

VASILEVSKY, Alexander Mikhailovich (1895–1977). Soviet general who occupied high rank as both chief of operations and chief of the general staff. Stalin (q.v.) entrusted Vasilevsky with one of the key roles in the strategic direction of the war, as the principal link between senior commanders in the field and the central planning of operations in the Kremlin. A tsarist officer in the first world war, Vasilevsky joined the Red Army in 1919 and the party in 1931. After inter-war experience in staff work, he was appointed deputy chief of operations in 1940 and chief of operations in 1941. At the same time he was deputy chief of the general staff during 1941 and the first half of 1942, when in June he replaced Shaposhnikov (q.v.) as chief of the general staff. His only relief from the burden and responsibility of staff work came in 1945 when he was given command of the Third Belorussian Front for the assault against East Prussia. He was commander-in-chief of Soviet forces during the brief Russo–Japanese conflict of 1945.

Major-General Alexander Vandergrift, US Marine Corps, on Guadalcanal Island shortly after his units had taken Japanese positions on Matanikou Beach.

Marshal of the Soviet Union, Alexander Vasilevsky, chief of the general staff. He was a competent and energetic commander, though at times guilty of over-compliance with the forceful Stalin.

Although not a front-line commander for most of the war, Vasilevsky spent much of his time at the front, planning operations alongside army group (front) and army commanders. This was by far the more interesting and exciting part of his work. At intervals he returned to Moscow where he attended the twice-daily conferences with the supreme commander, which were almost certainly as terrifying as front-line combat with Hitler's (q.v.) *Wehrmacht*. Vasilevsky's method was to get himself extensively and comprehensively briefed by the staffs of all the units concerned, so that he could answer unhesitatingly the questions on obscure detail which Stalin was apt to throw at his

advisers. Despite the confidence which this thorough preparation generated, Vasilevsky was reprehensible (although less than most) in not standing up to Stalin. He admitted implied liability for one notable failure in this area, in not proving to Stalin the dangers of an operation on which Stalin insisted. This was an advance in the Orel sector, at a time when overall policy was still to absorb the German attacks by strategic defence. Stalin's policy resulted in forces moving in both directions at the same time, which was both inadvisable and illogical, and led to the Germans regaining the initiative after their rebuff outside Moscow, and going on to besiege Stalingrad. If the offensive operation had been cancelled, Vasilevsky asserts, 'the country and its armed forces would have been spared serious defeats'. As Vasilevsky was deputy chief of the general staff and then chief of the general staff during this period, his fault was clearly either to approve the offensive operation, or to fail to dissuade Stalin from it by excessive deference. Vasilevsky has pointed to 'the difficult conditions under which the general staff had to work' as accounting for this failure – meaning Stalin's intransigence.

VATUTIN, Nikolai Fedorovich (1901–44). Soviet general, commander of the South-western Front which took part in the relief of Stalingrad. His forces began their critical move on 19 November 1942, advancing to the south-west behind a massive barrage from artillery and Katyusha rockets. They advanced seventy-five miles in three days, defeated the Third Romanian Army on the way, and on 22 November met Yeremenko's (q.v.) Stalingrad Front advancing from the south. The Germans at Stalingrad were encircled and trapped.

Vatutin carried out a similar move in early 1944, commanding the northern force of the pincers which cut off the Korsun salient in the Ukraine. This resulted in massive German losses, estimated

General Nikolai Vatutin, responsible for the northern pincer movement which led to German encirclement at Stalingrad. He was later shot by Ukrainians.

by the Russians themselves as 55,000 dead and 18,000 captured, with 400 tanks destroyed. Shortly after this battle, on 1 March 1944, Vatutin was assassinated by Ukrainian nationalists.

VIAN, (Sir) Philip (1894–1968). British admiral, commander of the destroyer *Cossack* which rescued 299 British merchant seamen from the German supply ship *Altmark*. He subsequently served in the Norwegian campaign, the Mediterranean and the Normandy landings, and during 1944 and 1945 went on to command the British carrier squadron in the Pacific.

VICTOR EMMMANUEL III (King) (1869–1947). King of Italy throughout the war. Victor Emmanuel was opposed to the war and opposed to Italy's fighting in it on the side of the Germans. However, Mussolini (q.v.) contemptuously dismissed his opinions and Victor Emmanuel remained aloof from politics until 1943. Then he was persuaded to act against Mussolini, and after making arrangements for the dictator's safe custody, signed the order in the Fascist grand council for Mussolini's arrest. He then appointed Badoglio (q.v.) prime minister. He escaped from Rome to the south just before Italy surrendered to the Allies and urged Italy to join with the Allies and declare war on Germany. On 5 June 1944 discontent with the continuing monarchy finally caused him to declare his son Umberto regent. He abdicated in 1946 and went into exile in Portugal.

W

WAINWRIGHT, Jonathan Mayhew (1883–1953). American general commanding in the Philippines at the time of the Japanese invasion. Wainwright took command of the Philippine forces when Douglas MacArthur (q.v.) was ordered to Australia in March 1942. He held out on Bataan and Corregidor until he was forced to surrender on 6 May 1942. He remained a prisoner of war until August 1945 when he was liberated from a prison camp in Manchuria by American parachutists. He was flown in by MacArthur, with the captured British general, Percival (q.v.), to witness the Japanese surrender ceremony on board USS *Missouri*. Wainwright was badly treated in captivity, and arrived at MacArthur's hotel on the night before the surrender ceremony an emaci-

Lieutenant-General Jonathan Wainwright (right) is greeted by General Douglas MacArthur (centre) after his release from Japanese captivity, along with Britain's Lieutenant-General Arthur Percival. Wainwright was taken prisoner in the Philippines, Percival at Singapore; both were freed in time for the Japanese surrender ceremonies on USS *Missouri* on 1 September 1945.

ated and weakened man walking only with the aid of a stick. He told MacArthur that he felt he had disgraced MacArthur and his nation by surrendering on Corregidor. In an emotional exchange MacArthur, shocked by this remark, assured him it was not so, and told him he could have his old corps back as soon as he wanted it. In September 1945 he was appointed to head Eastern Defence Command in the United States, and in January 1946 took over the Fourth Army until his retirement in 1947.

WALLIS, (Sir) Barnes (born 1887). British scientist of great imagination and creativity. Wallis invented the Wellington bomber with its 'geodesic' frame, and the 'bouncing bomb' which was used to destroy the Eder and Möhne dams in the low-level bombing runs led by Guy Gibson (q.v.) in 1943. He also created the block-buster ten-ton bombs 'Grand Slam' and 'Tall Boy', of high-penetration capacity, which destroyed the *Tirpitz* and U-boat pens. He was by training an aeronautical engineer and his creations included the airship R 100.

WATSON-WATT, (Sir) Robert (born 1892). Scottish scientist who developed radar. The system of 'radio detection and ranging' (abbreviated to RA.D.A.R.) gave the range, direction and altitude of aircraft, and by 1940 Britain had built a string of radar stations around the coast which gave Britain a clear advantage in the Battle of Britain. Watson-Watt was justly described by Tedder (q.v.) as 'one of the three saviours of Britain'. He also helped the Americans develop their radar defences in 1941. He was knighted in 1942.

WAVELL, Archibald Percival (First Earl Wavell) (1883–1950). British general, victor over the Italian armies in the early desert campaign, and traditionally considered the victim of Churchill's (q.v.) error in forcing through the abortive attempt to aid Greece in early 1941. Archibald Wavell was educated at Winchester and Sandhurst, and served in the Boer war and the first world war, losing an eye at Ypres in 1915. After the war he held a variety of posts at the War Office and on the army staff, and commanded an experi-

mental infantry formation, the 6 Brigade. He also served in 1937 and 1938 as commander in Palestine and Jordan. Shortly before the war began, in July 1939, he was given the task of creating the new Middle East Command. It was a small force in a vast theatre – little more than three divisions covering a third of a million square miles. During 1939 and early 1940, Wavell built up his force with limited troop reinforcements from India and other dominions, but when the German conquests of 1940 induced Mussolini (q.v.) to bring Italy into the war on 10 June on the Axis side, Wavell faced opposition from overwhelmingly superior forces, and on several disconnected fronts. In the western desert he appointed General O'Connor (q.v.) to command of the Western Desert Force, with instructions to bluff the Italians into believing that the British forces defending Egypt were vastly stronger than they in fact were. By aggressive patrolling, sudden attacks and withdrawals, and constant skirmishing the bluff succeeded, and the statically minded Italians frightened themselves with highly inflated rumours of vast British armoured strength. On 13 September, when the German domination of Europe appeared to be on the point of culmination with the invasion of Britain, Mussolini, still striving to extract the greatest possible capital from the Allied disasters, ordered an advance into Egypt by Graziani's (q.v.) Tenth Army. At the same time Italian forces made advances into the Sudan from Ethiopia, and in Somaliland. Wavell's response to these problems was a further brilliant process of bluff which convinced the Italians that the British were holding each front in strength, when in fact Wavell was forced to shuffle divisions about the theatre in order to campaign in barely adequate numbers. His main concentration was in the western desert where the Italians had established themselves in force with tanks and infantry. Wavell's orders to O'Connor were for a five days' raid, and he recommended a pincer movement attacking both Italian flanks. O'Connor preferred a penetrating thrust into the centre of the Italian positions, afterwards fanning out to take their camps in the rear. The result was a decisive victory in the battle of Sidi Barrani. It was followed by further victories at Bardia and Tobruk.

By this time Churchill was looking towards helping Greece, under the threat of a German invasion. Wavell warned that nothing the British could do could help Greece if the Germans invaded, but Churchill gave him a short answer: he expected 'prompt and active compliance with our decisions for which we bear full responsibility'.

For a time, however, the Greek enterprise faded into the background, and Wavell's various forces in Africa were able to continue their phenomenal successes, with victories in the western desert which finally eliminated the strength of the Italian Tenth Army, and in Ethiopia. O'Connor was desperate to mount a major effort into Tripolitania, but Wavell instead had new orders. A message from Churchill had congratulated him on O'Connor's victory against the Italians at Beda Fomm, but had ruled out any major effort against Tripoli, and ordered instead that Wavell's major effort should be to aid Greece and/or Turkey. The policy had come about as the result of the death of the Greek prime minister, General Metaxas, and the accession of Korysis, who brought up once more the request for British aid. Almost all the British politicians and staff officers who looked at the possibility thought, indeed knew, that intervention in Greece was an unsound military operation. Churchill remained the driving force. On 22 February Eden (q.v.), the British foreign secretary, Dill (q.v.), the CIGS, and Wavell consulted in Athens with the Greek king, prime minister and c-in-c. Eden, obviously voicing Churchill's enthusiasm, promised formidable resources, which he swelled by adding in non-combatant forces of doubtful value. Then Wavell was asked to give his view on the chance of success. He got to his feet and told the meeting that he thought the resources the British were offering would prove adequate to the task. The meeting ended, and arrangements for the Greek intervention went ahead. A few days later there was a significant development when the Greek c-in-c, General Papagos (q.v.), made it

Wavell (right) and O'Connor consider next moves in the desert after the capture of Bardia, January 1941.

known that he was not happy about the military situation and did not feel that the intervention of the British could save Greece. His view was now being shared by the British chiefs of staff, and even Eden was growing pessimistic. Wavell's own chief of general staff, General Arthur Smith, himself referred to Pagagos's opinion as 'providing ... the opportunity of withdrawing from what appears now to be an unsound venture'. Unbelievably, even Churchill was now growing less interested in the idea, and on 6 March he sent a message to Eden in Cairo outlining the various factors which made it difficult for the Cabinet to believe that the British now had any power to avert the fate of Greece.

His message included the words: 'We do not see any reason for expecting success, except that of course we attach great weight to the opinions of Dill and Wavell.' Eden consulted the chiefs of staff, especially Wavell as the army commander-in-chief, who all recommended sticking to the original commitment to Greece. At a lower level their own planning staffs were less optimistic, and on their own initiative began to draw up plans for an evacuation long before the troops had even landed. In due course, on 16 April, the invasion took place, and ended as almost everybody had predicted in a Greek surrender on 24 April and a British evacuation with the loss of vast quantities of equipment.

In the traditional historical interpretation, Wavell has been pictured as the innocent victim in this episode, forced to carry out the Greek operation by Winston Churchill against his own judgment, and shortly afterwards sacked by the true culprit, the British prime minister, as a scapegoat for the failure. The evidence, assembled by Sir Francis de Guingand (q.v.), then a member of the joint planning staff, shows that this is the opposite of the true picture. Although the politicians, Churchill and Eden, were forceful in pushing for the intervention in the early stages, they left ample room for it to be called off. And at all stages they relied heavily on the military judgment of Wavell himself. A word from him would have erased the enterprise at any of several stages, but he never gave it, and indeed he never presented any serious assessment of the military prospects. Furthermore, he was credited with commendable foresight in ordering plans for the withdrawal, when in fact his juniors drew them up themselves, virtually against Wavell's direct orders. Even if this reassessment of Wavell's role in the Greek fiasco is wrong and the orthodox theory correct, de Guingand prompts the following pertinent question: 'Can a general who allows himself to be pushed by his political masters into an operation which he judges will end in disaster be considered great? Should he not have made his protest known by his resignation?' Wavell was noted for his long

silences and his general inarticulacy. It seems that on this occasion everybody took him at his infrequent and scarcely audible word.

Unfortunately, Wavell's problems did not end there. During May Crete was invaded by the Germans and lost to the Allies with further heavy casualties, and Wavell was blamed for the state of its defences. Then he opposed the project to aid the Free French forces in Syria, but was overruled and forced to go ahead: that project ended in eventual success with the surrender of the Vichy French in July. Then he undertook the disastrous Battleaxe offensive on 15, 16 and 17 July, in which the British forces were defeated by Rommel (q.v.). Wavell seemed dogged by bad judgments ending generally in defeat, and Churchill and the Cabinet decided that it was time for a change in the Middle East. General Claude Auchinleck (q.v.) was called in, and Wavell sent out to replace him as commander-in-chief India. This job had the makings of a sinecure, except that Japan entered the war in December 1941, and Wavell once more found himself the central figure in a chapter of disasters. Wavell recognized the weakness of Singapore, and his view was vindicated as the Japanese fought their way southwards through Malaya in January. Then, as Singapore itself was attacked in February, Wavell suddenly became optimistic, sending messages to London saying that 'there is every intention and hope of holding' Singapore. His optimism was such that he reinforced the island with the landing of the well-equipped 18 Division, despite a warning from Auchinleck not to do so. Two days later the British surrendered in Singapore and the division was lost. From then on Wavell's role was reduced, and he was ultimately succeeded in the key British command in South-east Asia by Mountbatten (q.v.). Wavell was, however, promoted to field-marshal in January 1943, and given the political role of viceroy of India in June of that year.

Wavell (standing, left), ousted from his North African command, takes over as c-in-c India, and gets acquainted with his Far East troops in Singapore, November 1941.

WEDEMEYER, Albert Coady (born 1897). American army officer who served mainly in staff posts. Interestingly, his pre-war experience included a period at the German staff college (*Kreigsakademie*). He was concerned in organizing the expansion of the United States army in 1940, and in 1941 was appointed to the war-planning branch of the general staff, where he was involved in planning strategy and policy. In 1943 he went to the South-east Asia Command as deputy chief of staff to Admiral Mountbatten (q.v.). In 1944 he succeeded General Stilwell (q.v.) as commander of the United States forces in China, and was chief of staff to Chiang Kai-shek (q.v.) which he remained until the end of the war.

WEYGAND, Maxime (1867–1965). French general in command of all Allied forces in France after the initial stages of the German invasion in 1940. He was called from his post in the eastern Mediterranean on 19 May to take over from General Gamelin after the Germans had outflanked the Maginot Line. He soon realized, however, that there was no chance of holding the German advance and he persuaded Pétain (q.v.) to sign the armistice. He then became minister of defence. He was appointed to command Vichy French forces in Africa, but as he remained loyal to the Allied cause the Germans insisted on his dismissal in November 1941. He was arrested by the Gestapo after a year in retirement and offered, unsuccessfully, as a hostage for the escaped Free French leader General Giraud. He was liberated by the Allies, arrested again in May 1945, tried in 1948 by de Gaulle's (q.v.) government for collaboration, and acquitted.

WILSON, (Sir) Henry Maitland (1881–1964). British general responsible for directing many of the campaigns in the Mediterranean theatre. He was general officer commanding in Egypt on the outbreak of war, and was concerned in planning the operations against the Italians fought by General O'Connor (q.v.) in the field. He also commanded the British expedition to Greece, and conducted a skilful withdrawal. His subsequent tasks included suppressing the revolt in Iraq in 1941, defeating the Vichy French in Syria, and taking over the Persia–Iraq Command during 1942 and 1943. He became commander-in-chief Middle East in 1943, and supreme commander in the Mediterranean theatre in 1944 in succession to General Eisenhower (q.v.). In 1942 he went to Washington as head of the British chiefs of staff mission and took part in the Yalta and Potsdam conferences. Despite his succession of promotions to increasingly important posts, Wilson never achieved the key roles in the fighting which would have done justice to his abilities. He was widely known as 'Jumbo' Wilson because of his great size and ponderous gait.

WINGATE, Orde Charles (1903–44). British general, originator of the Chindit force which fought behind Japanese lines in Burma. Orde Wingate was brought up in a family with both religious and army connections. His parents were Plymouth Brethren, and both his father and his maternal grandfather were army officers. Wingate was educated as a day boy at Charterhouse School, and went to the Royal Military Academy at Woolwich, where he showed his characteristic individuality. He was impatient with traditional cadet activities, was no good at organized games, but proved exceptionally skilful in individual sports such as boxing, rifle shooting and swimming. He was also interested in wildlife and music, both unorthodox pursuits for a young cadet at the time. After passing out of Woolwich Wingate took a commission in the Royal Artillery in 1923. During his early military service he developed a passion for horses, especially for hunting in which he developed an uncanny instinctive understanding of the countryside. He also won prizes in amateur races and showjumping competitions. Wingate was keen to educate himself, and decided to learn Arabic. Eventually he secured an appointment in the Sudan in order to further his study of the language, and remained there for five years until 1933, when he returned for a three-year tour of duty in England. In 1936 he secured a post on the intelligence staff in Palestine, and before long developed strong sympathies with the Jewish settlers

Right General Maxime Weygand, who took over from Gamelin only to find the situation already too disastrous to save France from defeat. It was the start of a series of personal vicissitudes which outlasted the war.

Below General Sir Henry Maitland Wilson, supreme commander in the Mediterranean theatre, visits Fifth Army commander Mark Clark (centre) in Italy. At right is Lieutenant-General Jacob Devers, Wilson's deputy.

Orde Wingate (left), famous for his two Chindit campaigns, seen in 1941 with Haile Selassie during his earlier Ethiopian adventure which restored Selassie to the throne.

and became an ardent Zionist. He learned Hebrew and became friends with prominent Jewish leaders, including Chaim Weizmann. His main contribution to the Jewish cause was to organize the young Jews in the settlements into special night squads, infusing them with the offensive spirit needed to carry the fight outside the settlements and attack the marauding Arabs. His methods proved more effective than orthodox defence by regular soldiers, and because of his courage, ardent support and military contribution Wingate was known among the Jews as *Hayedid* (the friend). He was called the father of Israel's army. Wingate was awarded the DSO for his work in Palestine, although his unorthodox methods

and forthright manner made him unpopular among some of his superiors.

However, his experience proved a great asset and on the outbreak of war Lord Wavell (q.v.) asked him to organize resistance among the rebels in Abyssinia against the Italian occupation. Wingate worked with his characteristic single-minded energy to assemble the necessary arms and camels and organize the troops, and at the beginning of 1941 he crossed the frontier with a small force of Sudanese and Ethiopians under a handful of British officers, fewer than 2000 men in all. After a brilliant military campaign lasting less than five months, he had routed all Italian resistance and rode into Addis Ababa at the head of the column which restored the exiled Emperor Haile Selassie to his throne. After a period of illness, Wingate was again called in by Wavell, at that time commander-in-chief India, to help combat the Japanese invasion of Burma. Although the Allied withdrawal was almost complete by the time he arrived, Wingate visited the front and quickly formed an opinion of how the Japanese could best be fought. The result was his most original contribution to the war, the formation of long-range penetration groups. His intention was to harass the enemy's lines of communication, operating in support of the main forces while being supplied by air. Wingate was given a mixed force of British and Gurkha regular soldiers, and men from various local tribes, and in February 1943 they crossed the Chindwin to strike against the Japanese. The force remained in Burma for six weeks and, although large proportions of some columns were lost, either in battles with the Japanese or on the desperate march back, Wingate's theories were largely vindicated. Arriving back in England, Wingate was whisked away by Churchill (q.v.) to Quebec to meet President Roosevelt (q.v.), who was greatly impressed by his zeal and originality. Wingate was given a new force to train for a second Chindit operation, and this

time, in March 1944, they entered Burma by glider and transport planes to set up strongholds which could resist Japanese attack. During this operation, on 24 March, Wingate was flying over the hills in north Assam visiting his units when the aircraft crashed, killing Wingate and all the other occupants. No satisfactory cause for the crash was ever established, and in some quarters suspicions lingered that the aircraft had been sabotaged because of Wingate's unpopularity.

Wingate's contribution to warfare has never been fully acknowledged. His views were unorthodox and his personality colourful and too controversial for traditional military minds. The success of his expeditions was also misjudged because their aims were not clearly understood. His aim was to employ long-range penetration groups strictly in support of main force operations. Yet because of circumstances he was forced to undertake his campaigns unrelated to any main attack. His efforts therefore came to be judged as offensive operations in their own right, and inevitably were harshly and unjustly criticized. Nevertheless Wingate proved himself to be a true original, as Winston Churchill said: 'A man of genius who might have become a man of destiny.' (*See also* Slim)

Y

YAMAMOTO, Isoroku (1884–1943). Commander-in-chief of the Japanese combined fleet. In many ways the towering figure of Japan's navy, Yamamoto was the architect of the attack on Pearl Harbor, and commanded the vast Japanese forces engaged in the battle of Midway. He was killed when his aircraft was ambushed by American planes in 1943. Born in Niigata into a poor family with *samurai* antecedents, Yamamoto was virtually ordained to adopt a career in the armed forces. He chose the navy, and found himself rising rapidly through the ranks – captain at the age of thirty-nine and rear-admiral by the time he was forty-four. He was among the first officers in Japan to recognize the vital importance of air power in the navies of the future, and while his more reactionary colleagues were still devoted to the mighty battleships which would so soon prove obsolete, Yamamoto was arguing fervently for the construction of aircraft carriers. Although his views were outside the mainstream of Japanese naval thinking, he was appointed navy vice-minister in 1937, and forced through the construction of two new carriers, the *Shokaku* and the *Zuikaku*, which, together with the new generation fighter aircraft, the Zero, would put Japan in its highly competitive position at the outbreak of war.

Yamamoto also departed from mainstream thinking in another essential: he was opposed to war against the United States and Britain. Having studied at Harvard and been a naval attaché at Washington, he recognized the industrial might of the United States, and predicted that Japan would inevitably lose any war entered into against those enemies. His outspoken views made him enemies

but did not seriously affect his career, and on 30 August 1939, much to his own surprise, he was appointed to the senior command in the imperial Japanese navy, as commander-in-chief of the combined fleet.

Although his main responsibility was to carry out the established Japanese war plan to the best of his ability, Yamamoto quickly adapted that plan to incorporate his own ideas. Initially the plan had been to employ the fleet in conjunction with an attack on the Philippines, then to act defensively against any American move to relieve those islands. Yamamoto immediately began to add variations. He first planned to meet the threat of an American naval offensive as far east as the Marshall Islands. Then he altered the operational basis of the combined fleet by drawing its disparate units together under a unified command. He upgraded the training programme for aircraft operating from aircraft carriers, and brought the pilots up to a high standard of proficiency. And finally he took the most radical step of all. He reasoned that, although the American Pacific Fleet did not present a danger to the Japanese homeland itself, in the event of war against the United States, which the warlords seemed determined to force upon Japan, it would be perfectly possible for the American fleet to attack the extended lines of communication to the Dutch East Indies. And without the supplies of oil from that acquisition, Japan's capacity to wage war would be nullified. The answer, Yamamoto decided, was a pre-emptive air strike against the American Pacific Fleet in its base at Hawaii.

Yamamoto set about the detailed planning for

Admiral Yamamoto. The architect of the Pearl Harbor attack, and Japan's national hero, Yamamoto was unmoved by his popularity. He remained a professional seaman, operating from his cabin aboard the *Yamato*.

the air strike, accumulating a vast amount of intelligence and information about Pearl Harbor in his cabin on his own flagship *Nagato*, and putting his pilots through a special training programme in mock attacks against a Japanese bay south of Hyushu which closely resembled Pearl Harbor. By March 1941 the planning for Operation z was well advanced, and the force commander, Rear-Admiral Chuichi Nagumo, was selected. However, several problems remained. One was to secure the agreement of the Japanese high command to the plan. Another was that, despite his personal confidence, Yamamoto found that a large proportion of his own staff were against the idea, mainly on the grounds that it would jeopardize the safety of a large part of the Japanese navy which, if the Americans were forewarned of the attack, might find itself sailing far from support into an American trap. Yamamoto eventually silenced his own staff's arguments with a declaration that, so long as he was commander-in-chief, Operation z would go ahead. There still remained the ultimate authority of the general staff to convince. Yamamoto wrote them a letter assuring them of the high chances of success, but the operations sections still expressed doubts, and reiterated the objections which were by now becoming familiar to Yamamoto: sixty ships would be at risk, and surprise was essential, but the ships would have to be at sea for a month before the attack and would seriously risk being intercepted. It was after all unlikely that secrecy could be maintained in the light of active intelligence gathering by Britain, the United States and Russia. The objections went on, and Yamamoto was again obliged to deal with them firmly. He told the general staff that if the plan was not adopted he would not remain commander-in-chief. The plan was approved. It was 3 November 1941. By 17 November, after further intensive training, the force was ready, and after a ceremony aboard the *Akagi*, Yamamoto gave his pilots a brief and confident pep-talk, then watched them slip out to sea late that night on their way to Hawaii.

His part in the operation was finished. Despite his personal opposition to the war, Yamamoto had, against great pressure from virtually the entire navy, determined the form which the opening moves of the coming war would take. As events showed, his plan was abundantly vindicated, and his reputation at home was enhanced almost to the point of veneration, while to the United States he became the embodiment of villainy. Yamamoto himself disdained the adulation heaped on him at home, and continued to warn his countrymen that the war could still be lost. His own chance to fulfil his ambition of fighting the war at sea came at the battle of Midway in June 1942. Again Yamamoto was forced to impose his own fiercely independent view on senior navy personnel in order to get the battle fought at all. In Yamamoto's opinion this battle was crucial. If the imperial Japanese navy could knock out the American Pacific Fleet they would be free to land anywhere in the Pacific. If they failed, the American industrial machine would restore American control of the ocean within two years and Japan's defensive ring would be useless. Throughout the early months of 1942 the arguments had raged in Japan about the strategic moves to be followed when the early phase of expansion came to an end. Nothing was settled until, at the beginning of April, Yamamoto dictated a message to the naval general staff from his cabin aboard his new flagship *Yamato*:

In the last analysis the success of our strategy in the Pacific will be determined by whether or not we succeed in destroying the United States fleet, particularly its carrier task force.... We believe that by launching the proposed operation against Midway, we can succeed in drawing out the enemy's carrier strength and destroying it in decisive battle. If, on the other hand, the enemy should avoid our challenge, we shall still realize an important gain by advancing our defensive perimeter to Midway and the Western Aleutians without obstruction.

Faced with such a pronouncement from the most influential man in the Japanese naval hierarchy, both the naval and army general staff wilted.

Thus at the beginning of May the ships assembled for this mighty armada. Central to it was Nagumo's carrier striking force of *Akagi*, *Kaga*, *Hiryu* and *Soryu*, with the two fast battleships *Kirishima* and *Haruna*, three cruisers and fifteen destroyers. A main body commanded by Admiral Yamamoto himself consisted of three battleships, a light carrier, and two seaplane carriers with an escort of thirteen destroyers. There was also a Midway occupation force of twelve transports and supply ships with 5000 men, and they were escorted by a covering force of two battleships, the light carrier *Zuiho*, and four heavy cruisers with eight destroyers. The plan was to mount a strike against the Aleutians on 3 June, and thereby decoy the United States Pacific Fleet northwards, where it could be trapped between two carrier forces. In fact the American commander did not comply with Yamamoto's plan.

Aided by superior intelligence and reconnaissance, Admiral Nimitz (q.v.) made contact with Nagumo's carrier force early on 4 June. When the Americans attacked, most of Nagumo's aircraft were on board the carriers rearming after their initial strikes at Midway, and others were having their torpedoes changed to bombs to help neutralize the Midway airfields. Nimitz's first wave, torpedo bombers, was completely unsuccessful, and thirty-five of the forty-one were shot down. As a result the Japanese felt they had won the battle. But the next waves, consisting of dive bombers, transformed the picture. Launched from the carriers *Enterprise* and *Yorktown*, they destroyed three Japanese carriers in rapid succession that morning and a fourth late in the afternoon. Faced with these losses, on 5 June Yamamoto decided to call off the Midway operation. His plan had promised to overwhelm the smaller US Pacific Fleet, and instead had cost a great part of Japan's naval strength. The fault was partly Yamamoto's. He had divided his forces and at the same time had divided his objectives. Moreover, during the battle he had little control over his dispersed naval elements from his flagship *Yamato*.

The battle of Midway left the United States in control of the air over the Pacific, and therefore proved a turning point in the war. Yamamoto remained c-in-c of the combined fleet, and served in the naval battles associated with the struggle for Guadalcanal in October and November 1942. In April 1943 Yamamoto planned a tour of forward bases in the south-west Pacific, largely as a means of boosting troop morale after the disastrous losses they had suffered. American intelligence intercepted and decoded Japanese communications and learned of Yamamoto's exact itinerary. The details of his route and timing were flashed from Washington to fighter control at Henderson Field, Guadalcanal, with strict orders: 'Squadron 339 P38 must at all cost reach and destroy Yamamoto and staff.... President attaches extreme importance this operation.' Soon after 7 am on the morning of 18 April sixteen Lockheed Lightnings took off and made for Bougainville, where they surprised Yamamoto's aircraft. Yamamoto was flying in one camouflaged bomber, his staff were in a second, and they had an escort of six fighters. Yamamoto's pilot dived for the jungle and zigzagged above the treetops at 200 feet in an attempt to escape, while the Zeke escorts turned to engage the American fighters. They could do nothing. The Lightning pilots fired short bursts of cannon fire, and the two bombers crashed blazing into the jungle. The death of Yamamoto, Japan's most celebrated strategist and distinguished naval officer and the hero of Pearl Harbor, proved a great loss to the Japanese, especially in terms of their war morale.

YAMASHITA, Tomoyuki (1885–1946). Japanese general, who achieved his triumph as conqueror of Malaya, and was given command of the Philippines against the American invasion. Yamashita chose an army career by accident, having been an indifferent school pupil. But once embarked on army training he was successful, and passed out in a highly creditable fifth place from the Hiroshima military academy in 1908, and subsequently in sixth place from the staff college in 1916. Like many other young Japanese officers he travelled to Europe, and served in Switzerland and

Germany. In the 1920s he became enmeshed in one of the political cliques which were active at the time, the Imperial Way, dedicated to the establishment of military government and holding the emperor in reverence. In 1936 this faction attempted a coup, of which Yamashita certainly had prior knowledge, even if no direct involvement. Tokyo was thrown into chaos, and the position of the government remained confused until the emperor, enraged at the insurrection, ordered its perpetrators back to their barracks. More than 100 were court-martialled and fifteen of them shot. Yamashita, as a leading figure in the Imperial Way, was discreetly punished by having his name removed from the promotion lists and being banished to Korea in command of a brigade. It did not take him long to recover his position, and in less than two years, in November 1937, he was promoted to lieutenant-general. He had also by now established a great popular following among his junior officers, many of whom regarded him as the finest general in Japanese history. It was largely because of this popularity that his old rival Hideki Tojo (q.v.), then holding the rank of war minister, sent him out of the way again in 1940 on a tour of Italy and Germany. It was also without doubt the reason why, when Japan was on the point of going to war against the Allies in 1941, Yamashita was an obvious candidate for one of the key commands. He was appointed to lead the Twenty-fifth Army in the invasion of Malaya and Singapore. The plan which Yamashita inherited on his appointment called for a landing without prior bombardment in the interests of achieving surprise. Yamashita's principal amendment was to reject the offer of five divisions and confine himself to three, which he considered the maximum he could adequately supply in a jungle advance southward through Malaya as far as Singapore. The divisions chosen were Matsui's 5 Division, the 18 Division commanded by the redoubtable Renya Mutaguchi (q.v.), and the Imperial Guards Division commanded by Lieutenant-General Nishimura, whose loyalty to Yamashita was somewhat suspect. The main Japanese landings took place on the east coast of Malaya, beginning in the early hours of 8 December. Despite numerical inferiority (Yamashita had at his disposal 70,000 combat troops compared with the Allied defending forces of 88,000) the Japanese quickly crossed over to the west coast, and after taking the key defended roadblock at Jitra from the 11 Indian Division rapidly advanced down the peninsula. The Japanese tactic was not complicated: they either employed their superiority in tanks and artillery to overcome defended strongpoints, or moved strong forces behind the defences in outflanking movements, infiltrating men through the jungle in a left hook, or carrying them by sea to the right for a landing on the coast. By January the Allied rearguards had retreated into Singapore, and the Japanese had completed their conquest of Malaya in fifty-four days, at a cost of only 4600 casualties. Yet it would be wrong to convey the impression that the Twenty-fifth Army, or any other Japanese force for that matter, was an invincible war machine directed by brilliant and calculating military minds. Throughout January Yamashita himself had been worried to the point of paranoia about the manœuvring going on in Tokyo behind his back. He committed to his diary abusive comments on Tojo, Terauchi, the Southern Area Army commander, and several other people, and imagined at one stage that he was a candidate for assassination. Part of his problem was that the Japanese press was now boosting him to the level of a national hero, since the Malayan conquest was proving one of Japan's more successful land operations. He was also finding that the men under him were failing to measure up to his requirements. He complained that both Nishimura and Matsui had refused to obey orders and had delayed the advance. And he also observed that the troops lacked fighting spirit, talked in the jungle, and got lost because their NCOs and officers could not read maps. There remained the conquest of Singapore itself. The crossing to the island began on 8 February and the whole operation took precisely a week. In those seven days the defenders were forced back into the suburbs of the city of

General Tomoyuki Yamashita (seated, left) impatiently demands agreement to surrender terms from Britain's General Percival in Singapore, 15 February 1942.

Singapore, where they ran out of food, water, ammunition and the will to fight, and decided to surrender. Yamashita himself had faced serious problems throughout the campaign. In the course of the battle for Singapore his staff had reported to him that supplies were breaking down and artillery ammunition was running dangerously low. At one point he decided to gamble everything on an all-out artillery bombardment to delude the British into believing that he had no supply problems. But the British command had no idea how critical Yamashita's position was. They were forced to surrender on 15 February. The tally of prisoners was 130,000, compared with Japanese losses of 3000 killed and fewer than 7000 others

wounded. In his lightning campaign, seemingly so ruthlessly efficient but in fact a charter of organizational muddle and political obstruction, Yamashita had achieved possibly the greatest triumph in his nation's history. He had captured Britain's great base in the Far East, and eliminated the single most important obstacle to Japan's expansion to the south-west. In the historical context his achievement was even more significant, as the loss of Singapore to Britain signalled the end of the European empire in the Far East.

Yamashita might have expected his triumph to bring him honour and further important commands: in fact he was banished for the second time to impotent exile. The recollection of his involvement in the 1936 coup, and the public acclaim that came his way with the success in Malaya, made Yamashita much too dangerous for his enemies in Tokyo. He was refused an audience with the emperor and despatched to command the armies being formed in Manchukuo against the possibility of a Russian action – virtually a training and defensive command. It would be difficult to devise a more effective snub. Yamashita remained there until 1944, when the Allied advances in Burma and the south-west Pacific prompted the Japanese leadership to call again on the talents of their most successful general. He was given the job of defending the Philippines against the impending American invasion. Yamashita recognized that the mission was a hopeless one but, in accordance with the *samurai* code, suppressed his doubts and on 6 October arrived in Manila, resolved to defend as well as he could against the powerful American forces threatening the islands. The invasion of Leyte took place only two weeks later on 20 October, which gave Yamashita little time to improve the shaky defences. Yamashita wanted to abandon Leyte, which was eating up resources of men and materials as fast as it could be reinforced, and fight the main battle on the northern island of Luzon, but he was unable to secure agreement for such a radical step. The fighting on Leyte went on through November and into December, and Japan's chances of holding the islands were consistently weakened not only by losses on the ground, and not only by the parallel battle at sea and in the air which slashed their supply and support facilities, but also by further problems in command: Yamashita did not hold control over the 25,000 naval ground troops who were sent to Luzon, and he could not implement his own strategic decision because of the rigid instructions from Terauchi and Southern Army headquarters, now conveniently moved to Saigon. By the end of December the battle for Leyte was lost. Yamashita, preparing to fight it out on Luzon, twice relocated his headquarters, gradually moving it to the mountains in the north of Luzon. The landings on Luzon began on 9 January 1945, with four

divisions carried in the greatest American armada ever assembled and with powerful air support. There was little that Yamashita with his dwindling resources could do to prevent it, except ask his men to fight on with the frenzied determination which few troops anywhere in the world could match. The result was a slugging match lasting through the first half of 1945 in which the Americans gradually closed in on Yamashita's redoubt in the northern mountains. By the end of July the Japanese force had been reduced through illness, lack of supplies, and the fighting itself by two-thirds to a mere 50,000 men. On 14 August Yamashita heard by radio that Japan had surrendered, but he still held out until 1 September. On that day, after charging his staff with the task of rebuilding a new Japan, he walked out of his headquarters and down the hill towards the American lines to surrender.

On 8 October 1945 Yamashita was accused of violating the laws of war by failing to discharge his duty as commander 'to control the operations of the members of his command, permitting them to commit brutal atrocities and other high crimes against the people of the United States and of its allies and dependencies, particularly the Philippines'. His trial lasted six weeks and was subjected to some criticism as being unconstitutional. There was also a failure on the part of the prosecution to establish any direct connection between Yamashita and the incidents described in evidence. But in the climate of the immediate post-war period the niceties of the law were subordinated to international pressure for a clean-up, and Yamashita, held to be responsible for the actions of the troops in the Philippines, was sentenced to death by hanging. The defence offered strong and courageous arguments against the sentence, one of which bravely maintained that the military commission was unconstitutional and General MacArthur's (q.v.) orders regarding it were illegal. The case went before the Supreme Court, which decided that it had no power to enquire into the question of the prisoner's guilt. But even before it met, General MacArthur, exercising

Above Prisoners of war in a Singapore camp welcome the arrival of Allied forces.

Right Yamashita, 'the lion of Malaya', finds his role reversed at the capture of the Philippines, 3 September 1945.

quasi-dictatorial powers in the region, and carrying out his mission with unyielding severity, had decided to confirm the sentence. Yamashita, the 'lion of Malaya' who had proved himself in attack and defence to be one of the most capable of Japanese commanders, was hanged at Luzon prisoner-of-war camp at 5 am on 23 February 1946. (*See also* Percival)

YEREMENKO, Andrei Ivanovich (1892–1970). Soviet general: army commander in the relief of Stalingrad. An NCO in the tsarist army, Yeremenko rose to be an officer during the civil war. He was serving in the Far East at the time of the German invasion, and was hastily recalled to Moscow to serve in the defence of the city, during which he commanded first the Western and then the Briansk Army Groups. At the battle of Stalingrad in 1942 he was commander of the Stal-ingrad Front, responsible for the southern arm of the pincer movement which cut off the German Sixth Army. In January 1943 he handed over command of the Stalingrad Front to Malinovsky (q.v.), while he took command of the Kalinin Front. In 1944 Yeremenko commanded the special Black Sea Army which campaigned in the Crimea. Advancing along the south coast of the peninsula, the Russians enjoyed overwhelming superiority, and killed or captured some 60,000 German troops, who were admittedly demoralized and not especially keen to hold the Crimea while the German front to the north steadily retreated. In a rout of extraordinary completeness, German resistance collapsed against Yeremenko's advance. He commanded the Second Baltic Front from April 1944 until March 1945, then the Fourth Ukrainian Front for the advance into Czechoslovakia.

Z

ZEITZLER, Kurt (born 1895). German general who served as chief of the general staff, 1942–4. Zeitzler rose rapidly from infantry colonel, through staff posts during the French campaign of 1940 with Kleist's (q.v.) panzer army, to a staggering series of successes in the Russian invasion of 1941. A master of improvisation, he impressed Hitler (q.v.) with his vigorous approach, and was rewarded with the post of chief of staff in the west, when his forces repulsed the Dieppe raid. In September 1942 he became chief of the general staff. He was not a great success. Too rapid a promotion at first inhibited his independence, and he let Hitler impose the Stalingrad assault on the army, with disastrous results. In the end he began to press his own opinions, particularly in recommending withdrawal from round Stalingrad, and Hitler soon became disenchanted with him. They quarrelled frequently, and Zeitzler tried several times to resign. Eventually in July 1944 he went on sick leave to get out of Hitler's orbit. Hitler responded by dismissing him from the army, and humiliated him by depriving him of the right to wear uniform.

ZHUKOV, Georgii Konstantinovich (1896–1974). Legendary Russian commander universally known today as the 'general who never lost a battle'.

The son of a village shoemaker, Zhukov rose to the rank of deputy supreme commander to Stalin (q.v.). He was given the top military command in the most important Soviet campaigns of the war, from the defence of Moscow against the German invasion to the assault on Berlin which brought the war in Eastern Europe to an end.

After the war he was removed from the public eye by Stalin, perhaps because his popularity was deemed to constitute a threat. He was returned to office in 1952 and rose to become minister of defence, then again was consigned to obscurity and disgraced, for allegedly challenging the party leadership of the armed forces.

Zhukov began his military career in 1915 when he was drafted into the tsarist army, and he quickly distinguished himself as a brave NCO. He rose rapidly through the ranks of the cavalry in the inter-war years, and experimented with the use of tanks in battle. He was called on to lead the Soviet counter-attack against the Japanese Kwantung army, which he decisively defeated, though with heavy losses. In the Russo–Finnish War of 1940 he was chief of staff to the Red Army, and became a general in May 1940. From then on he occupied the position of Stalin's favourite, as one of the few men the Russian dictator could bring himself to trust. He was frequently called on as a 'trouble-shooter' to sort out difficulties in key operations. In February 1941 Stalin made him chief of the general staff, at the age of only forty-four.

It was in this capacity that Stalin sent Zhukov, at the height of the German invasion, to take over the Western Front, guarding the approaches to Moscow. Under Zhukov's command, the Russians succeeded in halting the German advance within thirty kilometres of Moscow itself. But Zhukov did not escape without criticism. At the height of the battle Rokossovsky (q.v.), then Sixteenth Army commander, had devised a plan for reorganizing the defences to greater effect by falling back on the natural defence line at the Istra river, and transferring troops freed by that move either into a second echelon to give a defence in depth, or to another threatened sector. He took the plan to Zhukov, who instantly dismissed it and ordered the troops to stand to the death. Rokossovsky took the matter over Zhukov's head, to the chief of the general staff Shaposhnikov (q.v.), who studied it, agreed with it, and ordered Rokossovsky to go ahead. Rokossovsky was sure that Stalin had also seen and approved the plan. Now he looked forward to watching the German armour 'break their teeth' on the improved defence line, and lose their mobility as they bogged down in the impassable approaches to the Istra.

But no sooner had the sanction arrived from Shaposhnikov than it was followed by a telegram from Zhukov: 'The troops of the Army Group are under my command. I revoke the order withdrawing forces to the Istra reservoir and order that the defence be maintained on the present line without retreating a step backwards.'

Rokossovsky had no alternative but to obey. Later he observed that Zhukov's character was unnecessarily harsh, and that his severity exceeded permissible limits.

Zhukov himself later justified his decision to forbid the withdrawal on the grounds that he had issued the order in the interests of the army group as a whole, and that the right flank of Fifth Army would have been exposed by Sixteenth Army's withdrawal, leaving the area of Perkhushkovo devoid of cover.

However Zhukov did not invariably have his own way. On 5 January 1942, when the German offensive had been halted, Stalin called a conference to consult his senior generals about the question of moving on to the counter-offensive. Stalin had convinced himself, with support from Timoshenko (q.v.), not only that a counter-attack should be made in the western sector in front of Moscow, but that at the same time the Soviet armies should immediately go on to the offensive in the north, near Leningrad, and in the south. This would turn the counter-attack in Zhukov's sector into a general offensive along the

entire front. Stalin summed up the plan by stating that the Germans were now in a state of confusion after their defeat at Moscow, and were badly prepared for winter. This was therefore the most suitable time for launching a general offensive. He then invited comments from the generals. Zhukov stepped forward to give his opinion. They could continue the offensive in the western sector, he said, but to do so they would need reinforcements of personnel and war material, especially tanks. At the same time they should refrain from offensives in the other sectors. Stalin made remarks through Zhukov's talk which convinced Zhukov that Stalin's mind was already made up. After some further discussion Stalin eventually said: 'I have talked with Timoshenko. He is for the offensive. We must grind up the Germans more quickly so that they will not be able to attack in the spring.' Malenkov and Beria supported Stalin, and eventually he brought the conference to a close. Afterwards, as they left Stalin's office, Shaposhnikov confirmed Zhukov's suspicions that the issue had been decided before the meeting began. 'Then why was our opinion asked for?' asked Zhukov. 'I don't know, my dear fellow. I don't know,' said Shaposhnikov.

Another account by a junior colleague of Zhukov's, Colonel-General P. A. Belov (q.v.), the commander of 2 Cavalry Corps, illustrates how rapidly Zhukov gained strength in the Russian war command. In November 1941 Belov was called to a conference at which his job was to present his plan for a counter-attack. Not only was he surprised by the deterioration in Stalin's appearance since his last view of the leader eight years earlier, but even more by Zhukov's behaviour. Zhukov spoke in a sharp commanding tone so that it looked as if he were the superior officer. Stalin apparently accepted this as proper.

When the German assaults of the spring of 1942 threatened the Russian situation on the southern

Marshal Georgii Zhukov, leading military figure in the Soviet Union, although his popular reputation as 'the general who never lost a battle' overstates his talents.

front Zhukov was placed in overall charge of four army groups commanded by Rokossovsky, Chuikov, Vatutin and Yeremenko (qq.v.). The outcome was the battle of Stalingrad at which the Russian armies achieved a victory that proved the turning point in the war in eastern Europe. Zhukov followed it with a brilliantly organized victory at Kursk in 1943 where he brought up vast quantities of armour and infantry to counter-attack after the initial German attack was spent. He followed it in the winter of 1944 with another great victory at Korsun, and further operations in which by a process of assembling massive strength and committing it wholesale with little regard for losses he cleared the German armies out of Soviet territory.

In early 1945 he was in command of First Belorussian Front, and in April, commanding Koniev's (q.v.) and Rokossovsky's armies, drove a massive force of 4000 tanks, 5000 aircraft, and 22,000 guns in a fifty-mile-wide front against Berlin. The city capitulated to him on 2 May 1945 and on 8 May he received the surrender of all German forces from General Keitel (q.v.).

Zhukov's double banishment after the war did not impair his high reputation in the west, although how far that reputation is justified is open to question. Certainly it was not based on any strategic or tactical thrusts of special merit of the kind which wins western generals critical acclaim. Most of his victories were won by the assembly of overwhelming force, much of it supplied by the industrial machinery of the western Allies, and sending it at the enemy in the form of an undisguised hammer blow. He was greatly aided in this by Hitler's (q.v.) own myopic strategy in resisting all suggestions of tactical withdrawal by his generals, and in such a conflict Russian force was bound to triumph. Zhukov's military philosophy was perhaps best summed up by General Eisenhower's (q.v.) remarks. He described Zhukov as stern, harsh and ruthless, and prepared to accept losses if necessary to achieve the required end. Zhukov told Eisenhower that if his troops encountered a minefield they were ordered to attack as though it were not there. The losses were accepted as only the same as would have been incurred if the area had been defended by troops instead of mines.

Acknowledgments

The photographs in this book are supplied or reproduced by kind permission of the following:

Bildarchiv Preussischer Kulturbesitz *51*, *141*, *142–3*, *212*

BPC Publishing Ltd 98

Camera Press 29, 31, 66 (above & below), 72, 79, 94, 100, 122, 123, 148, 159, 204, 226 (above & below), 231, 239, 251, 254, 275, 278, 291 (below), 298, 310, 329, 349

Central Press Photos 32 (right)

ECP Armées 248, 341 (above)

Fox Photos 55, 61, 63

Franklin D. Roosevelt Library 57, 263, 267, 269

Fujiphotos 150, 328 (left)

Historical Research Unit 107, 197, 297, 321

H.M.S.O. (Crown Copyright) 47

Robert Hunt Library *33*, *293*

Imperial War Museum 10, 11 (left), 22, 23 (above), 28, 30, 45, 46, 64, 71, 74, 77, 83, 90, 99, 101, 102, 103, 111, 112, 115, 132, 133, 147 (left), 154, 157 (below), 169, 191, 193, 198, 200, 203, *209*, *210–11*, 225, 240, 242, 243 (right), 244, 245, 247, 256 (below), 258, 270, 280, 286, 291 (above), *294–5*, 305, 320, 323, 325, 342

Keystone Press Agency 25, 27 (left), 49, 84, 88, 91, 108, 113 (left), 134–5, 140, 147 (right), 151, 157 (above), 162, 167, 185, 186, 206, 215, 217, 246, 256 (above), 265, 289, 311, 312, 315, 318–19, 327, 331, 335, 341 (below)

John MacClancy 119, 125, 127 (left & right), 128, 130, 136, 176, 179, 180, 184, 190, 216, 232, 234, 235, 236, 252, 260, 272, 282, 300, 301, 317

National Portrait Gallery 15

Novosti Press Agency 50 (left), 324, 333, 355

Popperfoto 20, 23 (below), 32 (left), *34 (above & below)*, 37, 40, 43, 50 (right), *52 (above & below)*, 53, 97, 105, 113 (right), 117, *144 (above & below)*, 153, 163, 166 (left & right), 208, 214, 222 (left), 229, 230, 241, 250, 262, 288, 292, *296*, 309, 337, 339, 351 (above)

Radio Times Hulton Picture Library 26, 27 (right), 42, 54, 87, 104, 120, 168 (above), 171, 172, 173, 182, 187, 188 (above), 195, 222 (left), 243 (left), 273, 279, 281, 284, 326

Society for Cultural Relations with the USSR 59, 109, 165, 332

US National Archives 14, 56, 69, 75, 76, 82, 85, 92, 93, 160 (below), 170, 188 (below), 189, 223, 314, 345, 351 (below)

Weidenfeld & Nicolson Archives 11 (right), 12, 17, 139, 249, 328 (right)

Zeitgeschichtliches Bildarchiv 218

Numbers in italics indicate colour illustrations.
Maps drawn by Tony Garrett.

All possible care has been taken in tracing the ownership of copyright material used in this book and in making acknowledgment for its use. If any owner has not been acknowledged the publishers apologize and will be glad of the opportunity to rectify the error.

Glossary

AA anti-aircraft

AAF Army Air Force (United States)

ABWEHR German military intelligence

AEAF Allied Expeditionary Air Force

ALLEGEMEINE SS General *SS* force, formed as the military arm of the *Wehrmacht*

ANZAC American–New Zealand–Australian Command

AOC Air Officer Commanding

ARABIAN NIGHTS codename for thousand-bomber raids on Germany

AUTOBAHN German motorway system

AWOL absent without leave

BAA Burma Area Army

BEF British Expeditionary Force

BGS Brigadier General Staff

BIA Burma Independence Army

BLITZKREIG sudden attack against enemy airfields, communications and military installations, using bomber and fighter aircraft followed by fast mobile armour and infantry, first used by Germans in their invasion of Poland

BLOCKBUSTER British 8000-pound bomb

BODYGUARD codename for deception plan for Operation Overlord

BOLERO codename for build-up of United States forces in Britain for Operation Overlord

CASH AND CARRY ACT American arms act, passed in November 1939, allowing sale of American arms to Allies if arms collected from America

CIGS Chief of the Imperial General Staff

C-IN-C commander-in-chief

COBRA codename for the American breakout at St Lô, Normandy

COLONEL WARDEN Winston Churchill's codename

COSSAC Chief of Staff to the Supreme Allied Commander

CROMWELL signal for the invasion of Britain by Germany

DEUTSCHES AFRIKA KORPS special German unit formed to aid Italians in North Africa, which became part of Panzer Armee Afrika in January 1942

D/F direction finding (radio navigation)

DSO Distinguished Service Order

DUKW amphibious craft, colloquially known by these factory serial letters, viz., d = year of origin (1942, fourth year of war); u = utility; k = front-wheel drive; w = six wheels

EEC European Economic Community

FFI *Forces Françaises de l'Intérieur* (the armed French resistance)

FORTITUDE codename for cover plan for Operation Overlord, to convince Germany that the landing would be in the Pas de Calais

FÜHRER leader

GEE British radar aid to target location

GESTAPO Nazi secret police

GOC General Officer Commanding

GRAND SLAM 22,000-pound bomb

H2S (H2X in United States) radar aid to navigation and target location

JCS Joint Chiefs of Staff (United States)

KRIEGSAKADEMIE German staff college

KRIEGSMARINE German navy, so named from 1935–45

LANDWEHR German Territorial Reserve

LCA landing craft, assault

LCI landing craft, infantry

LCT landing craft, tank

LEBENSRAUM German territory (literally, 'room for life')

LEND-LEASE American act, passed in March 1941, allowing American aid to Allies in form of arms and ancillary equipment, on basis of its being returned or paid for at the end of the war

LMG light machine gun

LST landing ship, tank

LUFTWAFFE German air force

MAGINOT LINE line of forts built by French in 1920s

in Lorraine, designed to check a German invasion of France

MC Military Cross

MILLENNIUM codename for thousand-bomber raid on Cologne

MILLENNIUM II codename for thousand-bomber raid on Bremen

MULBERRY artificial harbour used in Operation Over-lord

NATO North Atlantic Treaty Organization

NATOUSA North African Theater of Operations, United States Army

NCO non-commissioned officer

NKVD Russian secret service

NSDAP *Nationalsozialistische und Deutsche Arbeiterpartei* (National Socialist German Workers' Party), abbreviated to Nazi Party

OC Officer Commanding

OKH *Oberkommando des Heeres* (German high command of the army)

OKM *Oberkommando der Marine* (Naval High Command)

OKW *Oberkommando der Wehrmacht* (German high command of the entire armed forces)

OSS Office of Strategic Services

PANZER formations of tanks or tanks themselves (literally 'armour')

PLUTO pipeline under the ocean

POLITBURO principal committee of the Communist party

POW prisoner-of-war

RAAF Royal Australian Air Force

RAF Royal Air Force

REICHSTAG German Parliament

ROUNDUP codename for early Allied plan for the in-

vasion of Europe, 1943

RSHA *Reichssicherheits-Hauptampt* (German department containing the intelligence division, the Gestapo and the *Kripo*, or criminal police)

R/T radio telephony

RTC Royal Tank Corps

SA *Sturmabteilung* (literally 'storm section'; Hitler's first bodyguard and Nazi party army, led by Röhm)

SAAF South African Air Force

SACSEA Supreme Allied Commander South-east Asia

SAMURAI feudal warrior class of Japan

SAS Special Air Service

SD *Sicherheitsdienst* (Nazi party intelligence service)

SD State Department

SEAC South-east Asia Command

SHAEF Supreme Headquarters Allied Expeditionary Force

SIS Special Intelligence Service

SOE Special Operations Executive

SS *Schutzstaffeln* (literally 'protection squads'; Hitler's personal bodyguard, led by Himmler)

SWPA South-west Pacific Area

TALLBOY 12,000-pound penetration bomb

TUBE ALLOYS codename for atomic bomb research programme

UNO United Nations Organization

USAAF United States Army Air Force

USN United States Navy

VC Victoria Cross

VICHY GOVERNMENT French government during Nazi occupation of France, established by Pétain

VICTOR President Roosevelt's codename

WAFFEN SS Armed *ss* (élite German force formed from various *ss* divisions in 1940)

WEHRMACHT German army

Main Allied Conferences during Course of the War

PLACENTIA BAY: August 1941, between Churchill and Roosevelt, in which Britain attempted unsuccessfully to persuade America to join in the war against Germany

WASHINGTON: December 1941–January 1942, between Churchill and Roosevelt, to discuss further America's possible involvement in the war

CASABLANCA: January 1943, between Churchill and Roosevelt, to discuss the invasion of Sicily and preparations for the cross-Channel invasion, following the success of Operation Torch

WASHINGTON: May 1943, between Churchill and Roosevelt, to discuss the priorities of the invasion of Italy and the cross-Channel offensive, and policy on the Pacific arena

QUEBEC: August 1943, between Churchill and Roosevelt, to continue discussions of Washington conference

CAIRO: November 1943, between Churchill and Roosevelt, to discuss strategy in the Mediterranean and set the date for Operation Overlord. Chiang Kai-shek was also present

TEHERAN: November 1943, between Churchill, Roosevelt and Stalin, to continue discussions about Operation Overlord begun in Cairo

YALTA: February 1945, between Churchill, Roosevelt and Stalin, to discuss the post-war settlement, including the terms to be imposed on defeated Germany, the establishment of the United Nations Organization, and the entry of Russia into the war with Japan

POTSDAM: June 1945, between Churchill, Stalin and Truman, to discuss fate of Germany and eastern Europe

Important Military Operations referred to by Codenames

OPERATION SEELÖWE
(*Sealion*): proposed German invasion of Britain, ordered 16 July 1940, postponed 12 October 1940

OPERATION BARBAROSSA: June 1941, German invasion of Russia

OPERATION BATTLEAXE: June 1941, British offensive in North Africa which failed against Rommel's advancing Afrika Korps

OPERATION CRUSADER: November 1941–January 1942, Eighth Army offensive against Rommel in North Africa

OPERATION TORCH: November 1942, Allied invasion of north-west Africa

OPERATION HUSKY: July 1943, Allied invasion of Sicily

OPERATION OVERLORD: June 1944, Allied invasion of north-western Europe

OPERATION ANVIL: August 1944, Allied invasion of southern France

ARDENNES OFFENSIVE: December 1944, last major action between Allies and Germans in France

Military Organization

ARMY GROUP: largest command, comprising at least two armies

ARMY: major formation, comprising at least two corps, commanded by a general

CORPS: between two and four divisions, with other independent troops attached, usually commanded by a lieutenant general

DIVISION: 12,000 to 20,000 strong, comprising tanks, or infantry and tanks, with supporting troops such as engineers and signals, commanded by a major general

BRIGADE: three to eight battalions

BATTALION: 600–1000 strong, commanded by a lieutenant colonel

COMPANY: 100–250 strong, usually comprising three platoons, commanded by a captain

PLATOON: small unit, commanded by a lieutenant

Equivalent Officer Ranks

In this book, the ranks under which servicemen fought are deliberately left unspecified. Many of them occupied several different ranks in the course of the war as promotion came their way. Frequently, they only acquired the ranks by which they were subsequently known in the years after the war. A further complication arises out of the fact that different terminology is used. The man who reaches the highest rank in the British army holds the title of field marshal, while in the United States army he is known as a general. The same man in Moscow would be known as marshal of the Soviet Union, which is not quite the same as either. The problem has been dealt with by using the term 'general' in an overall descriptive sense, to signify the work of a commander in land warfare. Similarly 'admiral' and 'air commander' are used, along with various other terms, to denote an officer's role in the fighting, rather than to describe his specific rank at any time.

The lists of comparative ranks below are intended to aid the reader with background information on hierarchical structures. It must be remembered however that armies do not necessarily draw up their organization with direct reference to enemy, or even allied, practices. Ranks which therefore appear to be direct translations may not always involve precisely the same levels of responsibility, and readers should exercise discretion and judgment in approaching these tables. In some armies, ranks below officer-level, that is warrant officers and non-commissioned officers, proliferate to such an extent that even the most indirect comparisons are impossible. They have therefore been omitted.

ARMY RANKS

German Army	Waffen SS	British Army	United States Army
Generalfeldmarschall	Oberstgruppenführer	Field marshal	General of the Army
Generaloberst	Obergruppenführer	General	General
General der ... (unit concerned)	Gruppenführer	Lieutenant General	Lieutenant General
		Major General	Major General
Generalleutnant	Brigadeführer	Brigadier	Brigadier General
Generalmajor	Oberführer	Colonel	Colonel
Oberst	Standartenführer	Lieutenant Colonel	Lieutenant Colonel
Oberstleutnant	Oberstunnbannführer	Major	Major
Major Hauptmann	Sturmbannführer	Captain	Captain
Oberleutnant	Hauptsturmführer	Lieutenant	First Lieutenant
Leutnant	Obersturmführer	Second Lieutenant	Second Lieutenant
	Untersturmführer		

NAVAL RANKS

German	British	United States
Grossadmiral	Admiral of the Fleet	Fleet Admiral
Generaladmiral	Admiral	Admiral
Vizeadmiral	Vice Admiral	Vice Admiral
Konteradmiral	Rear Admiral	Rear Admiral
	Commodore	Commodor
Kapitän zur See	Captain	Captain
Fregattenkapitän	Commander	Commander
Korvettenkapitän	Lieutenant Commander	Lieutenant Commander
Kapitänleutnant	Lieutenant	Lieutenant
Oberleutnant zur See	Sub-Lieutenant	Lieutenant Junior Grade
Leutnant zur See	Acting Sub-Lieutenant	Ensign

AIR FORCE RANKS

German Air Force	**Royal Air Force**
Reichsmarshall	Marshal of the RAF
Generaloberst	Air Chief Marshal
General der ... (unit concerned)	Air Marshal
Generalleutnant	Air Vice Marshal
Generalmajor	Air Commodore
Oberst	Group Captain
Oberstleutnant	Wing Commander
Major	Squadron Leader
Hauptmann	Flight Lieutenant
Oberleutnant	Flying Officer
Leutnant	Pilot Officer

United States Marine Corps and United States Air Force officer ranks are the same as United States Army ranks.

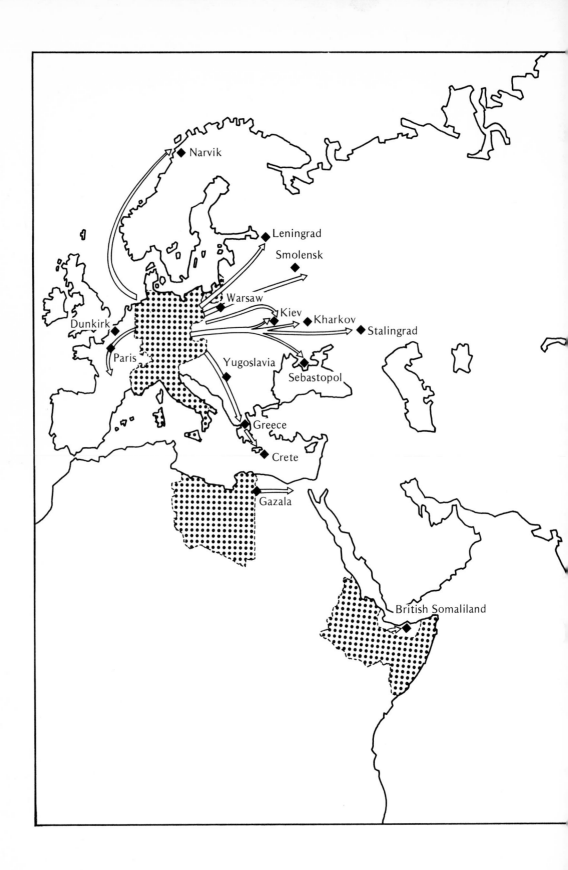

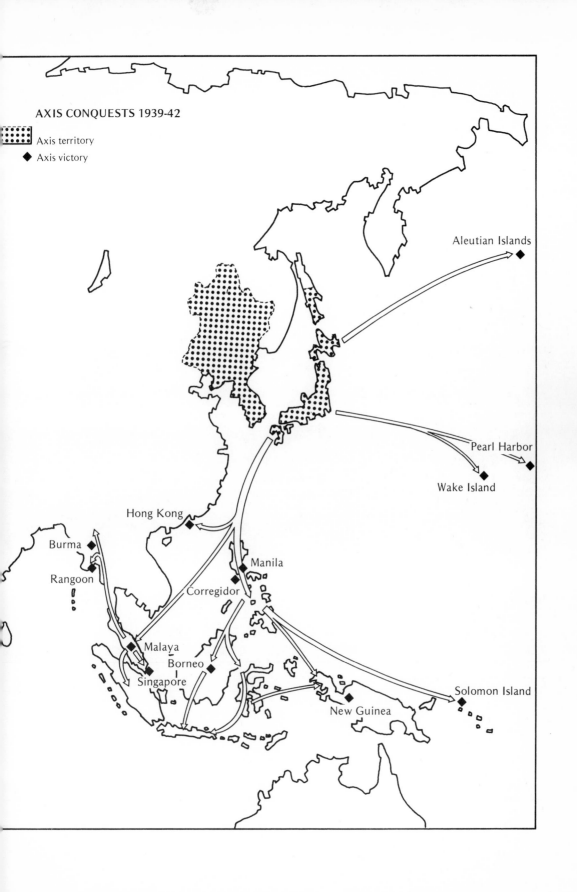

AXIS CONQUESTS 1939-42

Axis territory

Axis victory

Aleutian Islands

Pearl Harbor

Wake Island

Hong Kong

Burma

Rangoon

Manila

Corregidor

Malaya

Borneo

Singapore

New Guinea

Solomon Island

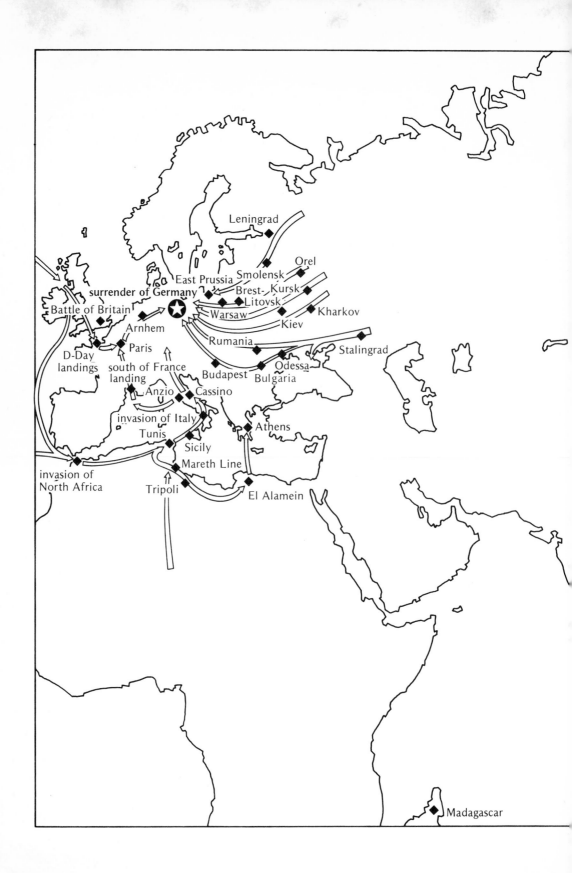

Leningrad

Orel

Smolensk

East Prussia

Brest-
Litovsk

Kursk

surrender of Germany

Battle of Britain

Warsaw

Kharkov

Kiev

Arnhem

Paris

Rumania

Stalingrad

D-Day
landings

south of France
landing

Budapest

Odessa

Bulgaria

Anzio

Cassino

invasion of Italy

Tunis

Athens

Sicily

Mareth Line

invasion of
North Africa

Tripoli

El Alamein

Madagascar

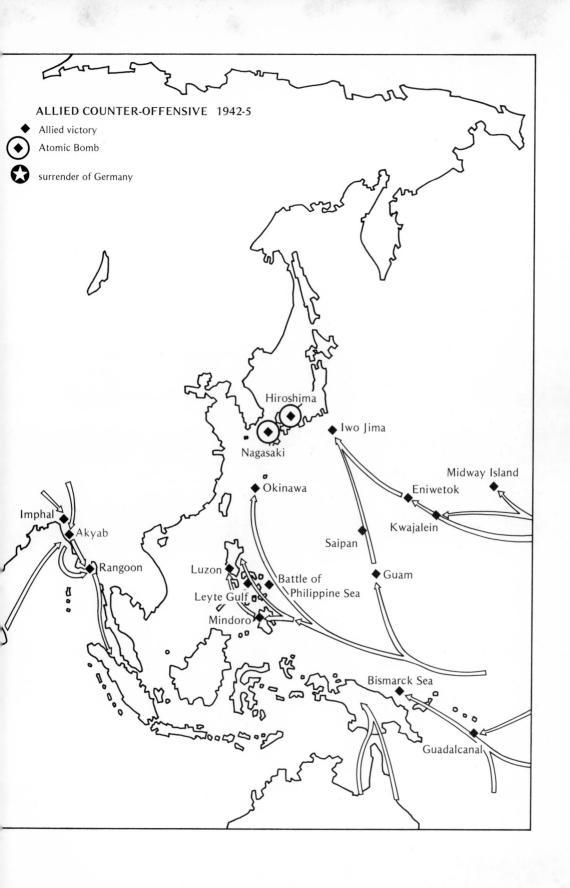

ALLIED COUNTER-OFFENSIVE 1942-5

◆ Allied victory

◉ Atomic Bomb

⊛ surrender of Germany

Hiroshima

Nagasaki

Iwo Jima

Midway Island

Okinawa

Eniwetok

Saipan

Kwajalein

Guam

Imphal

Akyab

Rangoon

Luzon

Leyte Gulf

Mindoro

Battle of
Philippine Sea

Bismarck Sea

Guadalcanal